WORK, INCOME AND INEQUALITY

The main thesis of this book is that the system by which production, access to work and income from work is organized is of critical importance to the determination of income distribution and of poverty. It is argued that this system – described as "the payments system" – is neglected in much economic analysis. It is suggested that the often observed deterioration in income distribution as development proceeds, the so-called "Kuznets curve," is due to the combined effects of economic and institutional changes.

The essays in this book explore the impact of the payments system on employment and income distribution in a wide range of different cases. A chapter by Eckart Ehlers looks at the traditional land tenure system in Iran; John Weeks examines changes in income distribution following the military reforms in Peru; Gustav Ranis describes contrasting developments in the Philippines and Taiwan; José María Caballero considers developments in cooperatives in Peru; two essays by David Morawetz and Joseph Zarfarty explore the various types of agricultural co-operative in Israel; Rehman Sobhan describes the role of the public corporation in Bangladesh; essays by Dharam Ghai and Azizur Rahman Khan and by Peter Nolan and Gordon White review the experience of agricultural cooperatives in parts of Russia and in the Communes in China.

The final chapter by Frances Stewart brings together the conclusions of the wide-ranging essays. The rules of the system are shown to be of vital significance to the determination of income distribution and development. That being so, the formation of the rules becomes a highly political process, which deserves greater study.

Frances Stewart is a Fellow of Somerville College and Lecturer and Senior Research Officer at the Institute of Commonwealth Studies, Oxford.

She has been consultant to many international organizations including the ILO, the OECD, UNIDO, UNCTAD, and the World Bank. She is a member of the Board of Directors of the Intermediate Technology Development Group.

Frances Stewart is editor of *Employment, Income Distribution and Development* and author of *Technology and Underdevelopment*.

WORK, INCOME AND INEQUALITY

Payments Systems in the Third World

Edited by
Frances Stewart

St. Martin's Press   New York

Printed in Hong Kong
First published in the United States of America in 1983

ISBN 0–312–88943–7

Library of Congress Cataloging in Publication Data

Main entry under title:

Work, income, and inequality.
    Includes index.
    1. Underdeveloped areas – Income distribution –
Addresses, essays, lectures.   2. Underdeveloped
areas – Agriculture – Addresses, essays, lectures.
I. Stewart, Frances.
HC79.15W67   339.2′09172′4   81-24065
ISBN 0–312–88943–7   AACR2

Contents

Preface

The essays in this book all examine different aspects of payments systems in developing economies. The starting-point is Chapter 1, which sets out the basic hypothesis – that the collection of rules/institutions, which determine how people get work, access to the use of productive assets, and acquire income from work, is of fundamental importance to the determination of the distribution of income in the process of development. This collection of rules/institutions is described as the 'payments system'. Chapters 2–11 all examine different aspects of payments systems, in particular situations in the process of development. Chapter 2 looks at an example of a traditional system in Iran. Chapters 3 and 4 consider developments in Peru, the Philippines and Taiwan at a rather macro level. The remaining chapters focus on particular institutions: on the informal sector, on public enterprise in Bangladesh, on agrarian co-ops in Peru, on the moshavim and kibbutzim in Israel, on communes in China and on collective agriculture in Soviet Central Asia. Chapter 12 provides a short overview and presents some conclusions.

Many of the topics in this book were discussed at a workshop in July 1978 at the Institute of Social Studies in the Hague, at which most of the authors were present. We are grateful to Louis Emmerij and the Institute of Social Studies for being excellent hosts, and to Willem Floor and the Ministry of Foreign Affairs for financing the workshop.

Frances Stewart

Notes on the Contributors

Frances Stewart, the editor of this volume, is a Fellow of Somerville College and Lecturer and Senior Research Officer at the Institute of Commonwealth Studies, Oxford.

She worked as an economist in Whitehall for six years. She was lecturer in economics at the University of East Africa for two years. She has been consultant to many international organisations including the ILO, the OECD, UNIDO, UNCTAD, and the World Bank. She is a member of the Board of Directors of the Intermediate Technology Development Group.

She has written widely on questions of development. She is editor of *Employment, Income Distribution and Development*, author of *Technology and Underdevelopment*, co-author (with A. Sengupta) of *International Financial Cooperation, A Framework for Change* and co-editor of *The Economics of New Technology in Developing Countries*.

Jose Maria Caballero is a research officer at the Centre of Latin American Studies in Cambridge. He has worked in Peru for a number of years and has published two books on agrarian questions in Peru.

Eckart Ehlers is a professor of geography at the Philipps-University of Marburg, West Germany. His special interest is in the social and economic geography of the Middle East.

Dharam Ghai is chief of the Rural Employment Policies Branch of the Employment and Development Department of the International Labour Office. He has been Director of the Institute of Development Studies, Nairobi. His recent publications include, editing with others, *Agrarian Systems and Rural Development* and *Planning for Basic Needs in Kenya*.

Azizur Rahman Khan is chief of the Asian Employment Programme of the International Labour Office. He has been Research Director of the Pakistan Institute of Development Studies and the Bangladesh Institute of Development Studies. He is author of *The Economy of Bangladesh* and co-author of *Poverty and Landlessness in Rural Asia*.

David Morawetz teaches economics at Boston University. His writings range from a study of economic life in a small Chilean fishing town to a survey of twenty-five years of economic development in the developing world.

Peter Nolan is an assistant lecturer in Cambridge University and Fellow of Jesus College, Cambridge.

Gustav Ranis is a professor of economics at Yale University, where he directed the Economic Growth Center for nearly ten years. He has worked in many countries, including Japan, Pakistan, Taiwan, Mexico and the Philippines. His publications include (with John Fei) *Development of the Labor Surplus Economy* and *Growth with Equity: the Taiwan Case*.

Rehman Sobhan is Research Director of the Bangladesh Institute of Development Studies. He is a former member of the Planning Commission in Bangladesh. His publications include *Public Enterprise in an Intermediate Regime*.

Victor E. Tokman is Director of ILO-PREALC. He has written books on technology, income distribution, employment and the informal sector in Latin America.

John Weeks is a professor of economics at the American University in Washington, DC. He is author of *Capital and Exploitation*. He has worked in Nigeria, Kenya, Jamaica, Peru and Nicaragua.

Gordon White is a research fellow at the Institute of Development Studies at the University of Sussex, specialising in Chinese development policy. He is the author of *The Politics of Class and Class Origin: the Case of the Cultural Revolution* and (with Marc Blecher) *Micropolitics in Contemporary China* and *Teachers and Politics in Contemporary China*.

Joseph Zarfaty is on the staff of the Bank of Israel. He has written on income distribution and happiness, and the use of index-linked bonds.

Acknowledgements

The editor and publishers wish to thank the following who have kindly given permission for the use of copyright material:

United Nations Educational, Scientific and Cultural Organisation for the table from *Agricultural Planning and Village Community in Israel,* © 1964, edited by J. Ben-David.
International Labour Review for the tables from 'Income distribution at different levels of development: a survey of evidence', from vol. 108, nos 2–3, August–September 1973.
The World Bank for the table from *Size Distribution of Income,* copyright © 1975, by Shail Jain.

Every effort has been made to trace all the copyright-holders, but if any have been inadvertently overlooked the publisher will be pleased to make the necessary arrangement at the first opportunity.

1 Inequality, Technology and Payments Systems

FRANCES STEWART*

Summary – *The chapter considers the way in which the interaction between technology, population growth and the payments system is responsible for growing inequality in many poor countries. The payments system describes the set of rules governing property rights, access to work and income from work. Payments systems may be classified into traditional, capitalist, mixed and socialist, although most economies exhibit hybrid characteristics. It is argued that capitalist and mixed economy payments systems are largely responsible for those situations where poverty has increased despite growth in per capita income. Finally the chapter considers methods of reforming the payments system.*

This chapter is divided into three sections: Section I presents a very simplified view of the 'facts', as currently reported, on the relationship between economic development and inequality; Section II considers some explanation for these facts – with particular emphasis on three aspects, technology, population growth and payments systems, exploring the interrelations between these three sources of inequality. Section III considers policy conclusions that are suggested by the earlier analysis.

I THE FACTS

The one fact that everyone is agreed on is that the statistical basis of the evidence on income distribution is weak and that interpretation presents

* I am grateful for stimulating comments on some of these ideas from Keith Griffin, participants at a Queen Elizabeth House seminar, participants at the Bellagio workshop and Carl Riskin. This chapter first appeared in *World Development*, vol. 6, no. 3, 1978.

considerable theoretical problems. All the thorny problems of inter-personal welfare comparisons are present in income distribution calculations, while evidence on trends over time also raises the problems associated with new products and changing tastes. Notable practical (and theoretical) problems are how to devise appropriate price indices for different income groups, and whether to rely on data for the distribution of income or consumption where the two appear to give conflicting results.[1] I shall ignore these difficulties in what follows.

Three types of evidence have been collected about the relationship between economic growth and inequality: long-run evidence from the history of the now industrialised countries; cross-sectional evidence comparing countries at different stages of development at one point in time; and time series evidence from the recent history of particular developing countries. In this chapter I will not summarise the detailed evidence – which has been ably done elsewhere[2] – but highlight the conclusions to provide a basis for the later discussion.

The long-run evidence from the history of the developed countries suggests that these countries have passed through three stages. In the first pre-industrial and pre-capitalist stage there was relative equality; inequality increased as industrialisation got under way; in the final stage (the twentieth century for many industrialised countries) inequality of income distribution was reduced. However, there is some controversy as to whether the third stage represents a continuing process of increased equality or resulted from the discontinuous effects of a series of shock events – viz. the two world wars, and the change from heavy unemployment to full employment. Some twentieth century data for developed countries is reproduced in Appendix 1 of this chapter. The three stage interpretation of this (very shaky) evidence is consistent with the now widely accepted interpretation of the second type of evidence – cross-sectional evidence of income distribution in different countries. According to this the least developed countries (as indicated by *per capita* income of less than $100 in 1965) show less inequality (a lower Gini coefficient) than a middle group of countries (*per capita* income between $100 and $500–1,000); the most developed countries (*per capita* income above $1,000) have more equal income distribution than the middle-income countries and, from then on, on the whole, equality of income distribution appears to increase as *per capita* income rises. The analysis supports Oshima's conclusion that countries pass through four stages of development – undeveloped, underdeveloped, semi-developed and fully developed – and that inequality increases through the first three stages and diminishes in the fourth.

If this interpretation of the time series evidence for developed countries and the cross-sectional evidence for all countries is correct and applicable to present day poor countries, then one would expect their recent history of trends in income distribution to vary according to the stage of development. However, there are two reasons for suspecting that it might be naïve to expect their experience to fit in systematically with the historical evidence. One important reason is that there have been changes in technology and in population trends which make it likely that their current experience may diverge from the historical norm. The other is that the broad historical and cross-sectional generalisations take stage of development as the only variable affecting inequality. Not only does this neglect technology and population, as just suggested, but it also ignores social structure, including social institutions, the property and payments systems, government policies on taxation, public goods, relief payments and so on. While the evidence does suggest a strong relationship between stage of development and inequality, it does not suggest that this is an exclusive relationship as shown by the departures from the stage of development 'norm' by individual countries (see Table 1.2 in the Appendix). There is evidence, for example, that the socialist countries have less inequality for any given stage of development, than capitalist and mixed economies, while Adelman and Morris find six socio-economic variables to be significantly related to the degree of equality. The use of evidence from one set of countries (whether cross-sectional or time series) as a guide to likely developments elsewhere is extremely dubious methodologically. The required assumption of a mechanistical growth process applicable to all countries irrespective of historical and social circumstances is belied by experience and common sense.

Ahluwalia's (1974) summary of recent experience in trends in income distribution in poor countries suggests varying experience; some countries with high growth rates have experienced increased inequality (Panama, Brazil, Mexico), others have experienced increased equality (Taiwan, Iran, Bulgaria), while a similar variety of experience is shown among slow growers. The Griffin and Khan case studies come to apparently more startling conclusions. Income distribution worsened and poverty increased in *all* the countries in Southeast Asia that they studied, whether they were fast or slow growers, with one notable exception – China. However, their conclusions are not as starkly in conflict with those of Ahluwalia as might appear because the coverage of the two differ; Griffin and Khan agree that inequality was reduced in Taiwan, although it was not one of their cases, while some of the other countries they studied – Indonesia and Malaysia – were not covered by Ahluwalia. The two studies agree that inequality increased in India and the Philippines, though probably not about the extent of the increase. The most significant disagreement concerns Sri Lanka: Lee (in Griffin and Khan) believes that inequality increased there, rather than decreased, justifying this conclusion on the basis of trends in consumption expenditure, prices and real wages which he feels throw considerable doubt on the income data used in Chenery *et al.* Whatever the truth with respect to Sri Lanka, the debate highlights the dubious quality of the data and the necessity for in-depth country studies to take into account changes in relative prices as well as income and consumption expenditure, in analysing trends.

Griffin and Khan's findings are not in conflict with the cross-sectional or time series data in that all the countries they studied could be described as moving from the undeveloped to the underdeveloped stage of development and consequently inequality would be expected to increase. However, the uniformity of the changes, their magnitude, the extent of and increase in numbers whose incomes are well below any reasonable minimum poverty standards and the reduction in absolute incomes of the bottom 40 per cent and particularly the bottom 20 per cent of income receivers, which occurred *even in countries where per capita incomes were growing quite fast*, present a challenge to analysis and to policy. In particular, these facts challenge two strategies and their analytical underpinning, as Griffin and Khan point out. They make nonsense of a 'trickle down' strategy in any country structurally similar to those they examine; and they shed considerable doubt on the potential of redistribution through growth policies. If growth is likely to be accompanied by increasing immiseration, then redistribution is required just to offset this. Yet the analysis of the case studies suggest that policies accompanying immiserising growth are at best neutral *and at worst reinforce those immiserising trends.*

II ANALYSIS

The distribution of real disposable income amounts to the distribution of acknowledged claims over resources – what Sen describes as exchange entitlements.[3] How these claims are distributed depends on the institutional framework of the economy and the nature of the technology in use.

It is worth drawing a distinction between *primary* claims on resources which arise directly out of the productive process of work and accumulation, and *secondary* claims which result from the transfer of primary claims. These secondary claims may be administered by the government in the form of taxes or they may work through family, tribal or other channels on a voluntary or semi-voluntary basis. The distinction is somewhat tentative because in some societies there is no clear distinction between the types of payment. For a system of payment in which need enters directly into the rules determining the primary distribution of income – e.g. the kibbutz, or the communes, or some types of family work units – the distinction between primary and secondary claims may be inapplicable.

The distribution of primary claims is the outcome of the institutional system in being – which determines the rules according to which claims are distributed – and technological/economic factors which determine how these rules work out in terms of actual income distribution. Secondary income distribution is dependent on institutional/social and political factors which are often heavily influenced by the primary distribution.

Secondary claims of one sort or another tend to play a more important role at early and late stages of development, and the least role in the middle developing stage (or what Sen has described as PEST – the Pure Exchange Standard Transition). At the early stages of development, secondary transfers take place informally through family, tribe and so on. At the latest stage they take place formally through the state. It is in the middle stage – where most of the countries analysed are now – that primary income distribution is of greatest significance. At that stage formal state-organised secondary transfer is of relatively minor importance, and tends to reinforce rather than counteract primary inequality; informal transfers probably offset primary inequality but at a diminishing rate as industrialisation and modernisation proceed, thus contributing to a deterioration in income distribution over time. It is therefore to primary income distribution that one must turn to analyse the trends in income distribution.

There are many different sets of rules that have been or might be adopted which determine how primary claims are generated and distributed. The rules may be classified into three types:

1. *Rules governing how income from work is determined.* In some systems (e.g. self-employment) income from work is determined by the total revenue generated from the operation. In others (e.g. wage-labour) it depends on the supply and demand for the labour involved, which in turn depend on labour's marginal revenue product and alternative

income-earning opportunities for the labour concerned. In some systems of wage payment, wages are strictly related to hours worked; in others productivity while at work enters directly into wage determination. In sharecropping and similar systems income from work is some predetermined proportion of the value of total output. In communally organised productive units, income from work may be related to work performance (in hours or productivity) or need, or determined as some share of the product. In such systems, social and political frictions and pressures play a role in determining the rules governing income distribution. It has been noted, for example with reference to China, that within relatively small units these pressures tend towards egalitarian rules as being those minimising social friction.

2. *Rules governing access to work.* Access to work involves access to complementary assets – of land, machinery, other inputs, marketing channels and so on. Thus for any set of rules under the first category, which relate income from work to its productivity, the distributional consequences of the set of rules depend on the distribution of the quantity and productivity of the complementary assets to which people gain access. Again a wide range of rules may be observed ranging from hereditary access, access via caste or tribe, to access in the market system where it is dependent on a supply/demand relationship between employers and employees. In the market system, in contrast to most others, access to work is not guaranteed to all – those whose productivity falls below the wage rate are denied access. In communally organised systems access to work is normally guaranteed to all, but systems differ as to how the work is allocated.

3. *Rules governing the accumulation of assets* – often described as the system of property rights – which determine how property is held, the extent to which individuals or groups of individuals may accumulate assets and the rights (defined in terms of offering access to others and payment for their use by others) that asset accumulation confers. It is well established that systems of property rights vary enormously between societies ranging from completely communal ownership to completely unfettered private accumulation. In between there are innumerable traditional tenure systems and a variety of mixed economy systems with nationalisation of some assets, co-operative ownership of producers or consumers and so on.

There are obvious links between the three sets of rules described. Thus the significance of the determination of access to different types of work differs according to whether income is related or unrelated to labour productivity. The significance of the system of property rights in turn in part depends on how far the acquisition of property rights also involves the power to determine access to work via access to complementary assets, and so on. It is clear that, for any given technological and economic situation, the distribution of primary income will be closely determined by the rules in use, or what for brevity we describe as the payments system.

As suggested, societies have differed greatly in the rules adopted. Very broadly – and no doubt superficially – we may divide payments systems into four prototypes:

1. *Pre-capitalist, pre-industrial systems.* Property rights are held partly communally and partly privately and are determined by convention and force. The rights property confer are more limited than in the capitalist stage – and property confers obligations as well as rights. Access to work is determined largely by historically formed convention. Generally both access to work and access to income are guaranteed in one way or another to all. In a pre-industrial technology, the distribution of complementary assets is less important than in later stages because technological unevenness in opportunity is less; moreover to the extent that prices and incomes are partly determined by convention rather than the market, this may also limit the extent of inequality arising from differential productivity.

2. *Pure capitalism.* Here property is held privately and accumulation (and decumulation) is unlimited. Asset accumulation confers claims on primary resources by bestowing the right to earn incomes through the direct employment of others; through lending assets to others; and through investment in human capital. Those without assets are dependent on finding employers who will provide them with access to the complementary resources; this in turn depends on the relationship between supply and demand for their labour. Income from work is determined by these forces and by their underlying determinants – in particular technology, capital accumulation and the labour supply.

3. *Mixed economies.* These are economies which accept the basic market and capitalist framework but impose restrictions of various types on the unfettered operation of pure capitalism – for example, by minimum (and sometimes maximum) wages, restrictions on private asset accumulation, the development of some communally owned assets

and communally provided services. The right to work may be guaranteed by government intervention, or failing that the right to a certain minimum income may be guaranteed irrespective of the work situation. The variants of the mixed economy are more or less endless. Much political and economic debate within them is concerned with precisely how to vary the rules so as to get the best combination of economic efficiency and social justice.

4. *Socialist economies.* In such economies private asset accumulation is severely limited as are the rights asset accumulation confers. Work, as argued, is normally guaranteed to all. Within this broad structure the rules, as to distribution of work opportunities, organisation of production and determination of income, differ enormously. At one end of the spectrum they come close to a market system but without private asset accumulation on any scale, thus generating income differentials according to relative productivity and supply and demand – though because full employment is ensured and because private asset accumulation is limited, income differentials tend to be far narrower than in mixed economies. At the other extreme, the socialist ideal of 'from each according to his ability to each according to his need' is more closely approximated. However, such an ideal is normally only realised within small units – e.g. kibbutzim – leaving room for the emergence of inequality *between* units (see for example Khan's discussion on China in Griffin and Khan, and Lardy (1975)).

From a taxonomic view, it might be worth distinguishing between pure capitalist and market systems. In both the determination of employment and the wage rate occurs through the market, but a market system does not necessarily involve capitalist property rights. Hence (see, e.g., Lerner) some socialists have advocated a market system. However, in what follows, the two terms have been used more or less interchangeably. These four prototypes are prototypes of payments systems, *not* of economies. Most actual economies have hybrid characteristics – some from one prototype, some from others.[5] For example, in many poor economies, payments are traditional in some areas, notably parts of the agricultural sector, pure capitalist in others, with mixed economy characteristics in the modern sector, and with cooperative or communal organisation for some activities. A similar, though somewhat more limited, range is to be found in most industrialised countries. There is no unique relationship between the type of technology in use and the payments system, but there is a strong tendency for traditional techniques to be associated with a traditional payments system and modern advanced country technology to be associated with mixed economy or socialist payments systems.

All the economies which have exhibited growing impoverishment and inequality have been hybrid both in relation to their payments systems and to technology. In the advanced technology industrial sector, they tend to display mixed economy characteristics with minimum wage legislation, and social security systems, progressive taxation, control of profits, nationalisation and so on. The remainder of the economy – the urban informal sector and most of the rural sector – contains a mixture of traditional and pure capitalist characteristics, and a mixture of traditional and modern technology. The pure capitalist system has been making inroads into the traditional payments system. Those areas in which increasing impoverishment is most acute seem to be those in which the pure capitalist rules are most widely in evidence. This is true with respect to all three types of rules described above – viz. rules in relation to work access, to income from work and to asset accumulation. For the most part, those countries in Asia which have *not* suffered from worsening income distribution and increasing impoverishment have modified the operation of the pure capitalist rules. China replaced the pure capitalist system with a socialist one as did the other socialist countries. Taiwan, while retaining the capitalist system, introduced an effective land reform.

The Taiwan story is obviously more complex than this suggests, as will be discussed briefly below.[6] Nor is the growing impoverishment in informal urban and rural sectors, in those countries with capitalist payments systems, solely to be attributed to the payments system. The impoverishment can be seen as due to the *interaction* between the market payments system, technology and population increase. Technology and population alone are not sufficient to explain the emergence of poverty as shown by the example of countries facing a similar situation which have avoided impoverishment, and as seems obvious from *a priori* argument; i.e. with growth in *per capita* production it cannot be argued that growing impoverishment is inevitable. It must therefore in part be due to the payments system. But given the market payments system, the nature of technology has played a critical role in generating inequality – with different technology or different demographic factors much of the impoverishment might have been avoided.

In the remainder of this section I shall try to elucidate the interaction between payments system, technology and population growth and the consequent impoverishment.

Modern technology in the industrial sector involves high capital/

labour ratios, and an industrialisation process based on it inevitably means that total savings are largely concentrated on the minority who find employment in the modern sector. This sector offers high wages to ensure an efficient and stable workforce. Partly because of technological requirements and partly because of the nature of organisation of the large firms with strong foreign connections, the sector almost invariably acquires mixed economy characteristics in its payments system. Only a small proportion of the natural growth in population can be employed in the sector because of the lumpiness of the technology which is designed for the advanced capital-rich countries. The rest of the population who form a growing number, because of the rapid growth in population and the slow growth in modern sector employment, have increasingly few complementary assets to work with in relation to their growing numbers; both the capital/labour and the land/labour ratios tend to worsen for the majority. There is therefore likely to be an overall worsening in their incomes relative to those in the modern sector, which is compounded by the fact that the modern sector tends to produce inappropriately high income products and require advanced country style infrastructural services. Government services of education, health, roads, ports, airports and so on have to be concentrated on the modern sector which not only possesses the political force to secure them but also requires them if it is to operate at all efficiently. Concentration of resources on this sector deprives the rest of the economy, comprising the majority of the population, of both welfare and investment resources. The nature of the products the modern sector produces also works to the detriment of the remainder of the economy. While the high-income products designed for richer consumers in advanced countries meet the wants of the high-income groups who have the purchasing power, the goods tend to be of a quality far in excess of those appropriate to meeting the needs of very poor consumers. The modern sector supplies them with few goods appropriate for meeting basic needs either in respect of consumption or of investment.[7] The worsening capital/labour and land/labour ratios outside the modern sector are likely to contribute to worsening absolute *per capita* incomes in these sectors, unless offset by technical progress. In the urban informal sector there is little technical progress to record; in the agricultural sector recent technological breakthroughs have succeeded in raising *per capita* agricultural output, as recorded by the Griffin/Khan case studies, despite the worsening ratios. But the worsening ratios are reflected in worsening incomes for those on the margin – those who rely on wage-employment, those with very little or no land. Worsening incomes for these people may take one of two forms (or both): either real wages tend to fall, reflecting the lowering land/labour ratios, the rise in rents and fall in labour share; or, total quantity of labour demanded by landlords falls (or rises less than the supply) so that with the same wage rate, annual incomes decline. The Griffin/Khan case studies show both of these phenomena. Not only do the incomes of landless labourers (and those with very little land) tend to worsen but also their numbers tend to increase. This can be seen partly as a direct consequence of the rising population, and partly as a process of decumulation of assets which occurs as the very low incomes following land fragmentation and falling incomes, that accompany the worsening in the land/labour ratio, lead smallholders to sell their assets so as to maintain their consumption at a survival level.

In such a system accumulation and decumulation tend to become cumulative; initial decumulation or sale of assets, while providing temporary relief, also leads ultimately to reduced incomes and therefore the need to sell more to survive; conversely accumulation provides the wherewithal to accumulate further. Moreover there is a parallel effect on labour productivity; low nutrition resulting from low incomes reduces labour productivity and therefore incomes in the next period, while high incomes beget high productivity and high incomes. The same cycle can be seen in terms of education and training; the poor cannot afford the education, training or investment in health essential to raise their incomes; the rich can. A similar sort of cumulative cycle has also been observed in control over infrastructural services, finance for inputs, technical advice and so on. Control over the distribution of this sort of service tends to be secured by the relatively prosperous. Accumulation breeds power which breeds further accumulation.

Whether or not lower income groups become absolutely worse off over time (and for many countries there is much controversy over this question), relative impoverishment and worsening income distribution tend to occur.

The process of impoverishment and enrichment described is closely related to the rules of the payment system in a market economy; while lumpiness and bias of technology create the initial conditions, it is the payments system which causes these conditions to produce growing inequality. The accumulation and decumulation of land is possible only in an unfettered capitalist system of private property rights. The lack of work and starvation wages – leading to the vicious cycle described – emerges *because workers are paid according to their marginal product*; given the asset/labour ratios and the technology, their marginal product is abysmally low, even though average product may be at a quite reasonable level. (Appendix 2 provides diagrammatic illustration of this process.)

In both urban and rural areas – as already noted – elements of traditional forms of organisation and pay remain. Thus family production units protect their members to some extent by providing work irrespective of productivity and paying according to some sharing principle. In the rural areas, such forms of organisation are becoming proportionately of diminishing importance. In the urban informal sector, there are family productive units, as well as wage-labour, but the paucity of opportunities means that average incomes of family enterprises are often very low.[8]

There are both parallels and differences between developments in rural and urban informal areas. In both there are demographic pressures which exert a downward influence on average and marginal incomes. In both, output per head, taking the economy as a whole, has been sustained, indeed increased, by technical advances and investment. In the urban areas, the indivisibility of modern technology means that relatively few are employed with expensive and high productivity equipment, with the result of high labour productivity in that sector. But the payments system ensures that the fruits of this rising output and productivity are retained by those directly concerned with this part of the productive process. Growing numbers in the urban areas who are not employed with modern technology – the consequence of population growth, migration and the slow employment growth of the modern technology sector – have few complementary resources to work with, in the way of capital equipment, know-how and market channels. The resources they do possess tend to be of low productivity because of technological neglect. Both average and marginal product is consequently low. Incomes are consequently low both for those in family enterprises and for those in wage employment, making accumulation and enrichment very difficult. In the rural areas, there is less indivisibility of technology – indeed it has often been argued that agricultural technology *is* efficiently divisible. But although this is true in theory, in practice the need for various indivisible inputs, such as irrigation, leads to relative advantage for the larger farmers, as does the administrative machinery providing finance, fertilisers, new seeds, technical advice and so on.[9] In the rural areas the limited supply of land against the growing population, and the tendency for cumulative accumulation or decumulation leads to increasing enrichment of the landlord and growing impoverishment of the rural labourer. The parallel between the two sectors arises because in both cases high average *per capita* output may be combined with very low wage levels and lack of income earning opportunity for those who lack the capital or land to provide their own opportunities. Under these circumstances their marginal product is extremely low and such workers tend to be paid their marginal product.

It might be argued that such pessimistic conclusions are belied by the situation of high minimum incomes and reduced inequality of the now developed countries, and by the experience of such 'success' market economies as Taiwan and S. Korea. In some ways the success of the now developed countries and of Taiwan and S. Korea can be explained in the same way. In all these countries, the rate of growth of employment in the modern sector expanded sufficiently fast to reduce demographic pressures outside it, and eventually to absorb a large proportion of the labour force, thus bringing all incomes towards those generated in the modern sector. But now developed countries' experience offers little immediate hope to poor countries; they suffered a century of impoverishment before incomes of the poor began to rise. Moreover, their population increase was never as rapid nor their modern sector technology as inappropriate as that in poor countries today. In Taiwan, the improved income distribution stemmed partly from a radical land reform, as has already been mentioned. However, the sustained rate of growth of employment in the industrial sector – of 8 per cent p.a. in Taiwan, 10 per cent in S. Korea – which no other country looks like emulating (see Table 1.3 in Appendix 1) must be largely responsible for reduced demographic pressures both in rural and urban areas.

III STRATEGIES

The trickle-down strategy has been effectively demolished as a way of tackling poverty by the facts of increased poverty despite growth in *per capita* income. Of the remaining strategies, some are primarily aimed at tackling poverty and the distribution of income by changing the *secondary* distribution while leaving the *primary* distribution unchanged; some combine a change in secondary with a change in primary distribution; while some concentrate mainly on sources of primary inequality.

All policies which propose to use secondary transfers to offset inequality arising from primary income distribution suffer from a fundamental socio-political weakness. In situations where primary income inequality is increasing, then a major effort of secondary redistribution is required to offset this. But power over the machinery of government – both political and administrative elements – tends to be captured by those who have gained in the primary income distribution. Thus effective redistribution measures are thwarted and secondary transfers tend to reinforce rather than offset the initial primary inequalities. Many case studies attest to the truth and significance of this socio-political mechanism. If this is accepted, it follows that any strategy which is designed solely at the secondary income distribution level, and fails to tackle sources of primary inequality, is an extremely weak one, unlikely to do more than pay lip service to the need for redistribution, while providing a respectable façade for a system which continues to generate appalling poverty.

This criticism applies most obviously to strategies based on using progressive taxation and government expenditure to correct primary inequality. It applies also to the redistribution with growth strategy. In this strategy the forces making for inequality are left untouched; but the additional incomes generated among the elite are then to be taxed to provide investment resources for the poor. Thus *if* effective – and for reasons just given this is unlikely – the policy would subsequently affect asset distribution and therefore primary income distribution, but only marginally. The main forces making for inequality in primary income distribution – the payments system, technology and demography – would remain untouched.

Inequality can only effectively be tackled at the source where it arises – viz. by attacking the mechanisms making for primary inequality. Any policies which rely on secondary transfer and do not attack primary sources are not only unlikely to be put into effect to any degree, but also will be of minor significance in alleviating poverty so long as the main causes of increased poverty continue to operate. The policies suggested are like trying to put out a fire with ten men, while one hundred incendiaries continue to operate, and the ten men turn out to be in the hire of the incendiaries.

Policies designed to correct sources of primary income distribution will also be subject to considerable opposition from the potential losers. For this reason it may be as unrealistic to postulate effective reform in mechanisms making for primary inequality as in mechanisms of secondary transfer. Where a particular system has already established entrenched interests, this is bound to be the case. However, the advantage of reform of primary distribution is that it can take place *before* interests have become entrenched, whereas it is the nature of secondary transfer mechanisms that they operate *after* they have become entrenched. Therefore in some cases it may be more realistic to expect effective reform of the primary distribution than secondary distribution. For one reason before the event any group of people may not know whether they would become gainers or losers by inegalitarian developments, and following Rawls-like principles may therefore want a maximin strategy. This idea of getting in at the beginning and preventing primary inequality developing (or at least developing to the extent it does under the market system) is particularly relevant to the policies that ought to be pursued by a country which has just emerged from an egalitarian revolution: in the immediate post-revolutionary situation a market system might produce near equality, or much greater equality than in the pre-revolutionary situation. But it would be likely eventually to lead to emerging inequalities – which was clearly foreseen by Mao in the 1950s in China, who therefore instituted his major payments reform in the form of the communes.

Even in these societies where the system has already generated substantial inequalities, it may be possible to institute changes in the primary distribution system which prevent a worsening in inequality without meeting the vested interests that are likely to arise if the whole system appears to be threatened: for example by organising marginal farmers into cooperatives before some become gainers, more losers through the process of land accumulation and decumulation.

Policies towards primary distribution

It was argued above that there were three (interacting) sources of increasing inequality in primary income distribution: the technology, population growth and the payments system. Effective policy towards any one of these would do much to alleviate the situation, even without changes in the others.

With a much more labour-intensive, divisible (i.e. small-scale), poverty-orientated technology, inequalities in productivity in different occupations would be considerably reduced; in theory, it should be possible for each member of the labour force to find employment with comparable technological resources; appropriate products designed to meet basic needs would lessen inequality and imbalances in consumption. With such technology, the market payments system would produce much greater equality in income distribution. In theory then technological reform could make a substantial contribution. But the continuous advance in the productivity of advanced country technology owing to concentration of R and D there, the poor performance of most alternative technologies owing to technological neglect, plus the many pressures – internal and international[10] – leading to the adoption of advanced country technology, make this a very problematic approach on its own.

Demographic factors are significant because with a much lower growth in population, the pressure on the informal urban sector and the rural sector to absorb extra manpower would be less, and so therefore would the downward pressure on low incomes. However successful demographic policy is more likely to be the consequence than the cause of improved income distribution, as indeed is also true of an appropriate technology policy.[11]

We now turn to the payments system, which was the central focus of the analysis in Section II. It was argued there that it was the interaction between technology, population growth rate, and payments system that was responsible for increasing inequality; and that with the same technology and population growth, the primary income distribution could be transformed by transforming the payments system.

In the case of developing countries experiencing increasing impoverishment on a major scale, the following features of the payments system were argued to be particularly responsible: first, the free market in land and other assets allowing progressive accumulation/decumulation of assets; secondly, the system of access to work dictated by the employer/employee relationship, such that people could only work if employers considered their marginal revenue product was likely to exceed their wage – this aspect of the system means that many able-bodied people are idle much of the time, when this condition is not met. Thirdly, the fact that determination of income from work depended on the supply/demand relationship, so that low productivity resulting from a high labour/resources ratio led to low incomes, and a consequent vicious cycle of asset decumulation, malnutrition and low productivity.

Changes in the payments system to modify or eliminate any or all of these features could radically alter the picture. Let me illustrate by taking some arbitrarily chosen, and in some ways absurd, proposals. There are many variants of possible changes. Take the first feature. Suppose land sales of any kind were totally forbidden. This would prevent increasing alienation of land. While today it would be too late to do much in most countries, had it been rigorously adopted twenty years ago, rural income distribution today might be quite different. Or take the second feature: suppose everyone were guaranteed the right to work at some predetermined reasonably set wage. This would eliminate poverty due to lack of work, much insecurity and increase productive capacity. Or take the third and suppose income from work were to be fixed by some convention, or at, say, some fixed relationship to average product, or determined by need. It is immediately obvious that any of these changes would have major and beneficial effects on income distribution. It is also obvious that they would have other implications for distribution of resources and so on that would need careful thinking out. These *particular* proposals are not intended as serious propositions. Obviously better reforms could be devised than, for example, just freezing the sale of all assets. The point is to emphasize one very simple idea: that reform of the payments system is of fundamental importance to effective attack on poverty.

Once the principle of payments system reform is accepted then considerable detailed work would be required on the economic and political feasibility of different schemes and on the potential for piecemeal reform in part of the economy as against wholesale reform. Payments reforms have been introduced throughout the world in economies at varying stages of development, both in a wholesale way and in a piecemeal way. In Tanzania, the Ujamaa experiment provides an example; while there has been considerable criticism of the experiment from the point of view of economic efficiency and participant popularity, little attempt has been made to compare the success of the villages in terms of primary income levels and distribution, as compared with what would have emerged in a free market system. The kibbutz provides an example of alternative payments schemes in the context of a mixed economy. Many other examples could be cited. A major research priority is to examine these experiences from two points of view: (1) their effectiveness in countering poverty, and (2) the conditions required to make such experiments successful. The socialist countries – particularly China – provide plentiful and varied case studies of wholesale reform of payments systems.

In reform of the payments system, the question of *motivation* has also to be considered. This is not simply a matter of work incentives and efficiency, but also critically of the acceptability of the rules to those who have the power to enforce or pervert them. The question of motivation is a complex one where historical developments, education and values interact, making the possibility and form of effective reform depend on these variables and therefore vary from society to society.

Reforms of payment schemes differ with respect to feasibility, and with respect to their likely efficiency in preventing impoverishment.

Feasibility is not just a question of political acceptability but also of administration; many schemes that are on the statute book are defeated on the ground. If the reforms are to be effective, reform of the system of property rights in the relevant areas has to have priority because the changes needed in access to and income from work are unlikely to be put into effect so long as private landlords/employers continue to have the right to accumulate assets and to determine conditions of work. Thus minimum wage legislation is notoriously ineffective in the context of a market economy. The state could in theory act as employer of the last resort guaranteeing work to all at some minimum wage. But if such work is to be productive enough to be self-financing, or nearly self-financing, the state has to provide the complementary assets with which to work – hence a corresponding portion of assets must be socialised. One reason underlying the comparative failure of many public works schemes is that they did not make use of sufficient land and machinery. They therefore proved a drain on resources and for this reason could not be expanded sufficiently or extended long enough to make any real inroad into the problem of poverty. It seems that some change in the system of property rights is a necessary precondition of successful change on the work/income side of the payments system.

One such reform that has been widely advocated is land reform. Griffin and Khan, for example, see it as essential for an attack on the problems they describe. The consequences of land reform clearly depend on the nature of the reform. If the reform simply consists in a once and for all redistribution of land from the large landlords to the landless without being ongoing or without changing other elements in the payments system, it will have short-run beneficial effects on primary income distribution but inequality and impoverishment are likely to re-emerge, since their underlying causes have not been changed. The policy could be made more effective in the long run by making it ongoing – i.e. having a major redistribution and then imposing rigid ceilings on holdings. However, even this may not be sufficient to prevent the re-emergence of poverty – with increasing population growth and land consolidation at the lower end of the holdings, and landless labourer will again become a major source of poverty. In any case, so long as the market system prevails, offering great rewards to accumulation, land reform is unlikely to be effective – as shown in the examples quoted by Griffin and Khan.[12] Other land reforms have had short-run benefits but have been drowned by inegalitarian accumulation in the medium term, as for example in Iran and Mexico.

What is needed is not just redistribution of land (and other assets) but a change in the way in which they are held towards communal or cooperative ownership. It is only with this sort of change, that work can be guaranteed and income fairly shared.

CONCLUSIONS

The main thesis of this chapter is that developments in the Third World – both in those countries where income distribution has improved and in those where it has worsened – can be explained as the outcome of the interaction between the institutionally determined rules and technological developments which together determine the primary distribution of claims. Secondary claims are regarded as being of secondary importance because of the evidence that secondary transfer policy rarely effectively counteracts primary tendencies. The multi-dimensional nature of the determinants of income distribution has important policy implications: it means interactions between the various dimensions may render policies ineffective, which appear superficially plausible. It also means that different types of policy are likely to be effective under different assumptions about some of the other variables – for example, the appropriate technology policy will differ according to the institutional setting, while the most effective institutional setting will differ according to the assumptions made about technology.

In the discussion of policy the chapter emphasised the need to tackle the problem of income distribution at the source by changing the rules according to which the product is distributed; the distribution of productivity from work could be made much more equal by a fairer distribution of the assets with which people work; the distribution of income from work could be made much fairer by a system which related earnings to average productivity rather than marginal product; both distribution and productivity would be improved by a system which guaranteed productive work to all. The chapter placed prime emphasis on the payments system, but successful reform in technology could also play a critical role in contributing to improved distribution, even without a reform of the payments system. Any reform in the system would be made easier to achieve and sustain if technology were transformed so as to eliminate the enormous productivity differentials it currently generates, differentials which consequently tend to be reflected in similar earnings differentials.

Work, Income and Inequality

Similarly, effective control of population increase would help prevent impoverishment. But there are interactions between the different approaches in terms of their feasibility from a politico-administrative point of view. Thus population control does not appear to be a feasible policy on its own – but it might be the outcome of a transformed income distribution resulting from other policies. The dominance of large-scale, profit-oriented decision-makers with strong international links prevents the introduction of alternative technology; a radically changed income distribution which therefore changed both the nature of markets and the control over investment resources would make an alternative technology considerably more practicable. This leaves the emphasis on payments system as the starting point: but it does not of course follow that political and administrative forces will favour such a change.

APPENDIX 1

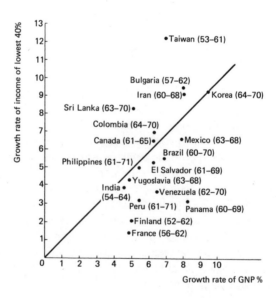

Figure 1.1   Growth and the lowest 40%
Source: Ahluwalia, in Chenery *et al.* (1974).

TABLE 1.1 Shares in national income of different income groups, for selected countries over long periods

Successive entries and dates

United Kingdom:

Income before tax	Bowley		Clark	Seers			Lydall	
	1880	1913	1929	1938	1947	1938	1949	1957
Top 5%	48	43	33	31	24	29	23.5	18
Top 20%	58	59	51	52	46	50	47.5	41.5

Prussia:

	Procopovitch				Reich Statistical Office	
	1854	1875	1896	1913	1913	1928
Top 5%	21	26	27	30	31	26
Top 20%		48	45	50	50	49
Lowest 60%		34		33	32	31

Mueller				
1873–80	1881–90	1891–1900	1901–10	1911–13
Top 5% 28	30	32	32	31

Saxony:

	Procopovitch			Reich Statistical Office	
	1880	1896	1912	1913	1928
Top 5%	34	36	33	33	28
Top 20%	56	57	55	54	50
Lowest 60%	27	26.5	27	28	31

TABLE 1.1 (*Contd*)

Successive entries and dates

Germany:

	Reich Statistical Office			Mueller		United Nations[1]		Wochenbericht[1]	
	1913	*1928*	*1928(adj.)*	*1928*	*1936*	*1936*	*1950*	*1955*	*1959*
Top 5%	31	27	21	20	23	28	24	18	18
Top 20%	50	49	45			53	48	43	43
Lowest 60%	32	31	34			26.5	29	34	34

Netherlands:

	1938	*1949*	*1954*
Top 5%	19	17	13
Top 20%	49	45.5	38.5
Lowest 60%	31	34	40

Denmark:

	Zeuthen I			Zeuthen II			Bjerke	
	1870	*1903*	*1935*	*1908*	*1925*	*1939*	*1949*	*1955*
Top 5%	36.5	28	26	30	26	24.5	19	17.5
Top 10%	50	38	36	39	37	35	29.5	27.4
Top 20%				55	53	51	45	44
Lowest 60%				31	25	27	32	32

Sweden:

Benzel

	1930	1935	1945
Top 5%	30	28	24
Top 20%	59	58	52
Lowest 60%	19	19	23

Norway:

	1907	1958	1948
Top 5% country districts	27	20	14
Top 5% cities	28–32	22	19

United Nations

	1935	1945	1948	1948	1954
Top 5%	28	23.5	20	20	17
Top 20%	56	51	47	45	43
Lower 60%	23	26	29	32	34

United States:

Kuznets

	1913–19	1919–28	1929–38	1939–43	1944–8
Top 1%	14	14	13	11	9
Top 5%	24[2]	25	25	21	17

Department of Commerce

	1929	1935–6	1941	1944–7	1950–4	1955–9
Top 5%	30	26.5	24	21	21	20
Top 20%	54	52	49	46	45	45
Lowest 60%	26	27	29	32	33	32

Source: S. Kuznets: 'Quantitative aspects of the economic growth of nations: VIII. Distribution of income by size', in *Economic Development and Cultural Change* (Chicago, Jan. 1963), Table 16, pp. 60 ff., cited in Paukert (1973). [1]Federal Republic of Germany. [2]1917–19.

Note: Data relating to after-tax incomes have been omitted.

TABLE 1.2 Size distribution of personal income before tax in 56 countries: Income shares received by quintiles of recipients in the neighbourhood of 1965

Country and level of GDP per head	Percentiles of recipients						Gini ratio	GDP per head in 1965 (US $)
	Below 20%	21–40%	41–60%	61–80%	81–95%	96–100%		
Under $100								
Chad (1958)	8.0	11.6	15.4	22.0	20.0	23.0	0.35	68
Dahomey (1959)	8.0	10.0	12.0	20.0	18.0	32.0	0.42	73
Niger (1960)	7.8	11.6	15.6	23.0	19.0	23.0	0.34	81
Nigeria (1959)	7.0	7.0	9.0	16.1	22.5	38.4	0.51	74
Sudan (1969)	5.6	9.4	14.3	22.6	31.0	17.1	0.40	97
Tanzania (1964)	4.8	7.8	11.0	15.4	18.1	42.9	0.54	61
Burma (1958)	10.0	13.0	13.0	15.5	20.3	28.2	0.35	64
India (1956–57)	8.0	12.0	16.0	22.0	22.0	20.0	0.33	95
Madagascar (1960)	3.9	7.8	11.3	18.0	22.0	37.0	0.53	92
Group average	*7.0*	*10.0*	*13.1*	*19.4*	*21.4*	*29.1*	*0.419*	*78.3*
$ 101–200								
Morocco (1965)	7.1	7.4	7.7	12.4	44.5	20.6	0.50	180
Senegal (1960)	3.0	7.0	10.0	16.0	28.0	36.0	0.56	192
Sierra Leone (1968)	3.8	6.3	9.1	16.7	30.3	33.8	0.56	142
Tunisia (1971)	5.0	5.7	10.0	14.4	42.6	22.4	0.53	187
Bolivia (1968)	3.5	8.0	12.0	15.5	25.3	35.7	0.53	132
Ceylon (Sri Lanka) (1963)	4.5	9.2	13.8	20.2	33.9	18.4	0.44	140
Pakistan (1963–64)	6.5	11.0	15.5	22.0	25.0	20.0	0.37	101
South Korea (1966)	9.0	14.0	18.0	23.0	23.5	12.5	0.26	107
Group average	*5.3*	*8.6*	*12.0*	*17.5*	*31.6*	*24.9*	*0.468*	*147.6*

$ 201–300

Malaya (1957–58)	6.5	11.2	15.7	22.6	26.2	17.8	0.36	278
Fiji (1968)	4.0	8.0	13.3	22.4	30.9	21.4	0.46	295
Ivory Coast (1959)	8.0	10.0	12.0	15.0	26.0	29.0	0.43	213
Zambia (1959)	6.3	9.6	11.1	15.9	19.6	37.5	0.48	207
Brazil (1960)	3.5	9.0	10.2	15.8	23.1	38.4	0.54	207
Ecuador (1968)	6.3	10.1	16.1	23.2	19.6	24.6	0.38	202
El Salvador (1965)	5.5	6.5	8.8	17.8	28.4	33.0	0.53	249
Peru (1961)	4.0	4.3	8.3	15.2	19.3	48.3	0.61	237
Iraq (1956)	2.0	6.0	8.0	16.0	34.0	34.0	0.60	285
Philippines (1961)	4.3	8.4	12.0	19.5	28.3	27.5	0.48	240
Colombia (1964)	2.2	4.7	9.0	16.1	27.7	40.4	0.62	275
Group average	*4.8*	*8.0*	*11.3*	*18.1*	*25.7*	*32.0*	*0.499*	*244.4*

$ 301–500

Gabon (1960)	2.0	6.0	7.0	14.0	24.0	47.0	0.64	368
Costa Rica (1969)	5.5	8.1	11.2	15.2	25.0	35.0	0.50	360
Jamaica (1958)	2.2	6.0	10.8	19.5	31.3	30.2	0.56	465
Surinam (1962)	10.7	11.6	14.7	20.6	27.0	15.4	0.30	424
Lebanon (1955–60)	3.0	4.2	15.8	16.0	27.0	34.0	0.55	440
Barbados (1951–52)	3.6	9.3	14.2	21.3	29.3	22.3	0.45	368
Chile (1968)	5.4	9.6	12.0	20.7	29.7	22.6	0.44	486
Mexico (1963)	3.5	6.6	11.1	19.3	30.7	28.8	0.53	441
Panama (1969)	4.9	9.4	13.8	15.2	22.2	34.5	0.48	490
Group average	*4.5*	*7.9*	*12.3*	*18.0*	*27.4*	*30.0*	*0.494*	*426.9*

$ 501–1000

Republic of South Africa (1965)	1.9	4.2	10.2	18.0	26.4	39.4	0.58	521
Argentina (1961)	7.0	10.4	13.2	17.9	22.2	29.3	0.42	782
Trinidad and Tobago (1957–58)	3.4	9.1	14.6	24.3	26.1	22.5	0.44	704
Venezuela (1962)	4.4	9.0	16.0	22.9	23.9	23.2	0.42	904

TABLE 1.2 (Contd)

Country and level of GDP per head	Percentiles of recipients						Gini ratio	GDP per head in 1965 (US $)
	Below 20%	21–40%	41–60%	61–80%	81–95%	96–100%		
Greece (1957)	9.0	10.3	13.3	17.9	26.5	23.0	0.38	591
Japan (1962)	4.7	10.6	15.8	22.9	31.2	14.8	0.39	838
Group average	*5.1*	*8.9*	*13.9*	*20.6*	*26.0*	*25.4*	*0.438*	*723.3*
$ 1001–2000								
Israel (1957)	6.8	13.4	18.6	21.8	28.2	11.2	0.30	1 243
United Kingdom (1964)	5.1	10.2	16.6	23.9	25.0	19.0	0.38	1 590
Netherlands (1962)	4.0	10.0	16.0	21.6	24.8	23.6	0.42	1 400
Federal Republic of Germany (1964)	5.3	10.1	13.7	18.0	19.2	33.7	0.45	1 667
France (1962)	1.9	7.6	14.0	22.8	28.7	25.0	0.50	1 732
Finland (1962)	2.4	8.7	15.4	24.2	28.3	21.0	0.46	1 568
Italy (1948)	6.1	10.5	14.6	20.4	24.3	24.1	0.40	1 011
Puerto Rico (1963)	4.5	9.2	14.2	21.5	28.6	22.0	0.44	1 101
Norway (1963)	4.5	12.1	18.5	24.4	25.1	15.4	0.35	1 717
Australia (1966–67)	6.6	13.4	17.8	23.4	24.4	14.4	0.30	1 823
Group average	*4.7*	*10.5*	*15.9*	*22.2*	*25.7*	*20.9*	*0.401*	*1 485.2*
$ 2001 and above								
Denmark (1963)	5.0	10.8	16.8	24.2	26.3	16.9	0.37	2 078
Sweden (1963)	4.4	9.6	17.4	24.6	26.4	17.6	0.39	2 406
United States (1969)	5.6	12.3	17.6	23.4	26.3	14.8	0.34	3 233
Group average	*5.0*	*10.9*	*17.3*	*24.1*	*26.3*	*16.4*	*0.365*	*2 572.3*

Source: Paukert (1973).

TABLE 1.3 Average annual rate of growth of economically active
population engaged in manufacturing and secondary sector

Countries	Manufacturing	Secondary Sector
Sri Lanka (1963–71)	1.29	1.91
India (1961–71)	−0.48	−0.37
S. Korea (1960–74)	10.66	9.91
Philippines (1960–74)	4.60	5.14
Thailand (1960–73)	7.47	8.15
Brazil (1960–70)	4.91	–
Costa Rica (1963–73)	4.43	4.61
Taiwan (1956–75)	–	8.06

Sources: (1) ILO, *Yearbook of Labour Statistics*, various years. (2) Economic Planning Council, Executive Yuan, Republic of China, *Taiwan Statistical Data Book* (1976).

Note: Secondary Sector = Mining + Manufacturing + Construction + Electricity, Gas and Water.

TABLE 1.4 Proportion of economically active
population engaged in mining, manufacturing,
construction, gas, electricity and water

Country	Date	%
Brazil	1960	13.4
	1970	17.9
India	1961	11.4
	1971	11.5
S. Korea	1960	9.1
	1974	21.1
Philippines	1960	12.3
	1974	13.9
Sri Lanka	1963	12.1
	1971	10.9
Thailand	1960	4.2
	1973	9.4
Costa Rica	1963	18.8
	1973	17.8
Taiwan	1956	15.0
	1975	35.5

Sources: (1) ILO, *Yearbook of Labour Statistics*, various years. (2) Economic Planning Council, Executive Yuan, Republic of China, *Taiwan Statistical Data Book* (1975).

APPENDIX 2: DIAGRAMMATIC REPRESENTATION

The diagram below relates average and marginal product to employment at a given point in time.[13] The flat portion of the curve, MM^1 represents high productivity employment in the modern sector; as employment/self-employment expands beyond that section, marginal product falls off rapidly, and average product also falls, although less rapidly. Workers in the modern sector receive some fraction of the total product, say OW. In the rest of the economy workers are assumed to receive their marginal product. Thus if total work force is ON^1, then they receive OP^1. The rapidly diminishing marginal product in the non-modern sector is the result of the low level of complementary resources in that sector – both investment and technology – and in the rural area the increase in labour/land ratios.

(a) **Demographic pressures**

Over time the work force expands due to demographic forces, thus ON^1 shifts to ON^2, and so on. Assuming nothing else changes and there are no additional opportunities in the modern sector, this depresses the marginal product and the wage so that it falls below subsistence, OS to OP^2.

(b) **Technology**

With changes in technology the relationships described change. Technical change increases productivity overall, but not equally for all types of activity.

For any given level of employment, *average* product rises. While marginal product outside the modern sector *may* rise a bit, it does not rise proportionately with average product since in the urban areas technical progress is concentrated in the modern sector, and in the rural areas a similar phenomenen occurs in that it is concentrated on intra-marginal labour and sometimes, though not always, intra-marginal irrigated land. Technical progress thus increases the divergence between average and marginal product. The combination of rising population and this type of technological change further pushes down marginal product in relation to average product, and makes for a combination of rising average product and declining marginal product, as shown in the

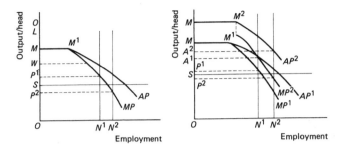

Figure 1.2.

diagram, where $OA^2 > OA^1$ but $OP^2 < OP^1$.

It can immediately be seen that the impoverishment that occurs – illustrated by the increasing proportion of employment at below subsistence if workers are paid marginal product – might be prevented in one of three ways: (i) by stopping, or reducing, the increase in population; (ii) by changing the nature of technology; and (iii) by changing the payments system so pay is related to average not marginal product.

NOTES

1. These questions have been widely discussed. See e.g. Atkinson (1975) and elsewhere; and Sen (1973) and (1981). In the latter Sen provides ingenious suggestions for improved measurements.
2. See Ahluwalia in Chenery *et al.* (1974) and Ahluwalia (1976), Paukert (1973), and Griffin and Khan (1977).
3. See Sen's fascinating analysis of the origin of famines and of exchange entitlements (1981), to which I am substantially indebted.
4. I owe this point to Carl Riskin.
5. It might be argued that the 'mixed' economy is already a hybrid – between socialist and capitalist payments systems. But this argument would, I believe, be wrong – the mixed economy payments system is a significant prototype of its own, being in essence a form of regulated capitalism with significant state participation in and (on balance) support for capitalist interests.
6. See Chapter 4 and Fei, Ranis and Kuo (1979) for a detailed account.
7. For much greater elaboration of this argument about the relation of advanced country technology to patterns of development see my *Technology and Underdevelopment* (1977).

8. The nature of organisation and opportunities in the urban informal sector has been subject to some controversy – with some, e.g. ILO (1972), seeing it as primarily organised on non-exploitative family self-employment lines and being a source of potential growth, while others (notably Leys (1975)) believe that it is a source of exploitation and impoverishment, with a wage-labour system predominating. It is clear that both forms of organisation operate, and, despite unevenness of incomes within the sector, both are a source of poverty rather than riches, because of the very low level of complementary resources within the sector.

9. But see Lipton (1978) for reasons why the technology need not be so biased.

10. The determinants of technological choice are discussed at length in my *Technology and Underdevelopment*, op. cit.

11. See R. Cassen (1976) for an extremely useful and detailed survey of the literature behind this dogmatic statement.

12. Several of the studies refer to land reform legislation that is on the statute book but not effective in practice – see the Bihar study and that on Tamil Nadu in particular.

13. The diagrams are, of course, a highly oversimplified representation of a complex situation.

REFERENCES

Adelman, I. and Morris, C. T., *Economic Growth and Social Equity in Developing Countries* (Stanford University Press, 1973).

Ahluwalia, M. S., 'Inequality, poverty and development', *Journal of Development Economics*, vol. 3 (1976).

Atkinson, A. B., *The Economics of Inequality* (Oxford University Press, 1975).

Cassen, R., 'Population and Development: A Survey' in P. Streeten and R. Jolly (eds), *Recent Issues in World Development* (Pergamon, 1981).

Chenery, H., M. S. Ahluwalia, C. L. G. Bell, J. H. Duloy and R. Jolly, *Redistribution with Growth* (Oxford University Press, 1974).

Fei, J. C. H., G. Ranis and S. Kuo, *Equity with Growth: the Taiwan Case* (Oxford University Press, 1979).

Griffin, K. and A. R. Khan (eds), *Poverty and Landlessness in Rural Asia* (Geneva: International Labour Office, 1977).

International Labour Office, *Employment, Incomes and Equality in Kenya.* (Geneva: ILO, 1972).

Lardy, N., 'Centralization and decentralization in China's fiscal management', *The China Quarterly*, no. 61 (1975).

Leys, C., *Underdevelopment in Kenya* (Heinemann, 1975).

Lipton, M., 'Inter-Farm, Inter-Regional and Farm–Non-Farm Income Distribution: 'The Impact of the New Cereal Varieties', *World Development*, Vol. 6, no. 3 (1978).

Paukert, F., 'Income distribution at different levels of development: a survey of evidence', *International Labour Review*, vol. 108, nos 2–3 (August–September 1973).

Oshima, H., 'The international comparison of size distribution of family

incomes with special reference to Asia', *Review of Economics and Statistics* (1962).
Sen, A. K., *On Economic Inequality* (Oxford: Clarendon Press, 1973).
Sen, A. K., *Poverty and Famines* (Oxford University Press, 1981).
Stewart, F., *Technology and Underdevelopment* (Macmillan, 1977).

2 Rent-capitalism and Unequal Development in the Middle East: the Case of Iran

ECKART EHLERS

I THEORETICAL BACKGROUND: THE CONCEPT OF RENT-CAPITALISM

Rent-capitalism is widely discussed in recent German-speaking economic and social geography. Developed in the late 1950s by the Austrian geographer Hans Bobek in connection with a theory of 'the main stages in socio-economic evolution from a geographical point of view', Bobek tried to discern six stages of social and economic evolution:

(a) the food gathering stage;
(b) the stage of specialised collectors, hunters and fishermen;
(c) the stage of clan-peasantry with pastoral nomadism as a subsidiary branch;
(d) the stage of feudally or autocratically organised agrarian societies;
(e) the stage of early urbanism and rent-capitalism; and
(f) the stage of productive capitalism, industrial society and modern urbanism.

Rent-capitalism, defined as a genuine socio-economic stage of its own, especially in the development of hydraulic civilisations (Wittfogel, 1956), has – according to Bobek – emerged in the early Middle East in connection with the upspring of the early city and temple-states both in Egypt and Mesopotamia and has persevered with slight changes and adaptions until our times. The theory of rent-capitalism is well suited for explaining certain aspects of the relationships between organisation of production, system of payment, income distribution and employment. The development and characteristics of rent-capitalism may be described as follows:

Rent-capitalism arose through commercialization and the transformation, undertaken in a plain profit-seeking spirit, of the original lordly (or feudal) claims on income from the peasant and artisan under-strata. Its elaboration was definitively promoted by the keeping of accounts and other forms of rationalization of rent drawing that were developed early in the large temple estates (Bobek 1961, p. 234).

It became practice for the ruling class and its representatives to split agricultural and/or other productive activities into a number of different stages or parts which were considered both as entities within and as part of the whole production process. Thus the peasants' as well as the artisans' productive economy became conceptually split into a system of different factors of production, for each of which a special part in the gross proceeds was calculated. Each was rewarded with a uniform share (in kind) of the proceeds. We shall see that this system is still widespread today.

In regard to its peculiar and characteristic quality in comparison both with the preceding feudal stage and that of the following stage of 'productive capitalism' Bobek argues as follows (op. cit., p. 237):

Rent-capitalism was a true capitalism in so far as it was characterized by a striving for unlimited gain and in so far as it adopted accounting practices and attained a high degree of accountancy and rationality-characteristics that are lacking in all the earlier stages of evolution of mankind, including the lordly order. Rent-capitalism differed from the more recent 'capitalism' (heretofore as a rule the only thing so called) in that it was not linked with production, but rather was satisfied with skimming off its proceeds. In regard to production it remained fundamentally sterile. For this reason it lent to ancient urbanism as a whole a definitely parasitical character, economically. On the other hand, since it concentrated a good part of the product of agriculture, mining, and other primary branches of production in the cities and put them within reach of a rather broad and differentiated element of the population there, it gave these cities the possibility of an unheard of rise not only in the number of their inhabitants, but also in material and cultural level.

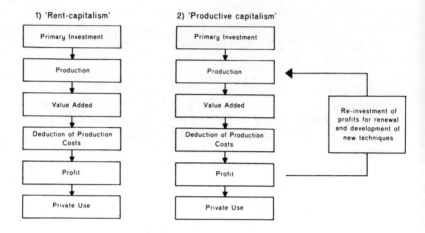

Figure 2.1   Descriptive representation of Bobek's concept of 'rent-capitalism'
and 'productive capitalism'

Although the characterisation of the term 'capitalism' and its
distinction into a 'rent-capitalism' in contrast to a 'productive
capitalism' may be unsatisfactory to the economist (cf. Fig. 2.1), the
concept of rent-capitalism nevertheless seems suited to explain a number
of phenomena connected with the problem of unequal development and
unequal income distribution in the Middle East. The following items
seem to be of special importance for understanding the organisation of
production and income distribution in the Middle East of today:

  – the splitting of one economic activity into different productive
    factors;
  – the commercialisation and free trade of these factors although they
    form part of *one* greater production process;
  – the resulting multiplication of a great number of personal interests
    in one economic activity without any individual responsibility for
    the whole.

The last factor seems to be responsible for the tendency *not* to invest
or re-invest any of the profits earned into existing economic enterprises
and thus the failure to enlarge and develop their economic foundations.
Any investment by an individual would at the same time benefit the
other partners through the resulting increase in productivity which,

then, would be split according to the rental shares of the different owners. This antagonism between individual responsibility and collective management (and profiteering) seems to be the main problem in reorganising the prevailing system of unequal payment, in many countries of the Middle East.

II ORGANIZATION OF PRODUCTION AND INCOME DISTRIBUTION

Rural land tenure

The rural sector has long been the most important basis of Iranian society and economy. Traditional forms of land tenure reveal typical aspects of the rent-capitalistic character of agricultural production and rural income distribution. There are two aspects of the organisation of agricultural production: first, traditional property rights in soil and water and other factors contributing to agricultural productivity and, second, the traditional relationships between owner of the land and worker. Four factors are held to be essential for any agricultural production and to be responsible for a 25 per cent share in total production: soil, seed, draught animals, and tools and human labour.

In cases where irrigation/water becomes necessary as an additional part of the agricultural production process, all factors are entitled to 20 per cent shares. Any of these four or five production factors can be split into subunits. For example, labour may be divided into plowing, tilling, harvesting, threshing or winnowing activities, each of which may be attributed to different persons who, then, will be compensated in corresponding shares of the 20 per cent harvest-share for the production factor 'human labour'. Thus according to Bobek (op. cit., p. 235), 'the concept of the enterprise or operating unit begins to dissolve, under such a system, into a series of individual titles, or rather tasks, and corresponding claims on income'.

Property Rights

Property rights in land are predominantly of two kinds: they are either fixed to certain parcels of land or they are 'ideal titles', i.e. imaginary shares or allotments of certain parts of the total agriculturally used lands, waters or whatever. In the first case, the relationships between owner and worker are clear. Where owner of the land and worker are one and the same person (*khordeh malek*), all benefits of work and management fall to him alone. This, however, has been the exception in traditional rural Iran, because landlordism and large landed properties have always prevailed. But again in cases where only *one* landlord owned a village and its land, organisational problems hardly arose: agricultural production was performed by individual share-croppers or groups of share-croppers (*boneh, bonku, sarah, haratta*, etc.) who received income shares according to the percentage of the production factors which they contributed to the production process.

Mostly, however, land-ownership of the villages and their usable lands was complicated by the fact that not one or two landlords, but several families and their members shared in the land-titles. The splitting of village lands was intensified in case of death of one of the proprietors. In this case all heirs received parts of the property of the deceased, according to the Islamic laws of inheritance. The result was, in most cases, that property-rights in a village, in certain parts of a village or even single fields or gardens were atomised among a great number of proprietors who only knew the share, not the hectarage of land which they owned within the village and its boundaries. The possession of shares of the total produce rather than regionally fixed parts of the land

TABLE 2.1   'Ideal' property-rights in the village of Sharafabad Safla (62 ha)

Land-owner (serial numbers)	Shares of land		
	Peas	Barley	Sesame
1	1	20	$7\frac{5}{13}$
2	3	16	$14\frac{10}{13}$
3	3	16	$14\frac{10}{13}$
4	3	16	$14\frac{10}{13}$
5	3	16	$14\frac{10}{13}$
6	3	16	$14\frac{10}{13}$
7	1	20	$7\frac{5}{13}$
8	1	20	$7\frac{5}{13}$
Total	18	140	96

Source: Plan Organization, Govt of Iran. Dez Irrigation Project. Report on Land- and Waterrights. Nederlandsche Heidemaatschappij, Arnhem/Holland (Jan.–March 1960).

was made possible by the custom of splitting each property or part of it
into 'ideal' or 'imaginary' shares or allotments. Thus, a village or a
certain field could be divided as follows:

$$1 \text{ village or part of it} = 24 \text{ 'peas'}$$
$$1 \text{ 'pea'} = 24 \text{ 'barley'}$$
$$1 \text{ 'barley'} = 24 \text{ 'sesame'}$$

This means that each village or any part of it could be divided into
$24 \times 24 \times 24$ parts, i.e. into a total of 13,824 property-titles. It is obvious
that under such circumstances regionally fixed land-allotments are
hardly possible so that the 'ideal' or 'imaginary' land-title has become
very common in many parts of the country. Two examples illustrate this
intricate system of traditional land-ownership and show its extreme
flexibility. The fact that an area of several thousand hectares size can be
as easily divided as a smaller unit of approximately 60 hectares (see Table
2.1) or a small garden plot (see Table 2.2) proves the feasibility of this
traditional form of property-right in Iran.

The whole village or the whole agricultural production-process was

TABLE 2.2 'Ideal' property-rights in a garden
plot (1 ha) in Gheblei

Land-owner (serial numbers)	Shares of land		
	Peas	Barley	Sesame
1	1	8	–
2	2	4	–
3	1	16	–
4	2	23	–
5	–	17	8
6	1	16	–
7	–	11	–
8	–	17	8
9	–	12	–
10	1	11	–
11	4	10	16
12	–	8	16
13	–	8	16
14	2	23	–
15	2	5	8
Total	16	189	72

Source: See Table 2.1.

considered as an entity, out of which the different land-owners were compensated according to their share in the whole property after deduction of the shares for the share-croppers. This system and especially the fact of ideal property-titles, which are not to be regionally fixed and located, meant that no landlord was interested in re-investing any of his profits into the improvement of the land or any other agricultural production factor. Thus, robber-farming and wasteful exploitation of the soil have been permanent consequences of rural land use in Iran for centuries or even millenia (cf. Lambton, 1977).

Share-cropping practices

As mentioned before, the majority of agricultural land in Iran has traditionally been worked on a share-cropping basis. The strict separation of land-property and land-cultivation must therefore be considered as the organisational prototype of agricultural production with far reaching effects both on payment and employment.

The basis of all share-cropping arrangements is the splitting of the agricultural production process into those four or five production factors which are considered to be responsible for 25 or 20 per cent of the final harvest. Utilising the fundamental work by A. K. S. Lambton on 'Landlord and Peasant in Persia', Planck (1962) has summarised a few of the most common share-cropping practices in different parts of the country (see Table 2.3).

TABLE 2.3   Shares and duties of share-croppers in different parts of Iran

Area	Shares of the agricultural production (%)	Duties
Arak/Isfahan	67	Labour, Plough,* Seed
Burujird	33	Labour, Plough
	53	Labour, Plough, Seed
Hamadan	75	Labour, Plough, Seed
Fassa/Fars	20	Labour
Niriz/Fars (Qanat!)	25	Labour, Plough
Dizful/Khuzestan	80	Labour, Plough, Seed
Shushtar/Khuzestan	67–75	Labour, Plough, Seed

Source: Planck (1962).

* Plough: tool and animals

While the extrapolations of Planck refer to different parts of the country, the investigations of Gharatchedaghi (1967), in the Veramin district of Tehran, show that this great variety of share-cropping arrangements occurs equally among a group of a few villages within one geographical region (see Table 2.4).

So far, we do not know much about the details of the share-cropping arrangements. However, the two or three cases for which data have been published reveal that these surveys are rather crude generalisations and that in reality the different claims to parts of the harvest are much more complicated. In line with Bobek's assumption that 'the ideal of rent-capitalism is attained when the share-cropping farmer does not touch more than a meager share of the work of his hands' (op. cit., p. 235), Planck (1962) demonstrated, for a village in Fars province, that out of a total of 77.5 quintal only approx. 63 per cent were available for distribution between the landlord and his two share-croppers. The remaining 37 per cent were deducted beforehand for different activities and claims in connection with minor production factors such as tilling and harrowing, for the water surveyor, the village headman etc.

The investigations of Ehlers-Safi-Nejad (1979) point in the same direction. The distribution of the winter grain (*kesht shatfi*) in the village of Goldasteh near the Iranian capital Tehran is undertaken in two steps. Taking the whole harvest as a 100-per-cent-unit, first of all 7.6 per cent is deducted for different claims such as shares for the blacksmith, joiner, the village headman and others. The remainder is split into the five traditional production-factors, each one counting for 18.48 per cent of the final production. These are allocated to landlord and share-croppers according to their contributions to the production process.

The share-croppers are reimbursed according to the area of land they are entitled to work. Although the general rule is that the size of land attributed to each member of, for example, a *boneh* is of almost equal size and productivity (for example a '*joft*', i.e. the land that a man with a plough of oxen can work alone), there are again considerable variations from 1/8 *joft* to 2 or more *joft* per share-cropper (Ehlers, 1975). These variations in size may be due to inheritance or to other factors such as indebtedness of one share-cropper to another. They are the cause of considerable differences in income among the members of a share-cropping unit. At the same time the almost stable and stationary character of the boneh-structure proved, in the past, a rather restrictive factor for those who were not members of such a working unit, inhibiting their access to work. Many of those not included in this system were forced either to abandon their rural living or to develop

TABLE 2.4 Traditional forms of share-cropping in the Veramin-district near Tehran

	Soil	Water	Seed	Plough	Labour	Fertiliser	Transport	Pesticides	Tools	Share in the harvest (%)
I. Grain-cultivation (kesht shatfi)										
1. Form										
Landlord	+	+	+	+		+	+	+	+	75
Share-cropper		+			+	+	+	+		25
2. Form										
Landlord	+	+	+	+		+	+	+	+	66
Share-cropper					+		+	+		33
3. Form										
Landlord	+	+		+		+	+	+	+	55
Share-cropper			+		+		+	+		45

Contributions of the production partners to the production

II. Cultivation of cotton, legumes etc. (kesht saifi)

1. Form											
Landlord	+	+	+	+		+		+	++	++	+	75
Share-cropper		+	+	+	+	+		+	++	++		25
2. Form											
Landlord	+	+	+	+		+		+	++	++	+	66
Share-cropper		+	+	+	+	+		+	++	++		33
3. Form											
Landlord	+	+	+	+	+	+	++	++	++	++	+	55
Share-cropper		+	+		+	+	++	++	++	++		45
4. Form											
Landlord	+	+	+	++	+	++	++	++	++	++	+	50
Share-cropper		+	+	++	+	++	++	++	++	++		50

III. Cultivation of vegetables (kesht saifi)

1. Form											
Landlord	+	+	+	+	+	+		+	++	++	+	55
Share-cropper		+	+	+	+	+		++	++	++		45
2. Form											
Landlord	+	+	+	++	+	++	++	++	++	++	+	50
Share-cropper		+	+	++	+	++	++	++	++	++		50

Source: C. Gharatchedaghi (1967).

TABLE 2.5   Splitting of a harvest of 77,50 quintals wheat (100%) in Fars

Total production	77,50 quintals (100%)
Deduction for	
Seed	11.00 quintals
Tractor-transport of wheat	0.75 quintals
Threshing	3.87 quintals
Village-headman	10.07 quintals
Water-surveyor, field-guards and others	2.26 quintals
Blacksmith and carpenter	0.75 quintals
'Net' production	48.80 quintals (63%)
Landlord's share	24.40 quintals (31.5%)
Share-croppers' share (total)	24.40 quintals (31.5%)
Share-cropper A	12.20 quintals
Share-cropper B	12.20 quintals

Source: Planck (1962).

TABLE 2.6   Splitting of a harvest in Goldasteh/Tehran

Shares/costs	% age of harvest
Blacksmith	0.16
Carpenter	0.16
Field-guard	1.0
Village-headman (kadkhoda)	1.0
Mullah	0.2
Ox-drover	0.08
Boneh and farm labourers	5.0
Total deductions	7.6
rest	92.4
Landlord (for soil and water)	$2 \times 18,48\% = 36.96$
Urban capitalists (for seed, plough and tools)	$2 \times 18,48\% = 36.96$
Farm-labourers (for human labour)	$18,48\% + 5\% = 23.48$
Other deductions	2.6
Total	100

Source: E. Ehlers and J. Safi-Nejad (1979).

other non-agricultural activity within the village (*khoshnishin*).

It is noteworthy that the organisation of labour on a share-cropping basis is even more complicated than that of income distribution (both in reaction to 'ideal' landlordism and to share-cropping farmers). In general, one can say that share-cropping contracts are hardly ever made between individuals, i.e. between a single landlord and a single share-cropper. The share-croppers organise themselves into working-units generally of 2 to 6 members (*boneh, bonku, sarah*, etc.) who work the land together. In many parts of the country (possibly in most) the total agricultural land of the village was therefore divided into several field complexes which were redistributed annually among the different working-units and their members. In order to guarantee a fair distribution of land to all share-croppers, it is a widespread practice to attach an equal number of field-complexes to the different working-units by lottery. Within the *boneh, sarah*, etc. a second lottery then takes place in order to provide each member of the working-unit with his special part or share of land. While Figure 2.2 is an attempt to model the system of

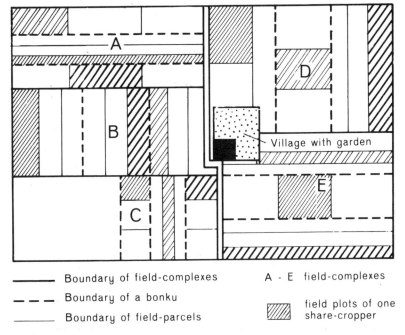

——— Boundary of field-complexes	A - E field-complexes
— — — Boundary of a bonku	field plots of one
——— Boundary of field-parcels	share-cropper

Figure 2.2   Model of a village with three bonku and three joft each

annual redistribution of lands among the share-croppers, Figure 2.3
gives an example of the actual results and problems: extreme fragmentation of fields, small size, long distances between the different parts
and – above all – an annual distribution pattern which will be entirely
different the following year.

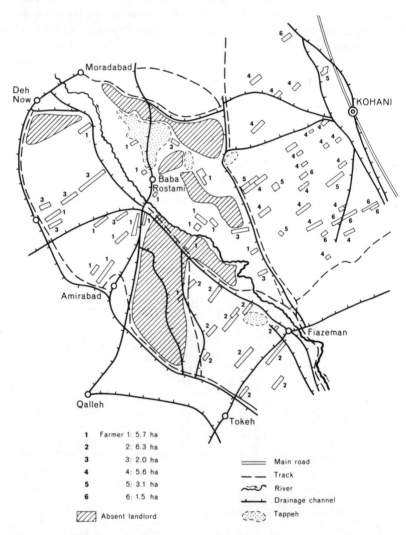

1	Farmer 1: 5.7 ha
2	2: 6.3 ha
3	3: 2.0 ha
4	4: 5.6 ha
5	5: 3.1 ha
6	6: 1.5 ha

Main road
Track
River
Drainage channel

Absent landlord   Tappeh

Figure 2.3   Pattern of land ownership: 1974. (From: National Cropping Plan,
Final Report, Tehran 1975)

In other words, in the same way that many landlords could not and still cannot point to any regionally fixed land-claims, the share-croppers did not have any regionally fixed tenure-rights: each year they received shares from other parts of the arable land of the village, each time amounting, however, to approximately the same amount that they were entitled to. The result of this practice is that at the level of the share-croppers, too, no one is interested in putting more efforts and means into the soil and its cultivation than absolutely necessary, because again all others – including the landlord himself – would benefit from any individual's endeavours.

Dallal and khoshnishin

In order to complete the picture of traditional rural land-tenure, two social groups have to be mentioned which are essential for the functioning of the rent-capitalistic system of rural production as well as for the analysis of the organisation of production, system of payment, income distribution and employment: the group of traders, dealers, brokers and hawkers (*dallal*) and the group of landless village-dwellers (*khoshnishin*). Both are of the utmost importance for the functioning of the system.

The group of the *dallal* will be dealt with in more detail in connection with rural-urban cottage industries. The *khoshnishin* participated in the traditional rural land-tenure as a kind of casual labour-force which, however, functioned as a permanent part of the whole system. *Khoshnishin* were used as seasonal labour or at times of special demand for labour. As such they became part of the division of the whole production process into different production factors and were compensated according to their share in the production process either in kind or in money (cf. Hooglund, 1973; Khosrovi, 1973).

Not all *khoshnishin*, however, are engaged in rural activities. Quite a few make their living as shopkeepers, taxi-, bus- or truck-drivers, or as middlemen of different kinds. As such they very often adopt parasitic attitudes, e.g. by selling on credit or lending money which has to be repaid in grain or other agricultural products. Takeovers of land or other properties of share-croppers or *khordeh maleki* by *khoshnishin* often occurred in cases where their loans were not repaid.

Rural-urban cottage industries

The same social and economic relationships, which are so characteristic of the traditional rural land-tenure, are prevalent also in the organisation of traditional manufacturing and cottage industries. Division of one economic activity into different production factors, commercialisation and free trade of these factors and skimming off the proceeds are also characteristics of the preindustrial manufacturing sector of urban Iran, as is illustrated by the traditional craft of carpet-manufacturing.

Organisation of carpet-manufacturing

The manufacture of Persian carpets, one of the most prestigious and important export articles with a long standing tradition and high reputation, has expanded considerably in recent years. Increasing demand in Europe and in America as well as in Iran itself led towards a revival of traditional carpet-manufacturing since the end of the nineteenth century. It seems remarkable that, although European and American companies were the organisers of this revival, they fully adopted traditional rent-capitalistic patterns in order to organise the production and marketing of the carpets (cf. Wirth, 1976).

Parallel with the great variety of forms of land tenure, there are also quite a few approaches to the organisation of the manufacture and marketing of carpets. This is illustrated by the example of the comparatively isolated oasis region of Tabas in southwestern Khorassan. Carpet manufacturing is comparatively recent in this area with origins of no more than approx. 20–5 years. Today, carpet-making is carried out in over 150 villages within the administrative area of Tabas or its hinterland, with altogether approximately 1,500 to 1,600 looms. Three examples demonstrate the wide variations in the organisation of this production. There are two qualities of carpets in Tabas and the surrounding region: one is a relatively coarse product, roughly equivalent to carpets of the Mashhad and Kashan types; the other is of high quality and value, comparable to the Nain and Isfahan carpets.

Example 1 represents the production of Mashhad and Kashan-type carpets for general use, organised by dealers in Tabas. This accounts for some 30–40 per cent of the 400-odd looms in Tabas and of the approximately 1,200 looms in the hinterland. Members of the carpet-dealers' guild and the numerous non-guild carpet-dealers enter into contractual arrangements with the carpet weavers, provide them with all supplies, including looms, and prescribe size, pattern and quality of the carpet. The wages are based on a unit of 12,000 knots, known as a *moghad*. A 2 × 3 metre carpet amounts to about 80 *moghad*. The weavers receive partial payment as the work progresses. The final wage settlement is made when the finished carpet is delivered to the dealer.

The dealers see to the supply of working materials in various ways. Individual dealers buy raw cotton and sheep's wool, and have them manufactured into yarn in Mashhad. There, too, or in Tehran, they buy natural and chemical colours in great quantities and have it transported to Tabas. The yarn is then dyed in Tabas. Other dealers buy finished yarn in Mashhad. Still others have the raw wool purchased in the villages, cleaned, spun and dyed comparatively crudely in town, then make it available to the weavers under contract to them.

Example 2 refers to the 60–70 per cent of the weavers of Mashhad-and Kashan-type carpets, who work independently and sell the finished products via the existing urban market mechanisms. Both urban and rural carpet-weavers obtain their working materials in the Tabas market. Two phenomena are noteworthy in this connection. First, among farmers who weave carpets as a sideline, there is no direct connection between their production of cotton and wool and the production of weaving materials. They sell their raw products in the market of Tabas or Mashhad, whence they also obtain their supplies of yarn – rendered dear through the urban-supplied services of cleaning, spinning and dyeing and profit-taking. Second, urban carpet-weavers frequently purchase their supplies after the first stages of refinement, then spin and dye the wool themselves, thereby achieving a much higher level of participation in the final value of the finished product than would otherwise be the case. But in so doing they put at risk the quality of their materials, due to the cottage-processing, thus affecting also the quality of the final product.

Many of the weavers – both urban and rural – who work independently but have little or no capital, are constrained to seek credit from urban or itinerant dealers or advances on unfinished carpets. As a result carpets frequently turn out to be smaller than planned (runners) in the interest of keeping the time-span between credit-taking and repayment as short as possible. Those with adequate capital sell their finished carpets to dealers in Tabas, whence 95–8 per cent are sold onwards to Mashhad. Direct sale by weavers either to final users or to wholesalers in Mashhad, Tehran or elsewhere is not common.

Example 3 represents the manufacture of carpets of the high value Nain type. It is externally controlled, but uses Tabas as a base, tapping the region's labour reservoir. On the surface it is hardly apparent as an economic element in the life of Tabas. Most of the 300 looms producing Nain carpets are located in the villages. Looms, yarns, patterns, wool and silk are 'imported' from Isfahan, Nain and Yazd by middlemen

TABLE 2.7   Urban processing of rural products and values added: cotton and sheep's wool (kg)

Cotton		Sheeps' wool	
Raw cotton	19 rials	sheep's wool (raw)	160 rials
Ginned cotton	21–2 rials	wool yarn (natural)	500 rials
Carded cotton	31–5 rials	wool yarn (dyed)*	560–1200 rials
Cleaned cotton	50 rials		
Natural cotton yarn	250 rials		
Dyed yarn*	300–400 rials		

Source: Ehlers (1977).

Note: * Price differences due to quality and kind of dye-stuff.

located in Tabas. Settlement between weaver and middlemen is made on a 50:50 basis of the wholesale price after the price of materials has been deducted. That Tabas serves merely as a 'staging-place' in the production and marketing of high-value Nain carpets is apparent also in the fact that fine wool and silk are as little in evidence in the Tabas market as Nain carpets: the finished products are moved directly from the villages to Isfahan or Tehran.

The few other studies so far that have dealt with organisational aspects of carpet manufacturing confirm the results and mechanisms of the Tabas area, so we may consider them as more or less representative of other parts of the country (Bazin, 1973, Costello, 1976, Darwent, 1965, English, 1966, Stöber, 1978). It is very probable that other traditional crafts are organised in a similar way, but corresponding investigations are lacking.

Marketing and profiteering

Considerable influence in the functioning of the whole system has to be attributed to the *dallals* and other types of traders and middlemen as indicated by the flow diagram (see Figure 2.4). They are essential for the organisation of the whole production process, and also responsible for the system of payment, for the unequal income distribution and certain aspects of employment. Above all, it is mainly due to this group that the price of the improved or finished products is rising disproportionately, the 'unproductive' partner in the whole production process is skimming off the main profits, while production labour is compensated with only small shares of the total revenue.

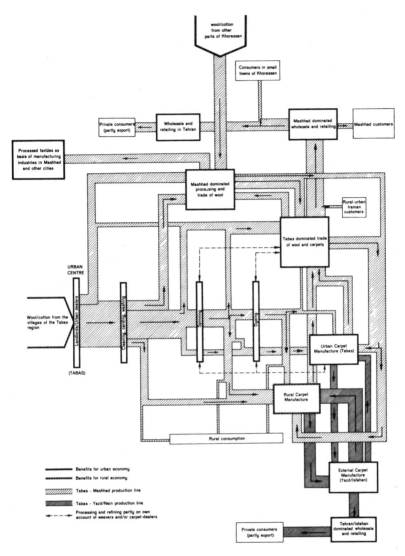

Figure 2.4　Simplified flow diagram of marketing processing and manufacture of wool (sheep wool/cotton) into carpets in Tabas/central Iran

On the basis of unpublished consular reports Stöber (1978) has recently tried to reconstruct the price-development of an America-sold Iranian carpet for the late 1920s (see Table 2.8). This attempt reveals that – in line with the results of the flow-diagram (see Figure 2.4) – of the total price of the sold product less than 30 per cent remained in Iran and only 20 per cent of the total price can be attributed to the different stages of its manufacturing. The craftsmen proper received only 1/7 of the total, a value which still seems high in comparison with present-day practices. For today, Wirth (1976) comes to the conclusion that a carpet, bought by a wholesaler in the Tehran bazaar, will approximately triple its price before it reaches the ultimate customer somewhere in Europe or in North America.

TABLE 2.8   Production costs and profits of a Kerman-carpet, sold in USA 1929

Production costs/profit	% of retail price
Sheep's wool	2.9
Cleaning and spinning	0.8
Cotton	1.2
Dyeing	2.3
Weaving	14.3
Commission of the dallal	3.2
Finishing	0.1
Packing	0.1
Transport in Iran	0.1
Taxes	0.1
Transport USA	0.1
Insurance	0.4
American customs	16.0
Chemical treatment USA	2.3
Wholesaler's profit	21.0
Retailer's profit	35.0

Source: G. Stöber (1978).

Both examples prove the extreme profiteering in connection with the marketing of the final product as well as the fact that the actual producers are compensated with a negligible share of the final price of the product. The almost ubiquitous presence of *dallals* has far reaching consequences for the problems of payment-systems and income distribution. As mentioned before, many *dallals* – be they mobile traders or bazaar-centred wholesalers – enter into personal contracts with the carpet-weavers providing them with working materials, designs and sometimes even looms. By paying them advances on the article to be produced *dallals* develop a kind of economic and social dependency which ties the carpet-weaver to the creditor and makes it impossible for him either to work independently or to dispose of his product when and where he wants to. Worst, however, such dependency-relationships cause bondages which sometimes bind a weaver to a certain *dallal* for a lifetime.

Similar to the relationships in the agricultural sector the mechanism of establishing such a dependency are that of *pish-foroush*: a weaver in need of money receives a credit in advance for a carpet, which then has to be sold more or less on the conditions of the *dallal* which are, by experience, much more unfavourable than those of free bazaar trade. But in times of carpet-booms many *dallal* pay for carpets in advance just in order to secure the labour-force and expertise of a certain weaver (*pish-kharid*).

III RENT-CAPITALISM, PAYMENT SYSTEM AND ECONOMIC DEVELOPMENT

The foregoing analysis reveals a remarkable persistence of old-established patterns and structures. A closer examination of property-rights and share-cropping practices in rural areas confirms the rent-capitalistic concept, with land-tenure traditions, which are in no way suited to develop and promote personal initiative and interest in any part of the agricultural production process. This is true both for landlord and share-cropper; both try to maximise advantage out of a production process in which they are not willing to invest anything. Wasteful exploitation and exhaustion of the soil are the consequence and cause of economic stagnation in the agricultural sector.

The same holds true for the pre-industrial structure of crafts and cottage-industries: here again we have the phenomenon that a unique investment is exploited as long as possible without re-investing any profits into the production process, be it in order to repair or uphold the equipment, to modernise existing techniques or to develop new ones. Again one of the main reasons is the fact that any individual investment may benefit others in the production process.

Rent-capitalism: its socio-economic and political background and consequences.

As far as we know, the rent-capitalistic system dates back well into pre-Islamic-times. Many of the main features of rent-capitalism (in Bobek's sense) can be traced back to the time of the ancient Middle East. Archaeological findings as well as analyses of ancient records and

economic texts prove that many of the prevalent practices of social
organisation were fully developed in Assyria and Babylonia from
whence they seem to have been introduced to Achaemenid Persia. The
main difference between that era and today seems to be that formerly the
hereditary nobility and especially the temples were the large landlords
while nowadays private landlords form the bulk of proprietors of soil,
water and technical equipment.[1]

The socio-economic and political background of present-day practices is the division between capital (soil, water, machinery, basic
materials such as seed in agriculture or wool, looms, dye in carpet-
manufacturing) and labour. Although the availability of capital never
includes seigneurial rights over the tenants or labourers (as it did in
European feudalism), both share-croppers and artisans as well as
labourers were and are entirely dependent on the capitalist. In rural Iran
the villagers' membership in one of the agricultural working-units is still
more or less hereditary, but all other decisions with regard to the
production process are in the hands of the landlord or his representative
(*mubashir*).[2] They organise and supervise the rotational cycle of
agriculture (as far as it is not determined by ecological conditions) and
manage the annual redistribution and allocation of lands to the share-
croppers. This traditional practice of land-rotation must be considered
as the decisive factor in socio-economic and political dependency: the
annual redistribution of the land guarantees that none of the share-
croppers could claim any 'traditional rights' through land-use to a
certain parcel of land or even claim property-rights. For this reason the
landlords always prevented the villagers from growing permanent crops
or planting trees. Such a fact would have established claims to the land
involved and was therefore in contrast to the economic and political
interests of the landlords, who were also in full command of political
power in their respective village(s).

Claims to rent-income were and are negotiable. Selling and mortgag-
ing of rents was and still is an extremely far-spread phenomenon in Iran, in
line with Bobek's assumption that the attachment of titles to the different
parts of the production process and their free trading, like goods, must
be considered as a decisive aspect of the rent-capitalism system. Thus for
example, one landlord could sell his claims to rent-income to another
one or to an urban businessman. The shares of the tenants and share-
croppers, especially, proved in the past to be an extremely negotiable
item: it was the basis not only for the far-spread granting of credits by
landlords and urban-based brokers and retailers (cf. Holmes, 1974,
Lodi, 1965), but also the basis of the afore-mentioned *pish-foroush-*

system and also the cause of a very common indebtedness of many villagers, farmers and labourers.

The main consequence of this system has been an almost complete stagnation in the technological, socio-economic and political development of rural Iran. Profit maximisation was based on an exhaustive exploitation of the soil without any reinvestment. Degradation of soil-fertility has been amply observed in all parts of the Middle East. The extreme flexibility of property-rights and a relative balance between demand and supply of agricultural land (partly due to comparatively slow population growth until recently) also resulted in economic and political stagnation, especially since there was a remarkable equality within the share-cropper-class.

On the whole, Bobek's assumption that the system of rent-capitalism was 'fundamentally sterile' seems to be valid not only with respect to technological, social, political and economic developments, but also to the cementation of centuries or even millenia old inequality between city and hinterland (Ehlers, 1978) and between landlord and peasant (cf. Haque, 1977, Lambton, 1953).

Payment system and economic development

The payment system is the outcome of the division of the production process into the different production factors or parts of them. But it is severely modified in two ways:

(1) the problem of indebtedness;
(2) the commanding power and influence of middlemen of different kinds.

The problem of indebtedness

The problem of indebtedness is a structural problem both in rural and in urban areas. Investigations in different areas of the country have shown that before the land-reform of 1962 large parts of the population were indebted. In the Caspian province of Gilan for example, 80,000 out of a total 137,000 farms were indebted, most of them to private creditors: 80 per cent of all creditors were urban-based shopkeepers and moneylenders, and 18 per cent landlords. In the neighbouring province of Mazanderan approx. 54 per cent of a total of 174,000 farm-units were indebted; the figures for other parts of the country are similar.

Indebtedness to shopkeepers, moneylenders or *dallal* is similarly far-spread among urbanites of different kinds and professions. Those examples mentioned in connection with carpet-manufacturing seem to be transferable to many other crafts: copper-smiths, engravers, weavers, carpenters, textile printers – they all work on different kinds of *pish-foroush* and/or *pish-karid* and are thus dependent on other persons.

The problems deriving from indebtedness are a certain *deformation of the payment-system* since considerable shares of the income are lost through interest rates of up to 40 per cent within a few months (cf. Lodi 1965). Even if these high interest rates are not paid in cash, but in kind (e.g. through *pish-foroush*), they cause considerable deviations of monetary flows with the result that the poor grow poorer, the rich, however, always richer. But it would be wrong to interpret indebtedness only as a phenomenon of poverty. It must be seen also as a policy by which landlords, shopkeepers, middlemen and other type of capitalists try to bind as many share-croppers, share-tenants or manufacturing labour-force (e.g. carpet-weavers) to themselves as possible. Indebtedness means dependency and dependency means a secure labour-force both in the agricultural and non-agricultural sector. It means, too, the obligation of the share-cropper, for example, to sell his grain under unfavourable conditions to the landlord or the urban creditor. In this respect the mechanism of indebtedness may be seen as a means of 'profit maximation' with a number of advantages for the creditors and disadvantages for the debtors.

Role and functions of middlemen

The commanding power and influence of middlemen of different kinds may be less apparent in the rural sector; it is prevalent, however, in almost all phases of urban trade and craft. The data presented for the process of carpet production and marketing seem transferable to many other small-scale industries. Price-increases due to the unproductive middlemen-activities occur not only in the marketing of the finished products, but even more so in the different stages of production. Because of the splitting of all stages of the production process into different autonomous parts, *dallal*, dealers, wholesaler, retailers and middlemen of different kinds are involved everywhere.

One may argue that similar activities are usual also in a highly rationalised and industrialised society. This is true, but with two decisive differences: first, *the 'unproductive' labour and middlemen demand a much higher percentage of the total cost of a product*, or, as Bobek (op. cit., p.

237) puts it: 'the constant skimming-off of a substantial part of the proceeds of production under the rent-capitalist system, without a corresponding economic return, proves a detrimental practice, impeding progress'. The second difference is to be seen in the fact that the presence of a middlemen of different kinds is invariably connected with *personal dependencies between productive labour*. In this connection the unproductive labour leads an almost parasitic existence in relation to the productive labour, which is bound to its sponger through the various mechanisms of indebtedness. The almost complete impossibility of escaping such a relationship must be seen as one of the main causes of the extremely stagnant character of general economic development in Iran and in the Middle East in general.

What then are the strategies for changing the extremely stagnant character of the traditional Iranian – or even Middle Eastern – economy? In line with Stewart's suggestion that 'inequality can only effectively be tackled at the source where it arises – viz. by attacking the mechanisms making for primary inequality' (see Chapter 1), one may make two suggestions:

   (a) a profound change of traditional land-tenure; and
   (b) a far-reaching reduction in the influence of middlemen.

(a) A first land-reform took place in 1962. Aimed at distributing the arable lands to those that work the land, the land-reform succeeded initially and in its different phases of implementation (cf. Ehlers, 1979; Lambton, 1969) in creating a number of small holdings. It also contributed to a considerable diminution of the political and economic power of the large landlords. Nevertheless, in the long run, its effects have been hampered by at least two of those three interacting sources of increasing inequality in primary income distribution: i.e. technology and population growth. While land-reform succeeded in changing the payment system considerably, it failed to meet the increased demands of Iranian society for agricultural products, due to a lack of modernisation in the equipment and production techniques. Worse, however, was the rapid population growth. In connection with traditional Islamic laws of inheritance this caused extreme fragmentation and diminution of many viable small-scale farms within a few years of land-reform.[3] Especially through the inheritance law, many of the traditional relationships of dependency were re-established, although between other partners. New relationships of dependency developed so that, on the whole, extreme social differentiation of the rural population and considerable social and

regional mobility can be observed. Or to put it in the words of the
sociologist Planck (1979, S. 57):

> Land reform in Iran has subverted the feudal class structure of
> landlords and share croppers to a large but not exactly determinable
> extent. But the land reform contributed little to the equalization of the
> villagers. On the contrary, the land reform set the social differenti-
> ation going. The number of social classes increased. The distances
> between the classes enlarged inside the villages. People in favour of the
> land reform climbed up. The majority of the khoshnishin had no other
> choice but to continue its rural life in utter misery or to migrate to the
> cities. The rural exodus extended enormously. The land reform set
> free the way for renewing the rural elites. The social positions which
> have been removed by the landlords and their local agents have been
> partly occupied by members of the new, rapidly extending
> bureaucracy.

The social and economic failure of the first land-reform legislation was
the cause of the re-integration phase of the Iranian agrarian reform
(Planck, 1975), as a result of which rural cooperatives, joint-farm
corporations and rural production cooperatives were created (cf. Table
2.9).

TABLE 2.9   Rural cooperative societies and unions, joint-farm corporations and
production cooperatives

	1969/70	*1972/73*	*1977/78*
Rural cooperative societies			
Number	8,102	8,361	2,925
Membership (thousand persons)	1,400	2,065	2,983
Capital (million Rials)	1,984	3,329	8,385
Rural cooperative unions			
Number	112	127	153
Number of member societies	7,542	7,961	2,907
Capital (million Rials)	781	1,580	3,665
Joint-farm corporations			
Number of corporations	–	43	93
Number of shareholders	–	15,250	35,444
Capital (million Rials)	–	685	1,515
Rural production cooperatives			
Number of cooperatives	–	0	39

Source: Bank Markazi Iran, Annual Reports and Balance Sheets (different years).

(b) Nothing has been done so far to crush the dominating influence of parasitic and economically unproductive middlemen. Various (mostly weak) attempts to minimise their influence have proven unsuccessful. The failure of an effective cooperative-movement that might have been able to replace the commanding influence of the class of middlemen and mediators, must especially be blamed as one of the main reasons for their persistently strong influence. Although the growth in the number of cooperatives and members seems impressive, their economic effect must be considered negligible. Mismanagement, disinterest of the bureaucratic leadership of these new institutions, a deep mistrust of the farmers towards the imposed management, corruption and a number of other factors contributed to the questionable effects of these new forms which, as Planck (1979) has shown, even increased inequality and injustice.

The Islamic revolution of 1979 that swept away monarchy and many of the recently grown socio-economic structures, will have deep effects on the situation not only of rural Iran, but also with regard to the functions of middlemen and their activities. The attempts to minimise the influence of the parasitic mediator-class is in accordance with basic religious thoughts. The intentions of increased development of rural Iran, on the other hand, are rooted in basic economic and social considerations. More than 50 per cent of the total population of the country still are rural; agriculture is, in terms of employment, the most important economic activity. It is therefore not surprising that the interest of the present government of the Islamic Republic of Iran has been focussed considerably on the development of agriculture and rural 'industries'. A new land-reform bill will not only dissolve all big holdings, but – again – provide 'for the distribution of agricultural land to the landless peasants of the country' *(Tehran Times*, 2.3.1980). In order to 'provide an uplift to the rural masses and stop the influx of the rural population towards industrialized centers' (ibid.) also rural industries such as carpet-manufacturing have received considerable financial funds (12.8 billion rials; *Tehran Times*, 16.2.1980). Whether all these measures will be sufficient to solve the problems of unequal development and the antagonism between cities and their hinterlands (Ehlers, 1978) remains to be seen.

IV CONCLUDING REMARKS

Rent-capitalism must be considered as a socio-economic system, which basically produces unequal development. As a specific Middle Eastern brand of the general phenomenon of feudalism, forms of personal dependency with resulting socio-economic consequences are common. On the other hand, there is a remarkable tradition of highly egalitarian and almost 'communistic' (in the proper sense of the word) behaviour among the traditional classes of small-holders and share-croppers: systems like the annual relocation of lands by lottery-system or communal cultivation of the land were retained after land-reform. They are interpreted as an extremely fair and democratic form of land-tenure. Also forms of neighbourly help in cases of sickness or death are very common. These systems persist in many parts of the country today. They remain unchanged as long as no individual endeavours to improve the soil (e.g. by drilling of wells) are undertaken. As soon, however, as one farmer or a group of farmers start improvements on their specific pieces of land in a given year, the rotational system of land-distribution is interrupted and the whole system collapses. The fact that many forms of communal land-tenure, of collective labour and of neighbourly help have a long tradition and have been functioning without problem in the past, raises the question of why these traditional systems have not been taken as bases for the improvement of the general social and economic welfare of the broad mass of the population. It may well be that, under the rules of an Islamic government, these possibilities will attract more interest than before.

Another aspect of the problem of unequal development in the Middle East is the lack of entrepreneurship which is often noted (cf. Meyer, 1959; Sayigh, 1957; Turner, 1974; Vaghefi, 1975). Industrialisation in Iran has, so far, had little effect on the existence of the traditional sector. Besides cementing inequality in the traditional sectors of economy, it has added a new dimension of inequality: that between traditional and modern Iran. On the whole, there is no doubt that forms of 'Islamic socialism' and of traditional forms of labour and property may well be suited to diminish the inequalities within the rural scene, but even more so between urban and rural Iran. If the statement of the Revolutionary Council that 'under the Islamic Republic of Iran . . . a peasant is as important as an industrialist, or a landlord' (*Tehran Times*, 2.3.1980) is more than just a slogan, then there may be hope that rent-capitalism and its inequalities may be abolished and be replaced by a more just social and economic order.

NOTES

1. Although the economic history of the ancient Middle East with regard to its influences on modern economic organisation and business practices has still

to be written, a few hints may serve to illustrate the surprising parallels between ancient and modern Middle East: M. A. Dandamayev, *Persien unter den ersten Achämeniden* (6. Jahrhundert v. Chr.). Beiträge zur Iranistik 8 (Wiesbaden, 1976); I. M. Diakonoff (ed.), *Ancient Mesopotamia. Socio-Economic History: A Collection of Studies by Soviet Scholars*, USSR Academy of Sciences, Institute of the Peoples of Asia (Moscow: Nauka Publ. House, 1969); H. T. Wright, 'The Administration of Rural Production in an Early Mesopotamian Town', Anthropological Papers no. 38, Museum of Anthropology (Ann Arbor: Univ. of Michigan, 1969). Interesting selections of articles are also to be found in *Iraq*, vol. 39 (1977) and in the *Journal of the Economic and Social History of the Orient*, vol. 18, pt. ii (June, 1975).

2. The best survey of almost all aspects of traditional agriculture in Iran is still A. K. S. Lambton, *Landlord and peasant in Persia. A study of Land Tenure and Land Revenue Administration* (Oxford, 1953).

3. The literature on the origin and different aspects of land-reform in Iran is very extensive. A collection of the most important books and articles is to be found in Ehlers (1979). Between 1962 and the early 1970s approx. 1 million farmers became owners of the lands, which they had worked before. More than 16,000 villages are said to have been distributed during the first phase of the land-reform. Exact figures are to be found in Planck (1975).

REFERENCES

Bazin, M., 'Le travail du tapis dans la région de Qom (Iran Central)'. *Bull. de la Societé Languedocienne de Géographie*, 7 (1973) pp. 83–92.
Bobek, H., 'Die Hauptstufen der Gesellschafts-und Wirtschaftsentfaltung in geographischer Sicht', *Die Erde*, 90 (1959) pp. 259–98. *Translated as:* 'The Main Stages in Socio-Economic Evolution from a Geographical Point of View' in Ph. L. Wagner and M. W. Mikesell, *Readings in Cultural Geography* (Chicago: 1961) pp. 218–47.
Bobek, H., 'Zum Konzept des Rentenkapitalismus', *TESG*, 65 (1974) pp. 73–8.
Bobek, H., 'Rentenkapitalismus und Entwicklung in Iran', in G. Schweizer (ed.), *Interdisziplinäre Iranforschung. Beihefte zum Tübinger Atlas des Vorderen Orients*, Reihe B (*Geisteswissenschaften*) Nr. 40 (Wiesbaden, 1979) pp. 113–24.
Costello, V. F., *Kashan: A city and region of Iran*, The Center for Middle Eastern and Islamic Studies of the University of Durham 3 (London-New York, 1976).
Darwent, D., 'Urban growth in relation to socio-economic development and westernization: A case study of the city of Mashad, Iran', unpublished Ph.D. dissertation (University of Durham, 1965).
Ehlers, E., 'Traditionelle und moderne Formen der Landwirtschaft in Iran. Siedlung, Wirtschaft und Agrarsozialstruktur im nördlichen Khuzistan seit dem Ende des 19. Jahrhunderts', *Marburger Geogr. Schriften*, 64 (Marburg, 1975).
Ehlers, E., 'Dezful and Its Hinterland: Observations on the Relationships of

Lesser Iranian Cities and Towns to Their Hinterlands', *Geography*, Journal of the Association of Iranian Geographers, 1 (1976) pp. 20–30.

Ehlers, E., 'Social and Economic Consequences of Large Scale Irrigation Developments: The Dez Irrigation Project/Khuzestan, Iran', in E. B. Worthington (ed.), *Arid Lands Irrigation in Developing Countries: Environmental Problems and Effects* (Oxford-New York, 1977) pp. 85–97.

Ehlers, E., City and Hinterland in Iran: The Example of Tabas/Khorassan, *TESG*, 68 (1977) pp. 284–96.

Ehlers, E., 'Rentenkapitalismus und Stadtentwicklung im islamischen Orient. Beispiel: Iran', *Erdkunde*, 32 (1978) pp. 124–42.

Ehlers, E., 'Die Iranische Landreform – Voraussetzungen, Ziele und Ergebnisse' in H. Elsenhans (ed.), *Agrarreformen in der Dritten Welt* (Frankfurt/Main-New York, 1979) pp. 433–70.

Ehlers, E. and Safi-Nejad, J., 'Formen kollektiver Landwirtschaft in Iran: Boneh' in E. Ehlers (ed.), *Beiträge zur Kulturgeographie des islamischen Orients, Marburger Geogr. Schriften*, 78 (1979) pp. 55–82.

English, P. W., *City and village in Iran. Settlement and economy in the Kirman basin* (Madison-Milwaukee-London, 1966).

Gharatchedaghi, C., 'Distribution of land in Veramin: An opening phase of the agrarian reform in Iran', *Schriften des Deutschen Orient-Instituts, Materialien und Dokumente* (Opladen: Leske-Verlag, 1967).

Goodell, G., 'Agricultural production in a traditional village of northern Khuzestan', *Marburger Geogr. Schriften*, 64 (1975) pp. 243–89.

Hamid, H. A., 'Marketing and business practices in Afghanistan', *Middle East Journal*, 14 (1960) pp. 87–93.

Haque, Z., *Landlord and Peasant in Early Islam* (Islamabad: Islamic Research Institute, 1977).

Holmes, J., 'Credit in Iranian villages', *Man*, 9 (1974) p. 311.

Hooglund, E. J., 'The khwushnishin population of Iran', *Iranian Studies*, 6 (1973) pp. 229–45.

Khosrovi, K., 'Les paysans sans terre: les khochnechin', *Sociologia Ruralis*, 13 (1973) pp. 289–93.

Khuri, F. I., 'The étiquette of bargaining in the Middle East', *American Anthropologist*, 70 (1968) pp. 698–706.

Lambton, A. K. S., *Landlord and peasant in Persia* (Oxford, 1953).

Lambton, A. K. S., *The Persian land reform 1962–1966* (Oxford, 1969).

Lambton, A. K. S., 'Aspects of agricultural organization and agrarian history in Persia', *Handbuch der Orientalistik*, 1. Abt. 6. Bd., 6. Abschn.: *Wirtschaftsgeschichte des Vorderen Orients in islamischer Zeit, Teil 1* (Leiden-Köln, 1977) pp. 160–87.

Lodi, H. S. K., 'Preharvest Sales of Agricultural Produce in Iran', *Monthly Bulletin of Agric. Economics and Statistics*, vol. 14, no. 6 (1965) pp. 1–4.

Löffler, R., 'The representative mediator and the new peasant', *American Anthropologist*, 73 (1971) pp. 1077–91.

Meyer, A. J., 'Middle Eastern capitalism', *Harvard Middle Eastern Studies*, 2 (Cambridge, Mass., 1959).

Planck, U., 'Der Teilbau im Iran', *ZfAL*, 1 (1962) pp. 47–81.

Planck, U., 'Die Reintegrationsphase der iranischen Agrarreform', *Erdkunde*, 29 (1975) pp. 1–9.

Planck, U., 'Die soziale Differenzierung der Landbevölkerung Irans infolge der Agrarreform', in G. Schweizer (ed.), *Interdisziplinäre Iranforschung. Beihefte zum Tübinger Atlas des Vorderen Orients*, Reihe B (*Geisteswissenschaften*) Nr. 40 (Wiesbaden, 1979) pp. 43–58.

Potter, D., 'The Bazaar Merchant', in S. N. Fisher (ed.), *Social Forces in the Middle East* (New York, 1968) pp. 99–115.

Sayigh, Y. A., 'Toward a theory of entrepreneurship for the Arab East', *Explorations in Entrepreneurial History*, 1 (1957) pp. 123–7.

Stöber, G., 'Die Afshahr. Nomadismus im Raum Kerman (Zentraliran)', *Marburger Geographische Schriften*, 76 (1978).

Turner, B. S., *Weber and Islam: A critical study* (London-Boston: International Library of Sociology, 1974).

Vaghefi, M. R., *Entrepreneurs of Iran: The Role of Business Leaders in the Development of Iran* (Palo Alto/Calif.: Altoan Press, 1975).

Wirth, E., 'Der Orientteppich und Europa', *Erlanger Geogr. Arb.*, 37 (1976).

3 The State and Income Redistribution in Peru, 1968–76, with Special Reference to Manufacturing

JOHN WEEKS

I INTRODUCTION

In late 1968, a military coup overthrew the civilian government of Peru, bringing to power a new government with General Juan Velasco as President. On a continent where coups are common, this was an uncommon coup, signalling not just a change of government, but a change in the class domination of the state. Before 1968, Peru had been ruled by a coalition of capitalists and pre-capitalist landlords, the capitalists having their investments in banking, finance, and export agriculture. This coalition was overthrown by the rising industrial bourgeoisie which, after 1968, sought to re-orient the economy to rapid industrialisation.[1]

Once having seized power through the military, the domestic industrial bourgeoisie embarked upon a series of structural reforms with the purpose of definitively breaking the power of the old ruling classes, establishing the profitability of production for the domestic market and winning the support of the Peruvian masses.[2] One professed goal of the new ruling class was to effect a more equal distribution of income,[3] and, to achieve this end in part, a number of major institutional changes were implemented: land reform, profit-sharing and, to a much lesser degree, nominal workers' ownership in industry, and substantially increased

62

state ownership and participation in the economy. These changes may not have had distributional equity as their primary motivation, as argued elsewhere,[4] but this was one of the professed goals.[5] The purpose of this article is to investigate the impact of these reforms on the distribution of income in Peru. Peru after 1968 is an important case study for evaluating the extent to which distributional changes can be brought about within given social relations of production. Despite a tendency of the post-coup government to speak of a Peru that was 'neither capitalist nor socialist', there is little controversy over the fact that the new government pursued a road of capitalist development[6] and that the reforms were aimed to alter the distribution of income within the capitalist mode of production, or capitalist 'system of payment'. In considering the impact of the reforms, we will not deal with the question of whether they were 'sincerely' intended to bring about greater distributional equality, whether they were 'sham' or 'real'. To the extent that they were instituted, they were, by definition, 'real'. Their implementation is precisely the question of their impact, and the zeal and extent of implementation reflects not the 'sincerity' or 'insincerity' of the ruling class's intentions, but the objective forces which delineate that which is possible within a given mode of production.

Because of the stress to be placed on the systemic limits to the impact of the Peruvian reforms, the analysis requires a theoretical consideration of these limits. This we save until after our empirical investigation of the impact of the institutional reforms in Peru after 1968, treated in Sections II and III. Section II briefly summarises the main reforms and estimates the extent of their coverage of the working population. In Section III, we measure the impact of the reforms on the functional distribution of income for the economy as a whole, and in manufacturing, where one of the most important reforms was instituted. In the final section, we interpret the empirical results in light of theoretical analysis.

Before entering into a detailed consideration of the Peruvian case, it is useful to place the distributional pattern of the Peruvian economy in context. In Table 3.1, we present the distribution of current income by quintiles for fourteen Latin American countries. The only Latin American countries of considerable size which are omitted are Guatemala and Bolivia. The data from different countries are not in all cases strictly comparable. While all refer to the entire population, rural and urban, the coverage is of households in five cases, and of individuals in the other cases (see note to Table 3.1). If we average across the nine countries for which coverage is more or less similar (last row), we see

TABLE 3.1 The size distribution of income in selected Latin American countries, 1961–71

Country & Data	Population Quintiles					Top 5%
	1st	2nd	3rd	4th	5th	
Argentina, 1961	5.1	9.3	13.1	18.6	53.9	32.0
Brazil, 1970	2.8	5.3	9.0	15.6	67.3	44.8
Chile, 1968	4.8	8.2	12.2	19.0	55.8	31.0
Colombia, 1970	2.9	7.1	11.6	18.9	59.5	33.7
Costa Rica, 1971	5.4	9.2	13.8	21.2	50.4	23.0
Dominican Rep., 1969	4.3	8.1	12.8	20.5	54.3	26.3
Ecuador, 1970	1.8	3.4	7.3	15.5	72.0	43.0
El Salvador, 1961	5.1	6.5	10.2	17.4	60.8	34.0
Honduras, 1967/68	1.6	4.8	9.5	18.8	65.3	32.9
Mexico, 1969	4.2	6.0	9.7	16.9	63.2	37.8
Panama, 1972	4.6	10.6	15.5	21.9	47.4	22.2
Uruguay, 1967	3.0	7.6	13.1	22.8	53.5	20.8
Venezuela, 1971	2.7	5.5	9.6	16.8	65.4	40.5
Peru, 1972	2.5	6.5	12.5	20.0	58.5	33.0
Mean*	3.4	6.9	11.3	18.6	59.8	33.4

Sources: For all but Peru, Shail Jain, *Size Distribution of Income* (Washington: World Bank, 1975); for Peru see Table 3.3.

Note: For Chile, Costa Rica, Dominican Republic, Honduras and Mexico these are household distributions. The rest are either for the economically active population (Ecuador and Venezuela) or income recipients (economically active less the unemployed).
* Mean of all countries except those using the household distribution.

that in Peru the poorest two quintiles of the population received slightly less than the nine-country mean. At the top of the income distribution, income in Peru was slightly (but very slightly) less concentrated than average. But particularly for the wealthiest 5 per cent (last column), the difference is so small as to be insignificant statistically. Thus, by comparison to other Latin American countries, income distribution in Peru in the 1960s and early 1970s was probably average in terms of inequality; more equal than neighbouring Ecuador, but considerably more unequal than Argentina, Costa Rica, or Panama.

II INSTITUTIONAL REFORMS IN PERU, 1968–75

A number of structural changes were introduced into the Peruvian economy after 1968 by the bourgeois government,[7] and here we consider only those relevant to income distribution: the land reform, social property legislation (workers' ownership), the industrial communities, and nationalisation of private capital. Since most of the discussion will be of the manufacturing sector, we consider the first only briefly.

The Peruvian land reform, in as far as it was aimed at definitively breaking the economic and political power of the pre-capitalist landlords in the highlands and the agricultural capitalists along the coastal plain, was a complete success. While land nationalisation was with compensation,[8] these classes played no significant role in the political life of Peru after 1970. The land reform involved the creation of a number of types of state-controlled agricultural institutions, from *de facto* state enterprises with nominal worker control in the case of the coastal sugar estates, to various types of producer cooperatives in the highlands.[9] With the exception of the former, which did not involve peasant production to any degree, the land reform was a disaster in terms of output and productive efficiency and probably accelerated the secular decline of highland agriculture, which had begun in the late 1950s and early 1960s.[10] Thus, the land reform probably contributed to the massive out-migration of the rural population from the highlands, and its distributional effects were swamped by this, whatever they may have been for those who remained on the land.

The introduction of full worker's ownership is best characterised as a 'social experiment', meaning by an 'experiment' something attempted on a very small scale for a brief period. While quite a bit of propaganda was given to the social property enterprises (Honda of Peru being the largest – 'Moto Andeno'), quantitatively they were insignificant. In 1973, far less than one per cent of the stock capital of Peruvian manufacturing was accounted for by social property enterprises.[11] A plan to convert bankrupt small and medium private mining companies into social property institutions was never implemented.

The most important institutional change which was formally aimed at directly affecting the distribution of income was the 'labour community' (*comunidades laboral*). The first form of these had been established in 1949 and 1950, as profit-sharing programmes. The reforms were applied wholesale to industry, fishing, mining, and telecommunications by four laws issued in 1970 and 1971.[2] With regard to distribution, the industrial laws provided that 10 per cent of the net income of each enterprise (before taxes) be annually paid to workers as a direct wage supplement; and, to effect ownership, that an additional 15 per cent be used to purchase stock in the name of the labour community. The latter percentage would end once the communities held 50 per cent of the company's stock. The laws were similar in the other sectors (fishing, mining, and telecommunications), with the special feature in mining that provided for redistribution between enterprises, prompted by the very large differences in productivity and profitability among companies in that sector. While the same uneven development existed in industry, this provision applied only to mining.[13] Finally, the distribution of the wage supplement in each enterprise was proportional to each employee's income, and every employee, up to the company president,

TABLE 3.2 Extent of coverage of the labour communities in Peru, by economic sector, 1974

A. *Absolute Numbers*

Sector	Total Estab.	Total Workers	Potential Coverage Estab.	Potential Coverage Workers	Actual Coverage Estab.	Actual Coverage Workers
Manufacturing	7780[1]	254,090[1]	6252	229,537	3535	199,179
Fishing	n.a.	n.a.	257	32,065	253	29,207
Mining	n.a.	68,847[2]	84	64,693	74	51,425
Communications	n.a.	n.a.	183	11,295	52	8,224
Total	–	–	6776	337,590	3914	288,035

B. *Relative Coverage*

Sector	Establishments Potential Total	Establishments Actual Total	Establishments Actual Potential	Workers Potential Total	Workers Actual Total	Workers Actual Potential
Manufacturing	80.4%	45.5%	56.5%	90.3%	78.4%	86.8%
Fishing	–	–	98.4	–	–	91.1
Mining	–	–	88.1	94.0	74.7	79.5
Communication	–	–	28.4	–	–	72.8
Total	–	–	57.8%	–	–	85.3%

Source: Centro de Estudios y Promocion de Desarrollo, Romanidad Laboral y capital-ismo (Lima: DESCO, 1976), pp. 88–9.

Notes: 1. These are from the industrial survey of 1974, covering all establishments hiring ten or more. The national accounts estimated there to be 444,300 wage and salary earners in manufacturing in 1974. The difference, 190,000, is accounted for by non-reporting enterprises, most hiring less than five persons.

2. All mining workers as reported to *Annuario de la Mineria, 1974*. The national accounts estimated 102,000 for the same year.

could be a member of the labour community.[14] Table 3.2 gives the extent of implementation of the labour community laws in 1974 by sector. The column head 'Potential Coverage' gives the total number of establishments and workers employed in them which fall under the labour communities laws. The 'Total' column gives the total number of enterprises and wage and salary earners in the sector; the difference arises from the exemption of extremely small establishments from the laws. If one eliminates the very small enterprises (see notes to Table 3.2) for which enforcement of the reform would have been extremely difficult, coverage, potential and actual, is quite high. In the two largest sectors, manufacturing and mining, slightly more than 75 per cent of all workers in enterprises hiring five or more were within labour communities. For fishing and communications, the proportions are probably quite similar if all workers were enumerated. Overall, the 288,035 employees covered in 1974 accounted for 11.1 per cent of all wage earners, and 15.6 per cent of non-agricultural wage earners. It can be concluded that by 1974, every enterprise of any size in these four sectors had labour communities.

Finally, our survey of institutional changes must consider the nationalisations of 1968–75. Elsewhere, it is argued that these nationalisations led to the *strengthening* of private capital in Peru,[15] but here we are only concerned with their implications for distribution. While nationalisation does not in and of itself affect distribution, it could be argued that it is an instrument of redistribution, since the state can pursue distributional policies *directly* through the payment system. Whatever the potential this instrument provides for distribution, the Peruvian state after 1968 played a much larger ownership role in the economy. Brundenius estimates that about 13 per cent of gross domestic product was state-owned in 1968, and 22 per cent in 1975. Further, if one includes the agricultural cooperatives and other forms of nominal worker-ownership, which must conform to state directives in all significant day-to-day operating decisions, the 1975 figure is 35 per cent.[16]

If one goes sector-by-sector, it is possible to be more precise. In 1973, the entire fishing industry (including processing) was purchased by the state. Before 1968, state ownership, sole control or joint ventures with private capital probably represented about 15 per cent of the financial capital of manufacturing companies hiring five or more workers. In 1975, 'mixed enterprise' (joint venture) state investment was 12 per cent of manufacturing financial ownership; predominantly or totally state enterprises were 34 per cent; and other forms of state ownership about one-half of one per cent.[17] In 1974 and 1975, significant portions of the mining industry came under state ownership, though expansion of foreign-owned mining subsequently left the state in minority control of the industry.[18]

Thus, by the early and middle 1970s, the Peruvian state established itself as a major economic factor in the productive sectors of the economy. In the following section, we will see if this had a measurable impact on the distribution of income.

III THE DISTRIBUTION OF INCOME IN PERU

Evidence from the functional distribution of income

Peru in the post Second World War period was a society perceived to be characterised by extreme inequality of income and wealth.[19] Until 1961, there were no data on the size distribution of income, but the national survey conducted in that year indicated that earlier perceptions had not been in error. In Table 3.3, we give the distribution of income from this survey and a second conducted in 1972. The two are not strictly comparable because of coverage and the definitions used. In addition; the major demographic changes that ocurred between the two years make comparisons difficult, even if the surveys had been conducted identically. The data indicate a society dramatically stratified, with the poorest 20 per cent earning an average 1/23 of the average income of the richest 20 per cent. Comparison of the 1961 and 1972 distributions

TABLE 3.3   The distribution of income in Peru, 1961 and
             1972

Quintiles	Income 1961	Shares 1972
0–20%	3.0%	2.5%
20–40	7.0	6.5
40–60	13.0	12.5
60–80	21.5	20.0
80–100	55.5	58.5
Highest 5%	26.0	33.0
Highest 1%	9.8	17.9
	100.0%	100.0%

Source: Webb and Figueroa, op. cit., and *VI Censo Nacional de Poblacion de 1972*, vol. 1 (Tables 43 and 44).

TABLE 3.4   The functional distribution of income in Peru, 1950–76

	Wage-Labour Income			'Independents'		
	Wages and Salaries	Wages	Salaries	Agricultural	Non-Agricultural	Profits
1950	38.9%	21.3%	17.6%	21.6%	14.2%	16.4%
1951	37.3	20.5	16.8	22.8	13.0	18.6
1952	38.9	21.0	18.0	21.7	13.4	16.8
1953	41.1	21.8	19.3	21.7	14.0	13.9
1954	42.3	22.4	19.9	19.9	14.8	14.4
1955	43.6	22.9	20.6	19.0	15.2	13.4
1956	44.9	22.5	22.4	15.9	15.7	14.9
1957	46.5	23.2	23.3	14.5	16.1	13.6
1958	47.9	24.3	23.6	16.4	16.1	10.3
1959	47.9	24.0	23.9	16.0	16.4	10.6
1960	46.2	23.4	22.8	13.7	15.7	15.3
1961	47.2	24.1	23.1	13.9	15.6	14.2
1962	46.4	23.6	22.8	13.9	15.6	15.5
1963	47.9	23.8	24.1	12.0	16.2	15.2
1964	47.7	22.9	24.8	12.1	16.8	15.6
1965	48.2	21.0	24.3	11.4	16.2	16.4
1966	47.8	23.4	24.3	11.1	16.4	17.4
1967	49.4	24.0	25.4	11.8	16.6	15.7
1968	49.5	23.5	26.0	11.4	16.6	15.4
1969	48.7	23.2	25.6	11.2	16.4	16.9
1970	46.7	22.0	24.7	12.0	15.4	19.8
1971	49.5	23.7	25.8	10.0	16.3	18.3
1972	51.2	24.7	26.5	8.8	16.7	17.4
1973	48.9	24.2	24.7	8.1	15.9	22.3
1974	47.0	23.8	23.2	8.6	15.5	23.6
1975	47.5	24.4	23.1	9.3	15.8	22.6
1976	46.4	24.1	22.2	9.0	15.7	24.7

Source: Banco Central de Reserva del Peru, *Cuentas Nacionales.*

indicate increase in inequality (the Lorenz curves do not cross), but this could be accounted for by the differences in method of the two surveys. In any case, Table 3.3 is of no aid in analysing the impact of the 1968 reforms, since it gives no guide to changes between 1961 and 1968, as opposed to 1969–72.

In order to measure the impact of the reforms, we must try to isolate their influence from other factors. We begin this process by treating the functional distribution of income over a sufficiently long period to separate out any secular or cyclical movements. In Table 3.4, national income is broken down into its functional shares for the years 1950–76, with wages and salaries separated, and a disaggregation made between rural and urban proprietor's income. Taking the 27 years as a whole, the major trends reflect a society in the process of industrialisation and proletarisation (growing wage and salary share), accompanied by a relative decline in the agricultural sector, as well as its progressive conversion to wage labour. In 1950, wage and salary-earners represen-

TABLE 3.5 Relative income shares of wage-labour and 'Independents', 1950–76

	Wage-Labour Income			'Independents'	
	Wages and Salaries	Wages	Salaries	Agricultural	Non-Agricultural
1950	0.86	0.60	1.80	0.54	1.00
1951	0.81	0.57	1.66	0.57	0.92
1952	0.84	0.58	1.74	0.55	0.95
1953	0.88	0.60	1.84	0.56	0.99
1954	0.89	0.61	1.86	0.52	1.04
1955	0.91	0.61	1.87	0.50	1.07
1956	0.93	0.61	2.00	0.42	1.11
1957	0.96	0.63	2.03	0.39	1.13
1958	0.98	0.65	2.02	0.44	1.12
1959	0.97	0.64	2.01	0.44	1.14
1960	0.93	0.62	1.88	0.38	1.08
1961	0.94	0.64	1.84	0.40	1.08
1962	0.92	0.62	1.80	0.40	1.08
1963	0.94	0.62	1.87	0.35	1.11
1964	0.93	0.60	1.87	0.36	1.15
1965	0.93	0.54	1.79	0.34	1.11
1966	0.91	0.61	1.74	0.34	1.11
1967	0.93	0.62	1.80	0.37	1.12
1968	0.93	0.60	1.82	0.36	1.11
1969	0.90	0.59	1.77	0.36	1.10
1970	0.86	0.56	1.68	0.39	1.03
1971	0.90	0.59	1.73	0.33	1.09
1972	0.92	0.61	1.74	0.30	1.11
1973	0.88	0.60	1.61	0.28	1.06
1974	0.86	0.58	1.48	0.30	1.04
1975	0.81	0.58	1.42	0.32	1.05
1976	0.80	0.58	1.36	0.31	1.02

Source: Same as Table 3.4, and Claes Brundenius, 'Remuneraciones y Redistribución de Ingresos' (Lima: Instituto Nacional de Planificacion, 1976) for labour force time series.

ted about 46 per cent of the total labour force and peasant farmers 40 per cent; in 1974, wage-labourers had become a majority of the labouring population, 56 per cent, and peasants only 30 per cent. This type of shift makes Table 3.5 of more use in considering distribution. Here, the income share of each class and sub-class is divided by that class's employment share. This statistic, the 'relative income share', has a convenient characteristic; since, by definition, the ratio of all income shares to all employment shares is unity, a number less than unity indicates that a class on average receives less than average national income per employed person, a useful benchmark. In addition, the 'relative income share' eliminates changes in income shares which are a result merely of a class increasing in relative size. In the case of wage earners, for example, we have eliminated the trend in employment growth.

A statistical inspection of Table 3.5 yields no evidence of any changes after 1968 which could be interpreted as leading to greater income equality, whatever their cause (with one possible exception considered below). In Table 3.6, we summarise the statistical tests for evidence of significant distributional changes after 1968. The table gives the average value of each relative income share (and the simple profit share) for 1950–68 and 1969–74, and the t-statistic for difference of two means. A positive 't' indicates that the average was higher in the *earlier* period. The table shows that the relative wage and salary share was actually *higher* in the earlier period, though the difference is not statistically significant. The same is true for the wage share of unskilled and semi-

TABLE 3.6   Test of significance for the difference in income shares, 1950–68 and 1969–74

	Mean Value		
Income Share	*1950–68*	*1969–74*	*t-Statistic*[1]
Wages and Salaries	0.914	0.908	t = 0.32, NS
Wages	0.608	0.604	t = 0.30, NS
Salaries	1.850	1.710	t = 3.07 sig.
Agricultural Independents	0.430	0.310	t = 3.10 sig.
Non-Agricultural Independents	1.080	1.090	t = − 0.387 NS
Profit Share	15.03	18.63	t = − 3.79 sig

Source: From Tables 3.4 and 3.5.

Note: 1. NS denotes that the difference is non-significant, and 'sig' that the difference is significant, in all cases at the 99 per cent level of confidence.

skilled workers (line 2). Thus, the reforms, taken together with other influences, had no effect in raising either the relative share of all workers nor of the lowest paid. The relative share of skilled workers did, however, *decline* significantly. Since this was not accompanied by an increase for the lowest paid, it probably represents a redistribution within the upper half of the income distribution.

Agricultural non-wage earners (peasants) were significantly worse off after 1968 in relative terms, and probably in absolute terms.[20] This reflects the general crisis in the agricultural sector coincident with the land reform. For the urban self-employed, there was no significant change, though the average value of their relative share was slightly higher after 1968. There was, however, a significant increase in the profit share, an increase that remains if we adjust for the very slight trend in that share. Thus, overall, the functional distribution of income indicates greater inequality after 1968: the relative position of the poorest, the peasantry, declined sharply, while profits rose substantially, and the situation of the other classes (the proletariat and urban petty bourgeoisie) remained the same.

One possible qualification to this summary might be made. Income shares, particularly those derived from capitalist production (wages and profits), are sensitive to the economic cycle. Characteristically in industrial capitalist countries the profit share rises during accumulation, and the wage share falls, and 1968–74 was a period of expansion. To see if this accounts for the movement (or non-movement) in the relative wage share, we have taken real gross domestic product and the simple wage and salary share and adjusted them for their secular trends. This allows inspection for a cyclical pattern, represented in Figure 3.1.[21] There is, in fact, a clear cyclical pattern in both. Up to 1967, there is a

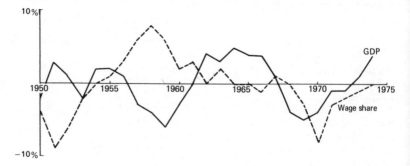

Figure 3.1   Trend adjusted movements in GDP and the wage share in national income: Peru, 1950–74

general tendency for the wage and salary share to move counter-cyclically. However, after 1967, the two move more or less together, indicating that the stability of the *relative* wage and salary share cannot be explained by counter-cyclical movements.

Evidence from manufacturing

It could be argued that it is too much to expect that the reforms of the new bourgeois government would manifest themselves in the functional distribution of income in just a few years. There are many factors operating upon this distribution beyond the control of the state, reflecting the laws of capitalist accumulation. Recognising this, we disaggregate, seeking sectors of the economy where state participation is quantitatively greatest and where whatever policy discretion the economic system allows would be greatest. Two possibilities are mining and fishing, since the Peruvian state assumed ownership of a major portion of the former and all of the latter. The mining industry must be ruled out for investigation, however, because of the recentness of the nationalisations (1974–5), which allows too little time for comparison.[22] In the case of fishing (nationalised in 1973), analysis is complicated by the disastrous collapse of the industry in 1972, because of over-fishing, a collapse which was nothing short of catastrophic. It should be noted that under state control of the industry, the Ministry of Fishing carried out a programme of lay-offs, wage-cutting, and union-busting rivalling anything occurring in the private sector.[23]

For manufacturing, there are considerable data, and it is possible to disaggregate in some detail. Overall for manufacturing, there is no indication that the industrial communities resulted in a rise in the wage share. However, this could reflect a number of other influences, such as a cyclical pattern. In order to control for these influences, we shall try to disaggregate to a level where the impact of state influence can be isolated. To do this, we have measured the change in money wages for all non-supervisory employees and the wage share in value-added for 54 sub-sectors of manufacturing and measured for each of these sub-sectors the share of state ownership of financial capital. Table 3.7 summarises this disaggregation, with industries divided into five categories, by the share of state ownership in total ownership. A brief glance shows that there is no evidence either that wages rose faster in industries with state participation, nor that the wage and salary bill increased (or fell less) in these sectors. The table compares wage changes

TABLE 3.7   Comparison of wage changes in Peruvian manufacturing, 1970–5

	Ratio, 1975 to 1970		
Share of State Ownership	*Average Wage*	*Wage Share*	*N*[1]
Over 50%	2.20	0.97	8
25–49	2.00	0.91	5
10–24	2.24	0.89	6
1–9	2.19	1.02	11
None	2.34	0.96	24
All sectors	2.16	0.98	54

Source: Ministerio de Industria y Turismo, industrial survey data, 1970 and 1975.

Note: [1] Number of sub-sectors in category.

between 1970 and 1975, for 54 branches of industry. The second column gives the average ratio of money wages in 1975 to money wages in 1970, by category of ownership. For all manufacturing, money wages rose by 116 per cent, and 134 per cent in sub-sectors with no state participation. In all industries with any state ownership, wages rose by less on the average. In four sub-sectors, state ownership exceeded 90 per cent. In three of these, wages rose more than the manufacturing average, but in each case within one standard deviation of the manufacturing mean. In the fourth, wages rose only 3 per cent (petroleum refining), the lowest for all 54 sub-sectors.

It might be argued that money wage changes are not the accurate measure of state action since they are limited by productivity change, demand conditions, and possibly other factors which vary across industries. For this reason, the ratio of the wage share in 1975 to that in 1970 is given in Column 3. Overall, the wage share in manufacturing fell by 2 per cent (last row), and the average for establishments in sectors with at least 50 per cent state ownership was virtually the same as for sectors with no state ownership. On average, the wage share rose in sub-sectors with the least, but some state ownership. But the average was not significantly different from that of manufacturing as a whole. Looking again at the four sub-sectors with 90 per cent or more state ownership, we find they rank 7th, 8th, 30th, and 41st among the 54 sub-sectors in terms of the ratio of the wage share in the two years. This indicates an absence of any consistent pattern among industries almost totally state-owned.

A commonly held view by commentators on the Peruvian reforms is that they tended to benefit wage earners in the 'modern' sector. The implication of this would be that the reforms affected a regressive distribution of income among the wage-employed. The foregoing evidence indicates that wage earners as a class did not benefit significantly but says nothing about the distribution within the class. To consider the possibility of intra-class effects, we break down manufacturing wages by size of enterprise in Table 3.8. If the reforms did benefit the better-paid more, we would expect to find that wages rose faster in large establishments (where wages are higher), and a consequent increase in the dispersion of wage levels by size of firm. Table 3.8 indicates no consistent pattern. The wages of unskilled and semi-skilled workers rose the least in the smallest establishments (see note 4 to Table 3.8) and in the largest (next to last column). The distribution of wage

TABLE 3.8 Movements in average money wages by type of labour and size of establishment in Peru, 1970–5

Size of Establishment (Employees)	Average money wages[1]					
	1970		1975		Ratio[5]	
	Obreros[2]	Empleados[3]	Obreros[2]	Empleados[3]	Obreros[2]	Empleados[3]
5–9	32.0[4]	32.0[4]	62.3[4]	62.3[4]	1.94[4]	1.94[4]
10–14	29.1	62.5	61.5	123.2	2.11	1.97
15–19	28.8	67.0	64.7	148.1	2.22	2.21
20–49	33.7	87.4	72.0	179.8	2.14	2.06
50–99	40.8	112.4	90.1	212.1	2.21	1.89
100–199	47.1	125.8	127.0	179.4	2.70	1.43
200–499	57.1	139.7	125.1	269.3	2.19	1.93
500–999	49.4	123.5	132.4	255.4	2.68	2.07
1000+	71.9	169.4	149.6	239.8	2.08	2.67
Simple mean[6]	44.7	111.0	100.9	200.9	2.29	2.03
Coef. of var.	0.333	0.331	0.337	0.259	0.251	0.17

Source: See Table 3.7.

Notes:
[1] Thousands of *soles* per year.
[2] Unskilled and semi-skilled workers.
[3] Skilled workers.
[4] For the smallest category of establishments, there was no adequate disaggregation of type of labour in 1970. The numbers are average wages for all workers employed.
[5] Ratio of the money wage in 1975 to 1970, by category of establishment and type of labour (see note 4).
[6] Smallest category omitted, see note 4.

levels increased slightly between 1970 and 1975, as measured by the coefficient of variation, but only slightly (.333 to .337). For skilled workers, average wages rose fastest in the largest firms, slowest in the category of 100–199 employees, and more than the mean increase in the 15–49 group. The dispersion of average wages around the mean industry value declined sharply (the coefficient of variation fell from .331 to .259). In summary, skilled wages were more equally distributed by

TABLE 3.9 Annual unskilled and semi-skilled wages, Lima Metropolitan Area 1957–78[1]

	Money wages[2]	Cost of living index	Price deflated wages
1957	31.0	24.8	125.0
1958	35.8	26.8	133.6
1959	41.0	30.2	135.8
1960	44.8	32.8	136.6
1961	49.1	34.8	141.1
1962	53.8	39.3	150.9
1963	59.3	39.3	150.9
1964	66.9	43.2	154.8
1965	74.6	50.2	148.6
1966	83.6	54.7	152.8
1967	90.7	60.0	151.2
1968	95.7	71.4	134.0
1969	108.6	76.0	142.6
1970	113.1	79.8	132.7
1971	131.7	85.2	154.6
1972	152.7	91.3	167.3
1973	183.8	100.0	183.8
1974	212.4[3]	116.9	181.7
1975	220.6	144.5	152.7
1976	271.9	191.5	142.0
1977	363.8	267.0	136.3
1978	508.7	459.0	110.8

Source: Servicio del Empleo y Recursos Humanos, *Sueldos y Salarios, 1969–1970*; Brundenius (1977) op. cit.; and Oficina de Estadistica y Censos, *Indice de Precios al Consumidor, Lima Metrolitana* (1976).

Notes:
[1] Index covers manufacturing, commerce, banking, construction, and non-government services, firms employing 10 or more.
[2] *Soles* per day.
[3] Average of 1st and 2nd quarters.

size of establishment in 1975 than in 1970, while unskilled and semi-skilled wages showed little change in their dispersion. Certainly the evidence does not support the hypothesis that 'modern' sector wage-earners gained substantially, if 'modern' sector can be approximated by size of establishment.

As a final note to our empirical analysis, it is instructive to demonstrate the very strong cyclical pattern of wage changes in Peru over the last twenty years. Table 3.9 gives indices of money and real wages (real purchasing power of wages) for unskilled and semi-skilled workers in Lima, 1957–78. The wages are for unskilled and semi-skilled in all sectors except state employment. Substantial real wage increases occurred 1970–3, but these were clearly part of an economic cycle, levelling off in 1973–4, and declining sharply in 1975–8. The cyclical pattern in wages is shown in Figure 3.2 where we have adjusted for the trend in wages over time. From 1959 to 1964, the Peruvian economy was in a prolonged expansionary period (see Figure 3.1 for the cyclical pattern in GDP), and real wages rose at a modest rate, relative to their trend value. Subsequently, GDP declined sharply relative to its trend (1966–9), followed by an equally sharp recovery (1969–74) and another economic crisis, far more severe than the previous one (1974 to the present). The wage movements reflect this economic cycle and suggest, particularly in light of our previous evidence, that any policy factors affecting wages are quite minor compared to the boom and bust of the economic cycle. We return to this point below.

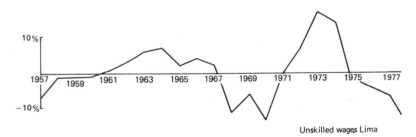

Unskilled wages Lima

Figure 3.2   Trend adjusted unskilled wages in Lima, deflated for cost-of-living 1957–78

Summary of the evidence

The statistics overwhelmingly indicate that the post-1968 reforms had no discernible impact on the functional distribution of income, except perhaps towards greater inequality. After 1968, peasant income declined sharply in relative terms, and the profit share rose. In fishing, wholly state-owned after 1973, employment fell, real wages fell, and worker protest was crushed. In manufacturing, sectors with state participation behaved no differently from those without state involvement, or worse, with regard to wage changes and the distribution between wages and profits. Wage movements in small and large establishments in manufacturing indicate no systematic variation.

One is thus left with the conclusion that distributional changes after 1968 seem dominated by secular and cyclical factors, with the reforms having little measurable impact. This finding in itself is not astonishing; all evidence from the industrial capitalist countries indicates that both the functional and size distributions of income are extremely stable. Peru seems to have conformed to this pattern, despite the post-1968 reforms. The interesting question is why this inflexibility should exist, and we consider that question in the final section.

IV   DISTRIBUTION OF INCOME IN THE CONTEXT OF ECONOMIC BACKWARDNESS

After 1950, Peru was a society well-advanced into the transition between pre-capitalism and capitalism.[24] As in the case of Britain, capitalism had begun in the agricultural sector,[25] though limited to the coastal plain. After World War II, the impetus of capitalist development shifted to industry and the society developed on the basis of rapidly expanding capitalist industrialisation and a relatively stagnant pre-capitalist agriculture in the Andean highlands. Distributional changes must be understood and interpreted in terms of the tension between these two modes of production. Economic backwardness is a consequence of the persistence of pre-capitalist institutions which provides a break on the dynamism of the capitalist sector.

It is beyond the scope of this chapter to deal fully with the transition to capitalism, but we can point out the major aspects of the process. Capitalist society represents the first mode of production in which society itself and the rule of the exploiting class[26] is reproduced through the circulation of commodities.[27] In previous class societies there was exchange but it is first under capitalism that exchange of products becomes both generalised and necessary. This is because in capitalist society production occurs by the advancing of money-capital for production; it is by the exchange of money against labour power and material elements of production that workers and the means of production are brought together, marshalled for production. Such is not the case under feudalism, where very little money need be put in circulation by the landlord prior to production. The peasant is not paid but, on the contrary, pays the landlord to the extent that there is a money exchange between them.[28] The land is not rented by the landlord, nor does he usually provide inputs to the peasant. But under capitalism, production is impossible without a prior circulation of commodities. The most important commodity in the capitalist context is labour power, the workers' capacity to work. When this labour power becomes a commodity on a growing scale, the conditions of capitalist accumulation follow.[29]

The capacity to work becomes a commodity on a large scale when people are separated from the means of production. The most important of these means in pre-capitalist society is land. Without land, the labourer must hire himself out to those who do have land, or to those who have the tools and other means for non-agricultural production. This social relationship of selling one's labour power has important consequences for both buyer and seller. The seller is thrown into a monetary world in which the condition of his continued existence depends not just upon his capacity to work but upon his *sale* of that ability. As a consequence, not only is the worker's labour power a commodity, but the products he consumes must also be commodities, purchased with his wage. Put simply, the labourer's social relations with the exploiting class changes from one in which he produces his own means of subsistence to one in which he must purchase them with money and, consequently, must enter into the wage contract. The process has analogous implications for the purchaser of labour power. Having advanced money for labour power, the capitalist must sell the product of the workers' labour, so that he can once again initiate production. Thus, the expansion of this simple exchange of money for labour power creates a wage labour force, products which must circulate as commodities, and the market for these products.[30]

Pre-capitalist relations, by holding labourers in social relations in which their capacity to work is not a commodity and the products they consume not commodities, blocks the development of commodity production and, thus, capitalism. For this reason, capitalists must attempt, as a class, to break down such social relations. Historically, this has been done in capitalist countries by undermining the viability of peasant or family farming. It should not surprise one, then, that the Peruvian land reform, instituted by a capitalist class, should be associated with a rapid decline in the relative position of the peasantry. Urban proprietors, self-employed, do not present the same barrier. While they may compete with capitalist enterprise in their artisanal production, their economic and social life is as monetised as that of the wage-earner. Thus we find their relative position stable, even improving, during the industrialisation of Peru.

An analysis of wages is much more complex since wages are basically determined in the process of capitalist accumulation, involving qualitative changes – economic crises, productivity change, the centralisation and concentration of capital.[31] These complexities can only be considered briefly. In the early stages of capitalist development, the working class is weak, both because the destruction of peasant life swells the ranks of the unemployed and because class consciousness itself is weak. Class consciousness is, by definition, the consciousness of individuals of their common membership in a class and of the common interests of that class, applicable to capitalists, workers and peasants. This consciousness develops for workers as capitalism develops, as they are thrown into large concentrations, and as their lives are increasingly ruled by the cycle of employment and unemployment.

Just as the working class is weak in the early stages of capitalist development, so is the capitalist class, particularly a national capitalist class faced with competition from capitalists of advanced industrial countries. Whatever the reformist sentiments of this class or its representatives, the task of overcoming pre-capitalist barriers, of ensuring adequate profitability (particularly *vis-à-vis* foreign capital) and the struggle to attain class hegemony severely limit possibilities of redistribution. Indeed, the Peruvian bourgeois state professed its commitment to greater equality most strongly during the period of economic expansion (1969–73). In this period, it is possible that some redistributive impact was felt, though there is no evidence of it. When the expansion of capital levelled off and then contraction set in and it became a question of redistributing a declining total, not even protestations of redistributive intentions were made. Well before any conditions were imposed by foreign lenders, the state unveiled an austerity package (the 'Baruha Plan', named after the minister of finance) in 1975. This and subsequent measures involved sharp devaluations, suspension of the right to strike, elimination of subsidies on basic necessities, and selective denationalisation (in the fishing industry, for example).

Flirtation with redistribution was over by 1975, even in words. While the Peruvian case does not demonstrate the impossibility of distributional reform, it does clearly demonstrate the weakness of such reforms in face of the economic cycle intrinsic to the capitalist mode of production.

NOTES

1. Elizabeth Dore and John Weeks, 'The Intensification of the Attack Against the Working Class in "Revolutionary" Peru', *Latin American Perspectives III* (Spring 1976).
2. Ibid.
3. This is stated in the *Plan Inca*, the manifesto and economic plan of the government for the 'transformation' of Peruvian society.
4. Dore and Weeks, op. cit.
5. For a description of the major reforms, see Richard Webb and Adolfo Figueroa, *Distribucion del Ingreso en el Peru* (Lima: Instituto de Estudias Peruanos, 1975).
6. Some have called it 'state capitalist'. E. V. K. Fitzgerald, 'The State and Economic Development of Peru Since 1968', Occasional Paper 49, Department of Applied Economics (University of Cambridge, 1976). This is, however, not accurate.
7. Some argue that the Peruvian state from 1968 to 1973 or 1974 possessed a 'relative autonomy' with respect to classes. See Giorgio Alberti, *et al.*, *Estado y Clase: La Comunidad Industrial en el Peru* (Lima: Instituto de Estudios Peruanos, 1977). This view is critised in Dore and Weeks, op. cit., and Elizabeth Dore and John Weeks, 'Class Alliances and Class Struggle in Peru', *Latin American Perspectives* (14) IV, 3 (Summer 1977) pp. 4–9.
8. For a discussion of the land reform, see José María Caballero, 'Sobre el Caracter de La Reforma Agraria Peruanos', *Latin American Perspectives*, IV (Summer 1977).
9. Ibid., pp. 148–9.
10. Tom Alberts, 'The Development of Agriculture in Peru, 1950–1975', Research Policy Programme, University of Lund, Sweden, Discussion Policy Paper No. 121 (April 1978).
11. Ministerio de Industria y Turismo, *El Capital Extranjero en el Sector Industrial, 1971–1973* (Lima, 1975) p. 15.
12. Webb and Figueroa, op. cit.
13. Centro de Estudios y Promocion del Desarrollo, *Communidad Laboral y Capitalismo: Alcances y Limites* (Lima: DESCO, 1976) Chapter III.
14. Webb and Figueroa, op. cit., p. 124ff.
15. Dore and Weeks, op. cit., and John Weeks, 'Backwardness, Foreign Capital, and Accumulation in the Manufacturing Sector of Peru, 1954–1975', *Latin American Perspectives*, IV (Summer 1977).
16. These figures cannot be considered too precise, since they are based on ownership of financial capital, taken as a portion of the total ownership in the economy. Given the difficulty in defining 'assets' in the rural sector, as well as estimating them, the figures must be taken as general indicators; Claes Brundenius, *Los 'Cambios Estructurales' en La Economica Peruana* (Lima: Ediciones Jose Maria Arguedas, 1977) p. 5.

17. Ministerio de Industria y Turismo, *El Capital Extranjero en el Sector Manufacturero*, 1973–1975 (Lima: 1977) p. 20.
18. Elizabeth Dore 'Crisis and Accumulation in the Peruvian Mining Industry, 1968–1974', *Latin American Perspectives* IV (Summer 1977).
19. Webb and Figueroa, op. cit., p. 157.
20. Output per worker in agriculture in 1971–2 was approximately the same as it had been in 1954–5, and real income 5–10 per cent lower. Claes Brundenius, 'Remuneraciones y Redistribucion de Ingresos', Instituto Nacional de Planificacion (Lima, July 1976) Appendix, Table 3.
21. The trend in the wage and salary share is best approximated linearly:

$$W = 40.51 + 0.49t \quad R^2 = 0.81$$

For gross domestic product:

$$\log \text{GDP} = 0.375 + 0.052t \quad R^2 = 0.993$$

Figure 3.1 is constructed by taking the ratio of each observation to its predicted value.
22. Elizabeth Dore, 'The Nationalization of the Mining and Fishmeal Industries in Peru: The Appearance and Reality', paper presented to the Latin Studies Association (Houston, Texas, November 1977).
23. The total catch was 10.2 million tons in 1971; 4.4 million in 1972; and 1.7 million in 1973. Fishing was suspended subsequently.
24. William Bollinger, 'The Bourgeois Revolution in Peru: A Conception of Peruvian History', *Latin American Perspectives*, IV (Summer 1977).
25. Ibid., pp. 20ff; and Rodney Hilton (ed.), *The Transition From Feudalism to Capitalism* (London: New Left Books, 1976).
26. *Exploitation* is used in the scientific sense of the appropriation by a non-producing class of part or all of the product of labour without compensation. Under capitalism, exploitation is veiled by the wage form, which is compensation for a certain period of a worker's time, but not for his labour (production).
27. Robert Brenner, 'The Origins of Capitalist Development', *New Left Review* 104 (July–August 1977) pp. 4–11.
28. Karl Marx, 'The Genesis of Capitalist Ground Rent' in *Capital*, vol. III (London: Lawrence and Wishart, 1974) chap. XLVII.
29. Ibid., vol. I, chap. 2, XXVI. This is the so-called process of 'primitive accumulation'.
30. For an excellent elaboration of this, see V. I. Lenin, 'On the so-called "Market Question"', *Collected Works* (Moscow: Progress Publishers, 1972).
31. Here we use Marx's terminology – concentration is the growth in size of individual capitals ('firms'), and centralisation the redistribution of capital among fewer capitals (mergers, etc.).

4 Alternative Patterns of Distribution and Growth in the Mixed Economy: the Philippines and Taiwan

GUSTAV RANIS

I INTRODUCTION

We assume here that the main societal objective is the rapid generation of growth in the presence of increased employment opportunities and the improvement of the size distribution of income – or at least an avoidance of deterioration in employment and distribution in the course of the transition growth process. This 'development task' is shared by all societies regardless of the social 'system' they have chosen for themselves on the spectrum between non-existent pure market economies and equally non-existent pure socialist economies. But the ability to achieve success in minimising conflicts among these objectives clearly relates to a society's initial conditions as well as the policies it brings to bear over time. Thus, while the definition of the development task may not be very different, the initial advantages or handicaps various countries face, as well as their ability to change the environment over time, will differ markedly. Countries always do have a range of organisational institutional choices open to them, as well as a range of economic policy choices which will affect their ability to solve their transition growth problem as we have defined it. Thus, given differences in the initial conditions, in the nature of the institutional/organisational choices as well as in the nature of the economic policy choices made over time, developing countries will end up with different 'payments systems', yielding different employment, distribution and growth outcomes at the closed end. It is the purpose of this chapter to examine this proposition in the context of two post-war Asian economies, the Philippines and Taiwan.

If we examine the overall performance of these two systems during the 1950s, we find that income distribution, while absolutely unfavourable in both, was actually more favourable in the Philippines (see Table 4.2, rows 17 and 18). Per capita income growth proceeded at relatively low but respectable rates in both, with a small edge going to Taiwan (see Table 4.2, row 16). Thus, during this early post-independence period, we find a not very substantial difference in performance with respect to either growth or equity. Yet by the end of the period under observation, i.e. the 1970s, the same table indicates that Taiwan had experienced consistently higher growth rates, i.e. at 6–7 per cent, and a marked improvement in the distribution of income, with the Gini coefficient falling to a remarkably low 0.28 level by 1970. The Philippines in contrast had lower, if still respectable, rates of per capita income growth, i.e. at about 2–2.6 per cent a year, but experienced no improvement, perhaps some deterioration from already poor levels, in the distribution of income. Our purpose here is to assess the importance of differences in the initial conditions as well as in the institutional and policy changes over time for this differential performance. A system's initial conditions do determine what early steps are possible, given human and natural resource constraints – while changes in both institutions and policies focus on the extent to which a system can organise itself over time to maximise the complementarity between growth and distribution objectives.

Section II will compare and contrast some of these initial conditions, which include such tangibles as initial infrastructure, spatial characteristics, size of country, and such intangibles as previous colonial experience in the two societies under examination – both placing constraints on any feasible set of actions once the economy is independent. For example, the existence of a rich, exportable natural resources base may determine, in the long run, the possibility of continuing on an import substitution path, oriented mainly towards domestic markets. Similarly, the extent to which transport and communication networks are urban-oriented and concentrated will affect the ability of a decentralised industrialisation effort to follow. To the extent that a country has experienced Japanese colonial rule focussed on the rural areas, relative to a Spanish or US colonialism with other objectives, the possibilities for a rural oriented decentralised development path may be quite different. Similarly, to the extent that land is more equally distributed as a consequence of earlier reforms, such as in Taiwan, this provides a clear advantage over an initially unequal distribution of such assets, as in the Philippines. Similarly, differences in the existence and utilisation of rural organisational infrastructure such. as the Taiwan Farmers' Associations, may play an important role in the type of payments system which ultimately emerges.

In section III we will try to analyse the primary distribution of income in relation to changes in the institutional/organisational milieu. While some dimensions of the organisational environment are fixed or at least not subject to rapid change, others, for example land reform, do make themselves amenable to public sector actions. Section IV concentrates on the economic policy changes which, in combination with the evolving organisational/institutional framework, permitted the primary payments system to take a very different shape in the two countries in the 1960s and 1970s, i.e. after the end of the primary import substitution subphase. Finally, section V will be devoted to some conclusions for policy.

II CONTRAST IN INITIAL CONDITIONS

Taiwan represents a relatively small, heavily populated and racially homogeneous entity poor in natural resources. As a former colony of Japan, and with food as the colonial product sought by Japan, Taiwan had the benefit of substantial prior investments in her rural areas, both in terms of physical infrastructure including irrigation, roads and electricity generation, as well as in terms of such institutional investments as land reform and the creation of farmers' associations. Sharing the common Chinese cultural heritage led to an emphasis on mass education and literacy and on the creation of a type of nominally unskilled human resources particularly suited for factory work. Indigenous entrepreneurial 'learning by doing' was, however, handicapped by the Japanese policy of reserving most industrial activity to themselves over the long years of Japanese occupation.

The Philippines, in contrast, represent a spatially disconnected pattern, with some major islands highly populated, others with a relatively abundant land and natural resources endowment. The colonial experience of the Philippines, both during the Spanish and US periods, was substantially different, focussing on the exportation of traditional cash crops, with food-producing agriculture relatively neglected and pre-existing rural industries discouraged by colonial imports in the course of the nineteenth and early twentieth centuries. In spite of being a somewhat larger country, the Philippines, it may be noted, were somewhat more export oriented at this stage, quite in contrast with the more recent period (see Table 4.2, row 14). A long history of centralised government, coupled with the erosion of the old barrio system, can be placed alongside traditional tight control by the landed elite.

In Table 4.1, we present some selected indicators showing the substantial headstart advantage of Taiwan over the Philippines in terms of the potential for achieving growth with equity over the years ahead. We may note the sharp contrast in the initial (1950) pressure of population on the land (see Table 4.1, row 1), favouring the Philippines, yet the substantially higher level of initial agricultural labour productivity in Taiwan (see Table 4.1, row 3). Taiwan's initially high and well dispersed level of electrification (Table 4.1, row 5), as well as its relatively much more extensive railroad net (Table 4.1, row 2), coupled with better roads and other overheads such as irrigation (Table 4.1, row 4) represent additional dimensions of Taiwan's relatively strong initial rural infrastructure.

Interestingly enough, in spite of many assumptions to the contrary, the percentage of the population enrolled in schools, the percentage of the population stock which is illiterate and the proportion of GNP expended on education dimensions all often seen as a substantial initial advantage of any Chinese culture based system, were not so different at this time (see Table 4.1, rows 6, 7 and 8). When it comes to the initial distribution of land, we see that Taiwan, as a consequence of the early (1905) land reforms under the Japanese, plus the 1949–53 post-independence reforms, had some, but not very decisive, advantages in terms of the initial distribution of this major asset (see row 9).

Finally, though these waters are much more murky, it is difficult to assess the initial entrepreneurial capacity of these two societies. Most observers credit the Philippines with a not much less favourable entrepreneurial base, given the pronounced Chinese/Malay racial mixture, due to the dominance of the Catholic religion on the islands, at least as compared with many of its Southeast Asian neighbours. On the other hand, the Japanese colonial presence probably inhibited the growth of indigenous industrial entrepreneurship on Taiwan, but there was a substantial entrepreneurial, along with civil-service and military, inflow at the time of the Communist takeover on the Mainland.

Overall, we thus have something of a mixed picture as the curtain rises in the early 1950s. The Japanese colonial heritage clearly gave Taiwan

TABLE 4.1   Initial conditions – 1950

	Taiwan	Philippines
1. Cultivated acres per worker	0.49	1.06
	(1952)	(1952)
2. Railroad activity		
ton/km per capita	118.5	7.6
passenger/km per capita	281.9	18.2
3. Agricultural labour productivity index;		
Phil = 100	214.0	100.0
4. Irrigation – % of cultivated land	54.2	13.9
	(1953)	
5. Electrification – installed capacity (KW per		
1000 pop.)	139.1	27.0
6. Education % enrolled (includes university)	17.0	18.0
	(1955)	(1955)
7. Literacy percentage	50.3	69.8
	(1956)	(1958)
8. Educational expenditure/GNP	2.6	2.4
9. Land ownership by top 10 % of owners	53.0	60.0
	(1952)	(1972)

Sources:
1. ILO, *Sharing in Development: A Programme of Employment, Equity and Growth for the Philippines*, ILO (Geneva, 1974); *Taiwan Statistical Data Book* (1975).
2. *UN Statistical Yearbook* (1952).
3. FAO, *Production Yearbook* (1953) vol. 4.
4. Ibid.
5. *UN Statistical Yearbook* (1953).
6. AID, *Economic Data Book for the Near East and South Africa* (June 1977).
7. UNESCO, *Statistical Yearbook* (1963).
8. UNESCO, *Statistical Yearbook* (1967).
9. (Philippines) ILO, *Sharing in Development: A Programme of Employment, Equity and Growth for the Philippines*, ILO (Geneva, 1974); (Taiwan) Samuel P. S. Ho, *Economic Development of Taiwan 1860–1970* (New Haven, 1978).

some initial advantages. On the other hand, the educational cum entrepreneurial strength of the initial population was not as severely biased in favour of Taiwan as may be generally supposed, nor was the distribution of land as different as one might have expected *ex ante*. One might thus be tempted to conclude that it was the post-independence policies which were followed, of both the institutional/organisational and of the economic variety, which had much to do with the sharply differentiated performance of the two systems over time. We now turn to an examination of this issue.

III   THE PRIMARY DISTRIBUTION OF INCOME:
      INSTITUTIONAL/ORGANISATIONAL CHOICES

The so-called 'primary' distribution of income is based partly on the
ownership of assets and partly on the way production and distribution
decisions are made. The distribution of assets, the technology and
output mixes chosen, and the rule by which owners of factor are
compensated, together determine the distribution of income as a result
of the production process itself, i.e. without regard to any 'secondary'
distribution, e.g. via the tax and/or expenditure system.

   With respect to the asset ownership dimension, Taiwan undertook a
highly effective land reform effort in the 1949–53 period – something
not duplicated in the Philippine case. Consequently, the land ownership
Gini in Taiwan declined from 0.62 in 1950 to about 0.46 in 1960; full
owners who represented 36 per cent of total farm families in 1950 in
Taiwan represented 80 per cent of total farm families by 1974. In the
Philippines the equivalent Gini figures are 0.58 and 0.53. The Taiwanese
land reform, only a portion of which is captured by land ownership
Ginis, consisted moreover of three steps: (1) a 25 per cent rent reduction
for tenants; (2) the sale of public land; (3) the redistribution of land to
private tillers. In the Philippines, in spite of some reforms, still only 58
per cent of the farmers in 1971 were owners of the land they tilled.

   A second important institutional reform which was effected in
Taiwan and not in the Philippines focusses on the conversion of pre-
existing decentralised farmers' organisations, both for the purposes of
encouraging small savings and technological diffusion, plus the maintenance of incentives for rural activities generally. The new Taiwan
Government found it possible to convert the farmers' associations,
which had been organised by colonial Japan for purposes of 'top-down'
tax and regulatory functions, into 'bottoms-up' groupings of farmers for
particular productive purposes, including the various financial, irrigation and technological tasks required by the rural economy. Working
in tandem with the Joint Commission on Rural Reconstruction at the
centre, these farmers' associations, which literally dotted the island,
provided a decentralised credit, investment and technology structure
which facilitated a strategy of rural development both in its agricultural
and non-agricultural dimensions. In contrast, the Philippines remained
a highly centralised agricultural economy with only some efforts made
by the mid 1970s to induce the growth of cooperatives, mainly from
above, i.e. by linking the cooperative form to participation in the
land reforms promulgated under martial law. The cooperative

legislation, the land reforms themselves, and the local government structure generally, continued to be comparatively weak and central-government dominated.

With respect to the initial distribution of the ownership of industrial capital, it is, however, impossible to obtain data. We do know, thanks to the taking over of the Japanese properties at the end of World War II, that most of Taiwan's large-scale industries were in Government hands and then in part distributed to medium-scale landlords as part of the land-reform programme. In the Philippines the distribution of industrial assets was probably more equitable initially but worsened over time due to the increased oligopoly power of the twenty most prominent families over three decades of import substitution and protectionism. Neither country, of course, experienced capital reforms during the period under observation, but a much more control oriented credit and foreign-exchange rationing system in the Philippines over these two decades undoubtedly favoured the larger scale establishments, i.e. there can be very little doubt that industrial concentration increased in the Philippines relative to Taiwan in this period. We do know that in 1960–1 the ratio of small to large firms was twice as high in Taiwan as in the Philippines, i.e. 5.6 versus 2.8; we also know that, over time, average firm capitalisation in Taiwan increased at a very slow rate and that the output growth of small firms actually exceeded that of large firms, which is quite remarkable by general LDC standards.

The fact that post-independence governments in the two cases continued to follow policies which further enhanced the gap in infrastructural construction in various areas is indicated in Table 4.2. We may note (row 1) that on the base of a smaller, spatially more concentrated, total population Taiwan increased its percentage of rural paved roads, which constitute about 2/3 of total roads in both countries, at a much faster pace over the period than did the Philippines. Moreover, Taiwan continued to increase its electric power capacity at a generally faster rate over the two decades (see row 3).

Coupled with this is the overall continued and growing reliance on local government and on local non-governmental organisations in the case of Taiwan, with little change from the colonial attitudes of centralisation and distrust of rural folk in evidence in the Philippines. Any effort to move a developing economy along a balanced growth path, with maximum participation of underemployed rural workers, requires a decentralised physical as well as organisational infrastructure.

A related dimension focuses on the marked differences in the educational structure of the two societies. There can be little doubt that

TABLE 4.2 Comparative performance 1950–75

	Taiwan				Philippines			
	1950	1960	1970	1975	1950	1960	1970	1975
Institutional/organizational changes								
1. % of paved roads	–	15.3	43.5	54.6	–	15.1	19.8	21.2
2. % school enrolment	–	21.1	26.5 (1973)	–	–	18.3	24.6 (1973)	–
3. Growth rate of installed electric capacity KW per 1,000 pop. (%)	5.7	11.5			8.3	4.8		
4. Educational expenditure/GNP	2.6	2.5	3.6	–	2.4	3.0	2.7	1.6
Economic policy changes and results								
5. Urban wage share	51.1 (1953)	53.2	52.5 (1968)	58.7	32.2 (1956)	26.7	20.9 (1971)	–
6. Effective rate of protection		59.6 (1966)				85.0 ('65)		
7. Multiple cropping index	1.65	1.84	1.83	1.81	1.26 (1948)	1.36	1.45 (1972)	–
8. Growth rate of production in manufacturing		15.0 (1951–60)	15.9	20.1	10.2 (1952–60)	6.1	6.0	
9. Growth rate of employment in manufacturing		3.8	5.4 (1960–8)		3.8	2.3	3.5	
10. Growth rate of agricultural labour productivity		5.3 (1954–61)	7.6 (1961–8)		.9	1.8	4.3 (1970–4)	
11. Index of agricultural labour productivity	100	135.4 (1956)	223.7		100	109.8	132.4	163.7
12. Savings/GNP	10.3	12.0	20.7	19.8	4.2	11.7	13.3	17.8

13. Investment/GNP	12.2	17.6	23.5	32.7	7.3	14.5	17.6	27.0
14. Total exports/GNP (%)	10.1	11.1	29.6	41.2	13.5	10.1	19.4	18.6
15. Agricultural exports/total exports (%)	—	51.7	22.5	17.5	88.9	86.5	69.8	65.1
16. Per capita GDP growth rate	4.8	6.3	7.1 (1974)	—	3.2	2.0	2.6	—
17. Income share of poorest 20%	2.9 (1953)	4.4 (1961)	8.8 (1972)	—	4.9 (1956)	4.8 (1961)	3.9 (1971)	—
18. Gini coefficient	.57	.46	.28	—	.49 (1956)	.50 (1961)	.49 (1971)	—

Sources:

1. Philippines National Economic and Development Authority, *Philippine Statistical Yearbook* (1978) UNCTAD, *Handbook of International Trade and Development Statistics* (1969).
2. AID, *Economic Data Book of the Near East and South Asia*, (1977).
3. UN, *Statistical Yearbook* (1953, 1962, 1971).
4. UNESCO, *Statistical Yearbook* (1967, 1976).
5. Republic of China, Directorate General of Budget, Accounting and Statistics, *Statistical Yearbook of the Republic of China* (1977); Philippines Bureau of the Census and Statistics, *Population, Land Area, Density and Percent Change in Three Censal Years 1948, 1960, 1970* (Philippines, 1972).
6. M. Hsing and J. Power, *Taiwan and the Philippines: Industrialization and Trade Policies*, OECD.
7. W. Galenson, *Economic Growth and Structural Change in Taiwan*, Cornell (1979); G. Ranis, *Sharing in Development: A Programme of Employment, Equity and Growth for the Philippines*, (Geneva: ILO, 1974).
8. UN, *Statistical Yearbook* (1976) World Bank, *World Tables* (1976).
9. ILO, *International Labor Statistics Yearbook* (1955, 1967, 1975).
10. *FAO Production Yearbook* (1971, 1975, 1966, 1955).
11. Ibid.
12. UN *Yearbook of National Accounts* (1957) pp. 185–6; (1978) pp. 1006–7; Republic of China, *Statistical Yearbook* (1978) pp. 298–301.
13. Ibid.
14. IMF, *Yearbook.*
15. UNCTAD, *Yearbook of Trade and Development Statistics* (1979).
16. AID, *Economic Data Book of the Near East and South Asia* 1974, at 1973 prices.
17. Shail Jain, *Size Distribution of Income*, World Bank Publication, 1975.
18. Ibid.

in both countries education is an important activity, taking up an unusually high percentage of the GNP (see Table 4.2, row 4). However, here the similarity ends. In the case of the Philippines, the educational structure is largely in private hands and not very well geared to the productive needs of the society, i.e. a large educational industry is mainly utilised not to produce needed skills but as a way to select candidates for unrelated scarce jobs via the so-called educational 'bumping' system. Moreover, the system is inequitable in the sense that it is a private fee charging system, with allocations largely by price, not merit, i.e. in terms of the ability of the wealthier families to place their children in the relatively few top-notch institutions. In the case of Taiwan, on the other hand, which continues to adhere to the old Imperial examinations system, virtually all children have equal access to educational opportunity at all levels, with educational costs financed by the state. Thus, over time, regardless of the initial distribution of physical assets, human capital resources are much more likely to be redistributed in accordance with criteria unrelated to family wealth or influence in the case of Taiwan. The tendency to maintain an educational meritocracy does not, of course, guarantee wage income equality, since members of some families are bound both to value education more highly and to benefit more from it than others, but it reduces the extent of 'unwarranted' or windfall profits going to members of some families just by virtue of membership.

In the mixed economy club, of which both the Philippines and Taiwan are members, differences in the organisational/institutional choices made over time are, of course, limited in their impact on the equity of the primary distribution system. They represent a necessary but not sufficient ingredient. Equally necessary is the extent to which the various factors of production, or, more precisely, the families which own those factors of production, are given access to productive employment opportunities in the course of the transition growth process. We will therefore now turn to a comparison of the policy settings over time which crucially affected the primary distribution of income in the two contrasting country cases.

IV   THE PRIMARY DISTRIBUTION OF INCOME:
ECONOMIC POLICY CHOICES

Both the Philippines and Taiwan emerged into independent transition growth after World War II. In both cases, as has frequently been observed, the initial post independence effort focussed on intervention by the national government along well known primary import substitution policy lines. This meant that, instead of continuing to let traditional raw material export receipts be used for reinvestment in these same sectors, as well as in the 'facilitating' ancillary service activities, an effort was made to produce previously imported consumer goods at home and supply them to the domestic market. In both instances, it is also correct to note that, given the customary substantial distortion of relative factor and commodity prices and the customary bias in favour of the new industrial entrepreneurial class, employment and income distribution objectives were on a back burner, with rapid industrialisation under protective cover the main game.

Nevertheless, we can already – even during the 1950s, which represent the primary import substitution decade in both countries – note two important divergences between the two countries. On the one hand, while the pro-industrial bias of this policy regime *ipso facto* amounts to an anti-agricultural bias, the extent of agricultural neglect in the case of the Philippines appears to be more severe than in the case of Taiwan – as illustrated by the divergent index of agricultural labour productivity growth in the two countries over time (see Table 4.2, rows 10 and 11). Taiwan's policy-makers clearly managed to continue to pay attention to the need of food-producing agriculture even during a policy regime which is characteristically focussed on driving resources into the hands of the new industrial elite. The severity of the virtually inevitable primary import substitution phase was clearly much less pronounced in the case of Taiwan, i.e. the level of protection was lower (see Table 4.2, row 6), the severity of intervention in the capital market etc. was less severe, and thus the ability of medium- and small-scale industrial producers and families, both in the rural and urban areas, to gain access to resources much enhanced. In fact, even as late as 1971 only 58 per cent of Taiwan's industrial establishments were located in urban or semi-urban areas, while in the Philippines more than 80 per cent of industrial activity continued to be located in the greater Manila area. As a consequence of industry's more decentralised location and less distorted endowment, labour's share in industrial value added amounted to 43.5 per cent for food, 53.8 per cent for textiles and 58.8 per cent for paper and paper products in the case of Taiwan, almost 50 per cent higher than in the Philippines.[1]

It should be clear that the usual syndrome of protection and overvalued exchange rates in the presence of budget deficits, inflation, import licensing etc. was common to both the Philippines and Taiwan

94

Work, Income and Inequality

during the 1950s; but the rate of effective protection was lower and real interest rates were substantially higher in Taiwan. Taiwan, in fact, enacted a monetary reform to keep interest rates substantially positive in real terms in the early 1950s, while the Philippines maintained rates of interest at low nominal and thus frequently negative real levels throughout the decade. The cooperative rural banking structure linked to the farmers' associations in Taiwan made credit available to farmers of all sizes at reasonable rates while, during this period, mainly the cash-crop-oriented, i.e. larger scale, farmers found themselves in that situation in the Philippines.

A marked contrast in the extent of multiple cropping and diversification towards a more labour-intensive agricultural output mix should also be noted. Land clearly continued to be much more intensively cultivated on Taiwan, both in terms of simple cultivated land/labour ratios – which differed by a factor of almost 4:1 in 1960 – but also in terms of the multiple-cropping index, which stood close to 1.85 in Taiwan in 1960 as compared to 1.36 in the Philippines (see Table 4.2, row 7).

Interestingly enough, the rate of growth of the industrial labour force was not so different in the two cases during the 1950s (see Table 4.2, row 9), with one fuelled more via domestic balanced growth and domestic, including agricultural, savings, the other more via traditional raw material export financing and foreign capital inflows (see Table 4.2, rows 12 and 13). Taiwan's agriculture was clearly able to 'hold' more of its people productively even during the 1950s as a consequence of the less severe relative price and output mix distortions during her primary import substitution sub-phase. Nevertheless, the relative centre of gravity of the economy was shifting towards the non-agricultural sector, as we would expect under conditions of successful balanced growth. In spite of the relatively smaller distortion of wages, interest rates and the prices of imported versus domestic goods, and the higher saving rates (see Table 4.2, row 12), Taiwan's ability to maintain a 3.8 per cent annual growth of her non-agricultural labour force, urban and rural, was about the same as that of the Philippines.

It is, however, when primary import substitution finally ran out of steam, which occurred in both country cases around the end of the 1950s, and a new expansion path had to be found, that a major divergence between these two developing systems could be observed. Once markets for non-durable consumer goods become exhausted, the typical dualistic economy faces essentially two options: one is to maintain the basic ingredients of the import substitution policy regime but to shift attention from non-durable consumer goods to consumer durables, the processing of intermediate goods, and capital goods, probably in that order, for the domestic market. The choice of this subphase, often called secondary import substitution, represents a system which continues to rely mainly on traditional land-based exports to fuel the production of increasingly capital and technology intensive industrial goods, mainly for the domestic market but sometimes also – with the help of subsidies – for export. This is basically the option followed by the Philippines during the 1960s, and to this day.

The second option is to give a new lease of life to the non-durable consumer goods industries, which, having benefitted from their initial protection in domestic markets, may now be ready to turn outward, into international markets – with, of course, the help of some key changes in the policy setting. Such a change in policy includes lower levels of effective protection and a greater market orientation generally, i.e. a more realistic rate of interest and rate of exchange. It usually also means a reduction in the neglect of the food producing agricultural sector as part of the maintenance of a balanced domestic growth process. This societal choice might be called export substitution since it gradually substitutes non-traditional labour-based for traditional land-based exports. This was the course basically followed by Taiwan.

It should, of course, be clear that in both Taiwan and the Philippines the same ultimate objective was and is to produce, and export, the whole range of industrial goods, shifting from labour-intensive to capital-intensive and technology-intensive items. But the difference in strategy as to how to get there makes all the difference with respect to the income distribution implications of the primary payments system. The Philippine decision, i.e. to shift directly from primary to secondary import substitution by maintaining, in fact, further raising, the temperature in its industrial hot-house had important implications for the choice of increasingly capital-intensive technologies and output mixes. Taiwan, in contrast, decided to shift first towards a more labour-intensive industrial export substitution phase before moving, in the 1970s, towards a similarly more capital-intensive secondary import substitution regime. It is this attempt to 'skip' the unskilled labour fuelled primary export substitution phase which created the much more inequitable primary payments system in the case of the Philippines.

Any effort to link the divergent growth patterns of the two economies to the differential equity performance of the primary payments system must, of course, be based on some causal analysis which links the different growth paths to the different employment cum equity outcomes as a consequence of the way in which production decisions are made. In an economy which seems to have a substantial agricultural sector and in which open urban unemployment is dwarfed by substantial rural as well as urban underemployment, it is, of course,essential to try to differentiate between rural and urban households as well as with respect to the spatial dimensions of economic activity which critically affect the primary payments system. While urban families are basically engaged in industrial and service activities generating wage and property incomes, rural families are engaged in both 'agricultural' activities generating a merged 'agricultural' income, and in non-agricultural (industrial and service) activities which generate wage and property income. The impact of a society's initial conditions, as well as of the organisational and economic policy changes it undertakes over time, can really be best assessed by examining the impact on rural and urban families separately as well as for all the society's families taken together.

While this chapter is not the appropriate place to go into the theoretical underpinnings of our analysis, we have used a Gini decomposition device to attempt to link the employment and distribution outcomes behaviourally to the nature of the growth path. For all families, and for rural and urban families separately, we can break down some overall index of distribution such as the Gini coefficient for all income into its various factor income components, e.g. rural agricultural income, rural non-agricultural wage and property income, urban wage and property income, etc., as well as the equity of distribution of each component, weighted by its relative importance in the families' total income, i.e. the relative functional shares. This general procedure[2] permits us to look at any change in income inequality as the weighted sum of changes in the functional shares and changes in the distribution of any one of the components. For example, if, for urban families, the wage share gains at the expense of the property share, such a change will obviously favour the overall equality of income distribution system if and only if wage income is more equally distributed than property income. Secondly, since a decline in the Gini coefficient of any component factor will, *ceteris paribus*, contribute to a decline in the overall Gini – in proportion to the weight of that factor – changes in the factor Ginis based on changing ownership patterns of capital and human resources, as impacted by both radical reforms and marginal changes in savings, i.e. physical and/or educational investment behaviour, represent, of course, an essential part of the explanatory nexus.

We shall proceed here in an admittedly somewhat casual fashion by citing some of the key conclusions which emanate from a comparative analysis of the primary payments system of the Philippines and Taiwan when examined in this context. First of all, as we would expect, wage income in both societies is clearly more equally distributed than property income, thus *ceteris paribus* the higher the labour share the lower the level of the overall Gini and the more the labour share is rising the more likely the Gini will decline over time. In the case of the Philippines urban labour's relative share lies between 0.21 and 0.32 and is declining substantially during the 1960s. Taiwan's wage share is substantially higher and rising gradually, reaching almost 0.60 in the early 1970s (see Table 4.2, row 5). At the same time both industrial output and employment growth, not so different in the two countries during the 1950s, began to diverge markedly thereafter (see Table 4.2, rows 8 and 9). This evidence would seem to provide substantial *a priori* support for the existence of more labour-intensive technologies and output mixes and their effect on employment generation, and thus the functional share of labour, in the Taiwan case. Especially telling for the outcome of rural family distributional equity is the rise of the relative share of labour in rural industries and services, which reached 0.75 by 1970 in Taiwan, about double that of the Philippines.

The tendency towards relatively more labour-intensive non-agricultural production functions and output mixes on Taiwan thus clearly became more pronounced in the 1960s when the policy regimes under which the two developing societies were operating began to diverge more dramatically. Once the (inevitable) end of primary (i.e. consumer non-durable goods) import substitution industrialisation had come upon both systems, the Philippine response of staying with the more protective package of policies, but redirecting it to the support of consumer durables, raw material processing and capital goods industries production, mainly for the domestic markets, made the output path even more capital and technology intensive. Taiwan, on the other hand, shifting to an export substitution orientation which entailed greater sensitivity to factor endowments and encouraged the penetration of foreign markets with labour-intensive non-durables under less distorted policy regimes, was able to absorb many more workers productively. One clear indication of this is the much more rapid rate of non-agricultural labour absorption (see Table 4.2, row 9) in the 1960s plus the continued increase in labour's relative share, both urban and rural, contributing powerfully to low and declining overall Ginis.

Thus, contrary to the general view, rapid growth in Taiwan was consistent with a rising share of wage income even while wage rates were kept low by the persistence of the unlimited supply of labour condition.

The crucial point thus is that income distribution does not have to get worse in the period of rapid growth before the labour surplus is exhausted, i.e. the rising leg of the Kuznetsian inverse U-shaped curve is not inevitable. By the end of the 1960s, having expanded her labour-intensive exports at a rather extraordinary rate (see Table 4.2, rows 14 and 15), Taiwan's unskilled labour surplus had become virtually exhausted. This led to a sustained rise of real wages for the first time, but this time for good and sufficient reason, i.e. due to labour's becoming a scarce commodity for the first time. This so-called 'commercialisation' of the economy, of course, represents a significant milestone along the transition growth path and is associated, in the so-called Kuznets curve context, with the advent of a more equal distribution of income.

In the contrasting case of the Philippines both the level and trend of labour's relative share were much less favourable, i.e. lower. Moreover, in the absence of a similar capacity to 'export' its unskilled, under-employed labour, the improvement of labour's share and of the overall distribution of income which accompanies the reaching of the com-mercialisation objective, of course, did not occur. As a consequence, we observe the continued maldistribution of income, possibly worsening over time as indicated in the equity indices of Table 4.2, rows 17 and 18. To reiterate, while we would expect any society which has exhausted its labour surplus to experience an improvement in its distribution of income, the really crucial difference between the two systems resides in the experience of the 1960s. It is this period which demonstrated whether or not combined institutional and policy environments can indeed yield rapid growth compatible with an improvement or at least a non-deterioration of income distribution equity long before real wages begin to rise in a sustained fashion. Our research clearly indicates that the absence of any iron law of worsening equity before the commercialis-ation is reached owes much to the rising relative share of labour, i.e. low wage rates being compatible with an increased share of wages as poor families have more members employed, working more hours per week.

A second effect contributing to this overall result which can be analysed with the help of our Gini decomposition analysis is the impact of the inevitable gradual shift from agricultural to non-agricultural income flows in rural families' total incomes, a common feature of both Taiwan and the Philippines, as well as virtually all developing countries. In the case of Taiwan the shift from agricultural to non-agricultural incomes meant that one was shifting from a less equally distributed to a more equally distributed income source. It is quite interesting to note that in Taiwan, given its relatively small family holdings, its extensive land reform, its virtual absence of landless workers, and its strong farmers' association structure, all previously referred to, rural industries and services income was still more equally distributed than agricultural income. And while we do not have equivalent good data on the Philippines, it is more likely to be true there, where there has been a more inequitable distribution of land to start with, no really extensive land reform, and a relatively much larger number of landless agricultural workers. Thus, in the case of Taiwan the more rapid reallocation from rural agricultural to rural non-agricultural activities helped improve the overall distribution of income, absolutely and relative to the Philippines.

Another important dimension of the primary payments system is the relative weight or importance of labour-intensive non-agricultural activities in the rural areas in relation to total rural family income. In the case of Taiwan, for example, the share of non-agricultural income in total rural household income was a substantial 32 per cent in 1964 and rose to a really remarkable 53 per cent by 1971. The Philippine data, on the other hand, indicate that the equivalent number was probably in the 15–20 per cent range and declining over the two decades. This phenomenon is extremely important for two related reasons: one, it indicates the large role which rural non-agricultural activity played in the industrial export substitution subphase of the more open Taiwan case; and two, it shows that the high and rising labour-intensity of these activities permitted a dramatically rapid absorption of the poorest rural unemployed and underemployed. Independent evidence indicates that it was, in fact, the smaller farmers in Taiwan who participated more than proportionately in these new non-agricultural activities, thus contributing to the overall shift in the source of rural household incomes and in the equity of its distribution across families. Facilitated by the already referred to infrastructural and organisational investments made in the rural areas, it was the growth of a decentralised and labour-intensive rural industrial and services sector which was heavily instrumental in eliminating any conflict between growth and equity in Taiwan. Rural industry and services employment grew at remarkable rates, even faster than its urban counterpart, during the overall rapidly growing 1960s. In the Philippines, by contrast, we find very little non-agricultural activity in the rural areas, i.e. very little interaction between agriculture and non-agriculture in the form of food processing etc., as well as very little subcontracting of urban industries to the rural areas using imported raw materials, as in Taiwan's Export Processing Zones. The Philippines' industrialisation path was much more urbanised and centralised in some of the bigger cities such as Manila; even her Bataan Export Processing

Zone has a completely different complexion, concentrating more on secondary import substitution industries, like automobile assembly, instead of the more labour-intensive textiles and electronics activities of Taiwan.

It is also necessary to note what was happening to the important, i.e. heavily weighted, agricultural income Gini itself over these more than two decades under observation. While, as we have already noted, Taiwan's agricultural income Gini was higher than that for non-agricultural income, it was also falling over time, partly due to the lagged effects of the 1949–53 land reform, mostly due to the shift within agriculture towards more labour-intensive crops. In fact, a substantial contribution to the lowering of the overall Gini in Taiwan was provided by a reduction of the agricultural income Gini from approximately 0.54 in 1953, to 0.35 in 1964, and 0.30 in 1972. It is difficult to obtain comparable data for the Philippines, but we would expect there to have been no decline from the relatively high agricultural income Ginis of the 1950s. In Taiwan we note the incentive effects of land reform, combined with the much higher extent of multiple cropping previously noted, and the shift to secondary, more labour-intensive food crops, such as mushrooms and asparagus, more labour-intensive than traditional sugar and rice. In the Philippines, on the other hand, commercial export oriented cash crops, which are much more land and capital intensive, remained much more important, leading to an apparently much larger conflict between respectable growth rates and the distribution of income in the course of the workings of the primary payments system.

Let us turn, finally and briefly, to the potential for secondary redistribution, i.e. the secondary payments system as a possible way of encouraging a diminution or elimination of 'equity with growth' conflicts. Our own analysis for the case of Taiwan indicates that government intervention through transfer payments and/or the tax system is not likely to have a very beneficial effect on income distribution equity in mixed economies.[3] Transfer payments are likely to be very small in quantity and, even more interesting, to be regressive, i.e. the rich receiving proportionately more than the poor of this type of income in all the developing countries which we have had a chance to examine. Yet more interesting is that, even in the overall highly egalitarian situation of Taiwan, the taxation system seems to be approximately neutral with respect to income distribution, i.e. the degree of inequality is about the same before and after taxes. This comes about through the fact that the quantitatively more important and regressive indirect tax payments just about cancel out the qualitatively less important and more progressive direct taxes.

While we have performed no similar studies for the case of the Philippines, the basic hypothesis, namely that LDC income distribution performance is largely a function of the outcomes achieved by the primary payments system and cannot rely very heavily on after-the-fact secondary reallocations via the secondary payments system, is strongly supported by the Taiwan study. The possibility of shifting from direct to indirect taxes, of course, runs up against a number of other practical considerations in most developing countries which rely heavily on tariffs, sales, and other indirect taxes, and are likely to be generally quite weak in the fiscal and tax collection areas. The fact that even Taiwan, which is presumably much better organised adminstratively than the Philippines, could not herself get much of an assistance from her tax and transfer system is but additional support for the need to place heavy reliance on the primary payments system, for better or worse, in the typical mixed developing economy case.

V SOME CONCLUSIONS FOR POLICY

Systems thus clearly do differ in terms of their initial conditions, the nature of the institutional/organisational policy choices over time, and the nature of the economic policy choices over time. Yet it is difficult to unravel precisely what contribution each of these three dimensions has made in yielding different payments systems and different distributional, employment and growth outcomes. Nevertheless, we are not interested in the Philippine and Taiwan cases just for their own sakes, but would like to learn as much as we can about the results of differently organised payments systems in terms of the 'growth with or without distributional equity' outcomes for other mixed economy cases during transition growth. It would also be interesting to know which features are so special in our two country cases to be irrelevant elsewhere, and which may give us some guidance as to what the scope for policy may be. While a country has very little choice about its initial conditions, including its colonial master, it does have some reasonable flexibility with respect to its institutional and organisational options, as well as its economic policy and strategy options.

We already know that most available cross sectional and country time series evidence is pointed in the direction of a payments system which inevitably tends to 'make things worse before they can get better' in the course of transition growth. Nevertheless, the demonstration of at least one exception to this general rule should provide some hope that we can identify the particular crucial elements and try to replicate them in other more typical developing economy cases to the extent technically and politically feasible. While there is no such animal as a 'typical' developing country or even a 'typical' Asian country, such search for generalisation must and will go on.

Starting with country-wide phenomena, we, of course, have noted, with respect to organisational/institutional factors, that Taiwan built on an already existent strong rural infrastructure, both in terms of its organisational and physical dimensions. Not only was prior land reform significant and the extent of dispersed irrigation, transport and power investment in the rural areas unusual, but the newly independent government clearly managed to utilise the colonial farmers' associations structure for its own purposes. The cooperative rural banks, the entire decentralised structure in Taiwan, from the Joint Commission on Rural Reconstruction at the centre to local functionally-oriented committees, constituted a rather unique network providing an ideal type of organizational/institutional regime for a mixed economy which maximised the scope for local decision-making in both the public and private sectors. The ability to move through the hot-house of primary import substitution, with, on the one hand, relatively less neglect than normal for food-producing agriculture, both via institutional land reform and the avoidance of excessive terms of trade manipulation against the sector, and the pursuit of a continuous strategy of encouraging decentralised industrialisation, on the other, must be given a good deal of the credit.

In the Philippines, on the other hand, initially less favourable conditions were further built upon by pursuing a more extreme and extended version of the import substitution policy syndrome. To the extent that Philippine land reform was effected, it apparently increased the number and worsened the situation of her landless agricultural workers. As has been pointed out by others, increased underemployment among such workers and a worsening distribution in the rural areas often result if land reform is unaccompanied by the appearance of new labour absorbing rural activities. The Philippine development strategy has basically not altered. It remains urban-industry oriented, with comprehensive land reforms never implemented, with the perpetuation of a highly centralised public sector, and expressly paternalistic attitudes towards once vigorous local government initiatives, as well as, on the private side, the superimposition of a top-down cooperative structure linked to participation in land reform.

Aside from the specific direct and indirect dimensions of public sector policies already referred to there is also the question of the different ways in which the public sector organises itself for action in the rural areas of the mixed economy. In Taiwan, while the central government was certainly strong, a good deal of decentralisation was achieved, most directly by use of the farmers' associations as instruments of rural development, but also with line departments and the Joint Commission on Rural Reconstruction providing technical and credit inputs, with decisions as to what infrastructure was required, and where, left to the local level. In the Philippines, in sharp contrast, decision making with respect to both the allocation and the character of public sector overhead facilities was always thoroughly centralised. The disdain for local public sector activities at the barrio or submunicipio level runs very deep. There is generally a dim view taken of the existence of requisite entrepreneurial and technical capacities among would-be medium- and small-scale rural industrialists in the private sector, as well as local government officials in the public sector. There is consequently very little evidence of any devolution of fiscal, planning or investment allocation functions to the appropriate local level in the Philippines, in contrast to Taiwan.

The dividing line between institutional and economic policies is, of course, itself hard to draw. The fact that agricultural output in Taiwan grew at an annual rate of 5.6 per cent between 1953 and 1973, and did quite well even during the primary import substitution 1950s, can be attributed in part to the colonial heritage and in part to policy which did not distort signals unduly against the tillers of the soil. As we have seen, moreover, in Taiwan both rural and urban industry and services were capable of absorbing especially the poorest of the rural labour force, while in the Philippines development was highly concentrated and much more capital-intensive in both its technology and output mix dimensions.

Taiwan clearly has the advantage of being a compact island with a homogeneous population and in receipt of superior physical and institutional infrastructure, especially in the rural areas. But the continuation of these policies during the post-war period built on prior strength and converted the network of farmers' associations and extension services to make it more amenable to expanded development-oriented uses. In the Philippines, in contrast, both nature and colonial policies were much less favourable; and yet the Philippine Government continued to build on weakness in terms of the absence of a real effort to mobilise the agricultural hinterland as part of a balanced domestic growth process. Here post-colonial policy continued to favour traditional exports but now channeled the proceeds toward a new indigenous industrial class. Little effort was made to make up for the colonial deficit; instead, attention was heavily focussed on the creation of a new urban industrial enclave gradually to take its place alongside the agricultural plantation enclave. One striking comparison is that in 1960 Taiwan had deployed 80 research workers per 100,000 population in food producing agriculture, in contrast to 1.6 in the Philippines.

Changes in the overall economic policy environment, i.e. a change to a more reasonable foreign-exchange regime, reduction of protectionism, interest-rate reform etc. around 1961 in Taiwan must be given a good deal of the credit, at least as much as the encouragement of rural industries via the maintenance of a strong rural electrification grid, the maintenance of equality in power and fuel rates in urban and rural areas, the establishment of rural industrial estates, bonded factories and export processing zones located with an eye to rural labour location and mobility. In the case of the Philippines both energy distribution and rate structure along with those covering the many other directly allocated inputs and favours were clearly biased in favour of the urban large-scale sector. Electricity rates, for example, were lower in the Greater Manila area, and enterprise tax incentives could only be obtained if you were large enough to afford a branch office in Manila. We may reasonably conclude that while geographic, cultural and historical antecedents, plus organisational choices, undoubtedly gave Taiwan an initial relative advantage, with respect to the balanced growth of her rural non-agricultural and agricultural activity at its source in a balanced growth context, her post-colonial institutional and economic policies continued to move the system in the direction of a markedly more equitable primary payments system than was the case in the Philippines.

Taiwan clearly moved from land-intensive import substitution to labour-intensive export substitution through less than two decades of balanced growth to reach the commercialisation or end-of-labour-surplus phase. An overall economic policy environment which increasingly forced output mixes and technology choices into greater harmony with changing endowment conditions thus undoubtedly played a very major role in the Taiwan case. The ability to maintain the import substitution policy structure because of her relatively more favourable natural resources endowment permitted the Philippines to achieve a reasonably respectable growth rate but rendered her unable to avoid unfavourable employment and income distribution outcomes.

This comparison lends further support to our basic notion that, in the mixed developing economy, primary payments systems have to be relied upon to ease the conflict between growth and distribution, and that can only be done through the kind of growth path which is pursued in the first place. 'Patching up', after the fact, even if the intentions are good, is not likely to work. The establishment of such a payments system, moreover, is partly based on the institutional, partly on the economic policy setting. While it is extremely difficult to allocate credit in a more precise fashion, we can offer some tentative conclusions for policy, nevertheless:

(1) Initial conditions do restrict the range of both the institutional/organisational and policy options available in open economy contexts.

(2) There are, nevertheless, substantial observable differences in behaviour traceable to the acceptance of different sets of institutional and policy choices.

(3) The question of asset ownership, public versus private and foreign versus domestic, may be less important than other organisational/institutional and economic policy choices.

(4) All developing societies will have to tackle the same basic problem. Mixed economies can generate a record of rapid growth in the presence of high employment and improving distribution of income, i.e. as in Taiwan, or rapid growth in the presence of increasing underemployment and a worsening distribution of income, as in the Philippines. The outcome depends in large part on the extent to which choices with respect to institutional, organisational and economic policy options can be made in the direction of utilising human resources extensively and avoiding the 'skipping' of the labour-intensive export substitution phase.

(5) Making these institutional and economic policy choices, in turn, depends in large part on the political capacity of the government to combine a decentralised, dispersed pattern of decision making with central authority to exercise major policy changes. It also depends on the ability to forge effective coalitions among shifting interest groups, e.g. the landed aristocracy, the new industrial class, or civil servants which are bound to lose power with policy changes which will reduce the scope for the discretionary allocation of scarce factors or final goods.

(6) Necessity, in terms of the absence of a natural resources or foreign capital bonanza to fall back on, may well be the mother of more appropriate policy choices, both of the institutional and economic variety. But even if such resources are in plentiful supply, a society may

be unable to tolerate a continued worsening of employment and income distribution in the presence of good overall growth performance.

A very important question, of course, is to what extent the Philippine performance has been an inevitable consequence of her initial conditions and to what extent of the perverse institutional and economic policies which followed; and secondly, depending on the response, we would like to know what can be done by those who are desirous of lifting man-made constraints on a better payments system.

Societies, like individuals, tend to follow the road of least resistance. Accordingly, the Philippines have traditionally been biased towards natural-resource-based exports and have continued to rely heavily on such exports in the course of the transition-growth process. It is this which translates into both a relative neglect of food-producing agriculture and the avoidance of the painful policy changes which might lead to a fuller utilisation of her unskilled human resources. It is the ability as well as the willingness to prolong the import substitution industrialisation phase which is at stake here. The skipping of labour-intensive primary export substitution is made possible by the relatively large availability of resources both via a 'natural' overvaluation of the exchange rate and the effects of trade and domestically oriented intervention policies tending in the same direction.

More natural resources and/or more foreign capital, public or private, can clearly be made use of to help ease the transition from one policy regime to another. Just as easily they can be used to avoid unpleasant changes along the growth path – at least for some interest groups. Certainly the availability and/or the discovery of additional natural resources, and/or booming raw material prices, and/or generous friends abroad, can make it all the more tempting to postpone any potentially unpleasant changes in structure.

In the final analysis the basic issue may be whether Filipino interest groups can be persuaded that a change in the direction of a more equitable payments system may be in their own longer term interest, e.g. an ability to persuade industrialists that a switch to export substitution may provide larger profits on expanded volume than subsidised export promotion on top of a smaller volume of sales for the domestic market under continued import substitution. Similar arguments can be made with respect to the civil service which may feel a threat to its discretionary powers, and organised labour which may be reluctant to substitute maximisation of total working family wage incomes for individual member wage rates as its objective.

A basic question, of course, is whether or not a more equitable primary payments system is the real or merely the rhetorical objective of the system. That in more protected and controlled economies like that of the Philippines hijacking by the middle class is a favoured indoor sport should be clear to all who wish to see. But even if the intentions are really clear, it may take a very strong government such as the one in Taiwan, combined with the constraints imposed by a natural-resources-poor environment, to effect the necessary reforms, both of the institutional and economic-policy variety.

NOTES AND REFERENCES

1. Mo-Huan Hsing, 'Taiwan's Industrialization and Trade Policies', OECD and ILO, *Sharing in Development: A Programme of Employment, Equity and Growth for the Philippines* (1974).
2. Fully explained in J. Fei, G. Ranis, S. Kuo, 'Growth and the Family Distribution of Income by Factor Components', *Quarterly Journal of Economics* (February 1978); and in their book, *Growth with Equity: The Taiwan Case* (Oxford University Press, 1979).
3. In socialist economies, of course, where property income does not exist, one is always likely to find lower overall Ginis; we are not proposing to discuss the inequality of power and other hierarchical proxies which may, however, substitute for income in such societies.

5 The Influence of the Urban Informal Sector on Economic Inequality*

VICTOR E. TOKMAN

I THE MAIN HYPOTHESIS

Following Kuznets (1955), it is widely hypothesised that the shift of the labour force from agricultural to non-agricultural sectors would affect the secular income structure, widening inequality in the early phases of transition from pre-industrial to industrial economies, becoming stabilised for a while and narrowing inequality in the later phases. This behaviour is expected as the result both of a greater degree of inequality and of higher incomes per capita prevailing in the non-agricultural sectors. According to Kuznets' estimates, inequality should increase until the weight of non-agricultural sectors reaches 60–70 per cent of the total labour force.

This analysis implicitly assumes that labour movements occur in a two-sector framework, yet one of the main characteristics of the process of growth of less developed countries is the existence of a significant and non-disappearing urban informal sector. Changes in the analysis are required to allow for more complex intersectoral mobility, since most of the agricultural labour force seems to enter into the urban economy

* This chapter was written at the Economic Growth Center of Yale University where the author was a visiting fellow from November 1979 to February 1980. The chapter is part of a broader programme which comprises academic essays on employment and which is supported by the Ford Foundation. The author wishes to thank C. Díaz-Alejandro, E. Klein, B. Schmukler, G. Ranis and F. Stewart for their comments; the Ford Foundation and the Economic Growth Center for the intellectual and material support received during his stay.

through the informal sector (PREALC, 1978). Some of them stay there for all their working life, while the rest shift to more modern occupational positions.

The presence of an important urban informal sector affects the present distribution of income and its evolution. On the one hand, income distribution within the sector is expected to be more egalitarian than that prevailing in urban modern activities. This may be due to greater competition between units within the informal sector, as well as the mechanisms of surplus distribution which prevail inside the productive units. One can, however, expect that the net effect would still involve a higher degree of inequality than in the agricultural sector, but the transition from pre-industrial to industrial economies would have smaller effects on inequality than in the absence of the informal sector. Over time in less developed countries the share of the informal sector in the urban labour force is not decreasing and, as a consequence of rural-urban migration its share in the total labour force is increasing (Tokman, 1979). These employment trends are combined with increasing income differentials between the modern and informal sectors. As a result, although inequality during the first phase may be smaller than that anticipated by Kuznets, it could indeed increase in the process of growth and postpone for a long period the expected improvement in income distribution.

Some of these issues will be tackled in this chapter. For this task we will follow Stewart's methodology in Chapter One trying to analyse the system of payment prevailing in the urban informal sector. The rules governing income determination within the sector will be discussed in the next three sections. The rules governing access to complementary resources will be examined in the fifth section, while the rules governing capital accumulation and organisation of production will be considered in the sixth section. Finally, an attempt will be made to analyse the implications of the system of payment prevailing in the informal sector on the degree of inequality and its evolution.

II MARKET SHARE: NATURE AND MAGNITUDES

To analyse how incomes are determined in the informal sector[1] one has to understand first, how the share of the sector in total incomes is determined and second, what are the conditions of entry to the sector. The former aspect is linked to the type of interrelationships which prevail between the informal sector and the rest of the economy, while the latter is related to the degree of heterogeneity which can be found within the sector.

Discussion about the kind of intersectoral links which prevail presents a diversity of approaches in the literature.[2] They vary from assuming dependency and exploitation (Quijano, 1974; Bienefeld, 1975; Gerry, 1974; Bose, 1974) to the assumption of the existence of benign relationships (ILO, 1972; Mazumdar, 1976; Sethuraman, 1975). The former approach sees the informal sector as the result of subordination prevailing both at international and national levels. In this approach the market for informal sector activities is subordinated, residual and without possibilities of expansion. It is argued that, given the inegalitarian international economic system, the possibilities of accumulation of less developed countries are restricted because increases in productivity tend to be concentrated and retained in developed countries, while the smaller increases registered in developing countries are largely transferred to developed countries by various mechanisms, from terms of trade to technological transfer and transnational corporations. In turn, international dependence generates a heterogeneous internal productive structure due to the concentration of technological change in modern activities and the limited capacity of diffusion derived from the low-income elasticity for wage goods of those who benefit from such a process and the labour-saving bias of the new technology. This process gives place to an informal sector which does not create surplus, or if it does, its surplus is extracted either by labour exploitation or by unfavourable terms of trade. In either case the market for the informal sector is seen as a subordinated one, since the prices for the goods and services produced as well as the size of the market are determined outside the sector, which cannot be influenced by the informal productive units.

The second approach assumes that informal activities are complementary to those of the modern sectors and that they will benefit from output expansion. Complementarity is derived from the sector's efficient use of resources available, since it uses abundant labour intensively and does not require too much capital or foreign exchange, presenting comparative advantage in relation to similar activities in the modern sector. Moreover, the informal activities play an important role in different aspects of the economic process – mostly in the distribution of goods and services, in transportation of persons, but mainly of commodities and in the supply of credit. This type of interrelationship implies that the market for the informal sector will grow *pari passu* with the economy, while price determination will depend on the organisation of production. According to this approach, the informal sector can increase its size either by autonomous growth or by expansion induced by growth in the whole economy.

Subordination at international and national levels is the characteristic of underdevelopment; the informal sector analysis is one way of looking at a more comprehensive phenomenon. The existence of subordinated relationships would be accepted even by those who argue that complementarity relationships predominate. The problem is to determine how strong is the subordination and whether there is room left for evolutionary growth.

Although a subordinated relationship with the rest of the economy will prevail for the informal sector as a whole, some degree of autonomy is expected not only because it supplies its own demand for most manufactured goods, but mainly because of the importance of informal commercial activities and second-hand goods. The former reduces the payment made to acquire goods not produced within the sector, while the latter enlarges the life of durable and capital goods hence reducing the need to purchase new goods outside the sector. The subordination of the sector as a whole is the result of different processes occurring within it. Here one should distinguish those informal activities operating in sectors where the modern sector has an oligopolistic structure from those where that is not the case. This division will generally, though not always, coincide with the breakdown of activities according to type of product (manufacturing goods, personal services, and services connected with distribution and finance).

Markets and price determination for those informal activities already operating under oligopolistic conditions will be subordinated to the decisions of the oligopolistic firms. The evolution of this type of market passes through different phases where informal activities will expand or contract depending on the rhythm of demand expansion, minimum scale of operation for different size of establishments, economies of scale, etc. Given their position in the market, they cannot benefit from short-term extraordinary profits and in the longer run they will tend to lose markets because of the cost advantages presented by the oligopolistic firms. This is the present or future case for most informal manufacturing activities.[3]

There are other informal activities, mainly personal services, where large concentration seems unlikely in the medium run. Technological change in these activities is more gradual and their survival in economies of higher income levels allows one to anticipate their expansion. However, income improvements based on productivity changes are not likely to occur.

An intermediate case is that of informal commercial activities. Technological change within this activity is also gradual and trends in concentration are generally slower. In addition the factors which determine the survival of informal units under oligopoly conditions are present in this case. Market imperfections, especially demand behaviour at low income levels, introduce a sort of product and geographical differentiation which ensures the permanence of these activities for longer periods than, say, informal manufacturing activities. Location, owner-customer personal relationships, credit, indefinite possibilities of product subdivision, permanent presence because of the non-existence of 'business hours', etc., are factors which allow them to maintain a share in the overall market. However, many of these factors are linked to low levels of purchasing power and, in the long run, the introduction of supermarkets may lead to similar conditions as in the case of manufacturing oligopoly markets. Developments here are, however, entangled with cultural patterns which make changes in consumption patterns more difficult to predict, as is well illustrated by the development of these activities in economies with higher levels of income.

To sum up, the different type of interrelationships that a group of activities within the informal sector has with the rest of the economy will determine its share in total income and its evolution. Given the previous analysis, only normal profits can be expected in most informal activities, while a diminishing trend of the share of the informal sector's output in the total can be envisaged in the long run. Such a trend may not be stable, and its rhythm is difficult to forecast given the mechanism of resistance which exists.

In order to have an idea of the quantitative characteristics of the informal sector and its interrelationships, it is necessary to estimate the balance of payments position with the rest of the economy. This we have done for Chile and Mexico around 1970 to illustrate the methodology and type of results that can be expected.[4]

The urban informal sector in both countries accounts for around 40 per cent of the urban labour force or between 27 and 22 per cent of the total labour force.[5] Its share in urban value added varies between 20 and 13 per cent and as a consequence, output per person employed in the sector is 0.57 and 0.44 of total output per person and 0.44 and 0.33 of urban output per person. That is, income differentials are, on the average, around 1:2 in relation to the total economy and 1:3 in comparison to the rest of the urban sector (see Table 5.1). Manufacturing industries in both cases account for 23 per cent of informal sector employment, while personal services and commerce activities generate around 70 per cent of total employment and 60 per cent of the value added by the sector. It must be noted that the informal sector contributes significantly to employment and output in most urban economic activities, being particularly important in commerce where it accounts for 57 per cent of employment and 34 per cent of value added in Chile and 58 per cent of employment and 22 per cent of value added in Mexico. In manufacturing industries its share in employment varies between 32 and 37 per cent and it generates between 12 and nine per cent of the output of the sector, in Chile and Mexico, respectively.

The informal sector should be seen neither as a completely integrated

TABLE 5.1   Employment and value added by the informal sector in Chile and Mexico, circa 1970 (in percentages)

	Chile		Mexico	
	Employ-ment[1]	Value added[2]	Employ-ment[1]	Value added[2]
Food, beverages and tobacco	21.2	6.2	35.7	6.4
Textiles, shoes, clothing and leather	47.8	20.4	43.4	7.8
Wood, cork and furniture	44.4	19.2	51.5	20.5
Non-metallic minerals	15.7	2.0	46.0	9.6
Metallic products, machinery and transport	28.0	14.0	27.7	8.4
Other industries	37.9	20.4	26.3	7.0
Total manufacturing industries	(32.3)	(12.0)	(37.2)	(8.5)
Construction	29.4	17.6	30.9	10.4
Personal services	44.9	24.8	42.5	10.4
Commerce	57.3	34.4	58.5	25.6
Transport	20.0	11.2	28.7	17.3
Total informal sector as percentage of urban total	39.9	19.7	39.3	12.8
as percentage of total economy	27.5	15.7	21.8	9.5

Source: Chile (Tokman, 1978). Mexico, estimates on the basis of national statistics.

Notes:
1. As % of total employment of each sector.
2. As % of total value added of each sector.

nor as an autonomous sector, but rather as one with significant links with the rest of the economy while simultaneously it also presents a considerable degree of self-containment. Exports of the informal sector as percentage of total goods and services available for the sector amount to 45 and 58 per cent, while imports constitute between 36 and 61 per cent. Exports from the sector mostly consist of personal services, but in addition between 50 and 60 per cent of consumer goods produced by the informal sector are sold to the rest of the economy. The main imports are raw foodstuffs from the agricultural sector and processed foods and inputs from the urban formal sector. The degree of dependence of consumption on imports is higher than that registered for inputs.

The balance of payments position in the case of Chile registers a surplus on current account which amounts to 20 per cent of the informal sector exports, while the opposite occurs in Mexico where a deficit of six per cent of exports is estimated. In the former case the informal sector is transferring resources to the rest of the economy, while in the latter it is a net receiver, although of an insignificant quantity. The sectoral disaggregation of the balance of payments shows a similar pattern for both countries, a deficit with the agricultural sector and a surplus with the rest of urban activities. The informal sector is then playing an intermediary role in the resource transfer from the agricultural to the urban modern sectors (see Table 5.2).

Given the dependence of the informal sector, a declining trend in its terms of trade might have been expected. While the formal sector is able to retain gains in productivity, the informal sector should pass them on as relative price reductions. Although it is clear that both prices and markets are determined outside the sector, its trade structure is diversified; the situation thus differs from that confronted in international dependence analysis. An examination of income elasticities of exports and imports shows that in Chile and Mexico the elasticity for exports is twice that registered for imports. This is partly because of the significance of low income elasticity items, like agricultural products and raw materials, in the imports of the sector and partly because of the high elasticity which characterises the demand for domestic services.[6] The high elasticity for domestic services does not necessarily imply higher incomes, given the existence of surplus labour. On the other hand, basic services (water, electricity, etc.) which also constitute a significant import of the sector are subject to public tariff policies which often involve a subsidy component. Weights, elasticities and prices of these balance of payments components will vary according to countries, but in the case of Chile the terms of trade (ratio of export to import prices) of

TABLE 5.2   Balance of payments of the informal sector in Chile and Mexico, circa 1970

	Chile		Mexico	
	Millions of escudos	*Percentages*	*Millions of pesos*	*Percentages*
With the formal sector				
Exports	2,581	100.0	27,153	100.0
Intermediate goods	615	23.8	7,694	28.3
Consumption goods	1,878	72.8	18,630	68.6
Capital goods	88	3.4	829	3.1
Imports	1,795	100.0	21,853	100.0
Inputs	344	19.2	8,566	39.2
Consumption goods	1,451	80.8	13,287	60.8
Surplus	786	80.5[1]	5,300	18.3[1]
With the agricultural sector				
Exports	457	100.0	1,830	100.0
Intermediate goods	339	74.3	850	46.4
Consumption goods	118	25.7	980	53.6
Imports	642	100.0	8,828	100.0
Raw materials	93	14.5	1,693	19.2
Consumption goods	549	85.5	7,135	80.8
Deficit	− 185	− 40.6[1]	− 6,998	− 24.2[1]
Total balance of payments				
Exports	3,038	44.7[2]	28,983	58.1[2]
Imports	− 2,437	35.9	− 30,682	61.5[2]
Balance	601	19.8[1]	− 1,699	− 5.9[1]

Source: Chile (Tokman, 1978). Mexico, estimates on the basis of national statistics.

Notes:
1. As percentage of exports.
2. As percentage of available goods and services (production plus imports minus exports).

the informal sector show an improvement of 12 per cent during the 1960–70 period, while in the case of Mexico they improved by 4 per cent between 1968 and 1977.

III   MARKET STRUCTURE AND INCOME DETERMINATION

The analysis above suggests three main subgroups of informal activities. The first operates at the base of a concentrated market where cost differentials, due to economies of scale, are significant. A second subgroup operates under monopolistic competition where product differentiation and location are important, but operative costs are similar. The third subgroup is characterised by those activities which operate in a perfectly competitive market. Examples of activities belonging to the first subgroup are manufacturing industries which, on the average, account for around 19 per cent of informal sector employment in Latin America. Retail commerce, repair shops and semi-skilled services are within the second subgroup, amounting to around 30 per cent of informal sector employment, while the rest of the activities, mostly constituted by services, confront competitive markets.[7]

The three market structures share one common feature: that is, equilibrium in the long run is reached at a point at which no supernormal profits are possible and only those profits which are just sufficient to induce the entrepreneur to stay in the industry can be generated. This is the case when oligopolistic firms in concentrated markets fix prices at the minimum cost level of the small firms operating at the base of the market, since at this point they ensure maximum profits. The oligopolistic firms have differential advantages over their competitors, but they also confront diseconomies of scale due to product differentiation and imperfection in factor markets which constrain their expansion. Hence, the oligopolistic firms are unable to extend their output indefinitely at minimal costs and encounter progressively rising costs beyond an optimal scale. The adjustment of the market in the long run will be reached at a price level which exceeds the minimal average cost of the oligopolistic firms ensuring supernormal profits for them; in general it will not exceed the minimal average cost of competitive (informal) firms, thus allowing only normal profits for these firms.

A similar situation is faced by those informal activities inserted in monopolistic competitive markets. In these cases, products are generally differentiated by the conditions surrounding their sale, including the convenience of each seller's location. Buyers are then given a basis for preference and will therefore be paired with sellers, not in a random fashion but according to their preferences. Each seller, however, is subject to the competition of other products sold under different circumstances and in different locations. There is not a single large market of many sellers, but a network of related markets, one for each seller (Chamberlain, 1948). Each seller faces a negatively sloped demand curve for his distinct product, but his output constitutes such a small part of the total market that his decisions will not affect his competitors.

However, simultaneous movements on the part of all sellers cause shifts in demand. The short-run equilibrium for the individual seller will be reached when costs equate revenues but the competitive pressure given by the large number of firms restricts the possibilities of obtaining supernormal profits and reduces them in the long run to a normal level.[8]

In the case of competition, the normal profit equilibrium position is ensured by the characteristics of the market since each producer confronts an infinite elastic demand and prices are given. Any supernormal profits will induce the expansion of existing firms or the entrance of new units in the long run, reducing profits to their normal level.[9]

Implicitly or explicitly the long-run condition for zero profit equilibrium is linked to easy entry. This condition, as noted by several authors (ILO, 1972; Tokman, 1977) seems to be one of the main characteristics of urban informal activities. That urban informal activities are characterised by easy entry has been questioned by other authors (Bienefeld, 1975; Raczynski, 1977 and 1978; Möller, 1979) arguing that barriers to entry exist for many informal activities.

The effects of easy entry characteristics on profits may be distinct from the possibilities of entrance of the population into informal activities. For the former, it is sufficient that there are a certain number of persons which fulfil the conditions of entry required to perform an activity, to ensure that competition is produced in such a market, and hence no supernormal profits will be obtained. In cases where a large number of units are already established, as in the majority of informal activities, the possibility of expansion of established firms will produce similar effects on profits and ensure that barriers to entry are ineffective. For example, it is sufficient that a number of persons can establish or expand auto repair shops, to whip away supernormal profits in this activity. The number of new entrants required is associated with the size of the market.

There is no doubt that entrance to the informal sector is easier than to modern sector activities, since most of the factors which determine restrictions to entry cannot be found in the informal sector. Such is the case of advantages for established firms derived from economies of scale or absolute cost advantages due to control over superior production techniques, imperfections in the market of productive factors, control over strategic factor supplies, or preferential access to capital markets (Bain, 1967). If such factors are not present in the informal sector the only cause of barriers to entry will be product differentiation. In the case of modern firms such differentiation is associated with sales promotion and advertising, as well as the design or physical quality of competing products, while in the case of the informal sector it is limited to offering auxiliary services to buyers and to location. This then is the only factor which could generate advantages for established firms, constituting a barrier to entry to the informal sector. But this barrier does not seem to be high, as is well illustrated by the rapid rate of turnover that is usually found in informal units devoted to retail and repair activities.[10]

Easy entry, from an economic viewpoint, does not mean equal access to opportunities for all surplus labour. This will depend on the possibilities of obtaining complementary resources, mostly capital and skill, as well as the capacity to surpass the product differentiation barrier, generally linked to producer-customer special relationships. Let us first examine the latter.

Product differentiation is an important factor for established informal activities like commerce and repair and for services performed by semi-skilled workers such as seamstresses, plumbers and electricians. The barrier generated by this factor can in most cases be explained by differences in access to complementary resources. The situation varies according to occupations, but generally the preference of consumers to buy from one firm or person rather than from another operates as a differentiating factor between sizes of firms rather than among similar units. In those personal services performed by semi-skilled persons the access to a clientele of higher income can indeed raise their income possibilities. Lack of transparence in the market seems to be the main explanation for those income differentials which cannot be explained by differences in capital or skill endowments. Given the imperfection in market information, informal networks tend to operate based on personal contacts and recommendations. The possibilities of access to these informal networks are generally wide, although they are not homogeneous for everybody. Relatives, members of the extended family, and friends play an important intermediary role (Lomnitz, 1978).

The situation is different for those who perform established informal activities. Product differentiation in this case is linked to conditions surrounding the sale of the product, including location. Such conditions can be met by most members of the community provided they have access to complementary resources. Retail activity, for instance, gives additional services to the customer such as product divisibility, personal seller-customer relationships, closer location to residence. Any new firm can provide the additional services required to compete for customer preferences within a neighbourhood. Income differentials can be generated by monopolistic factors arising between neighbourhoods of different purchasing power. Such differences will generally be due to rents, interest, and/or costs of products due to quality differentials, and the barriers will be the amount of capital required rather than 'product' differentiation.[11]

Skill requirements do not appear as important barriers to the entrance to informal activities. In general, they are concentrated among people with lower levels of education. In Asunción (Paraguay) and San Salvador (El Salvador), for instance, three out of four persons with less than three years of education, and two out of three between four and six years, are performing informal activities (PREALC, 1978). Formal education, as well as skill, seem to be distributed evenly by type of activities. Only two (laundry and domestic services) of the 12 informal occupations studied in Chile show a concentration of low level of formal education and low skill requirements, while the rest of the activities mostly require intermediate skill levels (70 per cent of total requirements) with similar tails at both extremes of the distribution (unskilled and highly skilled jobs). In addition, the time required for on-the-job training is less than two years in 90 per cent of the cases analysed; only in laundry activities, did all the cases require less than three months of training (PREALC, 1979).[12]

Examination of differences in the skill required in the four most important informal occupations (seamstresses, plumbers, retailers and mechanics) clearly show that such differences are not very large and can be made-up with experience on the job. Apart from highly specialised functions in three of the cases in all of the activities a person can start at the lower skill level and move with experience on-the-job to perform more skilful tasks. Formal training and experience are substitutes in skill upgrading.[13] That skills are generally acquired while working is demonstrated in many cases studied,[14] as well as by the small importance of formal training. Only 17 per cent of the cases studied in Chile received some formal training. On-the-job training is accomplished mainly by working as wage worker or apprentice, generally in small firms.[15]

Capital availability introduces a differentiation in the returns obtained by those working in the informal sector but it does not seem to constitute a significant barrier to entry. On average, capital requirements per productive units and capital labour ratios are substantially lower than those registered for the same activities in the modern sector. Around 95 per cent of the informal activities studied in Chile required less than US $3,000 per unit, while 80 per cent required less than US $1,000 per unit. There is also some capital requirement divisibility since around 60 per cent of the units registered levels below US $300 and almost a third operated with insignificant capital (PREALC, 1979).[16] The spread in capital requirements is not a result of the aggregation of different requirements by occupation, since each of them presents such a pattern showing differences in the floor and ceiling requirements. Street sellers and those established in open markets, laundry women and construction workers seem to reach the top level at US $300; most of the established commerce, tailors and seamstresses, mechanics and electricians require a minimum capital of US $30. To be a taxi owner would require a minimum capital of around US $2,000.

The process of capital accumulation and firm growth cycle can also be observed through the case studies available. They suggest that in most cases the persons start with little capital and then accumulate during the operation of the firm. This is clearly the case of auto repair shops which generally start as backyard garages with only few tools (PREALC, 1978 and 1979a) and for established retail services which show the same cycle of growth (PREALC, 1978a). Of course, there are cases which start with larger capital endowments but the general trend suggests that capital differentials are the result of the evolution of the firms. Low capital barriers to entry seem then to prevail. Although capital availability explains income differentials, the heterogeneity in the capital structure of the informal sector is generated by factors affecting the possibilities of growth of the firms rather than by different points of departure.[17] The process of growth seems to reach a ceiling, which constitutes a barrier for the informal firm from becoming a modern unit. Minimum capital requirements to become modern firms require a jump in capital availability even for the most prosperous informal units. This can be illustrated by the situation faced by retailers or auto repair shops when they attempt to expand activities beyond a certain level. In both cases changes in the structure of the business are required since it usually involves a different product mix as well as a different organisation of production. The consequence is a significant increase in capital requirements which cannot be financed with own sources as in the case of informal activities.[18]

IV SURPLUS LABOUR AND THE DYNAMICS OF THE ADJUSTMENT

Given the limited job opportunities generated by the modern sector, the subordinated share of the informal activities in markets and the relatively easy entry in the sector, surplus labour will lead to an increase in informal employment until the income per person approaches the opportunity cost of labour which will be close to the subsistence level. This is clearly the case for those informal activities performed with little or no capital and generally by individuals. The situation, however, becomes more complex when, as seen in the previous section, there exists the possibility of increasing capital in most activities. This growth process is often accompanied by the creation of a small firm on quasi-capitalistic or family basis. The adjustment process will not be restricted to variations in labour incomes but will also include returns on capital. These returns on capital will be generally lower than its opportunity cost and will be entangled with the returns to labour of the entrepreneur.

The entrepreneur in small firms usually offers an indivisible package composed of his own labour, that of his family, and some capital. The objective is the maximisation of total income. Capital, however, is partly non-transferable since it often serves a dual purpose of being a household and a productive asset, as is the case with shops installed in the household premises or vehicles which serve both purposes. In addition, capital usually does not involve a high cost since it is the result of past savings, sale of other domestic assets or free capital transfers.[19] The alternative return for such capital will be the amount that can be obtained if invested in other informal activities or in the modern sector. The rate of interest will be applied only to the fraction of such capital that could be transferred. In the case of the alternative investment in the modern sector, the minimum quantities required usually exceeds capital availability of the informal sector, reducing the alternative return on capital to the rate of interest paid on savings accounts by the banking system, applied to the part of his total capital which is transferable.

In an economy with limited employment possibilities in the modern sector, such capital provides work for the entrepreneur and his family in the case of family firms, while it allows the quasi-capitalistic entrepreneur to maximise his total income. The alternative to a family firm in the informal sector would be to close the firm, invest that part of the capital which is transferable and search for jobs for himself and the rest of his family. Generally, the rest of his family (mainly the wife and school-age children or old people in the family) are not available for full-time jobs since they share their work in the firm with occupations outside the labour market (house care, school) or with leisure. This, added to the job scarcity in modern sectors, implies that the alternative return to family labour will often be limited to the income that the head of the family can earn by working in the modern sector. Here his situation becomes similar to that of the quasi-capitalistic entrepreneur since, given the barriers to entry which prevail in the modern sector, his theoretical alternative would be to become a dependent in a modern establishment of the same kind of activity but where his entrepreneurial capacity would be mostly unused and not remunerated. In practice, however, such an alternative often does not exist since job availability in the modern sector is severely restricted. But even if he could find a job outside the sector, the income he receives by working in his own informal unit will often exceed the alternative capital and the labour return and as a consequence, he will be in a stable position (i.e., not searching for jobs).

Given imperfections in factor markets and the downward pressure on labour incomes produced by the existence of labour surplus, it should be expected that incomes earned in the informal sector will be lower than those which could be obtained in similar activities of the modern sector, if they were available. This, in turn, will imply the existence of incentives to move from informal to formal jobs. The distribution of incomes of the informal and formal sector will, however, present some degree of overlapping which can be partly explained by differences in personal factors (education, age, experience, sex) and partly by differences in capital availability. While capital differences within the informal sector generate income differentials, they are expected to be smaller than in the formal sector since economies of scale are not significant, monopolistic profits do not exist and a more equal access to the little capital they use is possible given its greater divisibility and its limited return due to imperfect mobility. These factors will ensure that income distribution within the informal sector is more egalitarian than.in modern sectors, being close to that prevailing for labour earnings in those sectors.

The scarce data available support the previous analysis. On the one hand, although the distribution of income of the informal sectors in the cases of Peru (Webb, 1974), El Salvador, Dominican Republic and Paraguay (Souza-Tokman, 1978) overlaps with that of the formal sector, the analysis made in the last three cases clearly show that such overlapping in most cases occurs among persons with different characteristics. It also shows that there are people who earn more than in the formal sector and hence will not be induced to move out of their present job, as is the case with those who operate a successful retail shop.[20] This latter case has also been analysed at a different level for Santiago (Tokman, 1978a), showing that the small entrepreneur is maximising his total income in the present occupation since the alternative would imply a reduction in the return on capital and he would be forced to search for a well paid job in a tied labour market. While in the case of family firms, part-time jobs would need to be found for the rest of the family labour force.[21]

In the cities analysed (Asuncion, Santo Domingo and San Salvador) significant income differences were found between the informal and formal sectors, even in very homogeneous categories such as persons with the same level of education, age and sex or persons with similar sex, education and occupational position. For instance, males, in the age of peak activity, with four to six years of education who are occupied in the non-domestic informal sector received around 60 per cent of the income of persons with identical characteristics employed in the private formal sector. Males, with four to six years of education, employed in manufacturing informal establishments received 70 per cent of the income earned by similar persons working in the same type of establishments, but within the formal sector. The same results are reached using a two-stage multiple regression model which shows that in Santo Domingo persons with identical personal characteristics received incomes 1.4 times larger if they were employed in the formal rather than in the non-domestic informal sector, in manufacturing industry or other

TABLE 5.3 Gini coefficients within sectors in four Latin American countries circa 1974

Countries	Informal sector	Formal sector
Colombia		
Total	0.48	0.53
Adjusted	–	0.62
Dominican Republic		
Total	0.47	0.50
Males	0.44	0.50
Females	0.45	0.37
El Salvador		
Total	0.61	0.67
Males	0.61	0.70
Females	0.53	0.47
Paraguay		
Total	0.59	0.65
Males	0.54	0.66
Females	0.58	0.54

Source: See text.

sectors. Similar results were found for San Salvador, for all sectors. The differences in manufacturing industry are larger (1.6 times).[22]

Income distribution for the informal sector as a whole is likely to be more egalitarian than in the modern sector. Although different capital endowments create income differentials, they are expected to be smaller than in the rest of the economy. This can be seen in Table 5.3 where within sectors Gini coefficients were calculated for four Latin American countries. In the cases of Dominican Republic, El Salvador and Paraguay, the data collected by PREALC around 1974 on the basis of household surveys in Santo Domingo, San Salvador and Asunción were adjusted for three common biases. First, the underdeclaration of non-labour income, which was estimated by comparing its share according to the national accounts and that declared in the survey. The underdeclaration was around 30 per cent of total income in San Salvador and around 40 per cent in the other two cases. As non-labour incomes declared were a higher percentage in the upper incomes of the informal sector, the correction was allocated to the top decile of the formal sector. Second, an income was imputed to those who said they were unpaid family members. Since this part of the labour force usually helps the head of the household without receiving an established wage, the total income of the household was divided by the working members of such households and the resulting figure was allocated to unpaid family members. Finally, the domestic servants' income was adjusted because of the underdeclaration of wages received in kind, mostly food and shelter. In the case of Colombia, the data discussed by Bourguignon (1979) were used only adjusting for the first type of bias which the author recognised as important. Underdeclaration was arbitrarily assumed by him to be 30 per cent of total income and it was allocated to the top decile of the formal sector.

In Table 5.3 it can be seen that in the four cases the estimated Gini coefficient within the informal sector is smaller than that calculated within the formal sector. In those cases for which data were available, the estimate of the Gini coefficients by sex within each sector shows that the smaller inequality in the informal sector is entirely explained by the males coefficients, since informal females register in all cases an index of inequality larger than females in the formal sector.

V PUBLIC POLICIES AND ACCESS TO COMPLEMENTARY RESOURCES

The capacity of informal activities to generate surplus which is limited by the factors affecting income determination in the sector could be expanded by providing easier access to complementary resources through public policies. This, however, is not an easy task since it confronts several constraints which are related not only to the economic and political power of those who take decisions but also to characteristics of the informal units and of the persons working in them. To illustrate the type of problems which arise, it is worth looking at credit and training programmes which, if effectively implemented, could increase access to capital and skills.

Informal units usually tend to be excluded from credit, both private and public. As a consequence, their possibilities of financing are restricted to their own savings, informal transfers or parallel capital markets with a cost of capital which greatly exceeds that prevailing in the rest of the economy. Examples of this higher cost are shown for micro-industries in Mexico which paid rates eight times those paid by larger industries (PREALC, 1979b) or the rates paid by street sellers in El Salvador to those who finance their daily working capital at 10 per cent per day (PREALC, 1978). The allocation of credit, usually involving a subsidy, is determined by several factors linked to the process of delivery which are biased against small informal units. The main criteria for credit worthiness is the ownership of assets to guarantee debt repayment and hence an unequal starting point tends to be perpetuated. In addition, fixed administrative costs discriminate against operations for small amounts but in the case of Mexico they only explain 30 per cent of the extra rate charged by the formal system, the remainder being attributed to risk premium, and the monopsonistic position of the lender. The low level of education and particularly of commercial training of the informal entrepreneur is also a disadvantage, given the complex paperwork involved in each credit application.

Training programmes for skill upgrading can also raise productivity of the informal sector. These programmes, however, tend to exclude persons working in the sector being biased in favour of the children of blue-collar workers of large establishments as has been shown for Colombia and Chile (Puryear, 1977; PREALC, 1978). This bias is the result of the programmes' definition and the characteristics of informal units and of the persons involved in such activities. The programmes are usually developed to provide skills for an industrial labour force which would be employed in the modern sector and as such, the main task to be filled is the knowledge of new and increasingly capital-intensive technology. This type of curricula becomes irrelevant for those who are working with traditional technology and who do not envisage the possibility of moving towards higher productivity occupations. The main difficulty is, however, to develop a relevant content for people working in units characterised by atomisation, rudimentary division of labour which implies few possibilities for occupational mobility within the unit and job instability. Personal characteristics add further difficulties, since the level of education of these people is low and their capacity to pay for training is practically non-existent. In the case of Chile (PREALC, 1978), for example, it was estimated that direct costs of training would absorb between 10 and 20 per cent of the average income of the informal sector. If transport costs were included, the proportion increased to half the average income.

The factors mentioned above can be solved by introducing special measures in policy packages. The added complexity, however, seems to favour inertia and public policy generally perpetuates the outcome determined by the primary characteristics of the economic structure.

VI INTERSECTORAL SHIFTINGS AND URBAN INCOME INEQUALITY

The differences in income distribution within each segment of the urban economy will affect the degree of inequality generated as the result of a rural-urban shift in the labour force. The migrants insertion in the lower income but more equally distributed informal sector will diminish the increase in inequality. If employment in the informal sector were only a temporary phenomenon arising from short-run limits on employment creation in the modern sector, once the urban labour market adjusted, income distribution would follow the U-shaped path. Rapid urban labour force increase, determined by the fast rate of population growth and migration from the rural areas requires an expansion of employment creation at higher rates than is usually registered in the modern sectors. The informal sector becomes then a permanent sector and constitutes one of the structural characteristics of less developed countries.

The theory explaining why the informal sector persists in spite of the high rate of economic growth registered by most Latin American countries has been widely debated in the literature and falls beyond the scope of this paper.[23] It will suffice, however, to remark that such behaviour is associated with the type of growth followed by these countries which, among other characteristics, involves a restricted internal technological diffusion. This process of restricted technological diffusion caused by the concentration in the distribution of incomes prevailing in most of the countries and by factors associated with imported technology, generates a concentration of modern, highly capital-intensive technology in subsectors and even in establishments within sectors (mostly large), while the rest of the economy continues operating with traditional technologies. This process is also associated with higher returns to factors of production in the modern sector, in part, derived from productivity differentials but also as a result of imperfections in factor markets. The outcome is that the initial concentration of income tends to be perpetuated.

The process occurs in a context where modern establishments do not face strong competition, either from the outside, because of high tariff protection, or from the rest of the firms, because of great market concentration. They then, do not pass on the gains in productivity through price reductions but rather retain them in the form of higher factor incomes. In addition, and not totally independent of the increase in factor incomes, capital intensity tends to increase and employment creation in the modern sector becomes insufficient to absorb the rapidly growing labour supply.[24]

The payment of higher wages in the modern sector in economies with relative labour surplus has been explained by several theories ranging from human capital differences to imperfections in labour markets due to trade union or government interferences. The main reason, however, seems to lie in the partial monopolistic conditions under which modern firms operate, which due to the existence of monopolistic profits allows them to pay high wages, while price instability in such markets would generate heavy losses. This is combined with other factors, such as the need to stabilise the labour force, the political need to control the labour force and the international mobility of hierarchical personnel (Tokman, 1978).

The fragmentary data available for several Latin American countries support the previous analysis suggesting that the size of the informal sector has not decreased in the process of growth. This trend has been accompanied by non-diminishing, and even, in several cases, increasing income and productivity differentials between the informal and the modern sectors and by an increase in the wage dispersion in the latter.

The share of self-employed and unpaid family workers in the total labour force of Latin America has increased from 9.6 per cent in 1950 to 11.7 per cent in 1970. The share of urban self-employed and unpaid family workers in the urban labour force remained constant around 20 per cent between the same years (Tokman, 1980). As these are the main components of informal sector employment, it suggests that the latter has not been decreasing. The census data on employment is confirmed by the few case studies which estimate the evolution of employment and output of the informal sector. Webb (1974) reports that in Peru the traditional sector's share of the labour force increased from 24.1 to 33.1 per cent between 1950 and 1970, while its share of value added decreased from 35.1 to 34.6 during the same period. Differentials in productivity per person between sectors increased from 3.6 to 4.4 times. Nelson *et al.* (1971) show a similar trend for Colombia. The share of the traditional sector in the labour force increased from 54 to 58 per cent, while the income share diminished from 45 to 34 per cent between 1951 and 1964. Productivity differentials almost doubled during the same period. Möller (1979) finds that self-employment in Santiago grew by 21 per cent between 1967 and 1977, while their income was reduced by five per cent; in comparison wage earners increased their employment by nine per cent and their income grew by 2 per cent.

The data available on wage evolution seem also to support the previous findings of increased intersectoral differentials, but they also suggest that average dispersion within the modern sectors has increased. In 9 of the 12 Latin American countries for which information is available, the ratio of minimum urban wages to average manufacturing wages decreased between 1966 and 1977. In some of them, like Chile, Costa Rica and Brazil, the reduction in the coefficient was around 40 per cent. Only in one of the remaining countries (El Salvador), was there an increase in the ratio (Tokman, 1979). Several case studies show the same results at a more disaggregate level. The Webb study of Peru recorded an increase of income in the modern sector at an annual rate almost twice that found for the urban traditional sector (4.1 and 2.1 per cent) during the 1950–66 period. The rates of growth by occupations suggest a greater dispersion since self-employed, non-manual employees in the traditional sector and domestic servants increased their earnings by 1.6– 1.9 per cent while government employees, white-collar and wage earners in the modern sector increased by 3.3–4.9 per cent per year. Nelson *et al.* reported an increased wage dispersion between 1951–64 in Colombia, since the lowest 50 per cent of urban wage earners raised their annual real wage by 0–0.5 per cent, the following 15 per cent by 2–3 per cent and the top 35 per cent, mostly workers in modern firms, by 5 per cent per annum.

The evidence available for Brazil also confirms these trends. Income differentials by occupations and by skills increased. The ratio between incomes of administrative and technical employees to other non-agricultural workers increased from 2.49 in 1960 to 2.86 in 1976. Incomes of unskilled workers decreased by 42 per cent between 1961 and

1976, while those of skilled workers increased by 8 per cent and managers remuneration increased by 22 per cent. Langoni (1973) shows that the average income of those with no school remained stagnant; the incomes of those with college level increased by 52 per cent between 1960 and 1970. A revision made by Pfefferman and Webb still shows a rate of income growth for the former group of one-fourth that of the latter. Wells (1974) calculates Gini coefficients on earnings by establishments, showing an increase of 25 per cent in the coefficient between 1959 and 1971. This is the result of losses of shares of the bottom deciles, together with significant gains of the top two deciles.

Bacha and Taylor (1978) also report increased wage differentials within manufacturing industry in Brazil. Technicians and hierarchical personnel increased their incomes between 1966 and 1972 by 7.2 per cent per annum, while unskilled industrial workers reduced their income by 1.3 per cent per annum and skilled and semi-skilled increased by 2.9 per cent per year. Other studies for the manufacturing sector in Chile (Gregory, 1967) and Mexico (PREALC, 1978c) show similar trends.

VII CONCLUSIONS

The main conclusion of this paper seems to confirm Stewart's (Chapter One) hypothesis that the payment system given by the institutional framework under which the informal sector operates determines the distribution of primary claims over resources. Such a payment system results in greater equity and lower income levels than could be achieved in a price capitalistic framework. It is also clear that technology and population growth play an important role in generating and perpetuating inequality.

That the payment system prevailing in the informal sector produces such outcomes can be seen by exploring the rules which determine income and its distribution within the sector. Informal sector activities are restricted in most cases to residual markets in which possibilities of expansion are limited. This, however, is not a homogeneous feature for all kinds of informal activities, but rather the result of different trends which generate such results. The balance of payments analysis for Chile and Mexico ruled out the treatment of the sector as an isolated parallel economy while also confirming that predictions about the future share of the sector are difficult to make given the many factors involved in its determination.

The type of insertion of informal activities in the market structure excludes the possibility of obtaining supernormal profits. Relative ease of entry is also a common feature of most of the informal activities. Given the size of the markets in which they operate, such easy entry is at least sufficient to ensure competition among activities and to rule out monopolistic profits. Most members of the labour force will find it easier to comply with the requirements presented by informal activities than to surpass the barriers to entry which characterise modern operations. Absence of scale economies, low capital requirements and divisibility contribute to widen the possibilities of entry to the sector.

Easy entry ensures competition in the determination of factor returns, differences being mostly explained by different access to complementary factors, mainly capital. Imperfections in factor markets together with the organisation of production, mainly on family basis, on the one hand, lower the alternative return to capital and on the other ensure a distribution of total income according to needs rather than to the marginal productivity of family members, since no employment alternatives exist for family members outside the firm because of job scarcity in the modern sector and their part-time availability. The income of the firm becomes then a household income and its distribution is made to cover the requirements of each member and not their contribution to the generation of such income. This ensures a more equitable distribution of income within the firm. The organisation of production which is characterised by atomisation, little division of labour and instability, forms an important constraint in the implementation of public policies designed to facilitate access to complementary resources.

The set of rules which govern the functioning of the informal sector result in a more equitable distribution of income within the sector than that prevailing in the rest of urban activities. The technological process characterised by restricted diffusion in a context of rapidly growing urban labour supply interact with the prevailing payments system to produce a worsening in income distribution. The main characteristics of this process are a non-decreasing share of the informal sector in total employment and non-narrowing productivity differentials both between the informal and formal sectors and within the latter.

The trends noted in this chapter also suggest that while the Kuznets hypothesis is still valid for analysing changes in income distribution in the Latin American countries, its prediction could be affected in at least three ways. Rural to urban migration will generate less inequality during the early stages of growth than anticipated because of the entrance of the newcomers to the city through the informal sector. The permanence of the sector as well as the maintenance and even widening of income differentials with the modern sector, as suggested by the data, will continue to cause a deterioration in the distribution of income for a longer period than expected and for the same reason the turning point will be reached at higher levels of inequality. We have shown elsewhere (Tokman, 1980) using a simple model and the log variance as a measure of concentration that first the Latin American profile shows increasing inequality at slower rates than that anticipated by the Kuznets hypothesis, until more than 40 per cent of the labour force is in non-agricultural sectors. Second, that while the Kuznets curve reaches its turning point at 50 per cent of the population in each sector, which is equivalent to US $560 GNP per person, the Latin American profile reaches its turning point when 70 per cent of the population is in non-agricultural sectors, at around US $950 per person. Finally, that the turning point is reached in the Latin American case at 0.105 points of higher log variance. This is also confirmed by Bacha (1979) who analysed changes in income distribution for 30 countries during the sixties. He concludes that the data suggest an outward movement of the Kuznets curve, while the turning point for the poorer 40 per cent is recorded at US $900 instead of the US $468 found by Ahluwalia (1976) using cross-country data.[25]

The analysis also suggests that increased concentration in the distribution of income will be the result of larger shares of managers, technicians, white-collar and skilled blue-collar workers, while those at the bottom will not be able to expand their share of total incomes. Within the lower income population, those who are able to migrate from rural to urban areas will also benefit. This kind of picture seems to emerge from the data on distribution of income for Latin America (ECLA, 1977). The lower 50 per cent of the population maintained their share at around 13.5 per cent between 1960 and 1970, while those in the eighth and ninth deciles increased their share from 24.6 to 28.0 during the period. This 20 per cent of the population was able to capture 40 per cent of the total income increase and the top decile, although losing share, retained 30 per cent of the increment. The remainder was distributed between the lower 70 per cent of the population resulting in an absolute average income increase of the poorer 50 per cent of US $30 (dollars of 1960) while the top 5 per cent increased their income by US $300. There was, however, a redistribution within the poor. Those who were in the lowest two deciles decreased their share and only gained US $2 during the period, while those in the third, fourth and fifth deciles, mostly migrants, were able to increase their share from 10.3 to 11.4 per cent and their average income was in 1970 US $50 higher than in 1960.

To conclude, one is tempted to recall the three questions posed by Kuznets (1955). The first question was: is the pattern of the older developed countries likely to be repeated in the sense that in early phases of industrialisation in the underdeveloped countries income will tend to widen before the leveling forces become strong enough first to stabilise and then reduce income inequalities? The second follows from an affirmative answer to the first: can the political framework of the underdeveloped societies withstand the strain which further widening of income inequality is likely to generate? Finally, he asked: how can either the institutional and political framework of the underdeveloped societies or the process of economic growth and industrialisation be modified to favour a sustained rise to higher levels of economic performance and yet avoid the fatally simple remedy of an authoritarian regime that would use the population as cannon-fodder in the fight for economic achievement?

This chapter is addressed to the first question. Not only did inequality tend to widen but the improvement is taking longer to arrive. Political events in most Latin American countries have answered the second question. The many proposals developed by academics and international organisations sleep in an abandoned drawer, while the search for economic growth is being experimented with at the high cost of sacrificing large masses of the population.

NOTES

1. We will not discuss here the different definitions of the informal sector. For a detailed discussion of this subject see Tokman (1977).
2. We have discussed this issue in detail elsewhere (Tokman, 1978).
3. This argument does not necessarily imply that informal activities operating under this condition will disappear, nor that they will do it in a fixed period of time. On the contrary, there are several factors which could produce a less pronounced trend or even a reverse one. These factors are mainly related to the constraints of expansion of the oligopolistic firms and to the existence of imperfect competition in product and, mainly, in factor markets (see Tokman, 1978).
4. For the purpose of this paper only the main results will be discussed. A more detailed discussion for the case of Chile can be found in Tokman, 1978. Indeed, the source of data as well as the assumptions that had to be included make this exercise more a methodological than an empirical one.
5. For the sake of simplicity when two figures are given and no mention of countries is made, the first refers to Chile and the second to Mexico.
6. If domestic services are excluded, the elasticity of exports of the informal sector in Chile is 36 per cent higher than the elasticity of imports, while in the case of Mexico it is 60 per cent.

7. One could argue following Chamberlain (1948) that all activities are inserted in markets under monopolistic competition, where factors influencing perfect competition are variable. This breakdown tends, however, to note those characteristics which are closely associated with each market organisation.

8. It is possible, especially in spatial differentiation, that monopolistic profits exist. Differentials in the rent of urban land will tend to absorb the whole or a large part of the monopolistic profit due to this factor (see Chamberlain, 1948; especially Appendices C and D).

9. When entrepreneurs are heterogeneous even if all other factors are homogeneous, some firms will be able to earn supernormal profits in the long-run. The only way in which these firms will be forced to earn normal profits is by the entrance of entrepreneurs as efficient as those already established with differential advantages.

10. This is so even in countries with more stable and higher income markets. In the US for instance, 80 per cent of all replacement jobs created between 1969 and 1976 were generated by establishments 4 years old or younger while 2/3 of the net jobs created during that period were generated by firms with 20 or fewer employees and 5 out of 6.7 million new jobs were in trade or service while manufacturers produced virtually none. (As reported by D. L. Birch, MIT, *New York Times*, 3 December 1979). In the case of Santiago, Chile, preliminary work for a survey undertaken by PREALC in 1976 shows that at least 50 per cent of small retail shops were replaced in less than 2 years.

11. Prices should not be the same in all neighbourhoods unless the distribution of buyers is a random one. Neither will be the sales volume. Each firm will tend to maximise returns over costs. These costs include normal profits and the differential remaining, which is due to the superiority of the profit-making opportunities afforded by one site as compared to another, is rent, and is put into the hands of the landlords by the competition of entrepreneurs for the best opportunities (Chamberlain, 1948; Appendix D).

12. The survey covered self-employment in the 12 most important occupations, established commerce, street sellers, laundry women, service workers, taxi drivers, seamstresses and tailors, shoemakers, mechanics, electricians, plumbers, construction workers and others. Two questions made to those interviewed inquire the level of skill required by their job. The first one refers to whether the person interviewed considered himself as an apprentice, unskilled, semi-skilled, skilled or highly-skilled. He was then asked how long would it take to convert an unskilled worker in his activity into a skilled one.

13. In commerce activities, little skill differentials were found. In the other three cases analysed, of the four levels of skill established within each activity, the movement from the third to the second level could be shortened in time if learning by doing is substituted by formal training. The passage from the second to the top category would in most cases require formal training.

14. This is shown, for instance, for household and small shops working under subcontract in the clothing industry (Schmukler, 1979) and for mechanics (Nun, 1978) in Argentina; for repair mechanic shops (PREALC, 1979) and for the self-employment activities (PREALC, 1979) analysed in Chile.

15. In the self-employment activities in Chile, 80 per cent of those who declared

acquired skills while working in establishments did so in small enterprises while the remaining worked in modern sector firms. The pattern seems to be somewhat different in the case of mechanics which became owners of their shops since the skill requirements are higher. They still learn with experience but a significant proportion acquired such experience while working in large firms (PREALC, 1979).

16. Capital in this study did not include land and buildings.

17. All the small auto repair shops analysed in Santiago (PREALC, 1979a) started with little capital in their houses or that of some relatives and with only a few tools. All of them had expanded in comparison to the starting size, some even over-expanded and had to reduce their size. The capacity to grow seems to be related more to the entrepreneurial capacity, skill and, in some cases, consumption propensities than to the initial capital endowment. The same seems to happen in retail service, where different business cycle can be deduced according to whether the entrepreneur is devoted full-time and has experience in the trade. Initial capital indeed helps to accumulate, but growth is not restricted to those cases only as is shown by the fact that while 7.5 per cent of those shops with larger capital and selling to higher income markets increased the size of the establishment, 35.4 per cent of the low capital selling to low income markets did the same in Santiago (PREALC, 1978).

18. When mechanics were asked what would be their next step to expand their establishments, their answers reflected the introduction of changes in the product mix (i.e., import of spare parts, auto trade, body repair). The same happened when they were asked whether they could become authorised agents for servicing a car brand or by establishing long-term arrangements for servicing large company cars. The main constraint mentioned was the minimum capital required mostly in tools and spare parts. The answers were consistent with differences in initial capital endowment observed in the case studies. The only modern garage analysed started with an initial capital of US $60,000 (PREALC, 1979a) with a product mix which included servicing, sales and inputs of spare parts. A similar situation is found for the retailers which, to surpass the informal sector boundary, have to become self-services. That kind of operation requires larger sales volume, bigger buildings and broader product diversification. All these factors imply greater capital requirements (PREALC, 1978a).

19. Private fixed capital costs will be then negligible. This explains why in many cases small firms operate with nil return to capital which, in turn, is one of the causes of the large turnover of establishments found in these activities.

20. The exceptions of higher incomes in the informal sector are concentrated in middle-aged and higher education groups devoted to established commerce activities. In Asuncion, for instance, the income of the owner of an establishment in the informal sector was 46 per cent more than persons with similar education working in formal commerce activities. If the comparison is made only with white-collars in such activities, incomes of the informal sector are 18 per cent smaller than those received in the formal sector. The same type of results is found in San Salvador and Santo Domingo (Souza-Tokman, 1978).

21. The estimated income of the informal retailer for Santiago was 3.3 times the prevailing minimum wage. If allowances are made for unpaid family labour,

the net income of the owner would be 2.3 times the minimum wage which compares unfavourably with the wage received by white-collar workers in supermarkets (3.2 times the minimum) (Tokman, 1978).
22. Similar results are found for Belo Horizonte, Brazil (Merrick, 1976) and for Colombia by Kugler (1977).
23. See, for instance, Pinto (1965), Prebisch (1978) and PREALC (1978b).
24. Nelson *et al.* (1971) presents a formal model of restricted technological diffusion.
25. This is the result shown by the regression equation between the ratio of changes in the share of the lower 40 per cent to the rate of growth of GNP and the logarithm of GNP per person in the middle of the 1960s.

REFERENCES

Ahluwalia, M. S., 'Inequality, Poverty and Development', *Journal of Development Economics* 3(3) (September, 1976).
Bacha, E., 'Más allá de la curva Kuznets: Criamiento y cambios en las disigualdades' in O. Munõz (comp.), *Distribución del Ingreso en América Latina* (Buenos Aires, El Cid Editor, 1979).
Bacha, E., and Taylor, L., 'Brazilian Income Distribution in the 1960s: Facts, Model Results and the Controversy', *Journal of Development Studies*, 14(3) (April 1978).
Bain, J. S., *Barriers to New Competition* (Cambridge: Harvard University Press, 1967).
Bienefeld, M., 'The Informal Sector and Peripherical Capitalism: The Case of Tanzania', *IDS Bulletin*, 6(3) (February 1975).
Bose, A. N., *The Informal Sector in the Calcutta Metropolitan Economy* (Geneva: ILO, 1974).
Bourguignon, F., *Poverty and Dualism in the Urban Sector of Developing Economies: The Case of Colombia* (Paris: Institut des Sciences Mathématiques et Economiques Appliquées, 1978) mimeo.
Chamberlain, E. H., *The Theory of Monopolistic Competition* (Cambridge: Harvard University Press, 1948).
Dupré, E., *Factores explicativos de la concentración del ingreso del trabajo en El Salvador-según segmentos del mercado del trabajo* (Santiago: PREALC, 1979) mimeo.
Gerry, C., *Petty Producers and the Urban Economy: A Case Study of Dakar* (Geneva: ILO, 1974).
Gregory, P., *Industrial Wages in Chile* (Ithaca: Cornell University, New York State School of Industrial and Labor Relations, 1967).
International Labour Office, *Employment, Incomes and Equality: A Strategy for Increasing Productive Employment in Kenya* (Geneva: ILO, 1972).
Kugler, B., *Pobreza y la estructura del empleo en el sector urbano de Colombia*, paper submitted to the Conference on Distribution, Poverty and Development (Bogota, 1977).
Kuznets, S., 'Economic Growth and Income Inequality', *American Economic Review*, 45(1) (March 1955).
Langoni, C. G., *Distribucào da renda e desenvolvimento econômico do Brasil* (Rio do Janeiro: Editora Expressào e Cultura, 1973).

Lomintz, L., 'Mecanismos de articulación entre el sector informal y el sector formal urbano', in Tokman, V. E. and Klein, E. eds, *Subempleo en América Latina* (Buenos Aires: El Cid, 1979).

Mazumdar, D., 'The Urban Informal Sector', *World Development* 4(8) (August 1976).

Merrick, T., 'Employment and Earnings in the Informal Sector in Brazil: The Case of Belo Horizonte', *The Journal of Developing Areas*, 10(3) (1976).

Möller, A., *Los trabajadores por cuenta propia en Santiago* (Santiago: PREALC, 1979).

Nelson, R., Schultz, T. P. and Slighton, R., *Structural Change in a Developing Economy: Colombia's Problems and Prospects* (Princeton: Princeton University Press, 1971).

Nun, J., 'Despidos en la industria automotriz argentina: Estudio de un caso de superpoblación flotante', *Revista Mexicana de Sociología*, 40(1) (1978).

Pfefferman, G. and Webb, R., *The Distribution of Income in Brazil* (Washington: IBRD, 1979) mimeo.

Pinto, A., 'Concentración del progreso técnico y de sus frutos en el desarrollo latinoamericano', *El Trimestre Económico*, 32(125) (1965).

Prebisch, R., 'Críticas al capitalismo periférico', *Revista de la CEPAL* (primer semestre, 1976).

PREALC, *Sector informal: Funcionamiento y políticas* (Santiago: PREALC, 1978).

PREALC, *Comercio informal en una comuna de Santiago* (Santiago: PREALC, 1978a).

PREALC, *Employment in Latin America* (New York: Praeger, 1978b).

PREALC, *Necesidades de capacitación de los trabajadores por cuenta propia en Santiago* (Santiago: PREALC, 1979).

PREALC, *Entrevistas en profundidad a empresas y trabajadores del sector informal en reparación de automóviles* (Santiago: PREALC, 1979a).

PREALC, *Diferenciales de remuneraciones y coexistencia de establecimientos de distinto tamaño, México 1965–75* (Santiago: PREALC, 1978c).

Puryear, J., *Formación profesional en Colombia* (Montevideo: CINTERFOR, 1977).

Quijano, A., 'The Marginal Pole of the Economy and the Marginalized Labour Force' in *Economy and Society*, 3(4) (1974).

Raczinsky, D., *El sector informal urbano: Interrogantes y controversias*, (Santiago, PREALC, 1977).

Raczinsky, D., *Características del empleo informal urbano en Chile* (Santiago, CIEPLAN, 1978).

Schmukler, B., 'Relaciones actuales de producción en industrias tradicionales argentinas' in Tokman, V. E. and Klein, E. eds *Subempleo en América . . .* op. cit.

Sethuraman, S. V., 'Urban Development and Employment in Jakarta', *International Labour Review* 94(1) (July–August, 1976).

Souza, P. R. and Tokman, V. E., 'Distribución del ingreso, pobreza y empleo en áreas urbanas', *El Trimestre Económico*, 45(179) (July–September, 1978).

Tokman, V. E., 'Las relaciones entre los sectores formal e informal', *Revista de la CEPAL* (primer semestre, 1978).

Tokman, V. E., 'Competition in Retail Services: The Case of Santiago', *World Development*, 6(9–10) (September–October 1978a).

Tokman, V. E., 'Dinámica de los Mercados de trabajo y distribución del ingreso en América Latina', *Colección Estudios CIEPLAN No. 3* (Santiago, CIEPLAN, 1980).

Tokman, V. E., 'Dinámica del mercado de trabajo urbano: El sector informal urbano en América Latina' in Katzman R. and Reyna, J. L. (eds), *Fuerza de trabajo en América Latina* (Mexico, 1979a).

Tokman, V. E., *Growth, Underemployment and Income Distribution* (Santiago, PREALC, 1980).

Uthoff, A., *Earning Inequality, Metropolitan Santiago, 1969–1978: The Role of Human Capital within a Segmented Labour Market* (Santiago: PREALC, 1979) mimeo.

Webb, R., *Income and Employment in the Urban, Modern and Traditional Sectors of Peru* (Princeton: Princeton University, 1974) mimeo.

Wells, J., 'Distribution of Earnings, Growth and the Structure of Demand in Brazil during the 1960's' *World Development*, 2(1) (1974).

6 Distributive Regimes under Public Enterprise: a Case Study of the Bangladesh Experience*

REHMAN SOBHAN

INTRODUCTION

Whilst much attention has been paid to the development of public enterprise (PE) there has been less discussion on the use of public enterprise as a distributive mechanism. This perhaps stems from the somewhat axiomatic assumption that the extension of public enterprise is itself an expression of the redistributive intentions of a regime. This chapter attempts to focus discussion on the assumptions behind the use of the PE instrument and to see how it has been or could be used for distributive purposes.

The arguments used in this paper have been elaborated elsewhere.* The factual base draws upon data specific to Bangladesh.

The central theme of this chapter is that the distributive regimes under public enterprise tend to be conditioned by the prevailing dispensation

* This chapter draws substantially upon arguments and materials presented in a paper by Rehman Sobhan on 'Public Enterprise as an instrument of policy in Anti-poverty Strategies in South Asia' prepared for presentation at a meeting of the South Asia Group on Strategies for the 1980s, convened by Development Planning Division, ESCAP at Bangkok in April 1979.

of class forces within the polity. This factor emerges as crucial to the emergence and role of public enterprise, its capacity to generate surplus and the manner in which the surplus is distributed between contending social groups.

The analytical framework for this interpretation of the role of PE has been articulated elsewhere.[1] In this chapter it is therefore intended to use empirical data drawn from the experience of PEs in Bangladesh to illustrate the analysis rather than to establish quantitatively the properties of a rigorously formulated model. The discussion should, however, give some indication of relevant questions which model builders may seek to incorporate in such an exercise. To the extent that the study uses social classes as stereotypes the argument cannot capture all the nuances of intra-class interests, nor the specific role of particular individuals as leaders, policy-makers or managers, who have contributed to giving a particular direction to policies or the affairs of some enterprises. Our analysis is concerned with the general direction of policy towards public enterprise and its relationship to the prevailing configuration of social forces within society.

The use of Bangladesh as a case study warrants certain caveats. Apart from the historical specificity and unique social characteristics of the scene in Bangladesh, the data used is itself somewhat dated even though it does in places use more recent material. The chapter mainly draws upon a fairly detailed study of the political economy of public enterprise in Bangladesh, covering the period 1972–5.[2] The data certainly needs to be updated. However, a qualitative review of current trends in Bangladesh indicates that little has emerged to warrant any modifications in the underlying premise.

In the general analysis the term public enterprise (PE) is used generically to refer to all instruments of economic activity where the state by virtue of ownership or control of the enterprise institution directs its policy and controls the disposal of its surplus. This generic definition would normally include a variety of juridical entities ranging from departmental enterprises run by ministries, to public corporations and joint-stock companies where the government is the sole or dominant owner. This chapter, however, draws on specific quantitative data, which is largely derived from the study on public enterprise in Bangladesh,[3] which adopts more limiting definitions of public enterprise.[4] To the extent then that we draw upon this study to illustrate our analysis of the role of PEs in Bangladesh we will be constrained by the definitions and measures of our data source.

PUBLIC ENTERPRISES AS A DISTRIBUTIONAL INSTRUMENT

The significant feature of public enterprise is that it represents command over productive resources by the state. This makes it possible for decisions relating to production, distribution, investment and consumption to be reconciled by the state within the framework of a socially determined set of policy objectives.

At the macro-economic level the net surpluses[5] generated by the public enterprises are directly within the control of the state and can be allocated to serve specific policy objectives. The distribution of the surplus as between consumption and investment or between projects for the poor and guns for the armed forces are social decisions. To the extent that a regime is committed to realise redistributive goals, public enterprise is potentially a powerful resource to realise this objective both indirectly through its capacity to expand the productive forces within the economy and directly through its allocation of the surplus to the lower income groups.

The full social potential of PE, however, does not stop at the surplus but relates to the entire allocative regime embodied within a public enterprise. Beginning from the regime of pricing and procurement of raw materials, and moving on to the compensation of employees, the terms on which capital is made available, the market regime and pricing of the output and ending with the budgetary appropriation of the surplus through direct and indirect taxes and decisions on the content and allocation of the post tax surplus, a regime has by virtue of its control over the enterprise, powerful instruments to benefit one group over another. Thus a regime wanting to benefit cultivators could pay them higher procurement prices. Alternatively it may raise workers compensation absolutely and relatively. It may choose to subsidise consumers of fertiliser, cloth, cement, edible oils or any other group serviced by a public enterprise. All are decisions which may be taken at the expense of the surplus of public enterprise but would represent a social decision designed to serve particular groups such as farmers, workers or consumers.

To the extent that a public enterprise by virtue of its publicness is not constricted by the compulsion to maximise its profits, latitude to serve specific interest groups becomes considerable. Its allocative decisions then become a function of the balance of power between contending social groups in relation to the product of a particular enterprise. When we therefore talk of public enterprise as a distributive instrument we must distinguish between its potential and the practice, which will continue to be influenced by the balance of power with society.

PUBLIC ENTERPRISE AS AN INSTRUMENT OF CLASS STRUGGLE

In addition to the potential uses of public enterprise as an allocative instrument it can also play a positive role in breaking or reducing the power of the dominant social classes in society. On the land, state and collective farms may be used to replace plantations or large feudal estates owned by private interests. Of course, such institutions may also pre-empt individual small holdings and thus reflect the aggrandisement of state power over those of small farmers. This may or may not be a progressive step depending on the nature of state power.

In the capitalist sector, state enterprise can be used more categorically as an instrument of class war directed against an established foreign or local interest. Extension of public enterprise may here be used to redistribute assets from private to public ownership through nationalisation. This may be supplemented by pre-emptive measures designed to exclude private enterprise from certain segments of the economy and/or above a certain level of investment, reserving them for public enterprise. Such measures may be designed to reduce concentration of assets in private ownership and/or the monopoly of power within society which goes with such concentrations of wealth. Such a move may seek to reallocate economic and social power away from the bourgeoisie to the masses, but power may end up in the hands of an aspirant petty bourgeoisie which uses public enterprise as its own particular instrument of class war to re-appropriate the surplus for its own sectional interests.

A review of the Bangladesh experience will make it evident that both distributive and anti-bourgeois motives have conditioned the role of public enterprise.[6] However, these objectives have not necessarily realised proclaimed distributive objectives and in some cases may have served a contrary objective.

THE NATURE OF THE STATE IN BANGLADESH

The nature of the post-colonial state in Bangladesh was decisively conditioned by the character of the nationalist struggle for realising its liberation from Pakistani rule. To understand the nature of the struggle one needs briefly to review the nature of state power in Pakistan itself.

The emergence of Pakistan out of the partition of India had a traumatic impact on the post-colonial state. The communal carnage saw the complete withdrawal of the Hindu bourgeoisie which had dominated trade and commerce in the regions which came to constitute West Pakistan. This vacuum was, however, rapidly filled by the arrival of immigrant trading communities from India, Memons, Bohras and Ismailis who first moved into trade and thence into industry with the full patronage of the state in both West and East Pakistan (now Bangladesh).[7] Their progression in the West was unchallenged and moved at an accelerated pace. In the East, however, they had to contend with the hitherto dominant Hindu and Marwari trading interests who contrived to retain a presence in the regional economy. But faced with the progressive withdrawal of the Hindu bourgeoisie from Pakistan, state policies were directed to establish a local bourgeoisie. By 1959 the structure of private ownership in Pakistan came to be dominated by a West Pakistan based bourgeoisie whose span of control also covered the Eastern region.

The marriage of interests between an immigrant trading and industrial bourgeoisie based in West Pakistan, and a West Wing based bureaucracy, armed forces and land-owning elite, created a pattern of state power highly conducive to the rapid growth of both the bourgeois and feudal classes of West Pakistan. This development was realised through the use of state power to monopolise resources for the development of the West Wing at the expense of the East Wing. In the process the economy of the East Wing came to be completely dominated by a West Wing based bourgeoisie. The structure of private ownership in the East Wing on the eve of independence (see Table 6.1) indicates that only 18 per cent of fixed assets in manufacturing, 18 per cent of bank deposits, 10 per cent of insurance business and 33 per cent of the jute exports were in the hands of an indigenous bourgeoisie.[8] Inland water transport, foreign and inter-wing trade other than jute, large areas of wholesale trade, along with banking, insurance and industry was completely dominated by a non-indigenous bourgeoisie. The protracted struggle to end this external domination of the region culminated in the emergence of Bangladesh. The violent denouement of this struggle precipitated the dramatic withdrawal of the West Pakistani bourgeoisie for Bangladesh and the emergence of a complete vacuum in its urban economy.

The domination of the Bangladesh economy by the West Pakistan

TABLE 6.1 Structure of asset ownership in Bangladesh on the eve of independence

		Percentage owned by	
	Bengali	*Non Bengali Pakistan and foreign*	*Public enterprise*
Fixed assets in the modern industrialised sector (1969/70)	18	48	34
Bank deposits	18	82	–
Insurance business (life) (1969/70)	10	90	–
Jute trade (share of exports) (1969/70)	33	37	30

Source: R. Sobhan, 'Public Enterprise as an instrument of Policy in Anti-poverty Strategies in South Asia'.

bourgeoisie had inhibited the growth of an indigenous bourgeoisie, the growth of an indigeneous bourgeoisie being a phenomenen of the 1960s. The liberation struggle was dominated by workers, peasants, students and petty-bourgeoisie elements led by the Awami League which was a classical petty-bourgeois-based party. Post-liberation policies reflected the course of the armed struggle. The Pakistani-based metropolitan bourgeoisie withdrew but the recently elevated bourgeois elements in Bangladesh could not fill the consequent vacuum in the urban economy. Indeed state power not only moved to nationalise Pakistani enterprises but to dilute the power of the nascent Bangladesh bourgeoisie through nationalisation of their holdings in the jute, textiles, sugar industry and in banking and insurance. Further legislation pre-empted the growth of an upper bourgeoisie by putting a ceiling of Tk. 2.5 million on ownership of fixed assets in industry, excluding them from equity collaboration with foreign enterprise and reserving the bulk of international trade, including jute to public enterprise. The sweeping impact of the nationalisation policies in the industry sector are presented in Table 6.2.

The thrust of state policy was thus explicitly directed towards frustrating the growth of a class of big capitalists in Bangladesh. This objective was substantially realised up to the change of regime in August 1975 in spite of some attempts to expand investment opportunities for the private sector.[9] The dominant groups within the bourgeoisie used

TABLE 6.2 Position of private sector in industry as a consequence of nationalisation[1]

Category of units	Number of units	Value of fixed assets (in million Tk.)	% Share of fixed assets
Total Number of Units in 1969–70	3,051	6,137.5	100
Situation in 1969–70			
Under EPIDC ownership	53	2,097.0	34
Under private non-Bengali ownership	725	2,885.7	47
Under private Bengali ownership	2,253	1,118.8	18
Under private foreign ownership	20	36.0	1
Situation on March 26, 1972			
Units under former EPIDC[2] nationalised	53	2,097.0	34
Nationalised abandoned/absentee units	263 ⎫	2,629.7	43
Nationalised foreign enterprises	1 ⎭		
Nationalised Bengali Units	75	910.8	15
Total nationalised units (1 + 2 + 3)	392	5,637.5	92
Bengali-owned private units	2,178	208.0	3
Abandoned/absentee units for disinvestment	462	256.0	4
Units with foreign participation	13	36.0	1
Total private sector (5 + 6 + 7)	2,659	500.0	8
Total industrial sector	3,051	6,137.5	100

Source: Sobhan and Ahmed, *Public Enterprise in an Intermediate Regime* (Dacca: Bangladesh Institute of Development Studies, June 1980), Table 10.1, p. 192.

Notes
1. Includes all industries registered under the Factories Act.
2. East Pakistan Industrial Development Corporation

their control of state power to extract surpluses from public enterprises through trading franchises. This trend in the development of the bourgeoisie did not, however, emerge as a consequence of official policy but in spite of it. Such acts of primitive accumulation could always attract punitive action when patronage was withdrawn. There was thus no scope for a trading bourgeoisie to consolidate itself as a social force within Bangladesh.

The military regime which assumed power in August 1975 sought to legitimise the trading bourgeoisie and resurrect the dispossessed bourgeoisie of the pre-liberation period whose aspirations has been drastically frustrated by the nationalisation policies. The current thrust of the state policy reflects an attempt to revitalise the private sector. This however can only be realised through massive doses of state patronage channelled through the state industrial financing agencies. Since the change of regime, loans sanctioned to private industry have increased significantly rising from an average of Tk. 11.9 million per year between 1973–5 to Tk. 243.5 million per year for the period 1977–80.[10] However, of the total investment involved in these loan sanctions only 18 per cent was derived from the owners' equity, with the balance of 82 per cent coming from state loan and equity financing agencies.[11] Notwithstanding this attempt to build up a capitalist class under state sponsorship the public sector still remains dominant in the urban economy, particularly in manufacturing and finance. The bias towards the private sector has however some implications for the distributive regime of the public enterprises, which we will discuss subsequently.

THE DISTRIBUTIVE REGIME UNDER PUBLIC ENTERPRISE

This dramatic escalation in the role of public enterprise in Bangladesh after liberation still left the major component of the economy under private ownership. In 1974–5 only 16.3 per cent of the GDP originated in the public sector.[12] This reflected the fact that agriculture accounted for around 60 per cent of the GDP of Bangladesh in 1972/73 and land ownership was completely under private ownership. The dominance of traditional occupations in transport, trade, housing and small and cottage industry further contributed to the preponderance of private ownership. The impact of the extension of public enterprise after 1972 was thus largely focussed on the modern sector in contrast to the traditional sector.

However, whilst the state sector was dominant in the modern sectors of industry, finance and transport, its development programmes were of considerable significance for the growth impulses in the traditional sector and other components of the private sector. For instance in agriculture, apart from the effects of weather, most of the growth in grain output due to the application of HYV technology was a result of state programmes for distributing fertiliser, pesticides and improved seeds, agricultural credit and installation of mechanised irrigation equipment through public enterprises at subsidised rates. A sizeable part of the grain market is influenced by official grain imports, local procurement and public distribution, which together involve state subsidies which amounted to Tk. 1650, 12.3 per cent of the budget for

1979/80.[13] Even in the case of cash crops such as sugar, cane and jute, the pricing and procurement policies of public enterprises are of considerable importance in determining the acreage and volume of output.

In the construction and trade sector where actual ownership of enterprises is in private hands the growth impulses again largely originate in state expenditure policies. A large part of the new construction which has taken place in the last eight years consists either of construction work by public enterprises, executed by private contractors, or private construction financed by state financing agencies. In both areas the main inputs of steel and cement are largely supplied by public enterprise producers or state trading agencies. Similarly in the trading sector distribution of public enterprise production and imports are an important source of earning for private traders.

It follows that notwithstanding its GDP share the state sector is the dominant impulse for economic activity at the margin in Bangladesh. This gives policies towards PE a critical role in determining the distributive regime.

SURPLUS GENERATION UNDER PUBLIC ENTERPRISE

Before we move on to a discussion of the distributive regime under public enterprise it will be useful to see how far public enterprises in fact have generated surpluses, which could be deployed to promote economic development in Bangladesh.[14]

In this paper surplus has been defined as that part of the value of a product which directly re-enters the economy to finance further growth. This is estimated as the surplus in product value over and above payments for material inputs and employee compensation. This residual is made up of payments by public enterprise to the exchequer through direct and indirect taxes and through dividends or levies from its post-tax profits, augmented by that part of the surplus retained within the enterprise under the head of depreciation and retained earnings and/or reserves. The underlying assumption of this approach is that the surplus which goes to the government can be used to finance development, while the surplus retained within the enterprise can finance expansion within the enterprise. The depreciation fund is seen as part of the surplus even though it is required in theory to replace worn out equipment. But the decision to replace worn-out plant in a state sugar factory has to compete with a decision to set up a new textile mill, so that the depreciation fund should be included as part of the aggregate investment fund of the economy.

We have attempted to compute an estimate of surplus generated by public enterprises in Bangladesh. For the PE set as a whole relevant data is only available for 1973–4.[15] This indicates that in 1973–4 the surplus generated came to 67.3 per cent of value added from public enterprises, as a whole. Within the manufacturing sector, the surplus came to 40.2 per cent of value added by PEs in this sector.

The estimate of surplus used above may be contrasted with the more conventional measure of enterprise profitability in Bangladesh. On aggregate, as between 1973 and 1977, figures for the manufacturing sector show that in only one out of five years, 1973–4, did public enterprise in aggregate show a net profit of 3 per cent on sales value.[16] However if we exclude the chronically losing jute industry, then profits were earned in all years except 1975/76, with a high of 10.5 per cent in 1973/74. The profile of loss was highly localized to jute, paper and board and tanneries, though fertilisers, forest product and textiles went into the red in some years. From these figures it is apparent that profits as shown on the balance sheets of public enterprises were substantially below the operational surplus generated in these enterprises. The differential measures the burden of indirect taxes, interest and depreciation charges carried by these enterprises.

UTILIZATION OF THE SURPLUS

The fact that public enterprise continued to generate surpluses even when it was making low or negative profits indicates that it retained a capacity to contribute to the development process. This may be directly estimated through its contribution to public revenues and internal financing of capital expansion and modernisation. During 1973/74 PEs contributed 68 per cent of all taxes accruing to the government. The contribution through direct taxes was negligible so that the main source of revenue was indirect taxes. Including non-tax revenues, the contribution of PEs to total government revenue of Tk. 3,939 million comes to 60 per cent. This figure may be contrasted with the share of PEs value added in GDP in Bangladesh, which came to only 8.2 per cent.

This disproportionate contribution to public revenues by public enterprise again reflects its overwhelming importance in the monetised sector of the economy and the peculiar incidence of taxation which leaves the non-modernised sector virtually untouched.

If we move on to look at the share of PEs in fixed capital formation, their dominance becomes apparent. In the years for which data is available, public enterprises are overwhelmingly the most important source of investment. Public sector investment in Bangladesh between 1972–5 accounted for 81–5 per cent of total investment. Of this figure, roughly 40 per cent was in public enterprises and the remainder other public sector agencies.[18] This breakdown roughly approximates the First Five Year Plan investment strategy which committed 85 per cent of investment to the public sector.

Between 1973/74 and 1976/77 the share of public sector investment in manufacturing industry amounted to 92 per cent.[19] On a year-to-year basis there is some slight acceleration in the share of private sector investment rising to 18 per cent in 1975/76, but in real terms the share of private investment remains low. As noted even this low share of private investment is largely financed by public sector loan and equity finance institutions.

The extent to which PEs finance their own capital expansion out of savings/surplus depends on the definitions adopted. In practice there is no causal nexus in any one year between what are defined as savings of PEs and their GFCF. Investment in any one year is the result of expenditure decisions taken in previous years.

Its financing may come in all or part from domestic and foreign loans and even fresh equity investments. In turn savings generated by PEs in that year may not go into investment within the PE sector but may be retained or appropriated in the general revenues of the government. Using conventional measures of savings, PE in Bangladesh could finance about 45 per cent of its investment, the rest coming largely from foreign aid. However, if we recompute PE's contribution in terms of its surplus we find that in 1973/74 public sector development expenditure was Tk. 1963 million whilst PE's surplus came to Tk. 2921 million.

POLICIES RELATING TO THE DISTRIBUTION OF THE SURPLUS GENERATED BY PUBLIC ENTERPRISE

Within a system of private ownership and management the initial objective is that of maximising the surplus accruing to the owners of the equity in the enterprise. Decisions on procurement, marketing and remuneration of employees are all subordinated to this objective. Government policies are generally taken as exogeneously imposed parameters. However, the owners of property as a class try to influence the course of these policies in a direction favourable to the objectives of maximisation of the surplus on their equity, while individuals seek to bend, evade or manipulate their way round these parameters. Their success in both tasks depends on their collective strength and individual influence. The single objective of surplus maximisation does not exclude ancillary objectives of consolidating power and control over the environment, since these are themselves part of the attempt to influence the parameters within which the goal of surplus maximisation can be pursued.

TABLE 6.3 Matrix of distribution and beneficiaries of benefits from public enterprise

Recipients of revenue classified as social groups	Sources of revenue		
	Material inputs	Employee compensation	Surplus
Foreign	*		
Agricultural sector			
Small farmers	*		Subsidized consumption
Big farmers	*		of PE goods
Employees in PE			
Workers		Wages	Bonus
Management		Salaries	Profit share
			Social amenities
			Subsidised consumption of PE goods
Public Enterprise			Depreciation fund
			Reserves
			Post-tax profits
Government			Interest on loans from public sector financial institutions
			Indirect taxes
			Direct taxes
			Post-tax dividend paid to exchequer
Middleman		Trading profit	Premium from procurement of PE goods at sub-market prices

Source: Sobhan, op. cit., Table 13.

Note: * Signifies recipient of revenues.

TABLE 6.4   Bangladesh: % share of various elements in production value at factor cost in various manufacturing sectors in 1973/74

	Employee compensation	Interest	Depreciation	Government	Surplus over costs	Raw material	Others
Cotton textiles	16.6	1.2	2.2	5.6	16.2	52.8	5.5
Special textiles	12.3	7.3	5.8	16.3	20.9	33.0	4.4
Jute textiles	29.2	6.4	7.4	0.2	(−6.8)	49.9	13.7
Edible oil	4.0	1.8	0.8	5.7	24.5	58.6	4.6
Tobacco	9.2	5.9	1.9	34.5	(−7.8)	30.1	26.2
Fish and cold storage	6.4	1.9	1.5	1.6	6.8	52.8	29.0
Miscellaneous food	6.0	0.4	0.3	6.1	16.2	58.4	12.6
Paper and board	22.2	9.5	12.0	18.5	(−14.9)	62.9	10.2
Steel (large)	10.3	12.8	12.5	6.1	11.3	28.8	18.2
(small)	6.6	2.7	2.3	2.3	12.5	48.3	25.3
Sugar	10.4	4.9	4.6	2.1	15.1	51.6	11.3
Petroleum	3.4	4.7	5.2	4.2	0.9	79.3	2.3
Cement	9.6	1.6	1.7	29.3	21.0	24.0	12.8
Shipyard	13.2	4.2	1.7	2.9	1.8	46.7	29.5
Other	13.8	8.5	3.8	9.0	2.0	55.4	6.9
Pharmaceuticals	15.5	4.2	1.4	7.1	2.3	46.8	21.7
Leather	16.0	5.5	0.2	0.1	(−14.4)	89.7	2.9
Fertiliser	10.3	9.0	16.3	20.7	2.3	15.3	26.1
Chemicals	6.5	1.9	1.6	27.5	7.2	45.4	7.9
Matches	4.0	0.04	0.5	48.5	7.4	28.6	12.0
Rubber	12.6	2.9	1.0	24.5	7.0	37.9	14.1

Source: Sobhan and Ahmed, op. cit., Table 16.20.

In contrast to the private entrepreneur, public enterprise executives have limited control over the determination of the surplus and none over its distribution. For PE's maximisation of surplus may be coincidental rather than by design. Since public enterprise is a resource in the hands of the regime, it can allocate income from public enterprise by virtue of its ownership, on the basis of social policy.

This point may be more easily understood if we note that the revenues from public enterprise may be distributed between a variety of social groups as summarised in the form of a matrix presented in Table 6.3. This matrix of distribution from PEs is obviously simplified but serves to illustrate how the distribution of revenues can be exogenously determined by policy and other influences.

We may try to explain the impact of these influences in terms of the respective social groups involved, drawing upon the Bangladesh experience by way of illustration. Our analysis is limited by the absence of any quantitative research which specifically seeks to define inter-class income flows. To the extent that our analytical framework is seen to be relevant to an understanding of distributive regimes the matrix may provide the basis for further research to enable these slots in the table to be filled in. The data for Bangladesh used here is available only for the manufacturing sector for one year, 1973–4. This is presented in Table 6.4. For comparison as between 1969/70 and 1975/76 another set of data is presented in Table 6.5. In contrast to the more comprehensive coverage for 1973/74 in Table 6.4, the breakdown of distribution categories in Table 6.5 is very limited being restricted to payments for materials, employees compensation and surplus.

TABLE 6.5   Distribution of product value of public enterprises in the manufacturing sector.

	1969/70	1975/76
Percentage share of material inputs in production value	56.2	68.4
Percentage share of employee compensation in production value	10.5	10.9
Percentage share of surplus in production value	33.3	20.7
Total	100.0	100.0

Source: Sobhan, op. cit., Table 14.

THE EXTERNAL SECTOR

Public enterprises in Bangladesh purchase a part of their material inputs from abroad in the form of raw materials, intermediate inputs and spare parts. Exogenously induced changes in world prices can influence the earnings of PEs with a high import component. In the short run PEs can do little about this. The data as available in Tables 6.4 and 6.5 makes no distinction for payments to the external sector for material inputs. The high rise in the ratio of payments for raw materials from 56 per cent in 1969/70 to 68 per cent in 1975/76 is largely due to the rise in the cost of imports.[20] This change in the import cost structure led to big increases in production costs which were not always compensated by corresponding price increases in Bangladesh.[21] In these circumstances there was a net transfer of resources to foreign suppliers by the PEs or, where the cost was passed on, by consumers.

The government retains considerable power to determine the cost of imports by PEs, and its impact on the surplus. The most obvious weapon is the external exchange rate. By devaluing the currency a government can effect a sizeable transfer of the surplus from PEs to the public exchequer through accretions in earnings from import based taxes. This may come out of the surplus of PEs through a rise in costs or from middleman's profits or both. By way of illustration the combined influence of the devaluation of the Taka and price controls on yarn sharply reduced the profits of the nationalized textile industry after 1974/75, where imported raw cotton was an important part of its costs.[22]

Apart from its capacity to influence the external value of the currency the government can influence the import costs of a PE merely by its allocative decisions in external resource programming. Decisions to allocate cash foreign exchange or multilateral commodity credits, in contrast to bilateral tied aid or barter, can substantially influence the relative costs as between different sectors and over time. Paradoxically in Bangladesh PEs are frequently discriminated against by being obliged to use harder sources of aid whilst leaving the free foreign exchange to the private sector.[23]

THE AGRICULTURAL SECTOR

Here again government policy – towards the external value of the currency, domestic procurement prices and pricing policy for the supply of inputs to the farm sector – has a big influence on the surplus of PEs. A look at Table 6.4 shows that in such raw material-intensive sectors as jute, fish products and tanneries both government policy and natural factors are important determinants of the terms of trade between the PE sector and the farm sector.

The Pakistan experience is quite instructive as to the implication of exchange rate policy. In the pre-liberation period the jute industry in East Pakistan, now Bangladesh, was dominated by the West Wing capitalists who were a part of the ruling elite. This class could ensure a policy which consistently overvalued the rupee, which subsidised the jute industry, moving the terms of trade against the Bengali jute growers.[24] Whilst the post-liberation period saw the elimination of the West Pakistan capitalist through nationalisation, a popular government with a big constituency of farmers could not discriminate against the jute growers by manipulating the terms of trade in favour of the jute industry. As a result the cost of jute rose from 42 per cent of production cost to 50 per cent between 1969/70 and 1973/74 and even further in subsequent periods, when raw jute prices rose from Tk. 55 per maund in 1973/74 to Tk. 159 in 1977/78 due to increases in the domestic market price of jute.[25] As a result in 1977/78 when the volume of production came close to an all-time record the jute industry made an all-time record loss of Tk. 605 million which is 17 per cent of its sales.[26] This operating loss in the jute industry has grown progressively since 1972/73 and has converted over-all profits for the nationalised sector into operating losses in all years except 1973/74.[27]

The changing balance of power within the Bangladesh polity was not without relevance to the fate of jute growers in the most recent period. During 1979/80 the Bangladesh Jute Mills Corporation recorded an operating profit of Tk. 1,167 million[28] for the first time in the post-liberation period. This owed less to any spectacular improvement in operating performance, though output levels were the second highest in the post-liberation years, than to a move in the terms of trade against the jute growers. A collapse in the price of raw jute paid to the growers from an average of Tk. 134.6 per maund in 1978/79 to around Tk. 50 in the 1979/80 harvesting season, resulted from a drastic change in the market regime for jute growers following the gradual privatisation of domestic trade in raw jute. The nationalised jute industry became the beneficiaries of this price fall. But the main gains were reaped by the private traders who were buying jute from the growers at the current market price of Tk. 50 per maund and selling it to the jute mills at the statutory minimum price of Tk. 120. The minimum price had been designed to provide price support for jute growers but yielded windfall profits to the trade. The traders also managed to benefit from a large dose of bank credit from the nationalised banks extended under the same policy of providing price support to the growers. Since the trading community is an important support base for the regime, the growers were driven to the wall and the much bigger gains which might have accrued to the jute industry were reaped by the traders.

The experience of the jute sector has been repeated in a variety of other industries in Bangladesh. The basic conflict between growers and public enterprise in all these cases is not always dependent on the interplay of market forces. Market imperfections tend to influence procurement price for a variety of raw materials such as sugarcane, tobacco, fish, hides and skins. Here the sectional power of the respective beneficiaries of these procurements have acted to influence public policy to move the terms of trade in their favour. Their capacity to do so depends on their power and the sources of support for the regime. In a number of cases a regime which seeks to help growers against PEs on grounds of equity ends up by helping rich farmers or middlemen at the expense of public enterprise. The experience of the nationalised sugar industry in Bangladesh is a good illustration of this tendency.[29]

The conflict between growers and farmers manifests itself over the question of pricing policy for the products of public enterprise. A review of the Bangladesh experience shows that public enterprise has on occasion been used as an instrument to subsidise the farm sector. Prices paid to PEs for such inputs as fertiliser are well below world prices.[30] The implicit subsidy to growers represents a transfer of surplus from PEs to farmers. In the case of Bangladesh there is also a budgetary subsidy involved in addition to the underpricing of procurement by the state fertiliser distributing agency from the Chemical Corporation. Here again the assumption is that 'farmers' are being helped by the PEs. But in practice studies show that big farmers are the main consumers of fertiliser, whilst this class, along with the local intermediaries sell supplies of the fertiliser procured at sub-market prices on the black market to poorer farmers and appropriate the scarcity premium.[31] As with sugar there is some indication that the PEs' loss is the inter-mediaries' gain.

THE MIDDLEMEN

In Bangladesh, the presence of a trading bourgeoisie which retains its dominance in the domestic trading sector has important implications for the distributive regime of PEs. The data presented in Table 6.6 attempts to provide some measure of the surpluses appropriated by trading intermediaries through the marketing of goods produced by PEs. These figures based on studies of the PE market in Bangladesh show mark-ups on the products of the PE's sold at the retail level, ranging from 80–400 per cent over ex-factory prices. The differential between the ex-factory price and the retail price measures the scarcity premium on PE products which is seen as the concealed surplus appropriated by intermediaries trading in PE products.

TABLE 6.6   Scarcity premiums on selected commodities produced by public enterprises in Bangladesh, 1974/75.

	Per cent
Hydrogenated vegetable oil	88
Toilet soap	121
Sugar	100–150
Cement	300–400
Tyres and tubes	100
Television sets	200–300
Longcloth	62

Source: Sobhan and Ahmed, op. cit., Table 21.2

The notion of a concealed surplus in the product value of PE assumes that there is in fact a scarcity premium to be earned by marketing its product.[32] A mark-up between retail price and ex-factory price may simply reflect the normal costs of distribution. The concept of surplus used here thus relates to the notion that the price realised by PEs is in fact less than might be obtained in the open market. This situation arises in a regime of price and distribution controls. Price controls set the ex-factory price below its scarcity price. This needs to be compounded by distribution controls which limit the number of distributors entitled to market public goods. Where these price controls operate at the ex-factory level, the premium is legally realised by the wholesaler. Where price controls are fixed on the retail price the premium may be appropriated by any or all of a class of wholesalers, retailers and privileged consumers who operate in the black market. Normally the blackmarket at the retail and consumer level operates when goods go direct to retail outlets. When this is reinforced by a system of sale by ration-cards or permits where designated consumers are entitled to obtain goods at controlled prices, then individual card holders may sell their quota or entitlement for its scarcity value. At the same time the designated retailers may divert supplies to the blackmarket by the expedient of listing phantom ration-card-holders on their books. This phenomenon has been a perennial factor affecting the distributive regime in Bangladesh through the operation of a rationing system for selected wage goods for some if not all segments of the population. At the retail level, however, the surplus tends to be much more broadly distributed between the many retail outlets and a much larger number of beneficiaries. For instance in 1975 there were over 4.5 million ration-card-holders in six statutory rationing areas.

The substantial premiums are to be earned at the wholesale level where a much smaller number of selected beneficiaries are given distributional franchises for a product in short supply relative to its controlled price. Here a policy of price controls represented a policy of transferring the surplus from PEs to private distributors.

In Bangladesh private distributors have and continue to dominate the marketing of PE products, at least in the manufacturing sector. Obviously such services as power, oil and gas, transport, banking and insurance are directly sold to the consumer. However, where demand for utility services exceed supply at the regulated tariff – an endemic phenomenen in Bangladesh – it has become common practice to pay part of the scarcity premium to some elements in the decision-making process. Payments for anything from scarce wagon space to a first-class sleeping berth are made to station-masters and booking clerks since public sector transport services have invariably been underpriced. Long waiting lists for telephone and electricity connections also follow from the policy of sub-market pricing. It is again common to pay the premium as bribes to anyone from the minister concerned down to the linesman giving the service connection. Similarly in the finance sector the standard practice of underpricing capital cost and service remains a continuing feature of policy within the state-owned and regulated banking and insurance sectors. Both access and bribery are not uncommon prerequisites to expedite processing of loans or obtaining prompt settlement of insurance claims.

In all these sectors the ubiquitous middleman traffics in access to the decision-makers. For a small cut he can obtain a phone connection, power line, a sizeable O/D or, if nothing else, at least entrée into the minister's or secretary's office. In the manufacturing sector, however, the intermediary comes into his own because here he can in principle lay claim to the entire scarcity premium in his role as the designated monopoly distributor.

In Table 6.7 we present fairly comprehensive data on the pricing regime of PEs in Bangladesh although it remains limited to the year 1973/74. The market regime is fairly diversified in the case of the manufacturing sector. Given the wide coverage of public enterprise in manufacturing, PEs are distributed in the consumer, intermediate and capital goods sector. Whatever the market regime, virtually the entire PE sector operated in a scarcity market of varying degrees of intensity. This provided considerable scope for both surplus generation by PEs and pressure to re-appropriate this to contending social groups.

The data in Table 6.7 shows that a system of administered prices applied to products constituting 52 per cent of production value in the manufacturing sector. If one excludes jute which sold only in the export market, then 75.5 per cent of production value of domestically marketed goods was contributed by 17 PE industrial products. Only two, trucks and buses and writing paper, set prices at a level where there was little scope to realise a scarcity premium. For the rest we have given some indication of the dimensions of the premium in Table 6.6. In the case of 11 of these products distribution was undertaken by private dealers who appropriated the scarcity premium derived from the difference between the controlled ex-factory price and the market price. In the case of two products, namely bicycles and motor cycles, a system of permits either subsidised the consumer or permitted the consumer to extract the scarcity premium through sale of the permit. Public distribution was attempted for fertiliser, part of cloth and yarn output and sugar.

In the case of fertiliser, distribution at the retail level was in private hands and gave considerable scope for the surplus to be vested in the hands of dealers and big farmers as consumers who also ran their own blackmarket. Since the retail price was subsidised and the ex-factory price was itself less than half the world price, the implicit reallocation of the surplus was appreciable. In the case of sugar, distribution and price were controlled with the benefit accruing to ration-card-holders in five urban centres and to sweet manufacturers. In the case of cement a large part of the output was sold to government agencies but private sales were handled through dealers who made sizeable profits through appropriating the premium.

In the case of cotton yarn, which accounted for about a quarter of the PE sales in the domestic market, distribution was done by a public corporation and by weavers' co-operatives. This system, however, not only led to distributional inefficiencies leading to large inventory build-ups in the mills but considerable surplus appropriation was carried out by middlemen who infiltrated the co-operatives in order to obtain control of yarn supplies. The induction of private dealers as of 1975 into

TABLE 6.7   Price controlled commodities in the public sector 1973–4 (*in million Taka*)

	Producer Corporation	Production value	Sales value	Price fixing agency	Marketing agency	Scope for Surplus extraction
1. Fertiliser	BFCPC	240.0	220.0	Cabinet	BADC	Yes
2. Soap	,,	71.5	70.7	Min. of Com.	Dealers/CSC	Yes
3. Pharmaceuticals	,,	12.7	12.7	Min. of Health	Dealers	Yes
4. Motor cycle	BESC	9.3	3.6	Min. of Com.	DC's permit	Yes
5. Bicycles	,,	3.7	3.6	,,	,,	Yes
6. Tube lights	,,	3.5	2.4	,,	Dealers	Yes
7. Ceiling fans	,,	7.4	7.4	,,	,,	Yes
8. Trucks & buses	,,	166.3	166.3	,,	Direct	Very little
9. Radio/TV/fridge	,,	12.0	12.0	,,	Dealers	Yes
10. Cloth	BTIC		342.7	,,	DC/CSC	Yes
11. Yarn	,,	1319.7	908.8		COOPS/BSIC	Yes
12. Sugar	BS_gMC	404.0	245.2	Cabinet	Min. of Food	Yes

13. Cement	BMOGC/BMEDC	26.9	26.9	Min. of Com.	TCB	Yes
14. Newsprint	BPBC	49.5	28.1	Cabinet	Corpn	Yes
15. Paper	,,	98.9	73.9	Min. of Com.	Dealers	Very little
16. Edible oil	BFAIC	164.6	164.6	Min. of Food	Dealers	Yes
17. Flour products		75.3	75.3	,,	,,	Yes
18. Petroleum products	BMOGC/ Petro–Bangla	208.5	205.0	,, Natural Resources	,,	Selected products.
19. Total		2873.8	2569.3			
20. Total for public sector		5563.4	5164.2			
21. (19) as % of (20)		51.6	49.8			
22. Total excluding Jute		3806.5	3597.5			
23. (19) as % of (22)		75.5	71.4			
24. Mass consumption Items (1+2+3+10+11 +12+16+17)		2287.8	2040.0			
25. (24) as % of (22)		60.1	56.7			

Source: Sobhan and Ahmad, op. cit., Table 21.1, p. 474.

the yarn distribution system slightly improved efficiency but did little to limit surplus extraction by this class now operating under cover of official policy.

The pricing and distribution policy relating to PEs in Bangladesh reflects the influence of the trading bourgeoisie within the system. They use their access to policy-makers to impose a pricing policy which in effect transfers a sizeable part of the surplus generated by public enterprise to the hands of selected members of the bouregoisie. This transfer of the surplus from the control of public enterprise to the hands of big farmers and elements of the trading bourgeoisie not only reduces the earning capacity of public enterprise but also the revenues of the government. Revenue shortfalls compel the government to resort to deficit financing and raise its dependency on external resource inflows. The deficit financing generated inflationary pressures which eroded the political standing of the regime between 1972–5, whilst growing external dependency made the regime vulnerable to pressure from aid donors. The sectional interests of some elements of the ruling elite thus served to undermine the political position of the regime as a whole. The incapacity to resolve this contradiction, through an assault on the trading bourgeoisie and/or the re-capturing of the surplus through appropriate pricing policy, was paid for in the progressive weakening of the public enterprise sector. This trend in turn was used to criticise the nationalisation policy itself and to undermine the ideological premise of the policy. The incapacity to pass on the benefits of price controls to the poor, by at least protecting them from inflationary pressure, not only eroded the popular support base of the regime but contributed to the declining public image of the nationalised sector. This followed because the high retail price for PE products was paid by the general public but the scarcity premium was appropriated by the middleman rather than the PEs.[34]

THE SHARE OF THE EMPLOYEES

The surrender of the surplus to material suppliers or middlemen is frequently paid for by the employees of public enterprise, both labour and management. We do not have the data to distinguish between these two categories. However, in Table 6.8 we present data for the share of employees compensation in relation to value added and production value. This data cannot take into account the concealed transfer of surplus to the middlemen. The figures show that after an initial upsurge in the share of the employees in terms of both value added and product

TABLE 6.8 Trends in the level and share of manufacturing PE and employees compensation

	1969/70	1972/73	1973/74	1974/75	1975/76
Trends in real wages[1]		100	100.9	96	
% share of employees compensation of value added by PE[2]	28.1	37.8	32.5	34.2	34.5
% share of employees compensation of production value of PE[3]	13.2	16.8	16.8	12.7	10.9

Sources: (1) Sobhan and Ahmed, op. cit.; (2) & (3) Computed from Tables 5.30, 5.36, 5.37 in *1979 Statistical Year Book of Bangladesh*, Bangladesh Bureau of Statistics, Dacca.

value as between 1969/70 and 1972/73, which may reflect the impact of nationalisation, in the post-nationalisation phase the employees were hard put to maintain their share of value added and indeed faced a clear decline, in relation to product value, against other social groups. The failure to compensate for increases in material costs through higher prices meant that at the other end the middlemen extracted the premium at the expense of the employees.

It would appear (from Table 6.8) that real wages declined in the post-nationalisation phase. Thus for all their militancy and initial political strength, the workers in public enterprise in Bangladesh failed to protect their living standards or to prevent an appropriation of the PE surplus by the trading bourgeoisie. It would thus appear that the extension of public enterprise does not always lead to an improvement in the conditions of the working class. All that one may conclude is that under private ownership their circumstances tended to be worse both absolutely and in a relative sense, as private owners ensured that they appropriated the lions share of the surplus.

THE SHARE OF THE GOVERNMENT

It has become apparent that the government as a whole remains an important claimant on the surplus of public enterprise. It claims its share through indirect taxes levied on the material inputs being consumed by public enterprise, through direct taxes on its post tax profits and through its claim on dividends against its equity holdings in public enterprise. Further claims on the revenues of public enterprise may be made through the pricing of intermediate inputs consumed by public enterprise. This includes capital supplied by publicly owned banks. Here monetary policy operating through the cost and supply of capital becomes an instrument to reallocate the surplus between different components of the public enterprise system. To conclude that contributions to the exchequer from public enterprise are inadequate by reference to estimates of their payment of direct taxes and dividends can thus be highly misleading since the government has a variety of intermediate pricing, fiscal and monetary policy options within its control, to realise its share from the PEs. These instruments may be used at the direct expense of the surplus generated by public enterprise.

A further way in which the government appropriate the surplus is through procurement and pricing policy. The government both as a distributor and consumer may choose to underprice its procurements from public enterprise. This was the case in Bangladesh for offtake of fertiliser, sugar, edible oil, kerosene and cloth which were all marketed in all or part by state distribution agencies. Similarly the government of Bangladesh as consumer of capital and intermediate goods from public enterprises producing engineering goods, steel, cement and other such items used its monopsony power to obtain products at sub-market prices. To the extent that government is a direct consumer, the implicit transfer of the surplus from one agency to another may merely involve an allocative decision within the government. However, where the government as distributor passes on the surplus from public enterprise to private retailers or privileged consumers from the elite groups, then the public distribution system ends up by penalising itself.

We do not have much data on the distributive biases of the Bangladesh government's own allocative policies. The data presented in Table 6.4 brings out some of the distortions introduced by government fiscal policy. Thus for instance the government realises 34.5 per cent of the production value from the tobacco industry through indirect taxes which appears to have contributed to a deficit of 6.8 per cent in the sector. Similarly in the case of the paper and board industry the government realised 18.5 per cent in taxes and 9.5 per cent in interest, whilst the sector went on to incur a deficit of 14.9 per cent. Of all the industries, the leather industry appears to be the only one with a genuine incapacity to cover its material and labour costs. In all other industries the government, either as banker or treasury, appropriated its share of the surplus. It is, however, significant that whilst the government appears to have been fairly successful in extracting its share of surplus from public enterprise, it has been relatively unsuccessful in recovering any part of the scarcity premium earned by traders benefiting from its pricing or procurement policy, through the tax mechanism.

THE SHARE RETAINED BY PUBLIC ENTERPRISE

It would appear from our framework of analysis that the part of the surplus actually left with public enterprise in Bangladesh is very much a residual item. Foreign suppliers, farmers, government, bankers, middlemen, consumers and workers are all accommodated within the distributive mechanism, with the share of each depending on their position to influence the market or exercise power on the government. Public enterprise seems the one agency in the mechanism which has neither autonomy to decide on what its share should be nor power to realise its interest.

Table 6.4 has shown that in only 8 out of 18 industries did the size of the surplus retained by public enterprise exceed 10 per cent of production value. In some of these industries such as paper and board, steel and fertiliser, the retained surplus within the enterprise was largely made up from its depreciation fund. Even in jute, which incurred a deficit of 6.8 per cent, the depreciation fund compensated for this so that there was no direct constraint on the cash flow of the sector in relation to its current operations.

THE NATURE OF THE DISTRIBUTIVE REGIME IN BANGLADESH

Our review of the allocative regime of public enterprise in Bangladesh suggests that there is no policy perspective within which public enterprise is used as an instrument of distribution. Public enterprise remains a resource within the control of the government but the social purpose for which this resource is used continues to be permeated with confusion and conflict within the ranks of the policy-makers.

Confusion in particular appears to prevail over the actual mechanism of surplus distribution. Ideally a government would gain from maximising the surplus contributed by public enterprise and collecting this at a single point as a profit or dividend. This could be realised through the elimination of indirect taxes and price controls on public enterprise. The consequential increment in public revenues could then be allocated by the government through the budget on the basis of the social priorities established by the regime. The opportunity cost of these allocative decisions as between consumption and investment, between subsidising different consumers and taxing others and between competing sectors could also be determined within a common policy framework. Public enterprise would then be limited to concentrating on improving its productive efficiency, and its financial performance would largely come to depend on its own managerial skills rather than on the shifting sands of public policy and private interest seeking to eat into its surpluses. In this situation all the conflicting interests within the administration would seek to assert their claims at a common point within the allocative system, namely the annual budget, which would become the focal point for both power play and conflict resolution.

Distributive policy relating to PEs in Bangladesh has hardly extended beyond the expedient of accommodating contending claims on the surplus through a series of *ad hoc* decisions taken in the specific context of the claims. It is easier to take a decision on subsidising fertiliser consumers, as opposed to raising the revenues of a public enterprise, rather than to expose the relative interests of fertiliser consumers to comparison with claims on the budget for setting up rural health centres. The policy of robbing Peter to pay Paul is thus elevated to the level of a national policy without ever having to evaluate the relative merits of their perspective claims.

In any given situation it would appear that the strongly organised interest groups appear best positioned to stake their claims on the surplus as long as they do not have to expose their claim to any sort of collective scrutiny by society or its representatives. To the extent that these interest groups can be aggregated into collective social interests, the class of rich farmers, trading bourgeoisie or industrial bourgeoisie, appear as net gainers from the system. However, within these classes there are intra-class conflicts, which lead to shifting coalitions of interests emerging over any given question of distributive policy. Even within these sub-classes some individuals or factions, by virtue of their access to the decision-makers, are likely to be more successful in asserting their respective claims over others who are less privileged. Power and influence, however, emerge as the common arbiters of the distributive regime under public enterprise in a bourgeois regime.

CONCLUSIONS

Our review of the Bangladesh experience with public enterprise does not indicate that public enterprise has been conspicuously successful as a distributive instrument. Whilst the chapter focussed on the 1972–5 period, a review of current trends warrants scant modification to this conclusion. A review of the PE record in Bangladesh points to some distributive achievements. These may include an element of regional dispersal of investment in backward areas.[34] It has to a limited extent benefited some elements of the working class. It has to some extent increased the earnings of the farm sector. It has contributed to the revenues of the government indirectly rather than by design of policy. Though such contributions have in many cases been made directly at the cost of the growth potential of public enterprise or the interests of its employees, these revenues have not always been used by the government for redistributive programmes. The investment strategy of public enterprise has not made any significant direct contributions to employment or the meeting of basic needs of the poor. The particular choice of sectors to be included under public enterprise have tended to be both aid- and capital-intensive and have concentrated on the provision of capital and intermediate goods. These investments have however had important secondary impact on both employment and the meeting of basic needs which has contributed both to growth and improvement in the conditions of life.

Public enterprise as an instrument designed to reduce the role of the private sector has again met with mixed results in Bangladesh. To some extent the growth of public enterprise was directly realised at the expense of a particular segment of the bourgeoisie. However, this anti-bourgeois bias proved to be short lived. The current configuration of power in Bangladesh has quite explicitly served to direct policy toward building up a capitalist class from within the ranks of the bourgeoisie. Given the low level of entrepreneurial skills and the reluctance of the local bourgeoisie directly to invest their surplus in industry, the public sector will have to play a critical role of entrepreneurial support to build up a viable capitalist class. Since the distributive regime of controls favoured for public enterprise had directly encouraged the growth of a trading bourgeoisie at the expense of public enterprise, this class is now staking its claim to state support to set up industries. To serve this policy it became necessary to discredit policies and positions relating to public enterprise in order to legitimise the growth aspirations of the bourgeoisie which have to be realised at the expense of public enterprise.

The Bangladesh experience thus appears to confirm the view that the nature of the state is a critical factor in determining the growth of public enterprise, the interests it will serve and its distributive regime. To the extent that policy-makers seek to use public enterprise as a genuine weapon of class war in the service of the poor it would appear to depend on a transformation in the configuration of power within the state. If such a configuration is realised, public enterprise could be much more effectively deployed as an instrument to redistribute both resources and power within Bangladesh.

NOTES AND REFERENCES

1. R. Sobhan, 'Public Enterprises and the nature of the State', *Development and Change* (January 1979).
2. R. Sobhan and M. Ahmed, *Public Enterprise in an intermediate regime: A study in the political economy of Bangladesh* (Dacca: Bangladesh Institute of Development Studies, June 1980).
3. Ibid.
4. Ibid., defined public enterprise as distinct from the public sector to involve the following criteria for inclusion: (a) government ownership, (b) government control, (c) decision-making unit identifiability, (d) marketed product.
5. The term 'surplus' is used to indicate the value created over and above the material and labour costs of the product and is not used in its Marxist sense. Where it is used as a quantitative measure the concept is more specifically defined.
6. Sobhan and Ahmed, op. cit., for a fuller discussion of the nature of state power in Pakistan and Bangladesh.
7. For a fuller articulation of this process, see H. Papanek, 'Entrepreneurs in East Pakistan', South Asia Series, Research Paper No. 16 (Michigan State University, Asian Research Center, 1969).
8. Sobhan and Ahmed, op. cit.
9. Ibid. for a discussion of the circumstances, nature and consequence of these attempts.
10. These figures have been computed from data presented in the *Draft Second Five Year Plan 1980–85*, Planning Commission, Govt. of Bangladesh (Dacca, May 1980).
11. Ibid.
12. Op. cit., Sobhan and Ahmed.
13. *Bangladesh: Current Economic Position and Short-term Outlook*, World Bank, March 1980.
14. The term 'surplus' has been used in various contexts ranging from the Marxist conception of surplus to estimates of enterprise profitability computed by accountants. Without entering into a discussion of the merits of these conceptions in this paper, the term 'surplus' is used in a limited functional sense which takes into account the actual availability of accounting data which can be used for estimating the PE surplus.
15. Sobhan and Ahmed, op. cit.
16. Ibid. for 1973–4 and *Bangladesh: Issues and Prospects for Industrial Development*, World Bank (December 1978).
18. Ibid. for all estimates of capital formation.

19. Op. cit., *Bangladesh: Prospects for Industrial Development*.
20. Op. cit., Sobhan and Ahmed for a discussion of the impact of import price-rises in the manufacturing sector.
21. Ibid.
22. Derived from data on profitability, op. cit., World Bank report, 1980.
23. Op. cit., Sobhan and Ahmed.
24. The political economy of this phenomenon has been discussed by Richard Nations in 'The Economic Structure of Pakistan and Bangladesh', in R. Blackburn (ed.), *Explosion in the Subcontinent* (Penguin, 1975); and by A. R. Khan, *The Economy of Bangladesh* (Macmillan, 1972).
25. Estimate for cost structure in jute industry for 1969/70 derived from a study by Q. K. Ahmad, 'The Jute manufacturing industry of Bangladesh, 1947–74', unpublished Ph.D. dissertation (LSE, 1976); figures for 1973/74 derived from Sobhan and Ahmed; for latest trend in jute prices from World Bank report, 1980.
26. Ibid. World Bank report.
27. Sobhan and Ahmed, op. cit.
28. Discussion on this section is based on data derived from Budget documents for the 1980/81 financial year, published by Ministry of Finance, Government of Bangladesh; World Bank report 1980, for a discussion of the change in the market regime for jute growers in 1979/80.
29. Sobhan and Ahmed, op.cit.
30. Ibid.
31. Ibid.
32. Ibid. for a full discussion of the concept of scarcity premium in the context of Bangladesh pricing policy for PEs.
33. Ibid. for a discussion of the political economy of pricing policy in Bangladesh.
34. Ibid.

7 Casual Labour in Peruvian Agrarian Co-operatives*

JOSE MARIA CABALLERO

I INTRODUCTION

In this chapter I present a simplified model of the behaviour of the agrarian co-operatives of Coastal Peru. The model is particularly oriented – and thus restricted – to explain the relationship between the member and non-member work forces, and to illuminate the reasons why co-ops tend to make a wide use of casual non-member workers.

A possible approach to analyse the demand for casual labour would consist of focusing attention on seasonality. Casual labour hiring would thus be rigidly determined by the technical labour requirements of the various crops throughout the year together with the internal (i.e. the co-op's own) availability of labour, for any given technology. There can be no doubt as to the merit of this approach[1] for seasonality certainly explains many aspects of casual labour employment. Nevertheless it has two shortcomings. First, it does not help to understand why most co-ops, including those with an excess member work force, systematically employ casual workers throughout the year over and above seasonal requirements. Second, it disregards the fact that the attitudes of members towards work and income, as well as the cost of hiring external labour, significantly determine the demand for casual workers.

Instead of following the seasonality-technical requirements approach I shall set up here a model of co-op behaviour where the equilibrium of the firm is linked to the maximisation of members' welfare, the employment of casual labour being an integral part of the maximisation

---

* This is a revised version of a paper appeared in Spanish in *Economia*, vol. 1, No. 2 (Lima, August, 1978).

process. It will be seen that: (1) notwithstanding the subjective nature of co-op equilibrium (members' welfare maximisation), the *total* amount of labour input in the co-op depends on objective variables – the marginal productivity of labour and the cost of employing additional workers; and (2) members' capacity to decide how much to work allows them to distribute that total amount of labour between casual workers and themselves according to their subjective income-leisure preferences.

While emphasising the peculiarities of co-ops as labour demanders, my model does not incorporate technological and seasonality factors, which is of course a serious limitation. A more comprehensive analysis would require a combination of both approaches.

To build the model I shall use the tools of conventional microeconomic analysis, particularly the scheme of time allocation according to income-leisure preferences. This neoclassical tool is misleading when applied to the proletarian in the capitalist economy, since selling his labour power is to the proletarian a matter of need, not of choice – his problem is not whether to work a bit more or a bit less but either to get a job (where he will work the customary working day) or to beg. Instead, in the co-op, as in the peasant farm with which co-ops have many aspects in common, members can in fact decide whether to put in more or less work, for they are self-employed. Their choice will depend on the evaluation of the additional income and sacrifice involved.[2] The income-leisure time allocation scheme is thus appropriate here.

II BACKGROUND

Co-operatives were formed as a result of the agrarian reform started by the military regime in 1969, which transferred some 35 per cent of the country's arable land to different types of worker-managed firms. Those in the Coast – a long desert strip on the Pacific side of the Andes interspaced by rich irrigated valleys which benefit from the small but tumultuous rivers flowing from the Highlands into the Pacific Ocean – inherited the most modern and technically developed estates producing export crops (sugar cane, cotton), feedgrains (maize, sorghum, soya beans), food-grains (rice) and various kinds of vegetables and fruits, all under irrigation. Former estates had a resident work-force but also employed casual workers in peak periods. Most resident workers plus some outsiders chosen by the Department of Agriculture became full members of the new co-ops. These are fully commercial enterprises belonging to the capitalist sub-sector of the Peruvian agrarian economy.

They vary considerably in size with an average of some 500 ha of farm land and 100 members. All land and other assets are collectively owned and farming is collective. The General Assembly, where all members have an equal right to vote, is the highest authority but it only meets once or a few times per year to discuss matters of general policy. Day-to-day affairs are conducted by a hired manager – jointly appointed by the Assembly and the Department of Agriculture, and responsible to both – and a Workers Council of five members elected by the Assembly. Decision-making is restricted by a set of regulations imposed by the Department of Agriculture and the close supervision of public officials.

One of the main difficulties in understanding Peruvian Coastal co-ops is that they have two different aspects. If on the one hand they certainly have a self-management element, on the other the numerous and cumbersome State controls with which they are burdened make them resemble public rather than private enterprises. Each of these elements implies contradictions of their own which moreover intertwine in a complex way.

The self-management element itself gives these firms an ambiguous and unstable character for the capital-labour contradiction is not settled in favour of one of these. The capitalist enterprise is of course contradictory in this respect too, but the capital-labour contradiction can there be settled in favour of capital which is able to take the labour process under its command and submit it to profit requirements. The authority of capital, based on its having bought the labour power of workers, and which is consistently applied in the labour process by the capitalist or his representatives (with their capacity to sack, fine, change posts, persuade, bribe, etc.), permits the contradiction to be solved and gives stability to the firm. Instead, in the co-operatives we are analysing, those means to discipline labour do not exist or if they do they could hardly be applied. Indeed, the requirements and pressures of capital are present here – to the extent that co-ops operate within the capitalist market and in a general capitalist environment – but they cannot be transformed into an effective capitalist organisation of the labour process (i.e. capitalist labour discipline) because capital lacks here the necessary leadership to make them effective – workers are called to impose upon themselves the discipline of capital, which they naturally resist. Their resistence renders the co-ops unstable, unleashing forces leading to their degeneration (in the sense of transforming them into capitalist firms) or their self-destruction. Sustained reliance on cheap casual labour is – we shall presently see – a form of degeneration. The tendency towards self-destruction expresses itself in the reduction of the working day, the decrease of labour intensity, the inability to take quick and efficient commercial and production decisions, the use of co-op's resources for the private benefit of members, outright corruption, and, in a considerable number of cases, a pressure in favour of parceling out the land.

However, these two tendencies are checked to a certain extent by the control exercised by the State. But State intervention has a double effect: if on the one hand it prevents the forces of degeneration and self-destruction from operating fully, on the other it reinforces and perpetuates in members' consciousness a feeling of alienation from the firm and therefore a tendency towards indiscipline. Members tend to consider themselves as proletarians working for *the* (as opposed to *their*) co-operative, and to look upon the State as finally responsible for its economic performance. This partly results from the fact that in the short run the wage they receive is regarded as independent of the effort they supply and of the general economic performance of the firm – members tend to regard the State as finally responsible for paying their wage through the loans of the State-owned agriculture bank. But if the State can control co-ops' major decisions, its ability to supervise the labour process, and hence to restrain indiscipline, has some limits. Department of Agriculture officials can prevent a co-op from parcelling out the land or from operating certain investment projects or can take definite action when profitability or the labour process are significantly and conspicuously impaired, but they can hardly check at what time labour gets started every morning or whether its quality or intensity are below normal standards. Hired managers may try to cope with indiscipline but they find it difficult since their position is weak as they can easily be dismissed. They normally prefer, therefore, to play along.

Within this framework, casual labour demand can be seen as a syndrome of the tendency of Coastal co-ops to degenerate into capitalist firms. If there were no limits to the substitution of casual workers for members' labour, a steady process of replacement would take place until only a few members would remain taking upon themselves the managerial and other well-paid tasks and sharing the surplus generated by contract workers. State control prevents this from happening. Although the State seems to be interested in maintaining the present rate of casual labour hiring as a way of countervailing the effects of members' indiscipline, it does not allow co-ops to dismiss members in order to replace them by contract workers and it normally forces co-ops to admit new members when old ones retire or leave. It is interesting to note that the labour indiscipline of members, particularly the reduction of the number and intensity of working hours and the reluctance to accept hard tasks, both calls for the employment of casual workers and is made possible by the existence of a large and cheap supply of them. Casual labour hiring acts as a stabiliser countervailing the tendency towards self-destruction, permitting a *modus operandi* characterised by the combination of a sub-optimally utilised member work force alongside a fully utilised less paid non-member work-force.

Such a complex setting clearly defies straightforward formal modelling. I shall therefore proceed in a roundabout way and consider two extreme cases: the 'pure co-op' case where there is no State intervention, where members can freely decide the amount of effort to put into the co-op, and where there is a clear relationship between effort and income; and the 'State-run co-op' where there is a fixed wage independent of the level of effort, and a certain minimum compulsion to work. The actual situation in Peruvian coastal co-ops is somewhere between these two limits, leaning more to one or the other according to the set of particular circumstances facing each co-op. But before we go into this let me present some evidence regarding the importance of casual labour hiring and discrimination between casual workers and members.

III EVIDENCE

Unfortunately, there are no statistics on casual labour employment. Partial data do however exist for different groups of co-ops and different years, from independent studies undertaken with various purposes and methodologies. This is far from satisfactory, but when the existing data are collected together they present a reasonable picture of the order of magnitude involved which suffice for the present purposes. The information is presented in Table 7.1.

Casual labour hiring varies considerably – from 55 per cent to 9 per cent of the total labour force used. Variations would certainly be bigger if single co-ops instead of valley aggregates had been used. It must be emphasised – although this is not shown in the Table – that there is a marked seasonal pattern.[3] The 23 per cent average, which seems reasonable according to my own experience, implies that, on average, the number of days worked by casual labourers is 30 per cent of that worked by members or, equivalently, that every member 'has a right' to some 82 casual work days per year.[4] These figures, however, under-estimate the effort put in by casual workers as compared with that

TABLE 7.1   Co-ops' use of casual labour in different coastal valleys

Valley	Number of co-ops	Period	Casual workers as %[a] of total labour force
Piura	6	75[c]	35
La Leche	2	72/3	30[d]
Chancay	10	72/3	19[d]
Zaña	3	72/3	27[d]
Jequetepeque	8	72/3	51
Sugar co-ops	8	72[c]	15
Santa-Lacramarca	8	74[c]	36
Huaura-Sayán	18	74[c]	27
Ica[b]			
Big (over 700 ha)	6	73/4	40
Med. (500–700 ha)	4	73/4	20
Small (under 500 ha)	8	73/4	10
Zona Agraria IV			
Big (over 1,000 ha)	23	76[c]	19
Med. (500–1,000 ha)	40	76[c]	17
Small (under 500 ha)	12	76[c]	9
Total	156[f]		23[e]

Sources: Piura: José Deniz, 'Reforma Agraria y Asalariados Rurales en las Cooperativas Algodoneras del Perú' (Tesis de Master Sociología Rural, Flacso-Universidad Católica, Lima, 1975); La Leche, Chancay and Zaña: C. Scott *et al*, 'Los Trabajadores Eventuales en la Agricultura Costeña', manuscript prepared for CENCIRA (Lima, 1974); Jequetepeque: J. M. Caballero and N. Flores, 'Problemas Post-Reforma Agraria en Algunas Zonas de Cajamarca y La Libertad', CEPES (Lima, 1976); Sugar Co-ops: S. Roca, *Las Cooperativas Azucareras del Perú*, ESAN (Lima, 1975); Santa-Lacramarca and Huaura Sayan: Ministerio de Alimentación, OSPAL, 'Materiales de Discusión sobre Desarrollo Rural Integral' (Lima, 1975); Ica: Ministerio de Agricultura, CENCIRA, 'Comercialización de Productos Agrícolas: Caso de la Central de Cooperativas Jose Carlos Mariátegui, Ica' (Lima, 1975); Zona Agraria IV: Ministerio de Alimentación, SINEA, 'Los Cultivos y el Trabajo en las Cooperativas Agrarias de Producción de la Zona IV', (Lima, 1977).

Notes:
(a) Man-days worked by casual workers as a percentage of man-days worked by members plus casual workers.
(b) Data for Ica and Zona Agraria IV are the only ones broken up by size.
(c) Refers to a point in time rather than an agricultural year.
(d) Weighted average of the co-ops considered in the valley; the number of cultivated ha has been used as weight.
(e) Weighted average of the percentages in the column; the number of co-ops included in each valley has been used as weight.
(f) Since the 18 co-ops in Huaura-Sayán also belong to the Zona Agraria IV they have been counted twice, but the surveys relate to different points in time.

supplied by members, for two reasons. First, casual labourers work more hours per day.[5] Second, they normally perform those hard tasks that members refuse to take (such as cleaning or opening ditches, picking cotton, cutting cane, or transplanting rice) or, when both perform the same tasks, they are forced to work more intensively.[6] That is, average man-daily effort is far larger among casual workers – the simple comparison of the number of days worked by each group is thus misleading.

Differences in the average direct wage received by each group are important albeit they vary considerably among co-ops. Since the wage paid to casual workers is market determined and does not therefore vary very much from one co-op to another, variations in average wage differences between the two groups depend mainly on the variations in the wage rates enjoyed by the members of the various co-ops. Thus, in rich co-operatives which can pay their members a high wage, the average wage difference between members and non-members is high. This was for instance the case in the sugar co-ops. In 1972 the direct money income received by the members of the eight larger sugar co-ops was, on average, four times that received by casual workers.[7] In Talambo – a large and rich rice co-operative – the average cost to the co-op in 1971–2 of a daily average agricultural task was 112.3 soles when performed by a member but only 49.5 soles when performed by a casual worker.[8] According to a survey of SINEA of the co-operatives of the Zona Agraria IV (valleys around Lima), the average monthly direct wage income in January 1976 of a blue-collar member was 3,723 soles, while that of a casual worker was 2,951 soles.[9] A situation which may be regarded as normal (modal) is that indicated in a survey undertaken by OSPAL in the Huaura-Sayán and Santa-Lacramarca valleys. The average direct wage of blue-collar members in six co-ops in Huaura-Sayán was 48 per cent above that of casual workers. A similar average for six co-ops in Santa-Lacramarca showed a 22 per cent difference.[10] In very poor co-operatives casual workers receive a wage similar to that of the worst paid members. This is for instance the case in some co-ops in the region of Ica. Scott *et al.* observe that in certain cases in peak periods co-ops have to pay to casual workers a wage slightly above that of the worst paid members, but they also notice that this is a very localised phenomenon and that it automatically sets in motion wage increase demands on the part of members.[11]

To the difference in direct wages between the two groups we must add others in indirect incomes. Casual workers do not enjoy any of the facilities and perquisites open to members, such as housing facilities, free education, medical care, free meals, personal loans, retirement benefits, etc. And, above all, they enjoy no stability on the job for they are normally employed for a short period of time and then dismissed (although they may be employed again and again for further short periods), in contrast to members who cannot (or can only with great difficulty) be dismissed and who have a right to be permanently employed (and paid) by the co-op.

IV THE MODEL

The main determinants of co-ops' demand for casual labour can be reduced to six: (1) pattern of crops; (2) man (i.e. membership size)-land ratio; (3) technology; (4) prices of inputs and products and institutional conditions affecting the transformation of effort into income (degree of administrative efficiency, tax and forced savings regulations, etc.); (5) income-leisure preferences of members; and (6) the wage rate per unit of effort (i.e. the effort wage) prevailing in the casual labour market. The land size of the co-op could, of course, be included as a variable, but I shall not consider it since rather than absolute numbers our interest here is the relative demand (i.e. in proportion to the effort supplied by members) of casual labour. I shall assume (1) to (4) to be constant and investigate the effects of determinants (5) and (6). The model consists of the following equations:

Utility function

(1) $$U = U(f, y)$$

It is assumed that the welfare of members, U, is determined by their personal income from the co-op, y, and the availability of free time ('leisure'), f, which is the reverse of the effort put in the co-operative. Free time must not necessarily be employed in 'leisure activities', it could be used in other income generating activities outside the co-op.

Effort is difficult to define. Vanek[12] considers three elements: quality, duration and intensity of work. I share the opinion that they are the relevant ones. To avoid circularity it is important to distinguish between intensity and duration, on the one hand, and productivity, on the other.[13] Intensity and duration determine the actual quantity of work performed, which I refer to here as effort. While differences in duration are self-evident, differences in intensity imply a certain 'porosity' in the labour process which permits a fixed labour time to be more or less rich in labour content according to the intensity of the labour performed.[14] Productivity, on the other hand, refers not to the absolute quantity of work but to the quantity of product resulting from a certain quantity of work, and depends on the technical conditions of the production process. I shall assume that, from the point of view of both members' welfare and income generation effects, duration and intensity substitute for one another in a specified way so that they can be merged into a single variable – effort. I shall further assume that, in welfare terms, differences in quality (i.e. different types of agricultural jobs) can always be reduced to differences in the quantity of effort.

U stands for the welfare of the 'representative member'. We could assume that members' utility functions (as well as their income earning opportunities outside the co-op) are all alike, in which case any member could be the representative member, or that there is a well organised decision-making mechanism, sufficient to produce collective agreements on the preferred income-free time combinations. We can imagine that members agree beforehand on the amount of effort to be supplied by each of them (which need not necessarily be the same), and the agreement is then compulsorily enforced by the Workers Council or the manager. In this case the representative member would be a member who for any possible equilibrium position would always choose to put in the co-op an amount of effort equal to the average of that supplied by all members. We further assume that net total income is distributed among members in proportion to the effort they put in the co-operative, and that the utility function of the representative member has all the desired differentiation and convexity properties.

Clearly, all these assumptions are designed to bypass the very thorny (but yet of great theoretical and practical importance in worker-managed firms) question of collective welfare and behaviour. The only excuse can be that we are interested here in the behaviour of members *vis-à-vis* casual workers, and it is justified therefore to abstract as much as possible from the problems arising from the relations among members.[15]

Income function

(II)
$$y = \frac{P_x X - F - w e_c N}{M}$$

The income received by the representative member results from dividing the net total income of the co-op, $P_x X - F - we_c N$, among the number of members, M. We assume that the co-op produces a single product, X, which is sold at a fixed price, P_x. There are certain fixed costs (payment of the land and other assets transferred by the reform, interests on and repayment of previous loans, the salary of the manager, etc.) represented by F. We abstract for simplicity from the cost of seeds, fertilizer, pesticides, etc., assuming that wage payments to casual workers, $we_c N$, are the only variable cost. N stands for the number of casual workers employed, e_c is the effort supplied by each casual worker, and w is the effort wage rate, i.e. the wage paid to casual workers per unit of effort. Since as employer the co-op has the capacity to discipline the casual work force, we assume that e_c is fixed.

Equation (II) could also be written in the following way:

(IIa) $$y = we_m + ph + p(1 - h)$$

where e_m is the effort supplied by the representative member; p is the profit share that would correspond to the representative member if members' received a wage income for their effort equivalent to that of casual workers, that is:

$$p = \frac{XP_x - F - Ew}{M}$$

E being the total amount of effort put in the co-op; and h the percentage of total effort supplied by members:

$$h = \frac{e_m M}{E}$$

In (IIa) the income of the representative member appears divided into three components: the equivalent wage income, we_m; the profit share corresponding to his own effort, $p\,h$; and the profit share corresponding to the effort supplied by casual workers, $p(1 - h)$, or the portion of the surplus extracted from casual workers that accrues to him. It is easy to verify that (II) and (IIa) are equivalent.

Production function

(III) $$X = X(E, A)$$

The production of X depends on the total amount of effort supplied to the co-op, E, and on the amount of land and other productive assets, which are assumed to be constant and are jointly represented by A. The production function is assumed to be continuous and differentiable, and to show first increasing and then decreasing returns with respect to E.

Effort components

(IV) $$E = e_m M + e_c N$$

Total effort is the sum of the effort supplied by members, $e_m M$, and by casual workers, $e_c N$. e_c is assumed constant and e_m variable.

Time distribution

(v) $$\bar{t} = e_m + f.$$

The time available to the representative member after taking into account all necessary rests is a fixed amount, $\bar{t}$ (say 13 hours daily), which can be freely distributed between supplying effort to the co-op and free time. According to our definition of effort, such distribution does not only refer to the number of hours worked for the co-op but also to their intensity.

(I) to (v) are the equations of the model. It must be noticed that they try to portray the 'pure co-op' case, where there is free decision-making of members, unimpaired by State intervention, and a clear relationship between effort and income. The main way in which the situation summarised by my model departs from the traditional idea of a production co-operative is in that non-members can be employed in any desired quantity, so that work is not solely restricted to members, although these are the only ones to share in profits.

Maximising (I) with respect to our decision variables, e_m, f and N, under restrictions (II) to (v), we obtain the following equilibrium rule:[16]

(VI) $$w = P_x X_E = \frac{U_f}{U_y}$$

This rule implies an important difference between the co-op with and the co-op without access to an external labour supply. In the latter case, income and effort levels are determined subjectively according to the income/free-time preferences of members by applying the rule $P_x X_E$

$= U_f/U_y$, i.e. by equating the marginal rate of substitution between free time and income to the value of the marginal product of effort. In contrast, in the first case, equilibrium is regulated by an objective condition: the market price that must be paid to engage casual workers' effort (together, of course, with technology and price conditions). Members' preferences, expressed in the form of the f–y indifference curves of the representative member, only determine here the part of the total equilibrium effort that will be supplied by the members themselves.

We may, thus, regard the determination of equilibrium in the case of casual-labour hiring co-operatives as a two-stage process. First, total effort is determined by applying the objective rule: value of the marginal product of effort = effort wage rate (as fixed by the casual-labour market).[17] Second, members decide how much of that effort they will supply themselves by applying the subjective rule: marginal rate of substitution between free time and income = value of the marginal product of effort.[18]

The model is graphically illustrated in Figure 7.1 where effort is

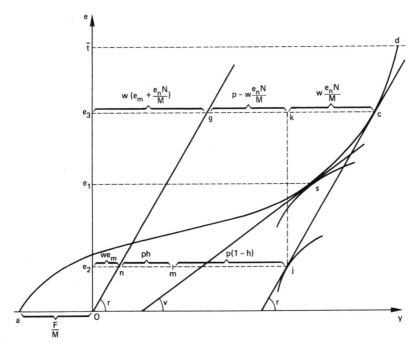

Figure 7.1   Equilibrium of the co-operative firm, with and without access to the casual labour market

measured vertically and income horizontally. Line $\bar{t}d$ indicates the maximum effort (say, per day) that the representative member could put into the co-op if he had no free time. Curve asd indicates the transformation of effort into income according to technical and price conditions; it starts to the left of O for we have assumed there are fixed costs, segment aO being equal to F/M. U and U' are two income/free-time indifference curves of the representative member.

Let us start by considering the situation where there is no casual labour market. Equilibrium would be reached at s where the representative member supplies Oe_1 effort in exchange for e_1s income. Let us assume now that the co-op is given the opportunity to employ any number of casual workers each supplying a fixed amount of effort and being paid a given effort wage rate equal to the cotangent of r. As a result, the income-effort combinations open to the co-op suddenly improve – the representative member can now choose any position along line jc which lies everywhere to the right of asd except at c where they touch. In equilibrium, the total amount of effort (measured per member) would be Oe_3, of which the representative member would supply Oe_2, the difference being covered by casual workers. The number of casual workers employed would be $N = (Oe_3 - Oe_2) M/e_c$. The gross income of the representative member would be e_3c, of which kc must be used to pay casual workers, remaining a net income e_3k ($= e_2j$). e_2n is what I called before the equivalent wage income, $w\,e_m$, while nj is the profit share, p, of the representative member. By choosing a point m on nj such that $nm/nj = e_m M/E = h$, we can break up nj into nm, which is the profit share corresponding to the effort put in by the representative member ($= ph$), and mj, which is his share in the profit generated by casual workers. e_2m is an 'earned income', while mj is a 'non-earned income' or the part of the surplus extracted from casual workers which is enjoyed by the representative member. Thus, we have been able to show on e_2j the three components of the representative member's income appearing in equation (IIa).

It is interesting to observe that Figure 7.1 implies that for effort wage rates above a certain limit, corresponding in the figure to the cotangent of v, members would hire themselves as casual workers rather than work as members. At the present moment this is a very exceptional case. But if the situation in the casual labour market become such that high wage rates persisted for a sufficiently long period of time, we might of course expect members to start abandoning the co-ops and hiring themselves out as casual workers.[19]

We turn now to the 'State-run co-op' case. As mentioned before, State intervention can be introduced into the model by assuming that members are paid a fixed wage which in the short run is independent of the level of effort and the economic performance of the co-op,[20] and that they are forced to supply some minimum amount of effort.

Let us then consider the effects of a fixed daily or weekly wage,[21] provisionally assuming that there is no casual labour hiring. The situation is summarized in.Figure 7.2. We start from the 'pure case' equilibrium position, s, where the representative member supplies Oe_0 effort and obtains e_0s income, and assume that he starts now being paid a fixed wage. If the wage is smaller that OW_0 it should have no effect: the equilibrium position would continue to be s where the level of satisfaction attained is equivalent to that derived from an income OW_0 without any attached effort. But it is unlikely that the fixed wage would be smaller than OW_0 (i.e. so small that receiving it without supplying any effort is not preferred to obtaining a larger income but with a considerable expenditure of effort), particularly since: (i) fixed wages in coastal co-ops are normally above subsistence income, and (ii) there are often other income-earning opportunities outside the co-op, so that the effort withdrawn from the co-op can be put into them. On the other hand, if the wage is bigger than OW_0, say OW_1, members will tend to stop supplying effort and move to a position such as i where they are on an indifference level U' higher than U. This 'zero effort drive' is, I believe, an underlying tendency in many Peruvian coastal co-ops.

The situation, of course, is untenable. The co-op in Figure 7.2 would be losing aW_1 per member.[22] With zero effort levels co-ops would in fact exist only as fictions, being simply an excuse for a transfer payment to members. The introduction of a fixed wage must therefore be accompanied by a certain compulsion to work. If losses are to be prevented, the compulsory effort must not be smaller than Oe_1 in Figure 7.3. How to enforce such a supply of effort on co-op members is a problem that obsesses Peruvian Department of Agriculture officials. From what has been said in Section II of this chapter, it is clear that they are in a bad position to ensure high effort levels. They can certainly force members to supply some minimum amount of effort and thus prevent the 'zero effort drive' from operating fully, but effort will normally be low, unable to guarantee profitability. Under the circumstances, the exploitation of casual labour is the best way to ensure profitability (or to reduce losses), and the State is therefore in favour of external workers being employed. The situation is illustrated in Figure 7.3 where line $W_1 W_1$ indicates the fixed wage and the compulsory effort level is Oe^*. Without casual labour hiring the co-op would be losing bq per member,

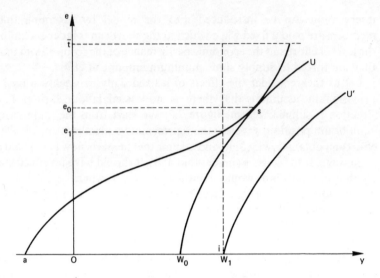

Figure 7.2   Effect of a fixed wage on the equilibrium position of the cooperative

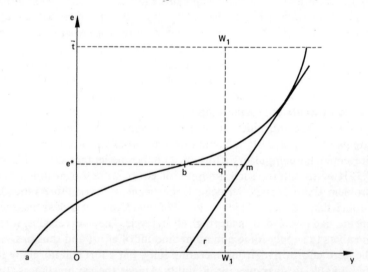

Figure 7.3   Effect of casual labour hiring on co-operative profitability

i.e. the difference between the wage received and the income generated
by the representative member. By employing external labour (at the
effort wage rate indicated by the cotangent of r) the loss is transformed
into a profit of qm per member.

V THE SUPPLY OF CASUAL LABOUR

Lack of data prevents a quantitative analysis of this fundamental question. I shall therefore limit myself to some general observations.

Some broad categories of casual workers can be established. The first one corresponds to the temporary migrant workers coming from the Highlands. There is a long tradition of this. Since the end of the last century until the late 1950s and early 1960s, a complex and well structured system of labour recruitment existed.[23] Before, labour requirements were satisfied by importing black slaves first and asiatic semi-slaves after. The system of casual recruitment, known as *enganche* (hooking), evolved in two directions: on the one hand, debt bondage quickly lost importance as the basic linking mechanism; on the other, the relative weight of casual workers coming from the coastal area itself increased. But Highland temporary migrants are still strong in numbers, although it is impossible to estimate the exact proportion. They tend to be semi-proletarianised peasants who need to complement the low self-employment incomes snatched from their small plots with a temporary wage in coastal valleys. They are often recruited by a middle man but they may also establish direct contacts with co-operatives and private farmers.

The other important group consists of coastal residents. Four categories can be distinguished here: (i) sons and relatives of co-op members who were not themselves absorbed as members; (ii) other landless agricultural workers residing in the coast who for whatever reasons were also not absorbed into the co-ops; (iii) coastal small owners who need to complement their incomes; and (iv) sons and relatives of coastal small owners or of the lower strata of urban workers in coastal provincial towns and villages. Workers in group (i) have more chances of being admitted as co-op members than any others. Indeed, they are sometimes accepted as permanent contract workers thus forming a third category between members and ordinary casual workers. Temporary migrants also exist within the coastal resident group, as is the case for instance, of the *golondrinos* (swallow migrants) from Piura in the north, who go as far down the coast as Ica and Nazca for the cotton harvest.

A large absolute number of workers seeking temporary employment in coastal agriculture together with seasonal factors and a high turnover rate,[24] jointly contribute to keep most casual labourers in a situation of underemployment. An average worker whose sole employment source is agricultural casual labour will probably be employed no more than six or seven months per year, although this is a personal guess which needs verifying. The pool of casual workers, all groups considered, is a much larger figure than the number of workers that could hypothetically be permanently absorbed by coastal co-ops and private farms under *ceteris paribus* assumptions.

VI   MACRORATIONALITY OF THE SYSTEM

There can be no doubt that the extensive use of casual labour by coastal co-ops entails the exploitation of casual workers by co-op members, who not only keep for themselves the surplus generated by the former but also impose comparatively harsh labour conditions and deprive them of any stability on the job.[25] And yet, when the system is considered as a whole, it becomes clear that it is advantageous from the point of view of the redistribution of income and employment opportunities. The structural characteristics of the co-ops that push members to withdraw effort, correspondingly open employment and hence income opportunities to casual workers that would not be available if the co-ops made full use of the member labour force.

Four things are redistributed: (i) the work withdrawn by members and performed by casual workers; (ii) the income thus forgone by members; (iii) the income forgone by the co-operative because of the reduction of internal collective savings; and (iv) the income forgone by the State because of the reduction of the profit tax base.

VII   CONCLUSION

In the early years of the agrarian reform it was thought that production co-operatives would be the best solution to the problem of how to reorganise Peruvian agriculture for, among other things (such as technically efficient size), they were considered to be very flexible in the use of their labour force and capable of inducing a big stimulus to work. Thus, for instance, it was expected that member labour surplus in slack periods could be mobilised without additional labour costs to operate long run maturing labour-intensive projects, whereas in peak periods high motivation and solidarity would ensure special dedication on the part of members and their families.

These predictions were not fulfilled. For sociological reasons that cannot be dealt with in this paper, partly having to do with the irresolution of the capital-labour contradiction in worker-managed co-ops, partly with the uneasy relations among members and partly with State intervention, co-op members have in fact shown very little work motivation. From the economic point of view, this could be traced to a lack of connection between personal effort and income. To the extent that members do not see a clear link between the two, they tend to withdraw their effort – what I called the zero effort drive – thus pushing the co-ops towards their self-destruction. State intervention and access to cheap casual labour prevents this – the former ensures that members will supply a certain amount of effort while the latter ensures that any necessary additional effort can be hired in the casual labour market. Apart from countervailing self-destruction forces and making co-ops more profitable (or less unprofitable), casual labour hiring has the effect of making the equilibrium total effort level independent of the income time subjective preferences of members (and the social factors on which they depend), since, as has been seen, in the external labour hiring co-op such preferences can only determine the distribution of effort (i.e. work) between members and non-members. This, of course, is important from the point of view of general economic efficiency. It entails that, at least theoretically, coastal co-ops satisfy the standard Pareto efficiency criterion of equating the marginal value product of labour to the ongoing market wage rate. Moreover, access to the casual labour market brings some positive redistribution consequences. It is indeed redistribution among the poor, but in the right direction – from better-off co-op members to worse-off casual workers. There is no denying that this system is exploitative in nature resting as it does on discrimination against casual workers, but yet, in its own perverse way, it fulfils certain socially useful functions.

NOTES

1. See C. Scott, "Agrarian Reform and Agricultural Labour Markets. Some Issues from Agriculture Production Co-operatives on the Northern Coast of Peru". School of Development Studies, University of East Anglia, Norwich, 1979, mimeo.
2. The sacrifice may consist of physical fatigue instead of rest – 'leisure' – or of the income forgone by not using that work time in other occupations such as cultivating a private plot.
3. Thus, for instance, in Fala, a rice co-op in Lambayeque, the relation between casual workers and members in 1973 was: January 2.0, February 1.7, March 1.0, April 0.5, May 1.1, June 0.7, July 0.4, August 0.1, September 0.4, October 1.5, November 1.2 and December 2.6. (See Centro de Estudios de la Participacion Popular, Monografía No. 33, Lima, 1974). This pattern is typical of rice growing co-ops.

4. Assuming 25 working days per month and one month holidays per year.
5. The normal working day for a casual worker is from 7am to 12am and from 1pm to 4pm, that is eight hours, whereas blue-collar members rarely work more than four or five hours per day.
6. L. Castro observes that in co-op La Viña (La Leche valley) a task that takes five hours for a casual worker would take two days for a member. (See Centro de Estudios de la Participación Popular, Monografía No. 41, Lima, 1974.) According to my personal experience, cotton harvesting in 1979 in all co-ops in the Huaura-Sayán valley was entirely done by casual workers – members refused to pick cotton. A similar situation has often been reported with respect to cane cutting.
7. See S. Roca, *Las Cooperativas Azucareras del Perú*, Table 7. ESAN (Lima, 1975).
8. See CENCIRA, 'Organización de la Cooperativa Agraria de Producción Talambo', unpublished manuscript (1975).
9. See Ministerio de Agricultura y Alimentacion, SINEA, 'Los Cultivos y el Trabajo en las Cooperativas Agrarias de Producción en la Zona IV' (Lima, 1977).
10. See Ministerio de Alimentación, OSPAL, 'Materiales de Discusión sobre Desarrollo Rural Integral' (Lima, 1975).
11. C. Scott, M. Manrique *et al*, 'Los Trabajadores Eventuales en la Agricultura Costeña', manuscript prepared for CENCIRA (Lima, 1974).
12. J. Vanek, *The General Theory of Labor-Managed Market Economies* (New York: Cornell University Press, 1970) pp. 235, 241–2.
13. See Marx on this. *Capital Vol. 1* (London: Penguin Books in Association with *New Left Review*, 1976) Chap. 17.
14. See C. Palloix, 'The Labour Process: from Fordism to Neo-Fordism', in *The Labour Process and Class Strategies*, CSE Pamphlet no. 1, The Conference of Socialist Economists, (1976).
15. I discuss the question of collective welfare and agreements in Peruvian Coastal co-ops in a separate work now being prepared.
16. We form the Lagrangean $Z = U(f, y) + k(\bar{t} - e_m - f)$.
    Taking the first derivatives with respect to f, e_m and N equal to zero, we obtain:

    (i) $$Z_f = U_f - k = 0,$$

    (ii) $$Z_{e_m} = U_y y_{e_m} - k = U_y Y_X X_E E_{e_m} - k = U_y P_x X_E - k = 0,$$

    (iii) $$Z_N = U_y y_N = U_y \frac{e_c}{M}(P_x X_E - w) = 0.$$

    From (iii) is clear that, since U_y, e_c and M are all different from zero,

    (iv) $$P_X X_E = w.$$

    From (i) and (ii) we obtain

    (v) $$P_x X_E = \frac{U_f}{U_y}.$$

    (iv) and (v) together give (VI).
17. In fact, since the model has been built around the representative member, it

is not the total amount of effort that is directly determined, but rather, given our definition of the representative member, that total amount measured per member, or E/M. However, M being a known parameter, E can be automatically calculated.

18. Santiago Roca has a different model of equilibrium determination for co-ops employing casual workers, which he applies to the Peruvian sugar co-ops. His model, I believe, suffers from two defects. First, it does not consider the income/free-time decisions of members, implicitly assuming that the amount of effort supplied by members is an exogenously fixed constant. Although this assumption fits the sugar co-ops better than the others it misses one of the most interesting elements in the mechanics of operation of Peruvian Coastal co-ops. Second, in the Ward-Vanek tradition, the number of members is treated as a variable entering equilibrium determination, and it is assumed that members can freely be dismissed or admitted in the number necessary to reach equilibrium. The lack of justification of this assumption is clear and has been repeatedly pointed out in the literature. It is particularly inadequate when applied to an external labour hiring co-op for it leads to a logical flaw. With decreasing marginal returns to labour, if the market wage rate is low enough to induce external labour hiring, the final equilibrium position must be such that only one member remains. The co-op is thus transformed into a private capitalist firm. This seems to me to be the only consistent solution with Roca's assumptions. See S. Roca, 'The Peruvian Sugar Co-operatives: Some Fundamental Economic Problems', *Economic Analysis and Worker's Management*, 1–2 (Beograd, 1975).

19. It is also interesting to investigate when casual workers would start being employed. Abstracting from land and other productive assets, which we assume to be fixed, if we assume the production function (III) to be of the Cobb–Douglas type:

(IIIa) $$X = aE^z,$$

casual workers would be hired to the point where

(VII) $$w = z\frac{X}{E}P_x.$$

If, for $N = 0$, i.e. for $E = e_m M$ in (IV) or in point s in Figure 7.1, w is bigger than zXP_x/E, no casual workers would be hired; they would only start being hired when w is smaller than zXP_x/E, and would continue to be hired until equality prevailed between both sides of (VII). For a conventional value of labour elasticity of $z = 1/2$, this implies that casual workers would only be hired when the effort wage were less than half the value of the average product of effort. If fixed costs are small and the number of members large, this approximately indicates that casual workers would only be hired when the effort wage were such that casual workers' effort were paid less than half that of members. This result is not inconsistent with the evidence presented above.

20. In general, wage determination in coastal co-ops resembles capitalist bargaining (industrial action included) more than worker-management

orthodox net income sharing. Although the State is not legally bound to pay wages to members of the co-ops, for political reasons, however, it does maintain a certain wage level in practice, and would certainly not allow co-ops to go out of business, keeping them afloat with credit from the State-owned agricultural bank.

21. Notice that we must distinguish between the fixed wage, W, received by members and the effort wage, w, received by casual workers. The first is measured per day or week (with a variable effort content), the second per unit of effort.

22. For simplicity we may assume in the development of the present argument that all members supply the same amount of effort as the representative member.

23. See C. Scott, *The Political Economy of Technique Choice in the Peruvian Sugar Industry 1954–1974*. Ph.D. Thesis. School of Development Studies, University of East Anglia, Norwich, 1978.

24. There is no systematic information on turnover rates. From information gathered for 1972/73 from eight co-operatives in the valley of Jequetepeque, I calculated an average turnover rate of thirty days. See J. M. Caballero and N. Flores, 'Problemas Post-Reforma Agraria en Alguans Zonas de Cajamarca y La Libertad', Monografía CEPES, no. 2 (Lima, 1976).

25. In a questionnaire applied to 315 casual labourers working for co-ops in Piura, more than 60 per cent regarded lack of job security as their main problem, and also more than 60 per cent attribute this and other problems to the boss-like attitude of members. See E. Rubín de Celis, *et al.*, *¿Qué Piensa el Campesinado de la Reforma Agraria? El Caso de Piura*, CIPCA (Piura, 1978).

8 The Moshav in Israel: Possibilities for its Application in Developing Countries

JOSEPH ZARFATY*

I INTRODUCTION

This chapter examines specific types of agricultural cooperative in Israel, with especial emphasis on the Moshav. At the end of the paper we elaborate why we believe it is possible to apply the system of agricultural cooperatives in developing countries. We also briefly describe the system's application in reality, as reflected in Israeli experience in developing countries.

It is possible to differentiate between seven different types of agricultural settlement customary in Israel: kibbutz, moshav shitufi (communal settlement), moshav ovdim (workers settlement), moshav olim (immigrant settlement), private settlement, moshava and farm.

The *kibbutz* (plural, kibbutzim) is a communal form of agricultural settlement which is based on a communal ownership of the means of production and property as well as on a cooperative economy both in production and consumption. Everyone participates in production according to his ability and consumes according to his needs. The basic unit is the kibbutz itself, whose members have the opportunity to influence its course by democratic means.[1]

* I would like to thank Jeremy Cohen of the Hebrew University and Eli Becher of Ben-Gurion University of the Negev for their fine assistance and advice. I alone am responsible for everything said or left out.

The *moshav shitufi* (plural, moshavim shitufim) is a combination of a kibbutz and moshav ovdim (see below). On a moshav shitufi, ownership of property and means of production are communal like a kibbutz, whereas consumption is private. Individuals who contribute to the communal farm – each one according to his ability – receive in return an equal monthly income according to their needs. The single criterion for determining the needs of the individual is the size of his family. The individuals can use their money as they see fit, and buy products and services with it according to their own scale of preferences. Here too, as in the kibbutz, the basic production unit is the moshav itself and its course is steered by democratic decisions accepted by its members.

In a *moshav ovdim* (plural, moshavei ovdim) the basic production unit is the individual farmstead. On a moshav ovdim there are between 50 to 150 private farmsteads, with an average of 80 farmsteads per moshav. Production is carried out individually but under certain constraints (such as mutual aid among different farmsteads on the moshav, cooperative purchasing and marketing, self-employment), and consumption is individual. Every farmer has to budget part of his time for a collective farming of the moshav's lands. Expensive agricultural tools are purchased collectively by the moshav. Like the two previous forms, the land upon which the settlers live is not their property but rather state lands leased to them for lengthy periods on easy terms.

Moshav olim (plural, moshavei olim) is a moshav ovdim whose members are new immigrants who came to Israel in large numbers after its establishment (especially from Asia and Africa). The moshav olim adopted most of the principles of the moshav ovdim.

In contrast to the four types of agricultural settlement surveyed above, which each have an element (strong or weak) of cooperation, three other types exist in Israel, characterised by private land ownership and lack of economic cooperation.

In the *private moshav* every farmer has his own piece of land which he farms as he sees fit. The farmer is free to sell his product at whatever price he wishes. He can employ hired labour and he consumes his income as a private unit.

The *moshava* (plural, moshavot) is a private moshav on a greater scale. Certain moshavot even developed into cities. What characterises the moshava as distinct from the private moshav is the large number of hired workers its members employ.

The *farm* is a type of agricultural settlement less prevalent in Israel. It is a single big farmstead which is self sustaining from both the economic and social standpoints. In this sense it is very similar to the typical farm in the United State.

TABLE 8.1 Types of settlement in Israel

Type of settlement	Ownership of means of production and property	Production	Consumption	Basic production unit	Land	Level of attainment in the equality of income distribution
Kibbutz	communal	communal	communal	the kibbutz	leased	complete
Moshav shitufi	communal	communal	private	the moshav	leased	complete
Moshav ovdim	private-coop.	private-coop.	private	single farmstead	leased	partial
Moshav olim	private-coop.	private-coop.	private	single farmstead	leased	partial
Private moshav	private	private	private	single farmstead	private	none
Moshava	private	private	private	single farmstead	private	none
Farm	private	private	private	the farm	private	—

Table 8.1 presents the principal differences among the seven types of agricultural settlement in Israel.

Two types of settlement principally concern this chapter: moshav ovdim and moshav shitufi. Another chapter discusses the kibbutz.[2] Pp. 195–8 will relate extensively to moshavei olim; the other types of settlement do not concern us since they lack any element of cooperativism within them.

II   THE ESTABLISHMENT AND DEVELOPMENT OF MOSHAVEI OVDIM AND MOSHAVIM SHITUFIM.

The background to the establishment of the first moshavim

With the appearance of the first kibbutzim in Palestine in 1909, there arose sharp criticism of their way of life. Critics argued that the kibbutz does not provide the opportunity for normal family life, that it suffocates all private initiative and that it violates the freedom of the individual. This is so since a decision taken by the majority of members is binding on everyone – even when the decision involves private life. There arose a need to create a new type of settlement whereby each family would have its own land, of a size that would not require hired labour. In this way the relative independence of each family would be preserved, subordinate to the cooperative framework in which it lived. The principle of mutual aid was suggested as a solution to the possible development of economic inequality among the various families. According to this principle, every member contributes an annual number of work days to the farmstead of a sick or backward colleague. In order to save each farmer the bother of purchasing raw materials and marketing agricultural produce, it was determined that all external purchases and marketing would be carried out in a cooperative manner by the village and its chosen representatives. Like the kibbutz, the moshav should be on state lands and not private ones. The settlers would be free to farm the tracts apportioned to them as they saw fit but could not trade or sell them..

The first successful attempt to fulfil all these principles was made in September 1921 when the first moshav ovdim, Nahalal, settled on the lands of the Jezreel Valley; the second, Kefar Yehezkel, was settled in December of the same year.

In the mid-1930s, a number of organisations which aspired to integrate the principal programmes of the kibbutz with those of the moshav ovdim began to crystallise. The members of these organisations aspired to a cooperative and productive way of life. At the same time they were not ready to give up individual life.

Thus burgeoned the idea of the moshav shitufi. On the basis of moshav shitufi common practice, every family has its own home which is independently run – both from an economic and social standpoint. All moshav property belongs to the membership as a whole. Everyone participates in communal production, similar to the kibbutz. The moshav's income is equally distributed among the members according to one basic criterion: size of family. In 1936 the first moshav shitufi, Kefar Hitin, was founded.

The development of moshavei ovdim and moshavim shitufim

The development of agricultural settlement in the 1920s was very slow, and only 13 moshavei ovdim were established in this period. Characteristic of this period was the attempt to preserve equality in income level among the members – whether by providing mutual aid to the backward members or by limiting possibilities for accumulation outside the general framework. For example, obtaining of private outside loans was stopped.

In the 1930s the number of moshavei ovdim and settlers grew considerably from 16 moshavim with a population of 3,400 in 1931 to 44 moshavim with a population of 9,900 in 1936. From the same period until the establishment of the state in 1948, almost no moshavei ovdim were added. This was due to the times – when emphasis was placed on security needs and on the desire to establish settlements which could combine agricultural and industrial production, that is to say, kibbutzim. With the state's foundation, there was a radical turning point with masses of immigrants from Asia, Africa and Europe arriving in Israel. As a consequence of this immigration the number of moshavim grew very rapidly (moshavei ovdim and moshavei olim) between 1948 and 1951, and amounted to 191 moshavim in 1951. In 1976 there were 350 moshavim in Israel, of which approximately 300 were moshavei ovdim and moshavei olim.

In contrast to the rapid growth of moshavei ovdim and moshavei olim the number of moshavim shitufim hardly grew after the first period of creation.

Between 1936 and 1945 23 moshavim shitufim were founded. In the stormy period between 1948 and 1951 only three moshavim were added and in 1976 there were 30 moshavim in Israel, with a population of 4,900 people. Unlike the moshavei ovdim and the kibbutzim the moshavim shitufim do not have their own settlement movement. They are attached to the moshav movement which invests most of its effort towards the development of moshavei ovdim and moshavei olim.

Table 8.2 shows the growth of the various types of settlement in Israel between 1922 to 1976.

TABLE 8.2   Growth of settlements, 1922–76

Year	Moshavei ovdim and moshavei olim No.	%	Private moshavim No.	%	Moshavim shitufim No.	%	Kibbutzim No.	%	Others No.	%	Total No.	%
1922	8	12	3	5	–	–	19	30	34	53	64	100
1931	16	16	14	14	–	–	31	30	42	40	103	100
1936	44	27	27	16	1	1	47	28	46	28	165	100
1948	44	13	35	11	25	8	177	54	45	14	326	100
1951	191	31	42	7	28	5	217	36	128	21	606	100
1955	273	37	43	6	27	4	225	31	164	22	732	100
1960	295	41	52	7	19	3	229	31	128	18	723	100
1963	299	43	47	7	21	3	230	33	102	14	699	100
1967	345	49	A	A	22	3	233	33	106	15	706	100
1972	347	49	A	A	27	4	226	32	104	15	704	100
1976	350	48	A	A	30	4	242	34	101	14	723	100

Sources: J. Ben-David (1964); M. L. Klayman (1970); D. Morawetz (1978); Yearbooks of the Central Bureau of Statistics (various years).

Note: A – the private moshavim in these years are included within the framework of moshavei ovdim.

The contribution of the various types of settlement to the total agricultural product cannot be determined with certainty. Yet on the basis of estimates,[3] in 1955 the moshavim contributed approximately 45 per cent of the product while kibbutzim contributed only 33 per cent. Kibbutz industrialisation developed partly at the expense of agriculture, while in moshavim there was no industrialisation at all. In addition there was a larger number of moshavim in that year.

With the consolidation and 'commercialisation' of the moshav and kibbutz there developed differences between them in production specialisation. While moshavim concentrated in labour-intensive branches such as livestock and their products, the kibbutzim specialized in branches which had economies of scale such as grain growing, field planting and fruits which required much investment and mechanisation. In addition, the kibbutzim developed industry extensively and today some 150 kibbutzim own approximately 270 industrial enterprises. Even within the specific agricultural areas there exist different specialisations for kibbutzim and moshavim. For example: in the poultry division the moshavim specialise in eggs while the kibbutzim specialise in meat. In this way it was possible to take advantage of economies of scale. The moshavim shitufim are closer in this respect to the kibbutzim than to the moshavim, and their economic behaviour is very similar to that of the kibbutzim.

The absorption of Jewish immigration from developing countries in moshavei olim

With the establishment of the state of Israel in May 1948 there was a large flow of new immigrants and within a short period the Jewish population increased from 650,000 people in May 1948 to 1,404,000 at the end of 1951.[4] At that time there was a great demand in the country for foodstuffs which the existing system found very difficult to provide. In addition there was security requirement for settling large areas, especially in the southern part of the country. These reasons, as well as the desire to solve the employment problems of the immigrants, led to the attempt to settle the greatest possible number of new immigrants in moshavei olim. The reason for the settlement of new immigrants in moshavim and not in kibbutzim is inherent in the immigrants' socio-cultural background. Most of the immigrants came from developing countries in Asia and Africa having a distinct patriarchal structure. They were not at all aware of the concepts of cooperativism and the kibbutz. Some of them came from communist countries and were not even willing to hear about complete communal life such as that of the kibbutz. The few immigrants who came from South America or North America were inclined to the moshav shitufi and indeed in the years 1948 to 1951 three new moshavim shitufim were founded. The rest of the immigrants were inclined to settle in moshavei ovdim (olim) because of their more flexible nature, and many others settled in the cities.

Table 8.3 shows the distribution of moshavim, and households in the moshavim, according to the region of origin of the settlers in the mid 1950s.

Unlike the pioneers who established the first moshavei ovdim, the new

TABLE 8.3   Region of origin of settlers

Region of origin	No. of moshavim	As %	No. of households	As %
East and Central Europe	72	28.1	4,831	29.8
Western Europe and Americans	2	0.7	136	0.8
The Balkans	10	3.9	739	4.6
North Africa	81	31.7	4,624	28.6
Remainder of middle Eastern countries	82	32.0	5,284	32.6
Others	9	3.6	575	3.6

Source: D. Weintraub and M. Lissak (1964), p. 98.

immigrants generally lacked pioneer spirit as well as agricultural experience. For them, the moshav was a foreign type of settlement to which they tried to accommodate as far as possible.

This fact created socio-economic problems and made suitable guidance necessary. To every new moshav a staff of counsellors was added in the first years whose function was to teach the new settlers the secrets of advanced farming and to train them to administer the moshav on their own. The staff consisted of agricultural, social and household counsellors.

The establishment and consolidation of new moshavim brought in its path deviations and irregularities in the principles of the moshav ovdim (principles which will be extensively detailed in the next section). For example, the hard economic condition of a number of moshavei olim resulted in an inability to pay their members on time what was owed to them for produce marketed by the moshav. This moved the members to market their produce privately, in contradiction to the principle which lays down cooperative purchasing and selling. Because many of the immigrants came from traditional countries, they were not aware of democratic procedures which should be customary in a moshav. Thus many difficulties arose in connection with the administration and decision-making processes in the moshav. The principle of mutual aid was also not completely fulfilled in the moshavei olim. The new settlers did not understand the egalitarian and social significance of this principle and it was only carried out by means of the moshav's governing bodies – particularly by giving larger financial assistance to backward farmsteads.

The primary economic development of moshavei olim was attained from 1954 onwards. On average 4–5 years passed from the establishment of the moshav olim until economic consolidation. With every additional year, the condition of moshavei olim improved in relation to moshavei ovdim. In 1954 the average net income of a farmstead in the moshavei olim was 20 per cent of the average net income of a farmstead in the moshavei ovdim; this ratio grew every year and in 1964–5 reached 60 per cent.[5] After a large dropout during the first four years of a moshav's existence, there was almost no dropout in the following years. For example, the dropout in 1964 was only 2 per cent.

The question is what are the reasons for the success of this great settlement enterprise? The answers centre on the high-quality guidance of the settlement bodies and the harmony between them and the settlers, as well as the character of the settlers. The moshavim which were most successful were those whose members came from small towns and villages and/or were used to hard work. For them, agricultural work did not represent a downgrading of their social status. Another type of moshavim which succeeded were those that were granted linked assistance and guidance from neighbouring veteran moshavim which adopted the new moshav and aided it in solving its socio-economic problems. The youthful age of settlers as well as a burgeoning young leadership from amongst them greatly helped the moshav's success. The same is to be said regarding moshavim whose members are from the same ethnic background or country of origin.

What has been stated heretofore is not an attempt to ignore the failures and crises which occurred in a number of moshavim. First, one must mention the crises of conditioning for tilling the soil which occurred among some of the settlers of urban origin. The second problem was connected to the adaptation required for administering a private farmstead. At one fell stroke, heavy responsibility fell on the shoulders of the individual farmer. Perhaps prior to his arrival in Israel he was a simple hired worker with limited obligations and responsibilities. An additional crisis occasionally occurred due to ethnic and family background with the breakdown in the traditional functioning of the woman in the family, of the power and solidarity of the 'Hamula' and transition to a completely different culture.

The settlement institutions regarded all these problems with great seriousness and developed various ways of dealing with them. One successful method was the system of a transitional farmstead. According to this, the settler worked for a specific period as a hired worker on his lands and the moshav bodies administered his farmstead. After the conclusion of the training and adaptation period, the settler took upon himself the responsibility and became a full fledged moshavnik.

III   SOCIO-ECONOMIC PRINCIPLES OF MOSHAVEI OVDIM AND MOSHAVIM SHITUFIM AND THEIR APPLICATION IN REALITY.

The organization of production, management and marketing and the payments system

Elizar Yaffe, one of the founders of the first moshav Nahalal and main moshav movement thinker determined four basic principles upon which moshavei ovdim were established.

The first principle: national land

The first principle comes from the belief that the land belongs to all of the people and therefore it cannot be the sole possession of one person. This principle lays down that land is given over by the state to the moshav and in turn leased to the settler. He has rights to the land but not ownership. He cannot sell or mortgage it. The leasing of the land is effected for 49 years and may be renewed at the end of this time period. The settler's right to farm his land depends on his readiness to accept the moshav's principles. The moshav can evict him from his land if he does not follow its basic tenets. It is forbidden for a member to divide his land among his children. This is to prevent the creation of small tracts of land which would augment the gap in income distribution. The father cannot bequeath his land to one or more of his children, but his children have a natural right to the land. The moshav generally confirms the land's transferral to one of them and tries to find additional tracts of land for the other offspring. If the father dies and none of his offspring want to continue to farm the land, it reverts to the moshav which passes it on to a new settler. He pays the family for improving on the land's value.

In order to create equal opportunities for all members, the moshav's lands are parcelled out according to a lottery among its founders. In this manner everyone receives his plot of land. If the village lands are of different kinds and quality, every farmer receives a few small tracts. In the end, everyone has lands of the same agricultural value. Because of this, the settler is eligible (with the consent of a special moshav committee) to exchange part of his land with another settler but in no case is he permitted to sell him the land.

The production unit in the moshav is the family and it is responsible for its production plan. Nevertheless there are a number of limitations which prevent the family from producing whatever it wants. First, for specific products there are production quotas. The moshav receives from the Ministry of Agriculture a total production quota and it divides the quota among the members. Secondly, settlers cannot produce products for which the moshav does not carry out organised marketing since it is forbidden for a settler to market these products by himself.

In addition to the lands leased to the settlers, the moshav holds some land tracts which are farmed cooperatively by all the settlers. On these tracts, grains and other crops with economies of scale are grown. Members whose tracts lay side by side may farm them cooperatively with the profits being distributed among them equally.

Second principle: self-employment

This principle comes from two basic aspirations of the moshav: not to exploit others and to preserve maximum egalitarianism. Josef Shapira, one of the founders of Nahalal, said, 'The inequality among men exists in the law of nature . . . it does not give one the right to live at the expense of another, to enjoy the fruits of his labour and to exploit his physical and spiritual powers.'[6]

Those who conceptualised the idea of the moshav ovdim feared that if hired labour were permitted in the moshav, it would develop into a village of Jewish middle-class farmers based on the labour of a Jewish and Arab proletariat. This would create richer and poorer members. Worse than that, the moshav could develop from a socio-economic body which emphasised collective values and mutual aid to a collection of families with private interests whose value is greater than that of the collective interest. In order to assist the preservation of the principle of self-work, the moshavim distributed to each settler, a plot of land big enough to sustain a family without requiring the employment of hired help. According to a survey held in 1954,[7] the average plot of a private farmstead in a moshav ovdim is approximately 10.4 acres.

Third principle: mutual aid

A large measure of economic security for the moshav members grows out of the principle of mutual aid. This principle assures immediate assistance to a member who because of sickness or for other reason is unable to work on his farmstead. Mutual aid ensures a continual decent level of living for members who have been overcome by economic difficulties. Thanks to this system there are no bankruptcies in moshavei ovdim. The desire to prevent disparities in members' economic conditions, comes from the general concept that the smaller the inequality of income distribution among members the better for the society as a whole.

In the early days of the moshav ovdim, mutual aid was expressed through the contribution by every member of a number of work days per month on the farmsteads of sick or backward members, according to the direction of a committee specially formed for this. In later periods, mutual aid was more 'economic' – the institution of progressive taxation in the moshav; the distribution of monies and equipment from outside the moshav to backward members; taking advantage of the moshav's credit opportunities and transferring it to members sunk in debt.

'A farm that takes cooperative responsibility for the fate of every member is more communal than a farm that has communal planting and cultivation of crops. Thus do I see cooperativism and its strength, in which is placed the ability of man to truly enjoy individualism.'[8]

Fourth principle: cooperative sale and purchase

The main reason for this tenet is the desire of the moshav to save its members the annoyances involved in each member's sale of produce and purchase of raw materials essential to his work. The early founders who arrived from Eastern and Central Europe wanted to escape from everything that symbolised their diaspora past: rootlessness, involvement in commerce, banking etc. They wanted to be pure farmers and not waste their time with anything else – especially not on commerce which was so contemptible in their eyes.

An additional advantage of cooperative purchase and sale is the large saving in market costs, especially since we are talking about agricultural produce which requires facilities and transport which have economies of scale (such as refrigerating milk and a large container to transport it). When the moshav cooperatively acquires the raw materials and the necessary commodities for its members, it receives large discounts.

The violation of this principle by the members is not only a moral problem but also an economic one. An end to marketing and purchasing, by means of the cooperative, cuts the moshav's income and can result in difficulties in providing essential services thereby damaging the moshav's welfare.

The farmers acquire all the essential raw materials they need via the purchasing cooperative of the moshav. Their account at the moshav is debited for the amount of the purchase. In addition in each moshav there is a small cooperative store which sells, for cash, food products and other household needs. The purchasing organisations also supply various services, such as credit, refrigeration etc., which the moshavim can use for a minimal charge.

The moshav's institutions and its services

The chief institution in every moshav is the general assembly which convenes every year. Every member of the moshav has the right to participate in it. The general assembly elects a council of 18–25 members from which 5–9 are elected as the secretariat which is responsible for the management of the moshav's day to day matters. The secretariat consists of the treasurer, book-keeper, external secretary and internal secretary of the moshav. The secretariat is assisted in its work by a number of sub-committees for education, culture, mutual aid, legal problems, acceptance of new members and control. The secretariat meets weekly and transfers decisions beyond its authority to the council. Primary problems which could affect the members of the moshav as a whole are handled by the general assembly.

In addition to purchasing services, the moshav grants its members a wide range of other services such as a tractor garage, incubator services for chicks, insurance and various municipal services such as education (kindergarten, grade school), culture (organising performances and motion pictures at the moshav), the paving of roads, street lighting, etc.

Credit arrangements at the moshav and payments for its services

The farmers purchase their inputs and sell their produce on credit. Every month an accounting takes place between the moshav and the farmers. If the farmer is found to have a credit balance, he is allowed to draw his money and make use of it. Debit balances are transferred to the following month. If the farmer needs credit to develop his farmstead he requests it from the secretariat.

The services that the moshav grants its members are financed in three ways: (1) acceptance of a lower amount for produce sold via the moshav; (2) payment of a higher sum for products that the farmer buys through the moshav; and (3) the levying of direct taxes. In general these taxes are uniform for all the farmers, though there are a number of moshavim where the tax rate is progressive according to the financial condition of the member. Expenditure of these services in most moshavim ranges from 11 to 15 per cent of the total yearly product.

A comparison between moshav's principles and reality

A comparison between the four principles of the moshav ovdim and developments during the 61 years since the establishment of the first moshav shows that these principles have not been fundamentally violated in practice. Both the principle of national land and mutual aid are operative today though mutual aid has somewhat changed from since the 1920s, and is principally expressed today by financial aid rather than by physical assistance. The cooperative purchase and sale principle is basically operative today as well, though there are irregularities here and there particularly in moshavei olim, where farmers sometimes (nowadays) sell their produce because they are in need of cash or wish to evade paying income tax and moshav levies. The principle of self-work is only partly applied. Because of seasonal demand for workers in agriculture, in some circumstances farmers hire one or two labourers for a number of weeks. In some of the moshavim there is a small reservoir of hired labour which is sent to farmers in need of temporary assistance. The members must have the approval of the moshav secretariat in order to make use of hired labour, and also in order to work outside the moshav.

Moshav shitufi: its principles, methods and organisation

The moshav shitufi attempts to limit the totality of communalism to the field of production. The moshav shitufi created a unified farm that cannot be divided nor does any member have a private or side income. On the other hand, it ensures family life as it gives each family a private home, with the management of the household and education of the children according to the member's desire.

The farmwork is cooperatively managed on a daily basis. This cooperativism concerns all branches and generally there is rotation of the duties among members.

As stated, every moshav shitufi family manages a household and the children eat and sleep at home. In order to cover the costs each family receives a monthly budget for living and clothing expenses which is based on the number of persons in the family and the children's age.[9] There is no valuing of workdays, profession or productivity. The kibbutz principle of 'From each according to his ability, to each according to his needs' holds. Each family is eligible, within the framework of the monthly budget, to purchase or order its commodities in the moshav's cooperative store where the price for products is especially low. The family can also travel to a nearby town and acquire electrical goods or expensive furniture. The family budget does not include costs for health care, education, culture, taxes and security. So as to avoid conditions which could bring about inequalities among members, health costs and expenses incurred by assisting relatives are taken up by the moshav.

Like the moshav ovdim, the moshav shitufi was established on national land. Members leaving the moshav shitufi return their homes to the moshav and receive a sum of money which should be sufficient for living in the city for a number of months. When the children of a moshav shitufi member wish to remain on the moshav and are accepted as fully fledged members, the moshav builds them homes or allots them homes which have become vacant.

In a moshav shitufi there is no obstacle to employing hired help, and some moshavim indeed do this. This is especially so regarding moshavim that have industrial enterprises. Lately there has been a tendency in moshavim shitufim and kibbutzim to reduce hired labour as much as possible, even at the expense of the moshav's development and profits.

Income distribution within moshavim and among them

In the previous section we saw the strength of the aspirations of the founders of the moshav ovdim to create conditions and tenets which would ensure maximum equality among moshav members.[10] The founders recognised the inequality existing between people, but they demanded that each member should be granted the same opportunity and aimed to prevent the possible development of extreme inequality among members, by forbidding the purchase of lands from other members in the moshav and by the principle of mutual aid. But their policies are hardly realised in relation to egalitarianism between moshavim. The moshav movement which is the roof organisation of the moshavei ovdim tries, nevertheless, to assist in the advancement of backward moshavim. But because it is a type of political organisation in which wealthy and established moshavim have a great influence, it cannot force them to carry out such moshav principles as mutual aid or limitation of the land area which each moshav can acquire for itself and its members.

A number of studies have been conducted regarding the nature of income distribution among farmers in veteran and new moshavim. A study conducted in 1958, with a sample of 66 farmsteads in 6 veteran moshavim, showed significant inequality in which 50 per cent of the farmsteads with the lowest income received only 27 per cent of the total income.[11] Another study conducted in 1961 showed that income variability within each moshav was greater than income variability among them. This study, with a sample of 54 farmsteads on 5 veteran moshavim, showed the following income variability among the farmsteads (see Table 8.4).

TABLE 8.4   Income variability within and among five moshavim

Moshav	1	2	3	4	5	Average of 5 moshav
Average farmstead	100	100	100	100	100	100
Highest income	164	232	196	156	311	218
Lowest income	26	21	39	35	49	36
Moshav average	100	98	86	50	163	100

Source: M. L. Klayman (1970).

Within the five moshavim the ratio of lowest to highest income varies from 1:11 to 1:4.5. In the comparison between the moshavim, the average income in the best moshav is 3.3 times higher than the average in the worst moshav.[12]

While the first moshavim were founded with the help of foreign capital and not from the settlers' funds, during the course of time more and more moshavim were founded whose members had their own capital from savings from prior work. This fact created inequality among the moshav members in the first years of the moshav and contributed to growing inequality over the years.

In the moshavei olim, the variability in income distribution is greater still, being the result of sharper deviations from the four moshav principles. Even in the youngest moshavim, in which uniform production plans for the various farmsteads were enforced, high income variances were created, both within each moshav and among the moshavim.

In conclusion, inequalities in the types of settlement discussed above has grown worse over the years despite the many attempts to curtail it. These differences in income are due to differences in skill, managerial efficiency and investments among the various households.

In contrast to the moshav ovdim and the moshav olim, the variance in income distribution in the moshav shitufi is zero. Every member receives exactly the same income as his peer with a family of the same size. The only difference in the income of various moshav families stems from difference in their size. Part of income is distributed in cash, in contrast to kibbutzim (see Chapter 9), but there are a number of products and services, such as medicine and education, aid to indigent relatives, housing services etc., which are distributed in accordance with needs.

Employment in moshavim

In principle, every moshav ovdim member is his own employer. He determines his own working hours and plans the agricultural branch in which he wants to be occupied. According to moshav principles, every member is allotted a tract of land which on the one hand would not require the employment of hired help and on the other would provide a fair livelihood for the farmer and his family so that they would not need additional means of support.

Two main problems arise in connection with these principles. The first is the seasonal character of agricultural work which requires a great deal of labour in certain seasons of the year in comparison to the minimal labour required in other periods. On average, a single farmstead requires 367 workdays per year or in other words 1.33 work years (on the basis of 280 workdays a year). Because of the uneven work curve, a different work burden is carried in different months. During the 6 most labour-using months, the household must provide between 36.5 and 46.5 monthly workdays, while during the three 'dead' winter months it provides 6.5–11.5 monthly workdays. It can easily be seen that the number of workers required by the farmstead varies from two workers in the peak months to less than one in the slack period. In most cases the household can provide such manpower by itself when all members of the family are recruited for work in the busy periods.

The second problem that arises is that of technological development. The question is whether it is possible to apply more efficient production systems in the moshav and if so how the surplus manpower, which might be created by using such systems, would be employed. New adaption systems which save manpower mostly require equipment that the private homestead cannot afford to purchase by itself. Attempts to solve this problem have focused on attempts to have cooperative ownerships, by the moshav itself or by a number of farmers, of sophisticated and expensive equipment (such as incubators for chicks or large field machinery). Less expensive equipment, such as tractors and milking machines, are becoming common among individual moshav farmers. The problem of discharging manpower because of technological improvements can be solved in a number of ways. The first is increasing the tracts of land and quantities of water allotted to farmers, in combination with growth in the size of their production quotas. This solution has serious limitations stemming primarily from the fact that such an increase would require a decrease in the number of moshav families, and thus would affect one of the principal goals of the State of Israel: proper distribution of the population, which includes preventing concentration in the major urban centres. A second possible solution is to try to control farmers' income, a process which would produce hidden unemployment and the non-optional exploitation of agricultural resources.

In every moshav ovdim there are a number of administrative posts such as treasurer, book-keeper, a marketing and purchasing official, teacher, nurse, etc. Many of these jobs are filled by people who live on the moshav but are not farmers. Their salaries are paid by the moshav. In some cases these jobs are distributed among members who are farmers and have temporary financial difficulties, so as to assist them to overcome their problems. Other posts are given to the sick or elderly, freeing them from the strain of agricultural labour.

The moshav women work side by side with their husbands on the farmstead, particularly in peak periods. In many cases responsibility is clearly divided between the husband and wife whereby the husband handles the main agricultural specialisation of the farmstead while his wife has responsibility for the lesser areas – as well as taking care of the house. The farmer and his wife work arduously. Whereas in the moshav shitufi and the kibbutz the members generally work eight hours a day and get a weekly day of rest, in the moshav ovdim the farmer works from sunup to sundown, an average of 12 hours a day. Farmers with livestock must work on Saturdays and holidays – 365 days out of the year. When they want to go on vacation they have to find someone who will replace them, whether a grown-up son or good neighbour.

On the moshav shitufi the work is organised as in a kibbutz. There is a work setting and every member works according to it. The possibilities for rotation among the members are very great, insuring variety and a lack of work boredom. The moshavim shitufim generally try to make do with internal manpower at their command, and to avoid taking on hired labourers. When the internal manpower is more than the amount needed, the moshav tries to find it some productive occupation – whether by extending moshav production or finding employment outside the moshav (e.g. by sending skilled members to work in other moshavim or in the cities). In these circumstances the member's salary is transferred to the moshav which gives him his monthly income like any other member, irrespective of his actual salary in the city. From an economic perspective it is worth while for the moshav to employ a member even if his marginal contribution to the moshav's income is almost zero. He represents a fixed cost for the moshav and any additional income that it gets either increases profits or decreases losses. In this sense the moshav shitufi has a large measure of economic justice in that income distribution is based on the average productivity of all the members and not on the marginal produce.[13]

In contrast to the kibbutz where the women work the same number of hours as the men, on the moshav shitufi where the family represents an individual consumption unit, they work less. The number of hours of every woman is a function of family status, number of children and their age. An unmarried woman who lives alone without children works like any male member. A married woman without children works 5 hours a day and a wife caring for many children works only 2 hours a day. The remaining hours are used to care for the children and household.

Measuring the success of the moshav ovdim and the factors contributing to it

The success of the moshav in Israel cannot be measured solely on the basis of economic criteria. Social, political and security criteria must be considered as well. The measure of success must be examined not only from the viewpoint of the individual moshav but also from the viewpoint of the state.

One of the best indicators for measuring the moshav's success is the extent of changeover in membership. The low percentage of members leaving shows that they are satisfied with their way of life or at least not so dissatisfied as to leave. This was not always the situation. In the early years of each moshav (both moshavei ovdim and moshavei olim) the dropout rate was very high, reaching 22 per cent crisis years. After the moshav's socio-economic consolidation, the percentage of those leaving dropped considerably, settling to an average of 0.5–2 per cent a year.

From a purely economic perspective the moshavim are not a failure, despite the fact that in the beginning they were not known for high productivity. Today, the standard of living of the average moshav's member is much higher than that of the average hired urban worker or of a hired agricultural labourer. Many moshavniks own private vehicles, fine homes and excellent agricultural equipment. There are of course backward moshavim where the standard of living is lower, but in general the term moshavnik arouses associations with economic strength and stability, a fine way of life in the bosom of nature and hard work.

Another considerable success achieved mainly through the moshavim is population dispersal. Because of the security problems and the desire to populate the desolate Negev desert with Israeli settlers, the slogan 'From the city to the village' was coined with the state's establishment. Thanks to the newly established moshavim the percentage of dwellers in the three major cities within the total population dropped from 52.1 per cent in 1948 to 31.1 per cent in 1967. At the same time the percentage of Negev residents grew from 0.9 per cent in 1948 to 11.2 per cent in 1967.

There are many causes for the success of the moshav in Israel, both exogenous and endogenous.[14] The main exogenous causes are: (1) the high quality of leadership. This was especially true of the moshavei olim which got a substantial cadre of counsellors and administrators in their early years. The institutions of settlement and the government were also characterised by excellent leadership and performance; (2) the support of the Zionist movement for settlement both from an ideological and material perspective; (3) the prestige of cooperative agriculture and its relative privilege in the economy. Despite the fact that Israel is an industrial state, its agriculture was not neglected with financial assistance being given openhandedly; (4) the development of a special place for moshavim within the framework of the cooperative agricultural sector. The moshavim specialised in labour-intensive breeding while the kibbutzim specialised in more expensive and capital-intensive farming; (5) national agricultural policy gave preference to the moshav type of settlement especially after the establishment of the state, combining macro agricultural planning at the national level with micro planning on the moshav level. The principle of national land also contributed to the moshav's success and prevented land speculation.

Among the endogenous causes the following should be mentioned: (1) the moshav's flexibility as an institution and the use of this flexibility by settlement bodies. Thus it was possible to utilise the principles of the moshav ovdim in application to the moshav olim; (2) the character of the moshav as a body for the integration of individuals in a cooperative framework, especially of those immigrants from traditional countries, into advanced Western agriculture; (3) the character and motivation of the farmers contributed considerably to the moshav ovdim's success. In contrast, the new immigrants generally arrived at the moshavim without any particular agricultural motivation, but slowly began to acquire the same enthusiasm that had characterised the moshavei ovdim.

IV APPLICATION OF THE MOSHAV SYSTEM IN DEVELOPING COUNTRIES

The transition from an autarchic to a mixed economy is an important feature of economic development. A supportive system in which a number of family farmsteads join together may be of great assistance to the establishment of such a transition. This system has to be responsible for the joint purchase and marketing of various commodities, the buying and maintenance of agricultural tools, etc. and in so doing to provide the single farmstead with the means to achieve the transition. The moshav ovdim principles may be used as a basis for such a system.

The question now is whether there is any chance of transferring the organisational principles of the moshav ovdim, and maybe even the ideological ones, to developing countries, or whether the factors that brought about the great success of the moshav in Israel are non-existent in these countries.

There is no doubt that the Zionist ideological background to the establishment of moshavim is special to Israel. There is also no doubt that the quality of leadership in Israel is especially high, although excellent leadership is not a necessary condition for successful application of moshav principles in other countries. The nature of the settlement institutions in Israel is special and inherent in its history. But this does not prevent the development and management of the moshav system in developing countries by existing bodies or those that would be set up for this purpose.

The national goals which caused the moshav to be preferred in Israel exist also in other countries. Many nations are interested in breaking the bottleneck of agricultural supply, raising the farmers' standard of living and dispersing political power. In many countries there is the minimum level of political stability which would make experimentation in the moshav system possible. Many are interested in advancing agricultural cooperation not from the ideals that were laid down by the moshav ovdim founders, but as a means to attain economic, social and political goals.

Among the different forms in which agricultural cooperation can be realised, the moshav appears to be the most suitable one. The moshav's structure produces a fruitful combination of individualism and cooperation. This combination and its aims can well be transferred to farmers in developing countries. It will provide them with a higher motivation for work and achievement. The moshav system can also aid in executing agrarian reforms. In many cases agrarian reforms represent redistribution of land without any attempt to continue providing the services previously given by the landowner. The application of moshav principles could aid in the execution of agrarian reform programs by creating organisational alternatives to the landowner and his services.

During the few years of its existence, the state of Israel has assisted many developing countries in developing and consolidating their agriculture. One of the areas of assistance has been in the field of agricultural cooperation.[15] In a number of countries, cooperative settlements were established, based on moshav ovdim, kibbutz and moshav shitufi principles. The aid was executed in two parallel channels: the despatch of agricultural counsellors with a cooperative background to developing countries; and in-training courses in Israel for these countries' representatives.

The transfer of moshav principles to the developing countries was done with great caution. The Israelis guarded against imitating the moshav in Israel and did not always use the term 'moshav'. They tried to apply moshav principles in a flexible manner in accordance with local needs.

An example is the establishment of moshavei ovdim in Burma. In 1962, an Israeli team began to plan Nemsang province in Burma and within a short span some ten moshavei ovdim were established there. In the beginning, the villages were structured on self supply, but slowly the problem of marketing produce arose; in the first stages the Israeli counsellors were forced to 'solve' the problem by purchasing the produce from the farmers. Today cooperative marketing principles have become institutionalised. In the framework of the regional centre, various enterprises were established such as transport and cooperative storage facilities for manures. School, kindergartens, cooperative store and garage, infirmary, etc. were opened. The success of the project arose despite its being in a distant and very backward region. Average family income in 1968 was double that of other agricultural settlements in Burma.

In the Ivory Coast two villages with 120 settlers were established in 1965. In these villages purchases and sales are carried out cooperatively. Services of agricultural machinery and communal grazing grounds are provided by the regional centre. But the property and farming are individual. The success of this project is measured primarily 'by the reciprocated positive attitude of public opinion to manual labour and agricultural work',[16] by building up the farmers' personal pride and by raising their motivation to work.

An interesting example of the application of moshav principles in aiding the implementation of an agrarian reform, occurred in Venezuela. Yitzhak Abt who went to Venezuela in 1961 helped establish cooperative settlements in the western part of the country. The programme succeeded beyond expectations. Moshav principles had an important role in this success.

A careful examination of the main success factors show that the quality of leadership in Venezuela was relatively high and assisted in implementing the project. The quality of assisting settlement bodies, which was very low at first, improved as their experience grew. The government and the various political parties in Venezuela consistently supported the programme. The strong desire to execute the agrarian reform and to improve the socio-economic conditions of the farmers was a suitable substitute for Zionist ideology, which had so greatly aided in the development of moshavei ovdim in Israel. The economic success of the farmers and their cooperative farmsteads contributed greatly to developing the cooperation concept in the country, as well as aiding the enforcement of the agrarian reform.

In the Central African Republic in the early 1960s, six moshavim shitufim were established. Every family in the moshav had its own room while singles still live in shared rooms. The work on the moshav is carried out communally on the basis of directives from the work committee. There are fixed work hours and days off as well as a yearly vacation. The farming is modernised as seen by the use of machines and advanced farming methods. Despite this, the moshav is not particularly successful. People evade work and do their best not to take on responsibility for running the moshav.

The case of the Guanabia tribe indians in Columbia has been totally different. A member of the tribe who visited Israel brought back the principles of agricultural cooperation in general and that of the moshav shitufi in particular. Forty families who were enthusiastic about the idea together purchased a large farmstead. They raise cattle, wheat, vegetables and fruit. The farmstead is managed by bodies elected at the yearly assembly. The moshav members come to work from their homes which are located at a certain distance from the farmstead. The wage is allotted to the member and his family according to the number of their work days. Profits are invested in improving and extending the farmstead. The members have strong self-discipline as they put all of their energies in the farmstead.

From these examples it can be concluded that while personal motivation is the decisive factor in the success or failure of the moshav shitufi in developing countries, with the moshav ovdim the importance of motivation decreases. Actually it is created in the farmer, as he begins to see the fruits of his labour.

SUMMARY AND CONCLUSIONS

Reality shows that under certain circumstances, the moshav ovdim system can assist considerably in the development of developing countries. By using this system it is possible to implement successfully an agrarian reform which will not represent just a land redistribution but also an opening for economic advancement, increase of food supply and rise in the standard of living of farmers. The moshav system creates a strong motivation to work and provides security for the farmer as well as the feeling that he is master of his own fate. Cooperation both at the village and regional levels gives the farmer the feeling of belonging and partnership in addition to its economic advantages.

The greatest advantage of the moshav system is the possibility of using its principles in a flexible manner and thus satisfying development needs of farmers from different cultural backgrounds and those of countries at different levels of development. There is no doubt that comprehensive application of the moshav system requires great outlays from public sources. In order to overcome this problem it is possible to limit the system at first to certain regions and to apply it in a limited and thrifty manner. Later on a mass settlement movement could be established after the first fruits have appeared and been publicised among the people. Grass roots cooperative organisation of the people could take form while the government's role would be limited to supplying the needed know-how and guidance in combination with suitable financial and organisational support.

NOTES

1. On the kibbutz, its development and principles see D. Morawetz, Chapter 9.
2. Ibid.
3. M. L. Klayman (1970), pp. 59–60.
4. N. Halevy and R. Klinov-Malul (1968), pp. 11, 39–44.
5. Regarding the income distribution within moshavei olim and among them see pp. 203 hereafter.
6. Moshav Ovdim-Anthology (1971), vol. 3, p. 340.
7. M. L. Klayman (1970), pp. 124–5.
8. D. Barash (1977), p. 28.
9. The computation of the amount due to the family or single member is carried out on the basis of the 'standard adult': A single member is one standard adult. A married couple is 1.5 standard adults and every child in the family represents from 0.14 to 0.40 standard adults according to his age. (D. Morawetz *et al.* (1977), p. 516).
10. An example of the founders' aspirations for equality is found in the fundamental decision made in the moshav movement: 'All members of a moshav ovdim have equal rights and obligations, and should enjoy to the extent possible, the same standard of living.' (J. Abarbanel (1974), p. 66.)
11. Y. Mundlak (1964), pp. 55–6.
12. M. L. Klayman (1970), pp. 102–3.
13. See also F. Stewart (Chapter 1).
14. This passage is based on the excellent analysis of M. L. Klayman (1970), pp. 238–44.
15. Such as the Cameroons, the Central African Republic, Benin (Dahomey) Ivory Coast, Tanzania, Togo, Ethiopia, Nigeria and Ruanda in Africa; Burma, Cambodia, Thailand, Sri Lanka (Ceylon), Nepal, India, and Iran in Asia; Argentina, Chile, Peru, Ecuador, Columbia and Venezuela in Latin America.
16. L. Laufer (1967), p. 118.

REFERENCES

Abarbanel, J. S., *The Cooperative Farmer and the Welfare State* (Manchester: Manchester Press 1974).
Barash, D., *Selected Writings* (Tel Aviv: The Moshavim Movement Publications (Hebrew), 1977).
Ben-David, J., 'The Kibbutz and the Moshav' in Ben-David (ed.), *Agricultural Planning and Village Community in Israel* (Paris: UNESCO 1964).
Halevy, N. and R. Klinov-Malul, *The Economic Development of Israel* (Jerusalem: Academon Publications (Hebrew), 1968).
Klayman, M. L., *The Moshav in Israel, a case study on Institution-Building for Agricultural Development* (New York: Praeger Publishers, 1970).
Laufer, L., *Israel and the Developing Countries: New Approaches to Cooperation* (New York: The Twentieth Century Fund, 1967).

Morawetz, D. *et al.* (1977), 'Income Distribution and Self Rated Happiness: Some Empirical Evidence', *The Economic Journal*, vol. 87, pp. 511–22.

Moshav Ovdim – Anthology (4 vols), The Moshavim Movement Publication 1969–78 (Hebrew).

Mundlak, Yair, *An Economic Analysis of Established Family Farms in Israel 1953–1958* (Jerusalem: The Falk Project for Economic Research in Israel, 1964).

Sternberg, A and N. Dinor, *Economic Analysis of Services in Cooperative Smallholder Settlements* (Tel Aviv Agricultural Publication Division no. 39 (Hebrew) 1961).

Talmon-Garber, Y. and E. Cohen, 'Collective Settlements in the Negev' in Ben David (ed.), *Agricultural Planning and Village Community in Israel* (Paris: UNESCO 1964).

Vitales, H., *A History of the Cooperative Movement in Israel*, vol. 4 of *Cooperative Smallholders Settlements (the Moshav Movement)* (London: Valentine Mitchell, 1968).

Wientraub, D. and M. Lissak, 'Physical and Material Conditions in the New Moshav', in Ben-David (ed.), *Agricultural Planning and Village Community in Israel* (Paris: UNESCO, 1964).

Weintraub, D. and M. Lissak, 'Social Integration and Change', in Ben-David (ed.), *Agricultural Planning and Village Community In Israel* (Paris: UNESCO 1964).

Weintraub, D. and M. Lissak, 'The Moshav and the Absorption of Immigration', in J. Ben-David (ed.), *Agricultural Planning and Village Community In Israel* (Paris: UNESCO 1964).

Weintraub, D., M. Lissak and Y. Azmon, *Moshava, Kibbutz and Moshav* (Ithaca: Cornell University Press, 1969).

9 The Kibbutz as a Model for Developing Countries: on maintaining full economic equality in practice*

DAVID MORAWETZ

The central question of this paper is: to what extent is the Israeli kibbutz experience relevant to other developing countries? Would it be possible to transplant the kibbutz to other environments, or are the conditions that enabled its establishment and continued existence in Israel too special? As a by-product of the discussion, some observations are offered on the problems of defining operationally and maintaining full economic equality in practice.

I INSTITUTIONAL DEFINITIONS AND COMPARISONS

Three main types of social and economic organisation exist in rural areas in Israel: the kibbutz, the moshav, and the moshav shitufi. All

* I am indebted for discussion of the issues and for comments on an earlier version to Frances Stewart, Balu and Rita Amir, David and Raheli Biale, Anina and Haim Korati, Dita and Evi Morawetz, and Martin Spechler; to Amir Helman, Amittai Niv and other faculty and students at the Ruppin Institute for Kibbutz Management at Emek Hefer; to the Participants in the Haifa University Conference on the Quality of Working Life and the Kibbutz Experience held during June 1978; and to the participants in the Workshop on the Organization of Production, System of Payment, Income Distribution and Employment held at The Hague during July 1978. I, alone, am responsible for all views expressed and for any remaining errors.

three are voluntary in nature; persons who are currently members may leave whenever they wish and non-members may join at any time provided their candidacy is approved by a stated proportion of the existing membership. All three rent the nationally-owned land that they occupy for a nominal fee.[1]

Table 9.1 sets out the differences between the three types of organization in a schematic and rather over-simplified way.

TABLE 9.1 Production and consumption in kibbutz, moshav and moshav shitufi

	Production	Consumption
Kibbutz	Collective	Collective
Moshav	Private-cooperative	Private
Moshav shitufi	Collective	Private

Kibbutz

The kibbutz (plural kibbutzim) is a communal village with a total population ranging approximately from 50 to 2,000 persons. Its two basic ideological principles are 'equality among all members' and 'from each according to his ability, to each according to his needs'. The means of production are owned communally and production is carried out collectively. No wages are paid; the kibbutz supplies basic needs (food, housing, social services and so forth) plus a personal allowance to all members on an agreed, equitable basis. A high value is placed on communal living: children of each age group are raised collectively in children's houses (though this has been modified to some extent recently on many kibbutzim), most meals are eaten in the collective dining hall, and a high priority is given to other areas of public consumption. The nuclear family still exists in the kibbutz, nevertheless, and it has in fact been growing steadily stronger over time.

Moshav

In a moshav (plural moshavim), or cooperative small-holders' settlement, land, buildings and small implements are held individually. All families have farms of approximately equal size and each undertakes its own production. The family is free to retain the cash income accruing from its efforts and to spend this income in whatever way it wishes. A moshav differs from a typical smallholders' village in many other countries in that there is almost always cooperative purchasing of inputs and marketing of outputs; there may also be communal cultivation of certain crops and collective ownership of tractors or other pieces of expensive equipment. There is little emphasis on collective living in a moshav.

Moshav shitufi

A moshav shitufi (plural moshavim shitufiim), or collective settlement, is a hybrid between a kibbutz and a moshav. The means of production are owned and operated collectively, as in a kibbutz. Incomes are equal for all members regardless of work input or productivity, again as in a kibbutz. But incomes are paid in cash and families are free to dispose of them as they wish, as in a moshav. The degree of emphasis that is placed on collective consumption and living arrangements in a moshav shitufi is midway between.that in a kibbutz and that in a moshav. Public sports areas, children's playgrounds, theatres and the like tend to be well-equipped and well-maintained. But children are raised at home by their individual families and there is no communal dining hall.[2]

From the above description, it is clear that there are several key differences between the kibbutz and the Chinese commune. The kibbutz is a voluntary organisation; the commune is not. One of the two basic principles of the kibbutz is 'from each according to his ability, to each according to his needs'; in the commune this principle reads: 'from each according to his ability, to each according to his *work*'. (*Peking Review*, 1978). Incomes in the kibbutz are received largely in kind and are equal for all members; those in the commune are received largely in cash and vary from member to member according to the type of job performed and the number of hours worked. All land is held collectively in the kibbutz, whereas the commune allows individuals to hold and cultivate small private plots. There is no collective eating arrangement in the commune; attempts to institute communal dining halls during the Great Leap Forward in the late 1950s failed for lack of popular support. Finally, the typical commune, which contains from 10,000 to 50,000 persons is between 30 and 100 times larger than the typical kibbutz. At a guess, China must have more than 15,000 communes; the total population of the 240 or so kibbutzim in Israel, 100,000 persons, would fit into fewer than a dozen of them. The average kibbutz is closer to the size of the Chinese production team, which generally has 100–300 members, than to the full commune.[3]

II GROWTH AND INDUSTRIALISATION

Growth

The first kibbutz was founded in 1909 but it was not until the late 1920s or early 1930s that the kibbutz movement can be said to have been firmly established. The 1930s and 1940s saw the movement's most rapid growth, as thousands of Jews who were refugees from anti-Semitism and war in Europe migrated to Israel and either joined existing kibbutzim or established new ones. Between 1931 and 1951 the number of kibbutzim in existence increased sevenfold from 30 to 203, and the total kibbutz population increased sixteenfold from 4,000 to 65,000. Since 1951 the total kibbutz population has increased by a further 50 per cent, but this reflects mainly growth within existing settlements rather than the establishment of new ones (see Table 9.2).

TABLE 9.2 Growth of kibbutzim and moshavim, 1921–76[a]

Year	Number of settlements			Total population (thousands)			Mean population of kibbutz (persons)	Kibbutz population as % of Israeli Jewish population
	Kibbutz	Moshav	Moshav shitufi	Kibbutz	Moshav	Moshav shitufi		
1921	11	n.a.	n.a.	1	1	n.a.	n.a.	n.a.
1931	30	n.a.	n.a.	4	3	n.a.	86	n.a.
1940	78	n.a.	n.a.	27	n.a.	n.a.	276	n.a.
1948	177	104		54	30		320	6[b]
1951	203	233	28	65	86	4	338	5
1961	228	346	20	81	121	4	382	4
1972	226	347	27	89	125	5	394	3
1976	242	350	30	106	133	7	438	3

Sources: Ben-David (1964), Mundlak (1964), Kanovsky (1966), Leviatan (1973), Barkai (1977), and Central Bureau of Statistics (various years).

Notes:
[a] Figures from different sources sometimes differ for particular years; thus, the precise absolute numbers should be treated with some caution. The trends, however, are not in dispute.
[b] 1949.

By contrast with the kibbutz experience, the most rapid increase in the population of the moshav movement occurred during the large-scale immigration to Israel from North Africa and Asia (including the Middle East) during 1948–51. During these three years immediately following the establishment of the State, immigration from these two continents approximately doubled Israel's population. During the same three years, the number of moshavim in existence increased by 150 per cent and the total moshav population trebled (see Table 9.2). Few of the newcomers from North Africa and Asia settled in, or established, kibbutzim.

Since the establishment of the State, the rate of growth of the kibbutz population has been somewhat lower than that of the non-kibbutz society. Thus, the proportion of kibbutzniks in the total Israeli population has fallen steadily from an all-time high of about 6 per cent in the late 1940s to about 3 per cent in the late 1970s. There are several reasons for this phenomenon. First, the birth rate of the non-kibbutz population has been somewhat higher than that of kibbutzniks. Note, though, that the birth rate of the non-kibbutz population is heavily influenced by the high fertility of those who are of North African and Asian origin. Indeed, the birth rate of kibbutzniks, more than 90 per cent of whom are of European origin, has been a little higher on average than that of non-kibbutz Israelis of European origin. This may partly reflect the fact that kibbutz parents receive more extra-family help in raising children than their non-kibbutz counterparts.

A second reason for the decline in the proportion of kibbutzniks in Israeli society is that only a small percentage of the new immigrants who have arrived in Israel in recent years have found their way to the kibbutzim. Immigrants from the Soviet Union, in particular, have been wary of getting involved in communal living. Third, the proportion of kibbutzniks who leave the kibbutz movement is greater than the proportion of Israelis who leave Israel. At present, about 50 per cent of kibbutz raised youth remain on their own kibbutz, a further 15 per cent move to other kibbutzim, and about 35 per cent leave the kibbutz movement altogether.[4]

Industrialisation

Whereas initially the kibbutz was an essentially agricultural community, the last decade or so has seen a significant trend towards industrialisation. In part, this is a simple reflection of the fact that employment had to be found for kibbutz members who were made redundant by the combination of constantly increasing technical progress and mechanisation in agriculture on the one hand and the relatively fixed supply of land and water on the other. But this is not the full story. Demographic, educational and policy factors have all played a part as well in the shift to industry.

The age distribution of the population of a long-established kibbutz is not normally shaped; rather, it tends to be double-humped like the back of a Bactrian camel. One hump represents the founders of the kibbutz; the second represents their sons and daughters (see Figure 9.1).

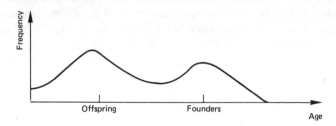

Figure 9.1   Age distribution on a typical long-established kibbutz

Because of this odd structure, it is by now not uncommon for fully one third of the members of a long-established kibbutz to be aged 50 and over. Agricultural work tends to be difficult for such people; hence, the kibbutz has had an incentive to establish light industry to provide them with employment. The sons and daughters of the founding generation have had more formal education than their parents: some 50 per cent of all kibbutz members have now studied for at least one year beyond the high-school certificate level. Although some of these second generation kibbutzniks have specialised in scientific farming, others have studied technical subjects relevant to industry and want to work in their fields of expertise. Finally, government policies of imposing quotas on some agricultural inputs and outputs and at the same time offering protection and capital subsidies to industry have clearly made industry more profitable than agriculture in Israel during recent years (Barkai, 1977).

As a result of this combination of circumstances, more than 150 of the 240 or so kibbutzim now own and operate at least one industrial plant, and there exist a few kibbutzim in which industry accounts for as much as 80 per cent of the community's total value of output. A small number of kibbutzim have recently taken the next step and specialised in the tertiary sector; one kibbutz in the north of the country, for example, has acquired a large computer and sells software services to urban clients.

Industrialisation of the kibbutz has solved some problems but at the same time it has created others. In particular, it has proved difficult to maintain high degrees of direct democracy, worker participation in decision-making, and rotation of jobs – all of which represent important kibbutz values – in the face of inflexible modern technology.[5]

III MAINTAINING ECONOMIC EQUALITY WITHIN THE KIBBUTZ

The kibbutz depends for its continued existence on each member feeling that he gets a relatively equal share of the fruits of the community's joint labours; anyone who feels he is getting less than this may want to leave the mini-society. The problem is that there are at least three plausible ways in which equality in the distribution of goods can be operationally defined. One is that each member should receive exactly the same goods and services as everyone else. A second is that each should receive goods and services according to his needs. Finally, it might be argued that all members should receive equal money incomes and that each should be free to dispose of his income according to his preferences. In the following discussion these three operational definitions of economic equality are referred to as the *identical goods definition*, the *needs definition*, and the *preferences definition*, respectively.[6]

The fact that there are three plausible ways in which economic equality can be defined would not be a problem if all three definitions led to the same distribution of goods and services in practice. Unfortunately, however, they do not. In particular, the identical goods and needs definitions will only lead to the same distributional outcome if all persons' needs are identical, and the identical goods and preferences definitions will only lead to the same outcome if all persons' preferences are identical. But of course, even people's basic needs differ because of differences in age, health, weight, and work activity. Once higher-order needs are taken into account, interpersonal differences in needs are even greater.[7] Similarly, people's preferences differ for a host of reasons. *Clearly, then, the interpersonal distribution of goods and services that is considered to be equal depends fundamentally on which of the three possible definitions of equality is used.*[8] One full slice of the history of the kibbutz movement consists of a continuing struggle to come to grips with this dilemma.

The kibbutz currently uses four distinct mechanisms to distribute different types of goods and services among its members: free distribution, equal quota distribution, unequal distribution according to needs, and allocation of equal money incomes.[9] Each method is problematical on one or another definition of equality.

Free distribution

Some commodities and services are bought or produced in bulk by the kibbutz and members are free to consume as much of them as they wish. The typical list of such free goods includes food, medical services, electricity, water, laundry services, and, at a slightly different level, social and economic security.

The standard economic problem involved in free distribution is that people tend to waste goods for which they do not pay. Such waste can be minimised by judiciously selecting for free distribution only goods that will be consumed in fairly constant quantities whatever their prices (within a reasonable price range). A glance at the above list suggests that the kibbutz has indeed selected its free goods according to this criterion, even if the selection was made on the basis of common sense reasoning rather than on economic theory.

But waste, an efficiency issue, is not the only problem that arises with free distribution. Even in Paradise, where there is no scarcity, free distribution does not assure equality on the identical goods definition, for different people are sure to consume different quantities of particular items. Furthermore, once scarcity is introduced, even equality on the preferences definition becomes problematical. Take food as an example. Food served in the dining hall is a free good on the kibbutz, and the type and quality of food to be bought and distributed freely is determined by the appropriate elected committee or official. But what of a member who would prefer to eat cereal and milk for breakfast or fillet steak and chocolate mousse for dinner instead of the tomatoes, cucumbers, eggs and cheese that are often provided for both meals in the communal dining hall. The needs of such a person for food-as-life-sustaining-material may indeed be fulfilled by the existing distribution system but his or her preference for food-as-pleasure-for-the-palate may not.[10] Indeed, a North American acquaintance of mine claims that his love of good, varied, well-prepared food was one of the main reasons that he and his family joined a moshav shitufi (where each family shops and cooks for itself) rather than a kibbutz after migrating to Israel.

Equal quota distribution

A second set of commodities is distributed in most kibbutzim on the basis of equal physical quantities for each member or for each nuclear family. These goods and services usually include expensive, lumpy items like housing space, refrigerators, television sets, air conditioning units and overseas trips. This form of distribution ensures equality on the identical goods definition but not on the needs or preferences definitions. Among expensive consumer durables, what if a person would rather have the kibbutz buy him a stereo system rather than a television set or an air conditioner? Such trading off of large items is generally not permitted. A television set is in a sense regarded like cheese in the communal dining hall; he who does not want it has no claim on any other commodity in lieu.[11]

As standards of living rise and the range of available commodities increases, the equal quota distribution principle becomes more and more problematical. Each member might be provided with an electric coffee-pot, but not everyone likes coffee; with an electric hair dryer, but not everyone has hair. One person wants to learn the guitar – should a guitar be bought for everyone? An artist needs time to practise his or her hobby or profession – should everyone be given the same amount of time off work as he or she is? One person wants to study, a second wants to travel, a third prefers to collect stamps. There seems to be no way that equal quota distribution can deal with any of these cases.[12]

A further difficulty for equal quota distribution arises in connection with items that the kibbutz cannot afford to provide to all its members at the same time, like overseas trips or new housing units. In such instances a queue has to be established. The two principles most commonly used to set up such queues are seniority of membership in the kibbutz and, to a lesser extent, the lottery.

The attitudes of kibbutzniks to the problems inherent in the equal quota distribution of goods were brought out in a survey of 1,600 men and women from 50 kibbutzim which is reported on by Helman (1975). Sixty per cent of the people interviewed felt that, at the time that the survey was carried out (1969), most goods and services tended to be supplied on the basis of an equal quantity of identical items to all. In response to a second question, the same proportion, 60 per cent, indicated that the most *desirable* way of distributing goods and services was not the current one; rather, it was to supply each person according to his or her special needs. And indeed, since the survey was carried out there has been a move in this direction.

Unequal distribution according to needs

Some commodities are distributed unequally among kibbutz members on the basis of particular needs of individuals – in some instances the distinction between a need and a preference is difficult to make – that are recognised by the group as legitimate. Cigarettes are one such item. Although cigarettes are rarely a completely free good in the kibbutz, in most kibbutzim smokers are subsidised to a large extent, with the particular arrangements varying from community to community. In some cases the kibbutz recognises the smoker's need for quantity but not for quality of smoking material. Thus, unlimited supplies of the cheapest cigarettes are made available *gratis* to all who want them, but those wishing to smoke more expensive brands have to pay the difference in cost from their personal allowances. In other cases, there is a subsidy to smoking in general. In still others, each smoker is allocated free the same quantity of cigarettes as he smoked the previous year, but he has to pay for any increase from his personal budget.

Unequal distribution of goods in this fashion clearly represents an attempt to attain equality on the needs (or preferences) definition but not on the identical goods definition. The problem is, of course, that whereas some needs are recognised for such unequal distribution, others are not. Some people need to smoke tobacco; others need to drink alcohol. Yet only the first of these needs is recognised by the kibbutz; drinkers have to pay for their need from their personal allowances. In a few kibbutzim non-smokers get partial monetary compensation for their abstinence, but in many they get nothing.

A second problem that arises when there is unequal distribution of commodities according to need is that, except in group cases like the above cigarette example, someone, or some committee or assembly, has to decide in each individual instance whether the applicant 'really needs' the item in question. This invites unpleasant personal confrontations. In the late 1940s, when resources were scarcer than they are today, kibbutz clothing was often allocated on a needs basis by the *mahsanayite* or clothing-store-keeper. If a particular member felt that his trousers or her woollen underwear were so worn that they needed replacing, the *mahsanayite*, who was usually short of funds, would examine the case and decide as she saw fit. Without claiming for a moment that it is typical, the following conversation recorded in a kibbutz during 1948–9 illustrates the type of interpersonal friction that this situation tends to generate:

[A woman walked into the clothing store and said to the *mahsanayite*,] 'I need a new dress.' The *mahsanayite* answered, 'Well, you can't have one; there are others before you who need dresses more than you.' The woman immediately burst into a loud, tearful, hysterical argument: 'How do you know that I don't need a new dress? You know very well what I have, or rather what I don't have. You may come into my room and see for yourself. Go into some other rooms and see what's in there! And anyway, why do I have to come here and beg for a dress I need? Don't you think I work enough? Do I work less than others? I have a right to get a dress and you should know it. What sort of a *mahsanayite* are you, anyway? Why do I have to go through this every time I need something?'[13]

A more recent example of the same 'who shall decide what a person really needs?' problem concerns a kibbutz member who was born in Eastern Europe and whose brother still lives there. In mid-1978, the member received notification that, after years of applying in vain to his government, her brother had finally been granted a visa to visit Romania, where he could spend two weeks with her. (Romania is currently the only East European country that Israelis can visit.) This was to be the third time that sister and brother would see each other in 40 years. Needing funds for the trip, and needing approval to take two weeks off from work, the member had to bring the matter up before the kibbutz general assembly. The night that the matter was discussed happened to be one on which a World Cup soccer match was being shown on television and many members were absent from the assembly . . . In the event, the trip was approved but the vote was close and the situation was invidious.

Allocation of equal money incomes

In terms of Western, individualistic, neo-classical economics, the solution to most of these problems would seem to be to give each member an equal money income or salary and let him or her decide how to spend it. This would ensure an *equal* right for all to develop their *different* potentials. The problems with such an arrangement in the eyes of kibbutzniks seem to be as follows. First of all, it is almost certain to lead to increased differences among members' consumption bundles and life styles. Such differences are feared because the maintenance of a high degree of real and perceived equality in consumption is so fundamental to the continued existence of the kibbutz that almost *any* differences that emerge among people are feared. (The latter, incidentally, helps to explain why the kibbutz tends to be, socially, a relatively conformist institution.)

Second, giving each person full control over the disposal of a money

income decreases the amount of collective decision-making and collective control over the individual's consumption. But collective decision-
making, it is felt, is one of the glues that holds the kibbutz community
together. If the member becomes less tied to the community on the
consumption side, the fear runs, is it not likely that he will identify less
with the community overall and thus work less hard, with the end result
being that the society will fall apart? The kibbutznik commonly
expresses his or her apprehension of the equal money incomes
arrangements by asking: 'But then how would we be different from a
moshav shitufi?' The implication, if I understand it correctly, is that in a
moshav shitufi there is much less communal living than in a kibbutz,
each family being relatively isolated from the others, rather like urban
dwellers.

Third, there is a feeling that one of the reasons that the kibbutz was
established was to escape from the pernicious effects on human beings of
money. In the first kibbutzim, members handled practically no money at
all. Even today, members do not pay individually for housing services,
food, education, medical services, electrical appliances, electricity,
water, laundry services, recreation services, phone calls, postage stamps
and much more. Introducing money to cover all of these items, it is felt,
would alter significantly the nature of life in the kibbutz.

Despite many kibbutzniks' strong reservations and fears with regard
to the monetisation of consumption, the kibbutz has indeed moved
rapidly in this direction in recent years. Once, the members' personal
allowance was enough only to buy sweets for the children. Then a
clothing allowance and a furniture allowance were introduced to give
members some discretion over the particular items that they would buy
within each of these categories. More recently, the clothing and
furniture allowances have been amalgamated, and several other specific
allowances have been added, to make up a single 'personal allowance'
which the member can dispose of in whatever way he or she wishes. This
personal allowance still only covers about 15 per cent of total
consumption expenditures (Helman, 1975, Appendix A), with the exact
percentage varying somewhat from kibbutz to kibbutz. But the trend
towards its increasing importance in recent years is unmistakable.

Supply-side problems

The discussion in this section so far has been devoted entirely to the
problems of maintaining equality while distributing a *given supply* of

available goods and services. But there is also an additional problem: some goods and services, by their very nature, become available to members (are supplied) in an unequal fashion, whichever definition of equality is used. With respect to many of these commodities, the kibbutz must necessarily discriminate against some member or members *whatever* distribution rules it lays down.

Personal transfers from outside the kibbutz are a case in point. One young couple, with rich relatives outside the kibbutz, might receive the most expensive modern Danish furniture, a five-piece stereo system and a large record collection as wedding presents; another couple, with no relatives outside, may have to be satisfied with the standard kibbutz furniture and no stereo or records. The first couple may have parents overseas who are willing to cover the costs of a yearly trip to the United States for their children during the 10–14 day annual vacation; the second couple may have to wait its turn for the once-or-twice-in-a-lifetime overseas trip that the kibbutz is currently able to afford its members.[14] Some members receive war-compensation payments from the German government or inherit large sums from parents outside the kibbutz, others do not.

In earlier days, any money or gifts that were received from outside the kibbutz had to be handed over in total to the community. More recently, this has been true only of larger sums (inheritances, Germans reparations payments), and even in these instances the individual member often receives a small amount personally and, depending on the kibbutz, may be able to claim the full amount if he or she should wish to leave the community at some future date. Smaller gifts, including wedding presents, are now usually kept by the recipients.

The biggest current dilemma in this regard concerns overseas travel paid from abroad. Overseas trips have a special significance for Israelis because of the country's small size, because of its geographical and political isolation, and because such a large proportion of Israelis either were born abroad themselves or have parents who were. Each kibbutz has its own rules on this question. In some kibbutzim, overseas-paid trips may be accepted but only once every three or five years. Sometimes, in a decision that can be particularly difficult for all concerned, a member with parents overseas may travel, but his or her spouse and/or children may not. Either decision puts the member who can travel at an advantage over fellow members who have to wait 20 or 30 years for a kibbutz-paid trip. But members who would like to visit their relatives (or who are invited to academic conferences) more than once every three or five years, and who would be able to travel at no cost to the kibbutz, are penalised as well. Incidentally, few, if any, of the participants in the conference at The Hague for which this paper was prepared would have been able to attend the meeting if they had been kibbutzniks. In no case had three years passed since the participant's last overseas trip. Even if this were overlooked, permission to leave at the appropriate time would have been difficult to obtain for some conferees because July is the fruit-picking season and their hands might have been needed at home.

Like the person with rich relatives outside the kibbutz, the member who works outside the community may also have preferential access to certain goods and services. Such a member may be able to visit relatives and friends in town after work on weekdays, whereas his fellow kibbutzniks have to use their one free day a week to do so. The same person may possibly have a telephone at home and may thus be able to receive calls from friends directly, whereas his fellow kibbutzniks can only receive messages and call back several hours later on the public kibbutz phone. Should the person who works in town be forbidden to see relatives and friends during the week and to receive non-work-related calls on his home phone in order to make his situation comparable to that of the others?

Despite the very real difficulties that are constantly encountered in maintaining intra-kibbutz economic equality, it would be a pity to lose perspective: in conjunction perhaps with a few religious communes, the kibbutz is still the most equal mini-society in material terms that exists today. Clear bounds on inequality are set by the fact that no-one can have a private outside income, no-one can live in a house larger or better than the latest batch built by the kibbutz for a group of members, no-one can own a private car, and no-one can buy his own time from the kibbutz to travel, work, study or simply live outside the kibbutz without the approval of the other members.

IV   MAINTAINING ECONOMIC EQUALITY AMONG KIBBUTZIM

In China, although the central government tries to give preference in infrastructure and the like to poorer communes, it recognises that it can do little to equalise standards of living among communes without seriously damaging work motivation. Thus, some communes are clearly better off materially than others. In Israel, by contrast, the kibbutz movement and the national government consider that it is important that standards of living should be relatively equal among kibbutzim.

They also feel, both for ideological and for morale reasons, that the average kibbutz standard of living should not be too different from that of middle class Israeli non-kibbutz society. The main three mechanisms by which these twin ends are achieved are: publication each year by the kibbutz movement of a so-called 'minimum standard of consumption' which all kibbutzim, including newly-established ones, ought to attempt to attain, and which richer kibbutzim ought not to exceed by too much;[15] provision of subsidies and technical assistance to new or struggling kibbutzim by the central government; and imposition by the movement on its member kibbutzim of taxes that rise progressively with kibbutz per capita income, and transfer of part of the revenue from these taxes to poorer kibbutzim.[16]

I know of no analysis in which the relative importance of these three mechanisms has been separated out. Nevertheless, the strength of their combined effect in equalising kibbutz consumption levels is not in doubt. This effect may be seen in two ways. First, the distribution of consumption among kibbutzim is remarkably equal in absolute terms, and it is also considerably more equal than the inter-kibbutz distribution of income. Gini coefficients calculated for consumption inequality among kibbutzim between 1954 and 1968 never exceed 0.09, and show no trend over time. Gini coefficients for income inequality, by contrast, increased somewhat from 0.11 to 0.18 in the mid 1950s (depending on the definition) to 0.16 or 0.20 respectively in 1968. The Gini coefficient for the inequality of the income distribution in Israel as a whole was about 0.37 in 1968.[17]

Second, and of course related, the short-run marginal propensity to consume that is estimated from three sets of cross-section samples of kibbutzim is very low indeed. It varied between 0.01 and 0.17 during 1956–65 on one sample of 200 kibbutzim; it was on average even lower in a second set of estimates for 40 settlements during 1961–72; and it was close to zero (0.02 and 0.03) in a third set of estimates for 98 kibbutzim during 1973–4.[18]

Just as increasing affluence poses problems for the maintenance of intra-kibbutz equality, so does it create difficulties for the maintenance of equality among kibbutzim. Kibbutzim that are richer and more profitably operated than the average have three options available to them. They can save and invest a higher proportion of income than average, thus ensuring that they will become richer still in the future. They can allow their standard of living to rise more rapidly than the average, in particular by providing themselves with more and better quality public consumption goods (Olympic swimming pools, art galleries, modern air-conditioned dining halls and the like) which are less strictly specified in the movement's minimum budget than private consumption goods. Or they can voluntarily put aside increasing proportions of their income for distribution to less wealthy kibbutzim. At present, the richer kibbutzim seem to be concentrating more on the first two options, which suggests that, in the future, inequality of living standards among kibbutzim may be expected to increase somewhat from its current fairly low level.

V OTHER PROBLEMS

The problems discussed above – maintaining equality within and among kibbutzim – are only a small sample of those that the kibbutz has had to face over time. In the initial stages there were physical hardships: the early kibbutzniks often had to live in tents for the first two years. There was, and for border kibbutzim remains, a security threat. There were the divisive ideological debates of the early 1950s, and the heated arguments a decade or so later over whether children ought to sleep in the children's houses or at home. Because of a shortage of manpower, some kibbutzim have broken the founders' code and employed hired labour, which has again caused dissension and the need for adjustments. Most recently, kibbutzniks have devoted much attention and ingenuity to the problem of youths who were born on kibbutzim but want to leave the movement. Although all of these are important and interesting issues in the history of the kibbutz, it is outside the scope of this chapter to examine them here.

VI FACTORS ACCOUNTING FOR SURVIVAL

The vast majority of voluntarily-established communes do not survive beyond the initial romantic stage.[19] What are the special conditions that account for the fact that the kibbutz has been able to overcome the many problems that it has faced, and survive, indeed prosper, for over half a century? The list is a long one.

1. The kibbutz is a *voluntary* organisation with free entry and exit. If membership were not voluntary, members would presumably have had to be given material incentives to encourage them to work (as is the case in the Chinese commune). But this would have created inequality of incomes, in which case the mini-society would no longer be a kibbutz. If the kibbutz were not voluntary and no material incentives were

provided, the work motivation problem would presumably have been insuperable.[20]

2. The early kibbutzniks had clear, strongly-held *nationalist goals*. They felt that they were returning to the land that their forefathers had left 2,000 years ago, and that they were building up a country that would be a haven for Jews from all over the world. They felt the need for such a haven particularly acutely as a result of the events that took place in Europe from the early 1930s onwards.

3. The early kibbutzniks also held a clear *socialist or at least egalitarian ideology*. Influenced by the Russian Revolution, they wanted to set up a society in which all people would be equal.

4. They had a high degree of *commitment* to these nationalistic and egalitarian visions. Further, since many early kibbutzniks formed training groups in Europe years before setting out for Palestine, these commitments were soon reinforced by the growth of a family-like commitment to the welfare of their fellow members.

5. The founding kibbutzniks had a strong *work ethic*. They appear to have believed that work is of value in itself and not just for the fruits that it bears. That this ethic is not yet dead is indicated by the fact that not even the richest kibbutzim seem to have considered working a five-day week instead of the present six days, or increasing the annual holidays beyond two weeks. The pressure to work hard in the kibbutz seems to be almost entirely informal. In China, slackers are invited to a formal self-criticism session; in the kibbutz, offenders are simply whispered about and looked down upon. A kibbutznik who consistently refuses to take on his or her share of the work burden can, in theory, be expelled by the kibbutz general assembly. But a two-thirds or three-quarters majority is usually required and this procedure is almost never resorted to in practice. Of course, in a community that is relatively self-contained socially, as a kibbutz is, informal social rankings and informal social pressures on non-conformists have much greater force than in an anonymous urban society.

6. The people who established the early kibbutzim were not developing-country peasants with long-ingrained ways of farming and living on the land and a resistance to change, but educated, middle-class Europeans. The fact that they had little advance knowledge of farming techniques was a hindrance at first, but later, in enabling *flexibility*, it may have been an asset.

7. The *balance* that has been maintained between stability of basic values on the one hand, and flexibility with respect to non-basic issues on the other, has been important in the kibbutz's survival. No effort has

been spared in attempting to maintain intra-kibbutz equality – a basic value. But two other values that were strongly held in the early days – the superiority of physical labour over mental labour and the superiority of agricultural work over other forms of physical work – were quietly abandoned when, because of the need to provide alternative forms of employment for members, their continued espousal threatened the survival of the kibbutz. The fact that there is a high degree of direct democracy in decision-making within the kibbutz may have helped to enable it to adjust flexibly to changing circumstances as problems have arisen.

8. The kibbutzniks had and still have a high degree of *awareness* of the importance of the social experiment that they have been undertaking. This awareness, which has been described as an elitist self consciousness, has acted a little like an extended 'Hawthorne effect'.[21]

9. The effectiveness of the kibbutz *education and informal socialisation system* in transmitting the values of the founders to their children (and, in some cases, to their grandchildren) has been important in keeping the proportion of youths who leave the kibbutz movement down to one third.

10. The central *kibbutz movement*, or umbrella organisation, has helped to ensure that, when new areas are opened up for settlement, part is set aside for new kibbutzim.[22] It has also been an important source of support for new and struggling settlements. The absence of such an umbrella organisation, together with the lack of a clearly articulated and strongly held ideology, may be one reason why the moshav shitufi movement has failed to grow over the years.

11. The constant *external threat* has no doubt helped to bind the border kibbutzim together.

12. Finally, given the high degree of contact of kibbutzniks with the outside society through relatives and friends and through business and professional relationships, it is doubtful whether the kibbutz movement could have survived if it had not succeeded in *raising the standards of living* of its members. Living standards in the kibbutz have risen faster than those in the rest of Israel during the past 25 years; the latter, in turn, have risen faster than living standards in all but a handful of developing countries during the same period (Morawetz, 1977). According to Barkai (1977, p. 149), kibbutz per capita consumption grew at an average annual rate of about 10–11 per cent during the thirty years 1936–65, and at about 5–6 per cent during 1954–65.

The subsidy issue

One factor that may partly underlie the success of the kibbutz movement is absent from the above list: assistance from the government. This is not because such assistance has not been forthcoming – indeed, no kibbutz has been allowed to fail for purely economic reasons – but rather because I know of no study indicating in quantitative terms how significant such assistance has been. The author of such a study would face formidable problems. At the conceptual level, there is a benchmark problem. All of Israel is in a sense subsidised: during 1973–6, for example, about 13–18 per cent of the country's total available economic resources were provided from external sources as cover for the balance of payments deficit.[23] Should the kibbutz situation be compared, therefore, with the current, subsidized situation of the rest of Israeli society, or should it be compared with the situation as it would exist if there were no subsidies in either sector? Further, world prices for agricultural products are distorted by the fact that agricultural commodities are subsidized in many of the most important supplying countries. How should the influence of these foreign subsidies be incorporated into the analysis?

At the empirical level, what price should the kibbutzim be charged for the land that they occupy and for the water that they use? Since both land and water are rationed, their true shadow prices are presumably above their current administered prices – but by how much? Should the government's policy of attempting to equalise the price paid for water throughout the country be accepted as legitimate, or should each kibbutz be charged its true shadow marginal cost? Note that kibbutzim in general pay about the same price for water as other agricultural users. What are the appropriate shadow prices for agricultural products that are currently subject to output quotas in Israel? Again the kibbutz and other Israeli agricultural entities both enjoy the benefits of these quotas. The kibbutz receives government loans at subsidised interest rates – but so do many other agents in Israeli society. Border kibbutzim receive special help – but at what prices or in what manner should one evaluate the contribution of these settlements to the security of the state? How can one quantify the significant contribution of the kibbutz movement in general to Israeli morale and psychic welfare, and so on?

It is known that the kibbutzim rate highly in world terms in productivity in particular sectors – in eggs laid per chicken, milk obtained per cow, cotton harvested per hectare, and the like.[24] It is also known that the kibbutzim produce some 40 per cent of Israel's total agricultural output with 25 per cent of its agricultural labour force; that they produce 6 per cent of Israel's total industrial output with 4 per cent of its industrial labour force; that they exported just over a third of their total industrial output in 1977; and that their industrial exports grew at 30 per cent a year during 1974–7.[25] This evidence suggests that, at the very least, the kibbutz system of collective production and equal distribution of income and consumption has not had disastrous effects on productivity. Unfortunately, the derivation of a more informative conclusion than this will have to await a full examination of the subsidy issue.[26]

VII RELEVANCE FOR DEVELOPING COUNTRIES

In a discussion of the alternative modes of production that might be adopted by developing countries (Stewart, chapter I) the kibbutz is of particular interest because it represents an extreme case: the complete separation of the organisation of production from the distribution of payment. It stands as a working example of the closest that people have been able to get to complete economic equality within a mini-society.

It seems most unlikely that the kibbutz could be transplanted, unchanged, to any other developing country. The extraordinary set of historical circumstances that converged to enable its creation and survival is unlikely to appear again in the same form in the future. It is, of course, debatable which of the long list of conditions outlined in the previous section was *necessary* to the survival of the kibbutz. Personally, I would argue that the voluntary nature of the institution, the strongly held nationalist and egalitarian ideologies, the work ethic and, indeed, almost all of the conditions that are listed other than the external threat fall into the 'necessary' category. Nevertheless, even if it is only the voluntary nature of the organisation that was necessary – and, as argued above, if the kibbutz were not voluntary, incomes would have had to be unequally distributed to motivate members to work,[27] and hence it would no longer have been a kibbutz – this, alone, is probably enough to ensure that the kibbutz is not transplantable on any significant scale to developing countries. After all, by revealed preference, even in Israel 97 per cent of the people do not want to live in kibbutzim, and this group includes almost all Israelis of developing country (North Africa, Asia) origin.

To avoid any misunderstanding, let me emphasise that what I am arguing here is *not* that *communes in general* cannot function success-fully in developing countries; the considerable economic achievements of the intelligently designed Chinese communes would immediately belie such a claim. What I *am* arguing is that *a kibbutz* – that is, a commune in which all incomes are equal regardless of work input and productivity – is not transplantable on a large scale to developing countries, whether such a transplant is attempted on a voluntary basis (because few people would have the ideological commitment necessary for it to survive in the long term) or by compulsion (because in the absence of material incentives many members would work well below full pace, inevitably causing an eventual breakdown).

If the kibbutz itself is not likely to provide the solution to developing countries' problems, can one learn anything of at least indirect relevance for such nations from the kibbutz experience? I believe that the answer is yes. Many of the following points emerge as well in different but related form from a study of the Chinese commune.

Problems and costs of maintaining full economic equality

It was pointed out earlier that it is vital for the continued survival of the kibbutz that each member should feel that he is receiving an ap-proximately equal share of total available kibbutz resources. But because of the fuzziness of the concept of full economic equality in practice (see Section III above), this means that each member must be fairly constantly aware of what the other members are obtaining and doing. The kibbutznik gives up a certain amount of control over his own life: he cannot always do what he would like to do when he would like to do it if the other members do not agree. In return, he expects, and receives, a greater degree of control over the lives of his neighbours than an urban dweller or a family farmer normally has. It is an indication of the strength of this interpersonal 'watching' element that, despite the high degree of material equality that has been achieved, envy has by no means been eliminated in the economic area in the kibbutz. 'If in other societies A envies B his big car', writes Helman (1975, p. 50), himself a kibbutznik, 'in the kibbutz C envies D his little new bicycle or recorder.'[28]

Communal living at the level of intensity of the kibbutz clearly is not for everybody. For every two kibbutzniks, it is said, there is another person who has tried the kibbutz and left. It is instructive to examine the responses of three different groups of Israelis who were asked in 1974,

1976 and 1978 why they do not live on a kibbutz.[29] To what was apparently an open-ended question, the most common first response was 'lack of freedom for the individual' and 'lack of privacy'. Among persons who gave reasons, these two categories combined accounted for about a third of all first responses in each year.[30] Nor can these objections be dismissed as representing solely European-American middle class types of concerns. Although a detailed country-of-origin breakdown is not presented for all questions asked in the surveys, it is noteworthy that, both in 1976 and in 1978, persons of developing country (North Africa, Asia) origin displayed a general attitude towards the kibbutz that was statistically significantly *less* favourable than that displayed by persons of European-American origin.[31] This is consistent with the fact that very few persons of developing country origin in fact live on kibbutzim.

I do not want to go overboard on this issue. The kibbutz *has* managed more or less successfully thus far to steer a path between 'equality as identical goods' on the one hand and 'equality as equal fulfilment of needs or preferences' on the other. Most of the people who live on kibbutzim seem to be reasonably satisfied with this path; if they were not, they could leave. Furthermore, it goes without saying that there are costs to maintaining an *unequal* distribution of income and consumption, and that many non-kibbutz societies could be made considerably more equal than they are now before being forced to confront the sorts of costs of equality that the kibbutz faces. What I do want to stress is that, if one examines complete economic equality in the first society that has tried seriously and systematically to implement it: (a) it is surprisingly difficult to define; (b) it takes quite special people with a strong commitment to a clear ideology to maintain it; and (c) maintaining it involves costs in terms of loss of freedom of action and loss of privacy that, while apparently not sufficient to outweigh the benefits in the eyes of the kibbutzniks, at least ought not to be totally ignored.[32]

Utilization of resources

A well-established kibbutz found recently that six persons out of its total labour force of over two hundred were consistently unemployed. The kibbutz had hoped that its existing, profitable factory would be able to expand to absorb these people, but there were problems in marketing additional output. After all attempts to make the factory grow had failed, the kibbutz decided to sell it and buy a different plant. The new plant employs all the old factory's labour force plus the six persons who were formerly jobless, and is believed to have good prospects of absorbing the increases in the kibbutz population that are likely to occur in the future.

As this example illustrates, the kibbutz, like the Chinese commune, treats labour as a fixed cost. Both communities assume that all of their members will have to eat, thus work is found for all members even in cases where the person's marginal product is below his or her cost of upkeep. Making small communities jointly responsible for their members' welfare may be one way of ameliorating (by internalising) the unemployment problem in developing countries. Of course, since developed Western societies pay unemployment benefits, and thus *de facto* treat labour as a fixed cost, there is no obvious reason why they could not learn the same lesson.

Industrialisation of the countryside

In most developing countries, if the urban areas are to be prevented from growing so rapidly that they become unmanageable, the only alternative is to industrialise the countryside. The kibbutz, like the Chinese commune, has done this. Once again, making the rural community responsible for the welfare of its members seems to have been the key.

Optimal size of rural communal settlements

After quite a deal of experimentation with different sizes has taken place, the great majority of the kibbutzim now contain between (approximately) 200 and 800 persons. It seems to be generally agreed that a kibbutz needs at least 100 persons to be viable economically and socially but that if it has many more than 1,200 or so persons the identification of the individual with the group tends to fade. These are only rough numbers and no doubt the optimal size will differ from society to society. But it is surely not coincidental that the Chinese quickly realised that the commune, with a population of tens of thousands, had to be broken down into brigades and teams to make it socially and economically cohesive, and that the team, the smallest grouping, and the one closest in size to the kibbutz, was selected as the basic accounting unit.

Stability and change

If organisations, from small rural communities on upwards, are to survive in a changing world, they have to be able to strike the right balance between stability and continuity on the one hand and experimentation and change on the other. The history of the kibbutz movement presents an excellent example of how just such a balance can be struck and maintained.

Viability of socialist islands

Finally, the success of the kibbutz suggests what was not obvious *a priori*: that it is at least not impossible for small islands of socialism to survive in an essentially capitalist sea.

NOTES

1. Private farms account for the balance of Israel's agriculture. These are devoted mainly to citriculture in the Jewish sector and to food crops and fruit plantations in the non-Jewish sector.
2. For a more detailed description of the kibbutz, the moshav, and the moshav shitufi, see, for example, Ben-David (1964), Weintraub and Lissak (1964), Kanovsky (1966), Leon (1969), Shatil (1972), and the references cited in Shur (1972–6). The kibbutz, being the most radical and the most egalitarian departure from the forms of social organisation found in most countries, is the main focus of this chapter. On the relevance of the moshav shitufi for developing countries, see Zarfaty, chapter eight of this volume.
3. For more detailed information on the Chinese commune, see Stavis (1974).
4. Data supplied at the Haifa University Conference on the Quality of Working Life and the Kibbutz Experience, June 1978.
5. On the kibbutz industrialization process and its problems, see Shur (1972–6), Leviatan (1973), Barkai (1977), and Golomb and Shelhav (1978).
6. A variant of the third definition which might be more strictly consistent with consumer theory is that *satisfaction* should be equal for all persons – but this is not an operational definition since satisfaction cannot be measured. (A similar objection applies to a lesser extent to the needs definition.) A fourth definition, distribution of goods to each according to his work, is ruled out by kibbutz ideology. The following discussion is focussed on the distribution of consumption rather than the distribution of income because, all kibbutz saving being collective rather than personal, that is the form in which the problem arises in the kibbutz.
7. On the concept of a hierarchy of needs, see Maslow (1954).
8. Frances Stewart points out that a parent wishing to give 'equal' gifts to young children sometimes confronts the same definition-of-equality

problem. Knowing the respective children's tastes well, a parent might bring home a toy car for one and a block of chocolate for another. This is an attempt to achieve equality on the preferences definition. Yet when the gifts are received, the children may be unhappy that they did not receive identical items: that is, they would have preferred equality on the identical goods definition.

9. This categorisation is adapted from Helman (1975), who provides an excellent discussion of the problems of maintaining material equality in the kibbutz.

10. The member is free, of course, to buy cereal, steak and mousse from his or her personal allowance.

11. Partly, this is because it is felt that strict equality should be maintained on a commodity by commodity basis for certain expensive items. But partly, too, it is because externalities tend to be present to a greater degree than usual in the close-living kibbutz community. The person who prefers a stereo system may not want to watch television but (it is assumed) his children probably will, and they are likely to crowd the houses of his neighbours to do so.

12. In practice, most of the goods and services mentioned in this paragraph are *not* distributed on an equal quota basis in most kibbutzim.

13. Rosenfeld (1957, p. 126). Rosenfeld presents a colourful, acutely-observed description of the role of the *mahsanayite* in the distribution of clothing, and of the clothing problem in general, in several kibbutzim during 1948–9.

14. Members involved in the export side of a kibbutz enterprise may travel overseas on business more frequently than this.

15. The movement's minimum consumption budget publication for 1976 included the following:

> It would seem to us that [this amount] is quite a respectable sum, and constitutes an increase of 50 per cent in comparison with the original budget of 1975, whereas the [cost of living] index rose by only 40 per cent . . . We know that some kibbutzim may think that they can very well afford a higher level. We think that these kibbutzim must keep in line in order to avoid a discrepancy process within the kibbutz movement. On the other hand, there are kibbutzim who would consider this budget to exceed – we hope temporarily – their possibilities. We suggest these kibbutzim enlist their best social efforts and maintain a slightly lower level of consumption than the one suggested here.
>
> (quoted in Helman (1977, p. 5).

16. The balance of the revenue is used by the movement to finance its own administration and operations. Payment of these taxes by each kibbutz is a condition for its continued membership of the movement. Kibbutzim also pay income taxes to the national government, though at a somewhat lower rate than non-kibbutz entities. For a detailed discussion of the reasons for the difference, see Barkai (1977, pp. 142–6).

17. Barkai (1977) and Simhoni and Shmueli (1974).

18. See Barkai (1977), Gan (1975), and Helman (1977) respectively.

19. Niv (1976) presents a fascinating analysis of some of the factors that account for the success and failure of voluntary communes.

20. In the 1970s, many kibbutzim increased the severance payments that are allocated to members who leave in an attempt to ensure that people remain on the kibbutz only because they want to do so. Nevertheless, older members who decide to exit are still likely to face a significant drop in their material standard of living.
21. On the Hawthorne effect, see Roethlisberger and Dickson (1939).
22. Although I have referred to 'the kibbutz movement' throughout this chapter there are in fact several kibbutz federations which remain separate for ideological and historical reasons. The separate federations work together on a number of issues.
23. Calculated from Central Bureau of Statistics (1977), Table vi/3, pp. 152–153.
24. In cotton, Israel ranks fiftieth among all producing countries in the total volume of output, but second in output per hectare (Khan and Ghai. 1977).
25. The first two sets of figures were supplied at the Haifa University Conference on the quality of Working Life and the Kibbutz Experience; the two sets of export figures are from Dean (1978).
26. Some of the data on which the subsidy calculation might be based are presented by Pack (1971), Helman (1975) and Barkai (1977).
27. Sen (1973) formulates the work motivation problem in a commune or cooperative in terms of the Prisoner's Dilemma:

> Suppose that a typical member of a cooperative considers two alternatives, viz., to work hard (I_1) and not to work hard (I_0). He may make two assumptions about others in the cooperative, viz., that they will work hard (R_1) or that they will not (R_0). Consider a system in which people are paid according to needs (and not work), whereas their main concern is with their own welfare. A typical ranking of alternatives may then take the form (in decreasing order of preference): $I_0 R_1, I_1 R_1, I_0 R_0, I_1 R_0$. By working hard oneself one adds very little to one's income since the principle of distribution is not work but needs, but there is still the hardship of toil. So given the actions of others, everyone may prefer not to work hard, i.e., prefer I_0 to I_1, no matter whether the others do R_0 or R_1. But at the same time they may each prefer everyone working hard to no one working hard, since the latter may be disastrous for all. In such a situation, however, guided by rational calculus everyone ends up not working hard, i.e., doing I_0, which is a strictly dominant strategy. But each would have preferred that all had worked harder. Individual rational calculations would seem to lead all to disaster. (Sen, 1973, p. 97)

Happily, if there exists a work ethic in the community – for example, if the ranking of the alternatives is changed to $I_1 R_1, I_0 R_1, I_0 R_0, I_1 R_0$ (the 'Assurance Game') or, even better, to $I_1 R_1, I_0 R_1, I_1 R_0, I_0 R_0$ ('socially conscious preferences') – the Prisoner's Dilemma can disappear (Sen, 1973, p. 98). The problem awaiting any attempt to transplant the kibbutz, of course, is how to transplant the work ethic along with it.
28. In a recent investigation into attitudes toward the income distribution in a moshav shitufi (which is similar to a kibbutz in that all incomes are equal),

the egalitarianism of the residents appeared to be based at least as much on envy as on altruism. The typical resident seems to have been saying, in effect: 'I am concerned that all persons in my society should have equal incomes. However, if this is not possible for some reason, I would be at least as unhappy (maybe more unhappy) to see everyone else richer than I am as to see everyone poorer than I am.' (Morawetz and others, 1977, p. 521).

29. Leviatan and Orhan (1978). 1,206 and 1,267 persons were interviewed in 1976 and 1978 respectively; the number of interviewees for 1974 is not reported.
30. In 1978, the other first responses given were: closed society (11 per cent), no private money (6 per cent), wrong ideology (5 per cent), doesn't fit my character (5 per cent), no chance for advancement (5 per cent), no challenges (4 per cent), social tensions (3 per cent), afraid of not being accepted (2 per cent), snobbishness of the kibbutz (2 per cent), other reasons (26 per cent).
31. Leviatan and Orhan (1978, p. 14). In the 1978 survey the reasons why respondents *might* want to join a kibbutz were also asked. The responses include: absence of economic worries (27 per cent), well-organised, proper or pleasant social life (the Hebrew *haye hevrah t'kinim* is ambiguous) (16 per cent), peaceful rural life (15 per cent), good education for children (11 per cent), and equality among people and collective living (7 per cent). The small proportion of non-kibbutzniks mentioning equality among people and collective living as an attraction of the kibbutz indicates once again the extent to which kibbutzniks, who have devoted so much energy to maintaining equality and living collectively, are truly unusual people.
32. These costs are perhaps a little less noticeable in a moshav shitufi (still a very egalitarian society) than in a kibbutz.

REFERENCES

Barkai, H., *Growth Patterns of the Kibbutz Economy* (Amsterdam, North-Holland 1977).
Ben-David, J., 'The Kibbutz and the moshav', in J. Ben-David ed., *Agricultural Planning and Village Community in Israel* (Paris: UNESCO 1964).
Central Bureau of Statistics, *Statistical Abstract of Israel* (Jerusalem: Israel Government Central Bureau of Statistics various years).
Dean, M., 'Rosy View of Kibbutz Industries', *Jerusalem Post* (17 July 1978), p. 7.
Gan, H., 'Consumption Patterns in the Kibbutz', mimeographed, unpublished Master's thesis (Tel Aviv: Tel Aviv University (Hebrew), 1975).
Golomb, N. and Moshe, S., 'The Socio-Technical Project of the Kibbutz Industries' Association', mimeographed (Tel Aviv: Kibbutz Industries Association, paper presented at the International Congress on the Quality of Working Life and the Kibbutzim, 1978).
Helman, A., 'The Distribution and Allocation of Consumer Goods in the Kibbutz', (London: London School of Economics, unpublished doctoral dissertation 1975); (also available from the Ruppin Institute of Kibbutz Management, Emek Hefer, Israel).

Helman, A., 'Income-Consumption Relationship Within the Kibbutz System', mimeographed (Emek Hefer, Israel: Ruppin Institute, 1977).

Kanovsky, E., *The Economy of the Israeli Kibbutz* (Cambridge, Mass.: Harvard University Press, 1966).

Khan, A. R. and D. P. Ghai, 'Collective Agricultural and Rural Development in Soviet Central Asia', mimeo. (Geneva: International Labour Office, 1977).

Leon, D., *The Kibbutz: A New Way of Life* (Oxford: Pergamon Press, 1969).

Leviatan, U., 'The Process of Industrialization in the Israeli Kibbutzim', in Givat Haviva, *Kibbutz Changes* (Summer Institute, Hakibbutz Haarzi 1973) pp. 1–37.

Leviatan, U. and Eliat, O., 'The Beliefs of the Public About the Kibbutz', mimeographed (Tel Aviv: The Kibbutz Movement (Hebrew), 1978).

Maslow, A. H., *Motivation and Personality* (New York: Harper and Row, 1954).

Morawetz, D., *Twenty-five Years of Economic Development, 1950–1975* (Baltimore: Johns Hopkins University Press for the World Bank, 1977).

Morawetz, D. *et al.*, 'Income Distribution and Self-rated Happiness: Some Empirical Evidence,' *Economic Journal*, 87 (Sept. 1977) pp. 511–22.

Mundlak, Yair, *An Economic Analysis of Established Family Farms in Israel 1953–58* (Jerusalem: The Falk Project for Economic Research in Israel, 1964).

Niv, A., 'A Search for a Theory About the Survival of Communes', mimeographed (Cambridge, Mass.: Harvard Business School, unpublished doctoral dissertation, 1976).

Pack, H., *Structural Change and Economic Policy in Israel* (New Haven: Yale University Press, 1971).

Peking Review, 'To Each According to His Work: Socialist Principle in Distribution', *Peking Review* 7 (17 Feb. 1978) pp. 1–8.

Roethlisberger, F. J. and W. J. Dickson, *Management and the Worker* (Cambridge, Mass.: Harvard University Press, 1939).

Rosenfeld, E., 'Institutional Change in the Kibbutz', *Social Problems*, 52, 2 (1957) pp. 110–36.

Sen, A., *On Economic Inequality* (Delhi: Oxford University Press, 1973).

Shatil, J., 'Kibbutz Changes in the 60's and 70's', *Israel Horizons*, 20, 3/4 (1972), pp. 1–6; also in Givat Haviva, *Kibbutz Changes* (Summer Institute, Hakibbutz Haarzi, 1973).

Shur, S., *Kibbutz Bibliography* (Tel Aviv: Federation of Kibbutz Movements, Histadrut and Van Leer Foundation, 1972, with supplements 1975, 1976).

Simhoni, Y. and S. Shmueli, *Inequality in the Kibbutz Movement in a Number of Main Economic Variables in the Years 1957–1968* (Tel Aviv: Cheshev (Hebrew) 1974).

Stavis, B., *People's Communes and Rural Development in China*, Special Series on Rural Local Government, RLG No. 2 (Ithaca, N.Y.: Cornell University Rural Development Committee, 1974).

Weintraub, D. and M. Lissak, 'Social Integration and Change,' in J. Ben-David ed., *Agricultural Planning and Village Community in Israel* (Paris: UNESCO, 1964).

10 Economic Distribution and Rural Development in China: the Legacy of the Maoist Era

PETER NOLAN AND GORDON WHITE

This chapter analyses the nature and extent of economic inequality in the Chinese countryside in the 1970s prior to the death of Mao Tse-Tung and the arrest of the Shanghai radical group in late 1976. Since then, important policy changes have taken place affecting all areas of socioeconomic life, including many aspects of rural economic distribution. Since the precise impact of the new policies and institutions is still hard to assess, this chapter does not provide a detailed evaluation of these changes but should provide a useful background for such an evaluation.[1]

We intend to situate the problem of rural inequality in the context of a comprehensive analysis of the Chinese rural political economy. Analysis of the structure and generation of inequalities will be undertaken within the framework of an integrated matrix of three basic sets of factors: the political superstructure, the nature and level of the economic productive forces and the social relations of production.*

The notion of superstructure is a complex one, including politics,

---

* We realise, of course, that this analytical framework is a relatively simple one and that each of the above concepts and the relationships between them are the subject of a voluminous literature, particularly the debate over 'modes of production'. Not wishing to be drawn into the intricacies of this definitional debate, we regard these three categories of analysis, which coincide in broad outline with Chinese categories, as sufficiently powerful to identify the key determinants of economic inequality in the Chinese countryside.[2]

ideology, law, religion and culture. In our analysis we consider the key superstructural variables to be the institution of the Chinese Communist Party, ideological and policy differences within the Party, and the nature of the political interaction between the rural population and the Party concerning issues of economic inequality.

By 'productive forces', we are referring to the context of labour (the geographic and ecological conditions of the Chinese countryside), the material means of labour and the human agents of labour. The social relations of production* have three basic aspects: juridical ownership of the means of production, the forms of organisation and nature of relationships between people engaged in production, and the modes of distributing products or income.

The reader should bear in mind several methodological caveats. First, the evidence available on rural inequalities is fragmentary and most unsuitable for systematic empirical analysis. Statistics, where they exist, are often organised in non-comparable categories or across non-comparable units of analysis or time-periods. Too often, moreover, they are provided for polemical or promotional rather than informational purposes. Since more evidence is available for micro levels (people's commune, production brigade and production team) than for higher regional levels (groups of communes, countries or supra-commune 'natural' economic areas), this chapter focuses primarily on differentiation between and inside collective units within relatively small localities. Second, there are several points of caution to be observed in interpretation. In assessing the impact of official policies, for instance, since there have been major gaps between policies and grass-roots realities, we cannot assume that a given policy is either implemented at all, or implemented correctly. Nor can we assume that institutions function according to their formal structure or designation – as the Chinese remark, formal labels may be no more than 'signboards' which conceal quite different realities. Lastly, we should not waste time searching for a 'typical' pattern of economic inequality. The Chinese scene is characterised by a bewildering diversity across and within localities. Our main aims are to elucidate the basic determinants of inequality and to make some assessment, albeit imprecise, of the range of variation.

---

* Throughout this paper, we use this term as an abbreviation of the broader concept of relations of production, distribution, exchange and consumption.

I THE POLITICAL CONTEXT: PARTY, IDEOLOGY AND POLICY

When viewing the Chinese political economy in the context of other Third World societies, notably those where capitalist relations of production are dominant, it is important to emphasise the distinctive role of the Chinese Communist Party as an autonomous institutional force. In China, economic development is defined in teleological terms — socialism does not evolve, it is constructed and the Party acts as the historical *animateur*. The Party was the organising force behind a process of fundamental structural, institutional and attitudinal transformation in the Chinese countryside between Liberation in 1949 and 1962 when the system of people's communes was consolidated and Party organisations gradually extended to penetrate all sectors of society. Formally, all organisations in China are obliged to accept the hegemony of the Party; in political terms, the degree of organisational control and thus the impact of Party policies has varied across time and sector.[3] By the mid-1970s, the Party's membership had reached 35 million, about 3½ per cent of the total population. All people's communes have a Party committee and it is likely that most production brigades (the second tier in the rural collective system) have a Party branch and most production teams (the basic-level collective unit) have at least one Party member. Through this network, Party ideology and policy are transmitted to the grass-roots and have a wide-ranging impact on rural economic realities, while patterns of consensus and conflict among Party leaders over rural policy are also communicated to the basic level. Since the consolidation of the commune system in 1962, there has been basic institutional continuity in the countryside. There has also been an underlying consensus among Party leaders on certain basic policy guidelines, notably 'agriculture as the foundation' of economic development strategy, the need to narrow rural-urban differentials, the priority of rapid technological modernisation in agriculture and the idea of 'distribution according to labour' as the principle of income distribution. Over the same period, however, the leadership has been deeply divided over many aspects of rural policy, differences defined by the radical 'Maoist' wing of the Party as 'antagonistic' issues reflecting 'the struggle between the two lines', and by the right wing Deng Xiaoping group in the late 1970s as a conflict between rationality and realism on the one hand and 'ultra-leftist' sabotage on the other.[4] We shall be discussing these disagreements in some detail throughout this paper. The 1970s was a period of general political instability and rural policies were fluctuating and ambiguous. As a result, controls over agriculture were relatively loose and there has often been a wide divergence between central policies and their implementation. In spite of this, however, at the basic-level Party policies play a fundamental role in shaping the pattern of rural socio-economic relations.

II MODERNISATION OF THE PRODUCTIVE FORCES AND ITS IMPLICATIONS FOR RURAL INEQUALITIES

In discussing the question of rural modernisation, we distinguish between agricultural and non-agricultural work and will discuss each in turn.

A steady expansion of the Chinese population over many centuries, a limited potential for expanding the area of arable land, combined with uncertain and uncontrollable climatic conditions and the absence of an industrial revolution provided traditional Chinese agriculture with its distinctive features: the relatively small size of farms, the overwhelmingly dominant role occupied by grain production and non-mechanical, labour-intensive cultivation.[5] To what extent had this pre-scientific, back-breaking toil been transformed by the 1970s?

During the 1950s, for reasons of both strategy and scarcity, the Party placed major reliance in its attempt to increase agricultural output on an intensification of traditional farming methods. The rapidly expanding industrial sector concentrated on maximising the rate of internal self-expansion, producing only a relatively small amount of modern inputs for the agricultural sector. The bottlenecks which emerged during the First Five Year Plan and the crisis in agricultural production in the late 1950s forced a reassessment of investment priorities. From the early 1960s onwards the pace of rural modernisation was accelerated and a greater share of resources was devoted to the production of capital goods and to infrastructural construction for agriculture.[6]

Mechanisation in the 1960s and 1970s has proceeded rapidly from a small base. Machinery has been introduced increasingly in important farm activities such as ploughing, rice transplanting, threshing, transportation and water control. In general, mechanisation has not resulted in the movement of labour out of rural areas, but rather has reduced pressures on labour at times of peak demand and released it for higher productivity work within the rural sector, both agricultural (notably farmland capital construction and more efficient planting and harvesting in multiple-cropping areas) and non-agricultural (notably in small-scale rural industry). In spite of the rapid rate of mechanisation most farmwork is still carried out manually and some tasks, such as weeding, collecting organic fertilisers and gleaning harvested fields, are scarcely mechanised at all. There has been also a rapid increase, again from a small base, in the application of other 'scientific' inputs, notably chemical fertilisers, pesticides and high-yielding seed strains.[7] Scientific research and especially extension work have expanded considerably since the early 1960s; it is likely that the latter has led to a more rapid spread of basic scientific knowledge to the village level than has been the case in many other Third World countries.

Turning to non-agricultural work, in pre-Liberation China the rural population was extensively involved in various forms of non-agricultural activity. For instance, it is estimated that in 1933 almost one-half of the working population combined agriculture with non-agricultural occupations such as petty trading or transportation, and most peasant households carried on some form of domestic sideline or handicraft production. Though there has not been a dramatic increase in the proportion of the rural population engaged in non-agricultural production since 1949, since the early 1960s particularly, important changes have taken place in the nature of non-agricultural work. The most significant development has been the rapid increase in the number of small mechanised factories in the rural areas.[8] There are now perhaps over half a million such enterprises and total employment in rural industries is in the region of 7.5 to 15 million, the latter figure accounting for about 50 per cent of total employment in manufacturing and mining.[9]

A great variety of new occupations has emerged in the rural areas. An extensive contingent of administrators has grown up, notably the network of local cadres engaged in either part- or full-time administrative work in collective units at each level, and a large force of full-time state employees working in local branches of organisations such as the state purchase and sales agency and the People's Bank. There is also a growing body of specialised personnel, such as mechanics who maintain and repair agricultural machinery, financial personnel such as accountants and cashiers, education and health workers and agricultural extension workers.

Gradual technological modernisation and an increasingly complex division of labour on the rural scene have important implications for various dimensions of economic inequality. In the first place, the 1960s and 1970s have seen the beginning of a new relationship between town and country. The extensive application of modern inputs has led to a greater interdependence between the two sectors. There has also been a preliminary erosion of rural-urban differences in the nature of work, not only as a result of the quantitative growth of industrial and other skilled workers in the countryside, but also of the general process whereby agricultural labour is being industrialised in terms of the material means of production, requisite levels of knowledge and training, and rhythm of work. Party policies have contributed to this process of intersectoral homogenisation in a variety of ways, notably the shift to a strategic emphasis on rural development after 1960 and successive efforts to transfer urban material and human resources to the countryside (including skilled workers, administrative cadres, professionals and urban 'educated youth') combined with restraints on urban investment and levels of consumption. It seems likely that these policies have served to restrain the severe rural-urban inequalities associated with the process of economic modernisation in many Third World societies.

Turning to the impact of the modernisation of the productive forces on *intra-rural* inequalities, it is widely accepted that the degree of rural modernisation has varied greatly from region to region, locality to locality. The impact of Party policies has been somewhat ambiguous. Technical logic has demanded that modern inputs be supplied in packages due to strong elements of complementarity between the constituent elements – notably new seed-strains, chemical fertilisers and a controlled water-supply – and the consequently lighter burden on scientific extension services. Economic logic has demanded a concentration of modern inputs in high productivity areas, notably a relatively small number of 'high and stable yield areas', which accounted for about one-fifth of China's area sown to food grain in the early 1970s. On the other hand, redistributive political logic, notably of the radical Maoist variety, has attempted to implement various modes of resource transfer in favour of poorer areas and units, as we shall see later in this chapter.

Underlying these policy ambiguities, which reflect arguments within the Party leadership over the ways in which the relationship between inequality and modernisation should be handled, are certain basic structural tendencies inherent in the process of modernisation which the Chinese development model has been unable to avoid. The underlying impact of differential rent has set in train tendencies towards a cumulative process of uneven development. Differential levels of productivity have meant different amounts of local funds available either to purchase modern inputs from the State or to establish local industries capable of producing them. Paradoxically, the radical policy of self-reliance may have accentuated this trend. The spatial pattern of modernisation, moreover, has been uneven.[10] The spatial advantages accruing to suburban rural areas, in terms of markets and communication, has contributed to inequalities between these and more remote areas.

Modernisation has also produced an increasingly complex social division of labour within rural communities. This social differentiation, based primarily on variations in political or administrative authority, level of skill and degree of functional importance for the productive process, has clear hierarchical implications in the eyes of the rural population. Hierarchical perceptions have led to various forms of nepotism and privilege seeking, particularly on the part of rural cadres and, more generally, to the desire among peasants, particularly the young with a smattering of education, to leave agricultural work.

Increasing social differentiation has in turn raised questions concerning the sexual division of labour in agriculture, with ambiguous results for the socio-economic position of women in the countryside. On the one hand, the exodus of male peasants into non-agricultural occupations has led to measures to increase the rate of female participation in farm work, thus raising their absolute if not relative incomes. On the other hand, Chinese sources have argued that the increased use of machinery in agriculture has increased the potential for women to move into more skilled jobs given the lower physical demands of such work.[11] This kind of thinking has encountered stiff resistance in the villages, for cultural and historical reasons, and more 'advanced' jobs are still the primary preserve of men.[12]

Such issues were discussed extensively in the Chinese press after the Great Leap Forward, and policies were promulgated, by the radical wing of the Party leadership, both to reduce the hierarchical elements of the new division of labour and prevent the development of tendencies towards the inter-generational transmission of privileged access to the higher reaches of the new rural opportunity structure.[13]

Measures designed to prevent the emergence of a hierarchical division of labour include mass discussion of new appointees to commune and brigade-run enterprises and a systematic effort to involve ordinary villagers in processes of basic-level decision-making, such as financial accounting and production planning.

III ECONOMIC INEQUALITIES AND THE SOCIAL
     RELATIONS OF PRODUCTION

The level of ownership, organisation, and accounting

Rural inequalities may be analysed within the framework of three
systems of social relations of production: state, collective and private or
household. Each is characterised by a distinctive form of ownership,
work organisation and method of distribution. The aggregate pattern of
economic inequalities and specific variations at the local level are
influenced both by the specific character of each system and the nature of
the relationships between them.

The period 1949–62 saw a major transformation in social relations in
agriculture from a pre-revolutionary system of private agriculture. The
extent of collective ownership in traditional agriculture was negligible,
though there were some limited forms of co-operation, mainly labour
pooling during the busy season or co-operative arrangements for water
control.[14] The vast bulk of the means of production were owned by
individual farm households and, while there was extensive renting of
land, the planning and organisation of agricultural production took
place within the framework of the household. Rural inequalities thus
depended overwhelmingly on the differential ownership of land and
capital assets between households. The degree of inequality varied
considerably over time and across areas ranging from grossly exploitative and unequal patterns of landlord-tenant relations to more equal
patterns of small owner-farmer production.

After liberation, there was a thoroughgoing agrarian transformation
which passed through several transitional stages. The first major attack
on the pre-revolutionary pattern of social relations was effected by a
radical land reform which was mainly completed between 1946 and
1952. This programme which redistributed roughly two-fifths of total
farmland, resulted in a considerable equalisation of income-earning
opportunities but left the system of private production intact. In the
early 1950s, basic co-operative farms known as 'mutual-aid teams' were
widely organised. Simultaneously larger 'semi-socialist' collectives were
introduced as 'lower-level agricultural producer co-operatives'
(LLAPCs), involving the pooling of land, labour and farm capital,
where production and income distribution were carried out collectively.
In the LLAPC, distribution of collective income available for household consumption was partly in accordance with the amount of land
contributed by the household, but primarily according to labour

contribution. The 'socialist high tide' of 1955–6 brought about a sweeping transition from private to collective ownership and income distribution. By the end of 1956, about nine-tenths of peasants had moved into fully collective farms, higher-level APCs (HLAPCs), in which the land dividend was abolished, and all collective income available for household consumption was distributed 'according to labour'. These collectives remained relatively small with an average of 200 or so households in each at the end of 1956 and peasant households were permitted to retain a portion of arable land for their private use.[15] A further dramatic change in the organisation of rural socio-economic life occurred with the formation of 'people's communes' in the Great Leap Forward of 1958. The level of ownership and the unit of production organisation and income distribution expanded massively in size, the number of collectives shrinking from 680,081 (HLAPCs) in 1957 to only 26,578 (communes) in 1958. The communisation movement mounted a major attack on the household economy, private plots being drastically reduced or eliminated. There was also a partial switch away from the 'socialist' form of distribution according to (unequal) labour contribution to the 'communist' principle of egalitarian remuneration based on need rather than labour. The communes did not survive long in their initial form, however, and between 1959 and 1962 a series of reforms radically changed their structure.[16] The basic unit of collective ownership, organisation of production and distribution was reduced first from the commune to the next lower level, the (production) brigade (roughly comparable to the former HLAPC) and ultimately to the (production) team, the lowest level. In the early 1960s, moreover, in many areas the household economy regained economic predominance *de facto*, with responsibility for production frequently descending to the individual households, working under a contract with the team. The private plot was again permitted and often was allowed to exceed the original 5 per cent ratio of arable land. The size of the communes was reduced, their number rising to 74,000 in 1963. The Socialist Education Movement between 1962 and 1966 and the Cultural Revolution attacked the enlarged role of the household economy, putting pressure on the size of private plots, but did not seriously challenge the notion of the team as the basic unit of ownership, production and income distribution nor the right of peasants to retain private plots. Since 1962, the basic contours of the rural collective system have remained intact.[17]

When we consider the social relations of production in the Chinese countryside in the 1970s, therefore, we are basically dealing with a system of collectives, flanked by a small state sector and a significant household sector. Direct state involvement in agricultural production takes the form of state farms which occupy less than 5 per cent of total cultivated land and tend to be situated outside the major agricultural areas (notably in border areas).[18]

The collectives in the 1970s

The average commune of the 1970s was composed of 2,900 households and contained, on average, about 15 production brigades and 100 production teams.[19] The official position on the relationship between the three levels of collective is clear: the team is the basic level of ownership, production and distribution. The official role of the production brigade is to run enterprises and other undertakings beyond the scope of the team. It also purchases larger means of production such as tractors and attends to matters of culture, public security, primary education and basic health care. Similarly, the commune level runs enterprises that are too large for the brigade and provides higher-level education welfare services (such as a small hospital and middle schools). Chinese leaders and commentators in the 1970s have agreed that over time the balance of collective economy will shift in favour of the brigade and eventually the commune, culminating in the eventual merger of a collective into a state system of production. They have disagreed, however, over the pace and concrete instrumentalities of this process.

What was the relative economic importance of these three levels in the 1970s? The rapid advance of rural industry seems to have brought about an important change in the sectoral balance of income generation within the communes, but the extent of the shift seems to have varied a great deal from commune to commune. Statistics on communes in Shanghai's suburbs suggest that gross incomes generated at the commune, brigade and team levels were 31.9 per cent, 17.2 per cent and 50.9 per cent of total income respectively.[20] Moreover, the rate of expansion between levels was uneven: between 1970 and 1974, the commune share of gross income rose by over 200 per cent, brigade by almost 400 per cent and team by only 17 per cent. However, this example is untypical because the communes around Shanghai city are among China's most highly developed, which would bias income shares towards higher levels within the three-tier framework; and suburban Shanghai was a testing-ground for the radical wing of the CCP leadership who probably forced the economic pace at the brigade commune levels. It is likely that the dominance of the team level is much greater in most other parts in China. For example, in 1978 in the 'advanced' prefecture of Yantai in

Shandong province, the team level still generated 67.1 per cent of total commune income.[21] In less economically advanced areas, the share of team level economy is likely to be correspondingly higher. There is still a significant household economy, the existence of which is guaranteed in the Chinese constitution. This includes private plots, sideline production, private livestock, and individual handicraft workers (such as carpenters, smiths, stonemasons, etc.). The long run objective is for this sector to wither away as an increasing proportion of household income is generated within the collective economy. Though private plots on average only occupy about 5 per cent of total arable area, they contribute much more than 5 per cent of total household income, since they are used for higher income-earning forms of production. Visitors to China have estimated that the private sector in the mid-1970s constituted anything between 10 per cent and 25 per cent of total team income.[22] But the proportion seems to be subject to considerable variation: between regions (higher in south than in north China and higher in technically advanced areas), between collectives, and between households within teams. One study in Guangdong province estimates, for example, that between a quarter and a half of gross family income derived from the private sector.[23] Data are fragmentary, however, and no firm conclusions can be drawn. It is likely, moreover, that any statistics may well *understate* the significance of the household sector given the difficulties of collecting information on basic-level economic activities and the incentive for evasion and understatement given the clear official preference for the collective over the household sector.

During this period there was a fundamental tension in the relationship between the collective and the household sectors. Central leaders disagreed over the issue; therefore policy messages reaching the basic-level were changeable, ambiguous and imprecise. As a result, local cadres have found it extremely difficult to work out a 'correct' balance. On the one hand, they were told that the private sector was a necessary ancillary part of the rural economy and on the other that it might 'corrupt the masses' thinking', provide the 'soil for the sprouts of spontaneous capitalism' and be a source of a new economic 'polarisation' of peasant strata within the collectives. It is perhaps unsurprising that some cadres found the problem of private plots so complex that they either wanted 'to directly let go control of them or completely abolish them'. Despite such vicissitudes, the household sector has remained a fundamental part of the rural system of production throughout the 1970s.

What can we say about the impact of this system of agricultural production on the nature, degree and dynamics of rural economic inequality? The production team, a small group of perhaps 30–40 families, was adopted as the basic unit of ownership, production and account, to a large degree because it fits most conveniently into a rural context characterised by considerable local variations in average per capita income. The hasty raising of the collective level of account to the commune level during the Great Leap had resulted in severe disincentives for better-off collectives and was an important cause of the widespread resistance and disorganisation during 1958 and 1959 and the decision to lower the unit of account first to brigade then team in the early 1960s. Official sources frankly admit the inequalities between teams.[24]

The size of inter-collective income differentials within one locality can be quite substantial. For example, in Shanghai county in 1974, the average per-capita income in the richest commune was 65 per cent higher than in the poorest, that in the richest brigade 130 per cent higher than in the poorest, and that in the richest team 270 per cent higher than in the poorest.[25]

Some Chinese commentators, particularly in the Party's left wing, feared that under team-based collective agriculture 'polarisation' between cellular units might occur. They warned that teams might act as 'collective capitalist organisations', trying to maximise the average income of their own members as quickly as possible, even at the expense of neighbouring collectives.[26] Because the early and mid-1970s was a period when leftist leaders exerted some influence, albeit partial, on rural policy, there was considerable political emphasis on measures designed to stem any trends towards the intensification of inter-collective differentials. These measures were based on the concept of 'self reliance' rather than mere 'hand outs' to poor collectives. The major model of bootstraps development was the Tachai production brigade in the barren hills of Shensi province.[27] The kind of economic aid was considered crucial: a simple transfer of cash or goods to increase the personal consumption of members of poor teams was deemed inappropriate because it created 'false' and non-sustainable wealth and encouraged an attitude of dependence. The key goal of aid policy was to direct assistance through channels which would require the exertion of productive effort on the part of collective members; such as aid for farmland capital construction projects, or giving priority to poorer units in allocating purchase quotas for high income commodities. Many examples of such assistance however, come from areas where leftist policies were more dominant – it is likely that they are not typical of actual policies in communes in many provinces and regions. Redistribution measures were clearly viewed with some lack of enthusiasm by many officials at all levels and seem to have encountered resistance from better-off collectives at the basic level. When questioned by a delegation of US China specialists in 1972, for example, a representative of the Hubei provincial department of agriculture seemed sceptical about the principle of equalisation and gave it a relatively marginal role. He stressed that aid to poorer collectives was predominantly in the form of repayable loans, not grants, that only 5–10 % of total agricultural loans in the province were earmarked for poorer communes and, when asked whether there was a provincial policy on the more advanced helping the more backward collectives, he replied 'No, we stress self-reliance. We educate the poor and backward collectives and let them make revolution themselves. We use state aid sometimes.'

An interview with representatives of the central Ministry of Agriculture in Peking revealed a clear hostility to the idea of the state or higher collectives undertaking equalisation projects on a non-reciprocal basis which the section chief said was 'a form of exploitation'. Hence the criticisms, current throughout the 1970s but intensifying after the death of Mao, of 'egalitarian' measures of non-reciprocal expropriation of team or brigade assets for higher-level projects – the sin of 'egalitarianism and indiscriminate transfer of resources' (*yi ping er diao*).[28]

Given this kind of disagreement and clear variations in policy, it is difficult to generalise about the effect of such measures on inequality between collective units. The same can be said of the more direct method of equalising income between collectives, viz. to raise the level of ownership, production and account from the team to the brigade. It is significant, for example, that the national agricultural model collective, Tachai, was a production brigade not a team. Thus, though pacemaking model collectives have tended to demonstrate the virtues of such a transition the actual incidence has probably been limited, cases of transition often playing a 'model' role in the localities and thus being untypical, harbingers of the future rather than prescriptions for the present. It seems likely that many cases of transition under the impetus of 'radical' pressure in certain periods (for example, in the late 1960s), reverted to the *status quo ante* when the 'wind had subsided'. In general, in the 1970s, the stress in most policy statements has been to emphasise the gradual, long-term nature of the transition and guarantee the independence of production teams from higher-level depredations. But if we take this literally and assume that one of the basic conditions for a 'correct' transition to brigade-level ownership requires that the average per-capita incomes of the constituent teams should *already* be relatively equal, then the transition would seem over the long term to be a result of equalisation (assumed to result from the development of the productive forces) rather than a possible *cause*.

Linkages between state and collective economies and their impact on rural inequality

The rural collectives are not autonomous entities; they exist as part of a complex political economy, linked by relations of administration and exchange with the state sector (overwhelmingly urban, industrial, commercial and bureaucratic). The nature of these relationships plays an important role not only in determining specific patterns of economic distribution both between and within rural collectives, but also the general ratio between accumulation and consumption in the economy as a whole and the balance of resource flows between agriculture and industry, town and country. Three elements are important for our purposes: first, the mechanism of agricultural planning; second, administrative extraction through direct taxation; third, relations of exchange between agricultural and industrial commodities.

Agricultural planning and determination of the product mix

Rural collectives do not enjoy autonomy in allocating resources to different lines of production. The structure of agricultural production is formally included in the Chinese planning mechanism. The planning process moves up and down the hierarchy of state and collective units, each level elaborating its own plan in co-ordination with superior and subordinate units.[29] There seems to be a significant degree of flexibility built into this process, but the amount appears to vary according to the nature of the product. Priority claims on the resources of the teams go to 'category one' items, including grain, edible oil and cotton, and planning demands are strict. There is progressively greater flexibility allowed for 'category two' (including sugar, pork and tobacco) and 'category three' items (a residual list).[30] As for the plethora of small sideline products, it is difficult to incorporate them directly into the plan: this is done indirectly by purchasing contracts signed with state commercial organs.

It is arguable, though not statistically provable, that this system of planning restraints exerted an equalising influence on the relative incomes of rural collectives. There is ample evidence that the return per labour-day and per unit of land vary considerably between different lines of production, even in respect to the official price structure of agricultural commodities determined by the state. The state sector aside, moreover, agricultural commodities marketed in local 'free' markets generally fetch higher prices. Given these unequal returns, one would of course expect notionally autonomous collectives to choose lines of production which maximise their incomes and, given unequal factor endowments, one would expect this to magnify inter-collective differentials. To the extent that income maximisation is restrained through planning and other mechanisms, inter-collective differentials are reduced. The main issue has been the degree of emphasis to be placed on the production of grain, which is relatively 'cheap' compared to other sources of income. During the 1960s and early to mid 1970s, China has sought, for economic, political and military reasons, to develop self-sufficiency in grain production. Under the slogan of 'grain as the key link', considerable pressure has been brought to bear on collectives to devote a larger share of resources to grain production than they would otherwise wish.[31] To the extent that this has precluded more profitable endeavours, considerable tension developed between state planning authorities and basic-level collectives, sometimes finding expression within the formal planning process (complaints or revisions submitted to higher authorities by teams, brigades and communes) or through various forms of evasion or concealment.

Administrative extraction: the agricultural tax

It is accepted generally that the agricultural tax in China has remained stable in terms of total physical amount (it is mostly collected in kind, in grain) since the early 1950s and may even have declined absolutely.[32] As a result of increased agricultural output, the agricultural tax is said to have fallen from 12 per cent of farm output in 1952 to only 5 per cent in the mid-1970s. The tax paid by each team is calculated on the basis of its yields in a normal year and, once fixed, this norm stays unchanged 'for a certain period of time'. In terms of its distributive impact, the tax is regressive since it declines steadily as a proportion of total output as production increases.[33]

Modes of exchange: the marketing of agricultural and industrial products

The most important agricultural product is grain and the grain trade is formally entirely under unified state management – private trade in grain during the period in question was illegal. A compulsory quota is fixed for each team to sell to the state. Compulsory purchase quotas apply in addition to cotton and edible oil. Above-quota sales of these items must also be made to the state, but the price on such sales is above that for the quota portion. Unlike the agricultural tax, compulsory purchase quotas of grain are raised at regular intervals following the growth of production. There has been an effort to bring many other commodities under state management through delivery contracts between collectives and state commercial organs, which may in fact have the character of compulsory sales.

This purchasing system has generally been applied only to collective production; peasants have been able to dispose of the produce of their private plots outside in the rural fairs. These fairs have themselves been subject to state regulation, however, in terms of location, timing, nature of goods sold and prices. But prices in rural markets generally have been higher than those in the state sector.

It has been accepted generally that the terms of trade between industrial and agricultural commodities have steadily moved in favour of agriculture since the early 1950s.[34] Purchase prices for agricultural commodities have risen at different rates, though the evidence on specific commodities is ambiguous.[35] In the case of industrial goods, the price of capital goods has been the main component in stabilising the general price index. Most price indices of capital goods supplied to the countryside show a significant secular decline in price per unit.[36]

The system of exchange procedures contained elements which both fostered and restricted inequalities between collective units. On the one hand, there was the basic contradiction arising from the relationship between unequally endowed collectives and a uniform price structure. One Chinese source described the problem as follows:

> Due to the fact that each collective economic unit has different production conditions and a different degree of technical skill, thus the labour-time expended to produce the same quantity and quality of products is unequal i.e. the production costs expended are unequal. Since, in a system of commodity exchange, an equal quantity of product in the same area can only be sold at the same price, in the process of exchange some collective units make money and some lose it.[37]

The inequalities thus generated become cumulative if the more prosperous collectives plough back their extra income into the purchase of agricultural inputs. On the other hand, through the compulsory purchase quota system, the exchange mechanism tended to restrict inequality, by controlling the ability of collectives to maximise their incomes within the given configuration of prices.

If we view this complex of administrative and commercial linkages as a whole, therefore, its impact on inter-collective inequalities was ambiguous, during the period under study. Any firm evaluation is complicated by the fact that realities often belied policy prescriptions, especially in the uncertain political atmosphere of the 1970s. It seems that many teams did not plant their crops according to the state plan, but 'planted, in a "free planting way", whatever would earn them more money'.[38] Others took on the role of collective entrepreneurs, selling agricultural and sideline products on local free markets where they fetched higher prices. Some teams even set up informal 'back door' marketing arrangements with state commercial organs.[39] Relationships between state and collective, moreover, were fraught with considerable tension during this period, with frequent reports of basic-level reluctance to comply with planning directives (notably over the ratio of grain to other crops) or official marketing requirements.[40] These tensions came to the surface in the aftermath of the 1976 anti-radical coup and can be seen as part of the reason for the sweeping changes in rural policy witnessed in the late 1970s.

Accumulation and distribution in the rural collectives

Process of accumulation

Accumulation takes place at each of the three levels of the commune structure. During the early and mid-1970s, there was considerable official pressure for high rates of accumulation for a variety of reasons, both developmental (for example, the desire to encourage the purchase of farm inputs and to promote rural industrialisation), strategic (notably the threat of war with the Soviet Union, particularly prominent at the beginning of the decade) and redistributive (the desire to smooth out the impact of harvest fluctuations on consumption levels, or restrain any sudden leaps in consumption levels in rich collectives).

There was particular emphasis on the importance of accumulation at the brigade and commune levels whose relative economic shares seem to have increased over this period. Bare statistics on relative shares require qualification. In the brigade and commune sectors, output per worker is generally considerably higher than in agriculture and output per unit of capital is probably higher also. Thus their contribution to total accumulation in the commune may well be much greater than either their share of output, of the labour force, or of the value of fixed assets. For example, in Liu-chi commune in 1971–5, commune-run industries and other enterprises were providing 37.9 per cent of total commune revenues, yet were contributing fully 73.3 per cent of total commune accumulation.[41]

Ideally, accumulation at the different levels is based on the principles of cooperation, mutual benefit and rational division of labour. Accumulation at the two higher levels depends on two sources: that derived internally and (leaving aside the complex question of state loans or grants) that derived from lower-level collectives. Given the fact that each level is under pressure to accumulate, the latter relationship has generated tension and conflict. According to official policy, higher levels may draw resources from lower levels but only according to strict rules. The transaction must be based on the principle of 'equivalent exchange' i.e. the higher level must offer the lower level a share in the proceeds of new enterprises in proportion to their contribution.[42] For example, if a commune requires labour for a basic construction project, the lower units contribute their labour quotas in direct proportion to the amount of benefit it is expected they will derive from the project. If a brigade calls on its constituent teams to provide funds to build a pumping-station which will permit the opening up of new land, then each team should receive a share of the new land proportional to its contribution. If this system works properly, then lower levels welcome the development of higher level sectors because they contribute directly to their incomes (through a share of profits of higher level enterprises) or to general levels of collective welfare (either through the construction of physical facilities such as schools and health centres or by subsidising the cost that peasants pay for such services).

On the negative side, however, the desire to accumulate at higher levels has led to competition between levels; there has been a tendency for higher levels to resort to pressure and expropriation or 'equalisation and indiscriminate transfer'. Particularly in more advanced areas, state authorities were at times obliged to intervene to halt the expansion of commune and brigade enterprises because they were draining too much labour away from agriculture.[43]

There has been strong pressure on the production team to maintain a high level of accumulation. Official policy statements laid great stress on the vital importance of accumulation for expanding production and establishing a stable base for long-run growth in living standards. Thus, in the sequence of decision-making processes that the team is supposed to undergo in working out its annual plan for income distribution, distribution for personal consumption comes last. Over-emphasis on consumption was denounced as 'revisionist', taking the form of 'three depletions' (distributing, eating and using up everything) and 'four non-retentions' (failure to retain for the public accumulation fund, the welfare fund, production expenses, and reserve grain).

A 'correct' relationship between consumption and accumulation was elaborated which assumed that the personal income of team members should increase gradually as production increases.[44] The basic principle is to 'deduct more and accumulate more' in good years while still allowing some increase in the personal income of team members. This extra accumulation not only increases output over the long run but also acts as a cushion for personal incomes in bad years. Implicit in this is the idea that teams which are growing rapidly and where incomes are relatively high should increase the level of accumulation accordingly – a provision which is crucial for questions of rural inequality.[45] In general, official policy during this period envisaged a relatively slow improvement in living standards along with a relatively rapid increase in public accumulation, the 'correct' ratio in any given context varying according to economic level and rate of economic growth. For example, in Liu-chi Commune, between 1957 and 1975, the total value of agricultural and sideline production at all collective levels rose by 250 per cent, accumulation by 547 per cent and per capita consumption by only 83 per cent.[46]

To summarise this section on accumulation, it seems that the distributive impact of both policy and practice in the 1970s was ambiguous. On the one hand, the logic of accumulation policy (notably the principle of 'equivalent exchange' and the provisions for differential accumulation ratios) and the nature of the long-term accumulation process which it envisaged, would seem to encourage growing inequality in per capita output between collectives. A partial qualification to this process is provided by the increasing contribution made by brigade and commune levels to the provision of welfare and educational facilities. The qualification is only partial since such services normally are not free and fees are often more than 'nominal'. On the other hand, CCP policy on accumulation has been egalitarian in that it has placed limits on the short-term possibilities for richer teams to convert higher levels of per capita output into higher levels of consumption, a source of not inconsiderable exasperation to many teams in the 1970s.

Processes of income distribution within the production team

Private income: As noted, the household economy provides a significant proportion of household income and an even higher proportion
of household cash income. Cash from sidelines is especially important
since cash receipts from the collectives are distributed usually only
periodically, at the time of each harvest. While evidence is limited, what
there is tends to suggest that the combined income from the private plot,
domestic sidelines and private outside work is a major source of
inequality. The degree of inequality, however, depends on various
factors, which we can group under two headings, viz. the nature of
individual households and contextual factors. Variations in the number
of able-bodied labourers per household make an obvious difference but,
probably more important, are variations in 'enterprise' and skill. Rural
skills in sideline, handicraft and other productions are still to a
considerable extent hereditary. This tends to reproduce pre-existing
patterns of unequal skill and, to the extent that these skills can be
converted into income, favours previous upper strata. This is reflected in
statistics from a survey of 100 households in Guangxi province which
showed that the total per-capita income of 70 poor- and lower-middle
peasant households was 46 per cent lower than for 22 upper-middle
peasant households,* a differential largely deriving from the difference
in private income which was over 100 per cent.[47]

The amount of inequality deriving from the household sector varies,
however, according to certain contextual factors. First, it varies
according to local differences in the level of demand for goods and
services generated by households and the amount and variety of
profitable opportunities for such activities in the locality. Second, there
are political constraints, viz. the local political environment (are team or
brigade cadres strict about enforcing controls over household enterprises or do they 'grasp politics loosely'?) and the national policy
environment. These are obviously connected, albeit rather loosely.
During the period in question, national policy was relatively tough on
the household sector and this was often translated into effective, if
unpopular, controls at the grass-roots. The change in rural policy late in
the decade and consistent criticisms of 'ultra-leftist' local cadres have led
to a more benign official attitude to private economy.[48] To the extent
that this new policy emphasis provides more scope for private economic
activity, it will contribute to inter-household inequalities, and slow the

_____
* In each case, the classifications into strata date from the 1950s.

process of eradicating inequalities left over from pre-revolutionary society.

Collective income: After the deduction of the agricultural tax, various forms of collective accumulation and production costs, the remainder of a team's total income, in cash and in kind, is available for distribution to individual members. This process is illustrated in Table 10.1, describing the year-end distribution in one team in 1973.[49] Of the total amount distributed to individuals calculated in the year-end account, a portion already will have been distributed in the 'advance distribution' coinciding with the harvests earlier in the year.

The basic principle for distributing collective income to individuals has been spelled out on innumerable occasions in the Chinese press: the socialist principle of distribution 'from each according to his/her ability, to each according to his/her work'. This means payment according to the quantity and quality of labour contributed by each worker to the collective. It is officially recognised that, within a production team, there will be differences between members in their level of physical strength, diligence and technical skill, so that each worker will be able to complete a different amount of collective labour in a given time. The principle thus produces unequal rewards, but this inequality is seen as historically unavoidable and economically desirable given the stage of development: on the one hand, economic scarcity still exists and the necessary material basis for 'communist' distribution 'according to need' has not been established; on the other hand, the consciousness of the mass of the population is not 'communist', i.e. they still allow calculations of material reward to influence their work. The principle of 'distribution according to work' is thus seen as an essential incentive which 'raises enthusiasm for collective production', increases the motivation to improve skills and work quality, consolidates labour discipline, penalises slackers and rewards the energetic and reduces tensions between team members.[50]

Though official policy statements make no mention of implementing the communist principle of 'distribution according to need' at the present stage, in reality there are elements of this principle in the actual process of distribution at the grass-roots level. This has three aspects. First, an increasing amount of resources has been devoted to improving the provision of collective health and educational facilities in the rural areas. To the extent that such facilities are increasingly available to all team members at nominal charges (as of the late 1970s this goal was still quite a way off), they tend to raise the collective component of

TABLE 10.1 'Diligent and frugal' production team: year-end final account (31 Dec. 1973)

Income			Expenses			Distribution		
Item	Amount of money	% gross income	Item	Amount of money	% gross income	Item	Amount of money	% gross income
Income total	24,000	100	Expenses total	6,000	25.0	Total amount for distribution	18,000	75.0
Agricultural income	18,500	77.1	(i) agricultural	4,000	16.7	(i) Tax money	1,030	4.3
Forestry income	500	2.1	(ii) forestry	100	0.4	(ii) Collective retentions	2,420	10.1
Animal income	1,800	7.5	(iii) animal	1,016	4.2	(a) Common accumulation fund	1,200	5.0
Sideline income	2,500	10.4	(iv) sideline	600	2.5	(b) Common welfare fund	480	2.0
Fishing income	580	2.4	(v) fishing	200	0.8	(c) Production expenses basic fund	360	1.5
Other income	120	0.5	(vi) other	34	0.2	(d) Grain resource basic fund	380	1.6
			(vii) management	50	0.2	(iii) 'Overall' fund	150	0.6
						(iv) Distribution to commune members	14,400	60.0

Source: Guangxi Branch of the Chinese People's Bank (ed.), *Rural People's Commune Production Team Financial Accounting* (Guangxi People's Publishing House, 1974) p. 96.

individual income and thereby reduce inequalities in real income between team members. 'Special consideration' is often shown in the distribution process to individuals or households who are in difficulties through no fault of their own. Special consideration can take the form of adjustments in workpoint ratings or operate through the 'five guarantee' system (food, clothing, fuel, a proper burial and school fees, recently a sixth guarantee, medical care, has been included in those villages that can afford it.) Most of the recipients of 'five guarantee aid' are old widowed women, but they also include the dependents of dead soldiers, the mentally ill, orphans, and so on.[51] The standard of living that the 'five guarantee' households are provided from collective coffers is generally relatively low, enough for survival and little more. Moreover the proportion of collective members receiving such benefits on a long-term basis rarely exceeds 2 per cent and is usually about 1 per cent. But to be able to provide even these limited welfare benefits is a major achievement for a poor country and is clearly one of the distributive benefits of the collective system.[52]

A third aspect of distribution that is effectively 'according to need' is the procedure for dividing up grain available for distribution. To ensure that all team members achieve a minimum of grain consumption, distributable grain is classified into two parts: a 'basic grain ration' and 'workpoint grain'. This method is supported as combining a 'basic livelihood' for all with adequate incentives for stronger and more skilled team members.[53] The size of the ration varies according to age – in one model example, it was divided into five categories ranging from 220 *jin** per capita at under one year to 470 *jin* for adult workers. The ratio between the grain ration and workpoint grain is clearly very important. In 1974, it was recommended in Guangdong province that the latter should not exceed 30 per cent of total distributable grain, though elsewhere ratios of 60:40 and 80:20 have been reported.[54] However, the ration is not entirely a system of distribution according to need since it has to be earned: it is deducted from the total income of the household which is calculated on the basis of work points. If the ration exceeds a family's total earnings, the family may receive a loan from the team, thus becoming an 'overdrawn household'.

Grain ration aside, however, the principle of 'distribution according to work' rules the allocation of collective income to individuals, the

---

* A Chinese catty, slightly over one pound or about ½ kilogram.

measure being workpoints.* The value of the workpoint is simply the total amount available for distribution to team members divided by the total number of workpoints earned by team members during the year. There is a great variety of methods for calculating workpoints but most fall into two major categories: allocation by the task (often called 'piecerates') and allocation by the person (also called 'dayrates'). Task-based distribution is a relatively complex system of remuneration based on different types of work. While this method is held to have certain advantages, notably greater efficiency in the allocation of labour and greater incentive for personal effort, it is also recognised that it widens differentials, rewarding the stronger and the more skilled. During the early and mid 1970s, therefore, allocation by the task was in official disfavour, for increasing inequalities and encouraging peasants to 'put workpoints in command'. The basis of the system of allocation according to person is a personal rating usually assigned democratically at meetings of the team membership – a person's total workpoints is his or her total labour-days multiplied by this rating. The model for such a system was the Tachai production brigade in Shensi province where the rating was assessed in an annual meeting on the basis of 'self-assessment and group appraisal'. This method seems to have narrowed differentials in workpoints because the public context of assessment encouraged modesty and the operation of a kind of 'maximin' principle and tended to foster the tendency to give 'special consideration' to individuals in the light of their particular circumstances known to other members of the team.[55] For this reason, the system of allocation according to the person was in official favour during this period and was an important component of the 'learn from Tachai' movement.

How unequal was the distribution of workpoints in the early and mid 1970s? Concrete information on differentials is limited, but it has been suggested that by the mid-1970s the range of work points between the highest and the lowest workers was 2:1.[56] If we translate this ratio into workpoints (10:5 per day), it is probable that most adult workers cluster within a range of only 2–3 points (i.e. 8–10 points). Most able-bodied male workers would receive 9 or 10, whereas women were likely to be rated lower at 7 to 9. Levels 5 and 6 were usually reserved for the old or sick. A most detailed analysis, in two villages in Guangdong, found that the earnings of the top decile of workers took about 16 per cent of collective income, and the bottom decile 6–7 per cent; the top quintile

---

* Table 10.2 shows the different components of collective income for four households.

took 29 per cent and the bottom quintile about 14 per cent. In each case, the middle three quintiles took about 57 per cent of collective income.[57] Judging from the assessments of Western scholars and official Chinese complaints of excessive 'egalitarianism' in workpoint distribution in 1971 and at the end of the decade, not only were differentials narrower compared with earlier decades but there was a trend towards equalisation in the first half of the decade.[58]

Within the workpoint structure, an important source of inequality has been the tendency for women to receive systematically less workpoints. Even in Tachai, a woman could at best hope to earn 8.5 per day (in 1973) compared to 11 for a man.[59] Despite extensive propaganda to overcome this problem in the early 1970s there were continued reports of widespread prevalence of differentials based on gender and grass-roots resistance to the principle of 'equal pay for equal work' from chauvinist cadres and team members.[60]

Western observers have suggested that the rise of small-scale industry at the commune and brigade level has not accentuated income inequality within the production team since the workers there generally receive their payment from the team rather than the enterprise, i.e. the wage from the enterprise goes into the team's funds, the industrial worker receives income on the basis of work-points like other members of the team and any surplus between wages and workpoints accrues to the team's funds. It is also suggested that an industrial worker receives the same welfare benefits as his fellow team members.[61] However, these arrangements are clearly not universal and there are tendencies working to separate industrial wages from the team's control and to increase differentials between industrial and agricultural income. In a commune in the Shanghai area, for example, workers in the commune's 'repair and construction brigade' prior to 1973 were receiving, in addition to their workpoints in the team, a bonus of 45 *yuan* and a daily food subsidy of 0.3. *yuan*. In this enterprise in 1972, the average income of staff and workers was 720.8 *yuan*, compared to an average of income of 500-odd *yuan* for ordinary commune members.[62] The cadres in one team in suburban Peking organised team members to do outside contract work (building houses). Apart from high work-points, these workers were given very high subsidies for food, tools and travel. These items accounted for 40 per cent of the total income from the contract and effectively became additional income. The extra income alone earned by two of these able-bodied contract workers in only two months was equivalent to the annual income of one able-bodied worker who stayed and worked in the production team.[63] Official policy discouraged such large differentials in cash income and welfare benefits both on principle and for the very practical reason that they had a bad effect on peasant morale (i.e. they wanted to leave agriculture and were tempted to leave their teams, legally or illegally, to seek 'better' jobs elsewhere).

While the data on inequalities in collective earnings per worker show relatively small differentials, it must be remembered that there are great variations between *households* in their 'dependency ratio', i.e. the relationship between able-bodied labourers and dependents.[64] Consequently, inequalities in average per-capita household income are likely to be significantly greater than those in earnings per worker. However, inequalities arising from such causes are likely to be fluid, varying significantly from one stage in the family life-cycle to another.

To summarise this section then there were important constraints operating on the potential development of inequalities within the collective unit in the early and mid-1970s. A basic floor had been established under rural incomes through the grain ration, collective welfare provisions and the 'five guarantees'. The degree of inequality in work-point earnings between collective workers may well have narrowed relative to the 1960s. Moreover, within the collective unit, everyone benefitted from an increase in the value of the work-point, in the manner of the Chinese saying, 'the boat rises with the water level'.

However, it must be acknowledged that there still existed an important private sector and that the income from this sector may well have been a major contributor to income inequalities within the production team. It is also possible that, to the degree that there was a compression of work-point differentials, the balance of incentives for the stronger and more skilled peasant may have shifted towards the private sector. Thus a narrowing of inequalities in collective income may have been counter-balanced to some extent by a widening of differentials in private income.

CONCLUSIONS

Most analysts agree that economic inequalities in the Chinese countryside have decreased significantly compared to the pre-revolutionary situation. Blecher has tested this hypothesis statistically and his figures support it, showing 'pronounced differences of income distribution before and after 1949'.[65] Analysts such as Khan and Byres/Nolan have argued that rural economic inequalities in China are low compared to many other Third World countries.[66] Moreover, differentials apart, the

Chinese have been extraordinarily successful in designing a system of rural distribution which puts a 'floor' under the incomes and welfare of all the rural population. We would argue that the relatively narrow extent of Chinese rural income differentials and the ability to provide for the basic needs of all the rural population are inextricable from the socialist elements of China's political economy. The establishment of a new system of social relations of production in the 1950s laid the social, political and institutional framework for a relatively egalitarian pattern of rural development.

As we have seen in this chapter, however, China's rural political economy in the 1970s contains its own distinct pattern of inequalities, based on a wide variety of causes, both ecological and institutional. Given the crucial autonomous role of the Party in the Chinese system, the role of Party policies has proven an important causal factor in both compressing and widening differentials. The late 1960s and early to mid 1970s was a period when leftist leaders had some impact on rural policy and various redistributive policies current during this period seem to have had a degree of success in reducing rural differentials or holding them in check. In the eyes of the post-Mao leadership, however, there was 'too much egalitarianism' in the Chinese countryside during this period and they blame the alleged 'ultraleftism' of the previous Maoist leadership for this. In the new leadership's view, such egalitarian policies and practices are developmentally harmful since they reduce incentives and thereby productivity. They have put redistributive priorities on the back burner and have introduced a new set of policies to speed agricultural growth and raise rural incomes.[67]

At this early stage in the new strategy, its impact on rural economic growth and overall peasant standards appears to have been favourable on most indices: gross output of key commodities, average rural incomes (rising from 117 *yuan* per capita in 1977 to 170 in 1980), volume of rural market activity and growth in rural savings. It appears likely, however, that the fruits of increasing prosperity have been shared unequally since many of the new policies have inegalitarian implications: an emphasis on product specialisation according to natural comparative advantage (as opposed, for example, to overall enforcement of the principle of 'grain as the key link') which should lead to greater differentials between agricultural regions; a tougher 'businesslike' approach to rural credit (notably a crackdown on individual or household 'overdrafts' and unpaid state loans to collectives) which implies a diminution of the redistributive element in the Party's financial policies; an effort to enforce strictly the principle of 'equivalent exchange' between levels in the commune structure; an attempt to expand the household sector by encouraging domestic sideline production and allowing more scope for rural 'free' markets; moves to allocate state investment funds (notably for mechanisation) preferentially to a small number of favoured areas; the decision to allow direct marketing of agricultural produce in the cities and to expand 'putting out' work from large urban factories to smaller rural factories which will favour the better-situated suburban communes; and a clear distaste for methods of intra-team income distribution based on 'assessment by the person' in favour of some form of piece-rate system. In short, the new rural strategy is likely to intensify the already existing pattern of inequalities at regional, local and intra-unit levels.

It would be myopic to view the new policies as the result of mere changes in the relative power position of a few key leaders in the CCP. Rural policy is at the centre of a complex political process involving a wide range of actors and interests. Focussing on the rural sector, some of these competing interests have come into view in this chapter: rich *vs.* poor collectives; workers and staff in rural industry *vs.* ordinary peasants; suburban communes as opposed to more remote and less favoured communes; households with higher or lower dependency ratios within the teams; individuals with greater or lesser strength or skills within the teams; and 'leftist' *vs.* more conservative rural cadres and Party members. While the relatively egalitarian policies of the late 1960s and early 1970s benefited certain collectives, households and individuals, they clearly ran against the interests of, and thus antagonised, other sectors of the rural population who were to provide a social basis for the policy changes of the late 1970s. These political factors pose crucial questions about the evolving rural political economy of the post-Mao era. Will rural inequalities be allowed to expand unchecked so long as the agricultural growth statistics are favourable, or will the pendulum swing back to a more egalitarian rural strategy? How likely is such a policy swing, given the fact that the leftist leadership in the CCP has been purged and the rural beneficiaries of redistributive policies, almost by definition, lack political resources compared with their opponents? If the political impetus for a return to egalitarian rural policies is lacking, is there not a danger that the growth-oriented policies of the post-Mao leadership will reinforce rural inequalities, creating constellations of powerful interests which will act to defend their advantage and prevent any return to redistributive policies? Policy and political issues such as these will be an important challenge for the CCP leadership in the 1980s and their outcome will

TABLE 10.2 'Diligent and frugal' production team (year-end final accounts): chart of calculations of income distribution to household (31 Dec. 73).

Head of household	Element	People	Labour power	Income for distribution		Total	Deductions						Current year accounts balance		Repayment or previous years over-spending		Final balance of accounts	Commune members seal
				Total work points	Equivalent in money		Grain ration amount		Oil ration amount		Advance distribution loan outlay	Total	Money that should be paid out	Over-spent money	Previous year's over-spending	Repaid money	Amount of ready cash that should be received	Accumulated over-spent money
							Grain ration	Money	Oil ration	Money								
Li Wei	Poor	4	2	5,500	400	440	2,455	233.22	16	12.80	80	326.02	113.58				113.98	
Chang Jian	Lower middle	7	4	10,000	800	800	4,400	421.80	28	22.40	150	594.20	205.80				205.80	
Chen Gong	Middle	5	2	5,000	400	400	3,000	285.00	20	16.00	20	321.00	79.00			30	49.00	
Li Quiang	Poor	7	2	4,600	368	368	3,680	349.60	28	22.40		372.00		4	40			44
Other households		127	58	154,900	12,392	4,392	76,425	7,260.38	508	406.40	1,550	9,216.78	3,175.22		30	30	3,175.22	
Total		150	68	180,000	14,400	14,400	90,000	8,550.00	600	480.00	1,800	10,830.00	3,574.00	4	70	30	3,544.00	44

Source: As Table 10.1.
Notes: (value of labour day = 0.80 yuan.)
(Units: jin (physical)
yuan (financial)

272   *Work, Income and Inequality*

have crucial implications for the claim that the Chinese version of socialist development is an egalitarian one.

NOTES

1. We have attempted a preliminary assessment in P. Nolan and G. White, 'The distributive implications of China's new agricultural policies', J. Gray and G. White (eds), *China's New Development Strategy* (London: Academic Press, 1982).
2. For two useful contributions to this debate, see A. Foster-Carter, 'The modes of production controversy', *New Left Review*, no. 107 (Jan.–Feb. 1978) pp. 47–77; and M. Godelier, 'Infrastructure, societies and history', *New Left Review*, no. 112 (Nov.–Dec. 1978) pp. 84–96. For an official (as of mid-1975) Chinese discussion of these concepts, see Chin Yuan, 'Terms of political economy explained', *Guangming Ribao* (Glorious Daily), (16 April 1975), translated in *Survey of People's Republic of China Press* (hereafter SPRCP) Hongkong: US Consulate General, no. 5844 (2 May 1975) pp. 197–207.
3. For an excellent discussion of the Party's role, see F. Schurmann, *Ideology and Organisation in Communist China* (hereafter Schurmann, *Ideology and Organisation*) (Berkeley and Los Angeles: University of California Press, 1968) pp. 105–72.
4. For a comprehensive, well-argued analysis of these differences, see J. Gray, 'The two roads: alternative strategies of social change and economic growth in China', in S. R. Schram (ed.), *Authority, Participation and Cultural Change in China* (Cambridge: Cambridge University Press, 1973) (hereafter Schram (ed.), *Authority, Participation*) 109–157. For a discussion dealing specifically with the late 1960s and early 1970s, see Dennis Woodward, '"Two line struggle" in agriculture', in B. Brugger (ed.), *China: The Impact of the Cultural Revolution* (London: Croom Helm, 1978) pp. 153–70.
5. For a vivid and penetrating description of pre-revolutionary Chinese agriculture, see R. H. Tawney, *Land and Labour in China* (London. Allen and Unwin, 1932).
6. Consider for example the following data on the production of selected agricultural inputs:

TABLE 10.3

	1964	1974
Powered irrigation equipment (1,000 h.p.)	860	5,984
Tractors (15 h.p. units)	29,347	133,263
Chemical fertiliser (1,000 metric tons)	5,780	24,880

Source: R. M. Field, 'Civilian industrial production in the People's Republic of China: 1949–74', in *China: A Reassessment of the Economy*, Joint Economic Committee, Congress of the United States (Washington: US Government Printing Office, 1975) (hereafter *China: A Reassessment*) pp. 165–6. For a comprehensive discussion of this process of agricultural modernisation, see B. Stavis, *Making Green Revolution* (Ithaca: Cornell University, 1974).

7. For a general survey of technical changes in Chinese agriculture, see T. B. Wiens, 'The evolution of policy and capabilities in China's agricultural technology', in *The Chinese Economy Post-Mao*, Joint Economic Committee, Congress of the United States (Washington: US Government Printing Office, 1978) (hereafter *The Chinese Economy Post-Mao*) pp. 671–703.
8. For an account of the evolution of this strategy, see C. Riskin, 'Small industry and the Chinese model of development', *The China Quarterly*, no. 46 (April–June 1971).
9. J. Sigurdson, *Rural Industrialisation in China* (Cambridge, Mass. and London: Harvard University Press, 1977) pp. 3–4. Sigurdson defines 'rural industries' as those located at the county, commune levels or below. They include both heavy and light industry, the former tending to be located at the county level. They can vary in size from less than 20 to over 200 employees.
10. See G. W. Skinner, 'Marketing and social structure in rural China', *Journal of Asian Studies* vol. 24: nos. 1 (Nov. 1964), 2 (Feb. 1965) and 3 (May 1965).
11. For example, see Chin Chi-tsu and Hung Sung, 'Equal pay for equal work for men and women', *Hong Qi (Red Flag)* (hereafter HQ) no. 2 (1 Feb. 1972), translated in *Selections from China's Mainland Magazines* (hereafter SCMM) (Hongkong: US Consulate General) no. 723–4.
12. For some details on rural female industrial employment, see The American Rural Small-Scale Industry Delegation, *Rural Small-Scale Industry in the People's Republic of China* (Berkeley: University of California Press, 1974) pp. 40–4. For a comprehensive discussion of rural female employment see Marina Thorborg, 'Chinese employment policy in 1949–78 with special emphasis on women in rural production', in *The Chinese Economy Post-Mao*, pp. 535–604.
13. For example, see 'Run well the commune and brigade-run enterprises in accordance with socialist principles' by the Shanghai County Revolutionary Committee Investigation Team, *Xüexi yü Pipan* (Study and Criticism) (hereafter XXYPP) no. 5, 1975.
14. R. H. Myers, 'Cooperation in traditional agriculture and its implications for team farming in the People's Republic of China' in D. H. Perkins (ed.), *China's Modern Economy in Historical Perspective* (Stanford: Stanford University Press, 1975) pp. 261–77.
15. For an overview of the process of collectivisation in comparative perspective see Peter Nolan, 'Collectivisation in China: Some comparisons with the USSR', *Journal of Peasant Studies*, vol. 3: no. 2 (Jan. 1976) p. 193. See also K. R. Walker, 'Collectivisation in retrospect', *The China Quarterly*, no. 26 (April–June 1966) and J. Gray, 'The high tide of socialism in the Chinese countryside', in J. Chen and N. Tarling (eds), *Studies in the Social History of China and South East Asia* (Cambridge University Press, 1970).
16. For a discussion of post-leap changes in the communes, see K. R. Walker, *Planning in Chinese Agriculture: Socialisation and the Private Sector, 1956–1962* (London: Frank Cass, 1965), Chaps. 5 and 6.
17. For useful accounts of this period, see Frederick W. Crook, 'The commune system in the People's Republic of China, 1963–74', in *China: A Reassessment*; and Byung-Joon Ahn, 'The political economy of the people's commune in China: Changes and continuities', *Journal of Asian Studies*, vol. 24: no. 3 (May 1978).

18. As of the end of 1977, there were 2,000 state farms: see Green and Kilpatrick, 'China's agricultural production', in *The Chinese Economy Post-Mao*, p. 619. In the mid-1970s, about 90 per cent of irrigation-drainage machinery and about 80 per cent of tractors and draught animals were under collective ownership (Source: Chang Chun-ch'iao, *On Exercising All-Round Dictatorship over the Bourgeoisie* (Peking: Foreign Language Press, 1975) p. 6).

19. *The Socialist Collective Ownership System* (Shehuizhuyi jiti suoyouzhi) (Guangxi People's Publishing House, 1976) pp. 27–8 (hereafter *The Socialist Collective Ownership System*); Crook, 'The commune system in the PRC' in *China: A Reassessment of the Economy*, p. 375.

20. Shanghai County CCP Committee, 'We must still struggle to fight – an understanding from studying "On the question of agricultural cooperation"', *XXYPP*, no. 7 (1975) (hereafter: Shanghai County CCP Committee, 'We must still struggle. . .')

21. Chin Chi-chu, 'Red Tachai flowers are blossoming everywhere', *Peking Review*, vol. 18: no. 50 (12 Dec. 1978).

22. W. L. Parrish, 'Socialism and the Chinese peasant family' *Journal of Asian Studies*, vol. 24: no. 3 (May 1975) p. 619.

23. J. Unger, 'Collective incentives in the Chinese countryside: Lessons from Chen Village', *World Development*, vol. 6: no. 5 (May 1978) p. 596. In respect to variations according to level of technical development, it is interesting to note that a study of seven brigades in Hubei province in central China, in the highly mechanised Liu-Chi commune, revealed that the ratio of collective to private shares in total household income changed from 70 : 30 in 1957, to 90 : 10 in the mid 1970s (sources, Agricultural Mechanisation in Liu-Chi Commune, Beijing: People's Publishing House, 1976; translated in *Chinese Economic Studies*, vol. II: no. 4, summer 1978).

24. *The Socialist Collective Ownership System*, pp. 45–6.

25. Shanghai County CCP Committee, 'We must still struggle . . .' In Liu-Chi Commune in Hupei province in 1968, the income level of 25 poor productive teams was 31.6 per cent lower than the commune average (Source: *Agricultural Mechanisation in Liu-Chi Commune*, p. 29).

26. By contrast, the CCP encouraged such 'collective entrepreneurship' in the late 1970s: for example, see 'Is money synonymous with capitalism?', *Beijing Review*, no. 3 (19 Jan. 1979) pp. 5–6.

27. For a detailed discussion of the role of Tachai as a model in the 1970s, see Neville Maxwell, 'Learning from Tachai', *World Development*, vol. 3: nos. 7–8 (July-Aug., 1975) (hereafter, Maxwell, 'Learning from Tachai').

28. James Nickum describes this process at work in his 'Labour accumulation in rural China and its role since the Cultural Revolution', *Cambridge Journal of Economics*, 1978, 2, pp. 273–86. He notes that 'a strict adherence to exchange at equivalent values has a dampening effect on inter-unit projects', therefore higher levels tend to ignore it and engage in 'the unrequited transfer of resources from the haves to the have-nots' (p. 284).

29. For an excellent analysis of the planning process, see Marianne Bastid, 'Levels of economic decision-making', in Schram (ed.), *Authority, Participation*, pp. 159–97.

30. V. D. Lippit, 'The commune and economic development in China', *Current Scene*, vol. 13: no. 12 (Dec. 1975) pp. 6–9.

31. For an example of the debate over this issue in one commune in Jiangsu province in the early 1970s, see Wu Chou, *Report from Tungting – A People's Commune on Taihu Lake*, Beijing: Foreign Languages Press, 1975, p. 22. According to this account, there was a 'two line struggle' between advocates of two competing principles: 'take grain as the key link' *vs.* 'rely on the state for food-grain and on oneself for cash'.
32. This is suggested by Perkins ('Constraints influencing China's agricultural performance' in *China: a Reassessment* p. 363) and Chinese sources claim that 'the state even adjusted and reduced the tax by one-third in 1965' (Wei Min, 'China's tax policy', *Peking Review*, no. 39 (12 Sept. 1975).
33. Joan Robinson reported the existence of a directive in 1971 to readjust the tax burden while leaving the total tax payment in each county unchanged. 'In one county I visited, the readjustment had been made, taking progressive proportions of income per head in each team. In other provinces, nothing seemed to be known about it.' (Joan Robinson, *Economic Management in China* (London: Chinese Educational Institute, 1975) p. 12).
34. It should be noted that this is not the same thing as "urban-rural" terms of trade. The two have become less synonymous with the increased production of industrial goods, especially farm inputs, in the rural areas in the 1960s and 1970s.
35. Here for example are the indices for changes in the purchase prices (per kg.) of various commodities in a commune in Hunan province in central China.

TABLE 10.4

Year	Ginned Wheat	Cotton	Jute	Pork	Fish	Eggs
1957	100	100	100	100	100	100
1965	156	113	114	120	132	155
1975	178	134	114	120	177	165

Source: Hsiang Jung and Chin Chi-Chu, 'A vast rural market', *Peking Review*, no. 32–3 (9 Aug. 1976).

36. The long-term movement of relative prices of agricultural and industrial price indices has been as follows:—

TABLE 10.5

Year	Amount of industrial commodities that could be purchased with a given amount of agricultural commodities	Agricultural commodity price	Sales price of industrial inputs for agriculture[1]
1952	100	100	100
1977	170	168.8	52

Source: Zhu Weiwen, 'With great effort organise the exchange of industrial and agricultural commodities' Jungji Yanjiu (*Economic Research*) no. 4 (1979).
Note: 1. Agricultural machinery, chemical fertiliser, pesticide.

37. *The Socialist Collective Ownership System*, p. 49.
38. Chiang Wei-ch'ing, 'Further strengthens the dictatorship of the proletariat in the rural areas', *HQ*, no. 5 (1 May 1975), translated in *Selections from PRC Magazines* (hereafter SPRCM) Hongkong: US Consulate, General, no. 823–4 (27 May–2 June 1975). See also *The Socialist Collective Ownership System*, p. 50.
39. For example, see the article by the Revolutionary Mass Criticism Writing Group of Anhui province, 'Carry out well the class struggle in the sphere of rural economy', *HQ*, no. 2 (30 Jan. 1970), translated in *SCMM*, no. 673–4 (20–27 Feb. 1976).
40. For example, see the article by the Party Branch of Hsiachia Village Production Brigade, Ch'utou County Shandong Province, 'The road of Tachai is wide and broad', *HQ*, no. 1 (1 Jan. 1971), translated in *SCMM* no. 69–8 (22–29 Jan. 1971).
41. *Agricultural Mechanisation in Liu-chi Commune*, p. 67.
42. There is an excellent account of relations between different levels in the process of capital accumulation in Unger, 'Collective incentives. . .', pp. 592–5. The following examples are drawn from his account.
43. For example, see Shanghai County Revolutionary Committee, Investigation Team, 'Run well the commune – and the brigade – run enterprises according to socialist principles', *XXYPP*, no. 5, 1975 (hereafter Shanghai County, 'Run well the commune – and brigade – run enterprises. . .').
44. This is in accordance with Mao's oft-cited recommendation: 'We should do everything possible to enable the peasants in normal years to raise their personal incomes annually through increased production' (Mao Tse-tung, 'On the correct handling of contradictions among the people', 27 February 1957, in *Selected Works of Mao Tse-tung*, vol. 5, Beijing (Foreign Languages Press, 1977) p. 401).
45. This recommendation is stated explicitly in Gong Dianbo, *A Discussion of Distribution Policy*, p. 7.
46. *Agricultural Mechanisation in Liu-chi Commune*, p. 70.
47. Socialist Collective Ownership, pp. 70–1; see also Unger, 'Collective incentives. . .', p. 601, where he argues (in note 15) that 'private activities provide the major cause of income differentiation between the households of a Chen village team'.
48. For example, see 'Discussion on rural economic policies', *Peking Review*, no. 9 (3 March 1978) pp. 18–20.
49. To provide a precise background to Table 10.1, here are some basic data on the team in question: (i) 150 people took part in the distribution and the average per capita income was 96 yuan, an increase of 6 yuan over 1972; (ii) the total number of labour-days calculated was 18,000 and the value of one labour-day was .80 yuan (compared with .72 yuan in 1971); (iii) the total amount of ready cash distributed was 5,370 yuan, 35.8 yuan per capita; (iv) total income increased 9.1 per cent over 1972 while production expenses increased 7.1 per cent; (v) the 'common welfare fund' expenditure included looking after the dependents of fallen heroes, and serving soldiers (3 households, 100 yuan) subsidies to distressed families (1 household, 20 yuan), subsidies to 'five guarantee' households (1 household, 30 yuan) and outlays on the cooperative medical plan (100 yuan).

50. For a detailed discussion of this principle, see Gong Dianbo, *A Discussion of Distribution Policy*, pp. 9–12.
51. For a discussion of this system, see D. Davis Friedmann, 'Welfare practices in rural China', *World Development* vol. 6, no. 5, pp. 609–19. This section is based on her account.
52. The total outlay by a team for 'five guarantees' may be small in general, but it is still significant. Davis Friedmann (p. 163) calculates that the annual opportunity cost of providing 'five guarantees' in a typical brigade would amount to the purchase price of a new tractor.
53. See Gong Dianbo, *A Discussion of Distribution Policy*, p. 23–5 for a favourable analysis of this system.
54. Ibid., p. 26. It is interesting to note that in the model production team's account in Table 10.2, the value of the 'basic grain ration' amounted to 41.6 per cent of the total income available for distribution by the team. This raises the interesting possibility that, as a team becomes richer (with a probable fall in the share of grain in total personal income derived from the collective) there is a tendency for the proportions distributed 'according to need' to decline.
55. For a useful discussion of the advantages and disadvantages of this method, see M. K. Whyte, 'The Tachai brigade and incentives for the peasant', *Current Scene* VII: 16 (15 Aug. 1969).
56. M. K. Whyte, 'Inequality and stratification in China', *The China Quarterly*, no. 64. (Dec. 1975) p. 688.
57. M. Blecher, 'Income distribution in small rural Chinese communities', *The China Quarterly*, no. 68 (Dec. 1976) pp. 805–11.
58. Maxwell argues the latter in his 'Learning from Tachai', p. 481. For a typical critique of 'egalitarianism' from the late 1970s, see 'Economic policies in rural areas' *Beijing Review*, no. 16 (20 April 1979) pp. 17 and 20–2.
59. 'Learning from Tachai', p. 478.
60. See, for example, Chin Chi-tsu and Hung Sung, 'Equal pay for equal work for men and women', *HQ*, no. 3 (1 March 1972), translated in *SCMM*, no. 725–6 (3–10 April 1972).
61. *Small-Scale Industry in the PRC*, pp. 51–2.
62. Shanghai County, 'Run well the commune – and brigade – run enterprise. . .'.
63. Investigation Team of the Peking Municipal Committee of the CCP, 'How the label of a "lame brigade" is removed', *HQ*, no. 8 (1 Aug. 1972), translated in *SCMM*, 735–6 (29 Aug.–5 Sept. 1972).
64. For discussions of this question, see M. Blecher, 'Income distribution. . .' and E. J. Croll, 'Chiang Village: a Household Survey', *The China Quarterly*, no. 72 (Dec. 1977). Out of 27 households in the village, she found that the ratio ranged from one household in which all three members were wage earners to four households where there were twice as many dependents as earners.
65. Blecher, 'Income distribution in small rural Chinese communities', p. 813.
66. A. R. Khan, 'The Distribution of Income in Rural China' (Geneva: International Labour Organisation, 1976); T. J. Byres and P. Nolan, *Inequality: India and China Compared, 1950–70* (Open University Press, 1976).

Work, Income and Inequality

67. For comprehensive reviews of changes in agricultural policy, see B. Stavis, *Turning Point in China's Agricultural Policy* (Michigan State University: East Lansing, May 1979) and B. Brugger, 'Rural policy', in Brugger (ed.), *China since the 'Gang of Four'* (London: Croom Helm, 1980) pp. 135–73.

11 Collective Agriculture in Soviet Central Asia

AZIZUR RAHMAN KHAN
AND
DHARAM GHAI

I INTRODUCTION

The territory that now forms the Soviet Central Asian economic region was annexed by Tsarist Russia in the second half of the nineteenth century. The present national boundaries were drawn in the decade following the Soviet Revolution. Although the criteria of delimitation were linguistic and cultural each of the republics is in reality today a multinational entity. The region consists of four republics: Uzbekistan (14.5 million people in 1977), Tajikistan (3.6 million), Kirghizia (3.4 million) and Turkmenistan (2.7 million). Together the four republics have a territory of 1.3 million square kilometres. The average population density of 19 per square kilometre is misleading. Vast parts of the region consist of desert or mountains where very few people live. In the fertile river basin the density of population frequently exceeds 200 per square kilometre.

A few decades ago Central Asia was an overwhelmingly rural and extremely poor society. In recent decades it has undergone a remarkable transformation. Social institutions have been transformed in un-precedented porportions: the rural society of the region was catapulted from the middle ages into modern collective farms and State farms at one go. In contrast to many other parts of the world, the development of the rural economy in Central Asia was an integral part of the material advancement. As a result, the region continues to be predominantly rural. Thus it is interesting to analyse the Central Asian experience in agricultural and rural development in order to determine the factors that led to such a different performance in the region as compared to that in the immediate neighbouring areas.

The two main forms of agricultural organisation in the USSR are Kolkhoz (the collective farm) and Sovkhoz (the State farm).[1] In a collective farm the assets are owned or held collectively by the members who provide labour and share among themselves the net earnings. In a State farm the assets are owned by the State and the labour force is paid wages just as in any industrial enterprise. Besides Kolkhoz and Sovkhoz there are certain other types (e.g., inter Kolkhoz and/or Sovkhoz enterprises) of agricultural organisation but they employ a small proportion of the agricultural labour force.

The main focus of the study is on the collective farms – the Kolkhoz – to determine their achievements from the standpoint of productive efficiency, egalitarianism of income distribution, generation of surplus and promotion of employment. The information on which the study has been based comes from two main sources: published official data and a limited amount of data generated by the authors during a field trip, in October 1977, to the republics of Uzbekistan and Tajikistan, the two most populous republics of the region,[2] where a considerable amount of detailed data was collected for five collective farms. Gaps in statistical information will be only too obvious to the reader. On many interesting questions we have been able to do little more than raise questions or suggest hypotheses.

In 1913 the region constituted only 4.6 per cent of the total population of the area that now forms the USSR. By 1977 the share had more than doubled to 9.4 per cent. In the last forty years or so, demographic trends in Central Asia have diverged sharply from those in the rest of the Union. While the latter experienced a demographic transition through sharply reduced birth rates, the rate of population growth in the Central Asian republics continued to accelerate.

On the eve of the Revolution the level of urbanisation in Central Asia was no lower than for the area that later became the USSR. Indeed the territory that now forms Uzbekistan was more urbanised than the territories of any other republic except Georgia. During the period of Soviet power, Central Asia experienced a much lower rate of urbanisation than did the USSR as a whole. Rural-urban migration within the region was remarkably small.

By any ordinary standard the growth rates of industrial production in Central Asia have been impressive. But they have generally been lower than the industrial growth rates in the USSR as a whole. Table 11.1

TABLE 11.1   National income, its composition and per capita income and consumption

Uzbekistan	1965	1970	1975	1976
National income (current price million rubles)	5495.9	8702.5	12483.1	13191.6
% share of industry	37	34	38	40
% share of agriculture	38	37	32	30
% share of transport, construction trade and services	25	29	30	30
Per capita national income (current prices)	544	738	912	937
Per capita consumption	412	543	675	698

USSR	1965	1970	1975	1976
National income (thousand million rubles)	193.5	289.9	363.3	382.0
% share of industry	52	51	53	53
% share of agriculture	23	22	17	17
% share of transport, construction and services	25	27	30	30
Per capita national income	843	1199	1434	1495
Per capita consumption	611	833	1052	1095
Uzbek per capita national income as % of USSR's	64.5	61.6	63.6	62.7
Uzbek per capita consumption as % of USSR's	67.4	65.2	64.2	63.7

Source: Narodnoe Khozyaistvo Uzbekskoi SSR Za 60 Let (hereinafter referred to as NK Uz. 60) and Narodnoe Khozyaistvo SSSR Za 60 Let (hereinafter referred to as NK SU 60).

compares national income, its sectoral composition and per capita income in Uzbekistan, the overwhelmingly largest Central Asian republic, with the corresponding measurements for the USSR during the decade since 1965. In both, the share of agriculture in national income at current prices declined rapidly, but the rate of decline was significantly greater for the USSR than for Uzbekistan. By 1976 the percentage share of agriculture in national income in Uzbekistan was three-quarters higher than that in the USSR. Correspondingly, the share of industry in national income in Uzbekistan is lower than that in the

USSR. A comparison between the rest of Central Asia and the USSR will give results which are qualitatively similar.

II THE ORGANISATION OF COLLECTIVE FARMS

Agriculture in the USSR was organised into collective farms on a major scale from 1930. In that year in Uzbekistan for example just over one third of rural households were in collective farms. By 1940 virtually all households were in collective farms. In the 1950s there was a substantial increase in the typical size of collective farm through a process of merger and amalgamation. In Tajikistan for example there were 64 households per Kolkhoz in 1940. This had risen to 861 in 1973. Hectares of sown land per Kolkhoz rose nearly eight fold in the same period. There has also been a trend towards an increase in the proportion of State farms (Sovkhoz) in collective agriculture. For the USSR as a whole Sovkhoz accounted for 43 per cent of all agricultural workers in 1976; in Central Asia the trends are in the same direction, but the absolute proportion accounted for by State farms is lower.

The organisation of Kolkhoz has evolved during the fifty years of their existence. In 1969 a Model Collective Farm Charter formalised the changes in methods of organisation that had occurred since the earlier (1935) Model Rules. The 1969 Charter defines a Kolkhoz as 'a cooperative organisation of voluntarily associated peasants for the joint conduct of large-scale agricultural production on the basis of communal means of production and collective labour'. As a voluntary, co-operative association of producers in a planned, socialist economy, the Kolkhoz presents some interesting and distinctive features. It differs from state enterprises which are the more usual form of organisation in a socialist economy not only in the ownership pattern of means of production but perhaps more importantly in the greater autonomy it enjoys, in principle, in production and management. By the same token, in principle, the Kolkhoz provides greater scope for participation and democratic decision-making than may be possible in a state enterprise which comes directly under a ministry and is, therefore, more liable to political and bureaucratic control. At the same time, however, the Kolkhozy operate within the framework of a centrally planned economy which must, by its sheer logic, provide for the regulation of their activities. This is so for two main reasons. Firstly, the Kolkhozy are important producers of food and raw materials and their contribution must be fitted into the planned supply and demand of these commodities. Secondly, the incomes and standard of living of the Kolkhozniki are matters of national concern as part of the over-all policy on income distribution and material welfare. The autonomy enjoyed by the Kolkhozy is thus circumscribed by the dictates of central planning and considerations of national policy. The external framework within which a Kolkhoz must conduct its activities comprises not only the macro-economic factors but also a whole host of laws, institutions and practices operating at the national, regional and local levels.

A combination of historical factors and the logic of a centrally planned economy have resulted in a situation where some of the key parameters defining the external framework of the Kolkhozy are determined by the State. These include the determination of delivery targets, the procurement price structure, the price and availability of most investment goods and the fixing of minimum wage and certain social welfare services. On the other hand, there has been a trend since 1953 away from direct state control through administrative methods and towards greater autonomy of the Kolkhozy.

Although there are differences of details, the Kolkhozy display remarkable similarity in internal structure and organisation. The main organs of a Kolkhoz are the general meeting, the board, the inspection committee, the brigades and firmas. The leadership personnel consist of the Chairman and members of the board, the specialist staff and heads of brigades and firmas. The structure of the Kolkhoz may be illustrated by the organisation chart for Kolkhoz XXII Party Congress in Tajikistan shown in Figure 11.1.

All the production workers are organised into *brigades* and *firmas*, which are the main production units. With the expansion in the over-all size of the average Kolkhoz over the past three decades, the size of brigades has expanded correspondingly. In many ways, the brigades of today are comparable in size and in respect of some functions with the Kolkhozy of the early 1950s. Brigades are charged with well-defined tasks, e.g., the cultivation of so many acres of grain, cotton or vegetables; raising of livestock; or operation and maintenance of tractors. Some brigades – the so-called 'complex brigades' – may combine several of these tasks.

The duties of these production units include organisation of work, assignment of daily tasks, quality control, supervision of equipment, fulfilment of production targets, keeping records of work done and payment of workers. They may make proposals concerning technological change, productivity improvements or payment schemes. However, they do not have powers to set production targets or evolve

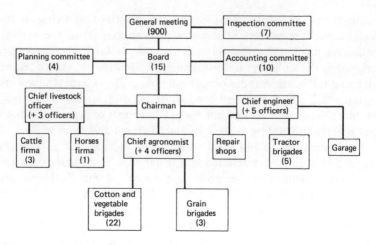

Figure 11.1   Organisation chart for Kolkhoz XXII Party Congress in Tajikistan
Note: The figures in brackets refer to number of persons or brigades and firmas.

their own payment and incentive schemes. Each brigade is led by an
elected or appointed brigadier. This is generally a full-time job and
entails responsibility for the fulfilment of tasks outlined above. The
brigades vary a good deal in size. In the Rossiya Kolkhoz, for example,
field brigades comprise 30–60 members, while tractor brigades have 50
members. Of the five Kolkhozy we visited, the average number of
workers per brigade varies from a low of 53 in Rossiya to a high of 103 in
Karl Marx.

   Zvenos are sub-units of brigades and firmas, comprising 2–6
members, which are assigned rather specific tasks. Their members
usually work on seasonal or temporary assignments and the unit ceases
to function once a given task has been performed.

III   TRENDS IN SECTORAL INCOMES

Table 11.1 shows that the per capita income in Uzbekistan in recent
years has varied between 62 and 65 per cent of the per capita income for
the USSR. The disparity in terms of per capita consumption has been
slightly lower. Table 11.2 contains some additional comparative
information about sectoral incomes.

   Table 11.2 compares payment per man-day in Kolkhoz in Uzbekistan
and Tajikistan with that in the USSR as a whole. The most striking

feature is that by 1965 payment in Central Asia was more than a fifth higher than that in the USSR as a whole. Indeed, the data available from an alternate source[3] indicate that in 1958 payment per man-day in the Central Asian Kolkhoz was 70 per cent above that for the USSR as a whole.

TABLE 11.2   Payment per man-day in Kolkhoz

	All USSR (rubles)	Uzbekistan (rubles)	Tajikistan (rubles)	Uzbekistan as % of USSR	Tajikistan as % of USSR
1965	2.68	3.29	3.21	123	120
1970	3.90	4.24	4.17	109	107
1972	–	–	4.10	–	–
1973	–	–	4.37	–	–
1975	4.54	4.60	–	101	–
1976	4.77	4.96	–	104	–

Source: *NK SU 60*; *NK Uz. 60*; and *Sovietski Tajikistan Za 50 Let* (hereinafter referred to as *ST 50*).

Thus we have the important fact that around the middle of the 1950s the Kolkhoz workers' collective earnings in Central Asia had reached a very high level in relation to that for the USSR. Unfortunately, we do not have comparable data for earlier years, but according to all available evidence the Central Asian agriculture in the early 1930s was less prosperous than the agriculture in most parts of the USSR. It would be reasonable to assume, therefore, that the disparity in Kolkhoz payments between Central Asia and the rest of the USSR started to move in favour of the former after these early years. Since the middle of the 1950s, the disparity between Central Asia and the USSR in terms of the earnings of the Kolkhoz workers has been narrowing. By the middle of the 1970s the disparity virtually disappeared.

When one looks at the regional disparity in industrial earnings, one finds a very different trend. In the earlier years earnings in the Central Asian industries were relatively low as compared to the rest of the USSR. Over the years this disparity has narrowed, but even in the 1970s earnings in the Central Asian industries remain significantly lower.

In summary, by 1970 the collective earnings per worker from Kolkhoz in Central Asia were still somewhat higher than in the rest of the USSR, although the disparity had come down from about 70 per cent in 1958 to less than 10 per cent. The earnings in State agriculture had by 1970 already become higher in the rest of the USSR than in Central Asia. Since earnings in Sovkhoz are higher than those in Kolkhoz and since the USSR has a higher share of Sovkhoz in total agriculture as compared to Central Asia the weighted average earning per agricultural worker in Central Asia was probably only a shade higher than that in the rest of the USSR. But the dependency ratio in rural Central Asia was much above that in the USSR as a whole. As a consequence *per capita* agricultural income in Central Asia was much lower than that in the USSR. Earnings per industrial worker were lower in Central Asia and this disadvantage was further aggravated by the unfavourable dependency ratio so that the per capita industrial income in Central Asia was much lower than that in the USSR. To this one should add the fact that the USSR has a higher share of industry – the high income sector – in total economic activity. The total effect of all these factors is to reduce the per capita national income and per capita consumption in Central Asia to about two-thirds of the corresponding quantities in the USSR as a whole.[4]

IV AN EXCEPTION TO THE STRATEGY OF PRIMITIVE SOCIALIST ACCUMULATION

In development literature the Soviet experience is frequently characterised as the strategy of 'primitive socialist accumulation' – extracting large surplus from the agricultural sector by imposing on it unfavourable terms of trade through the use of the monopsonistic power of the State as the buyer of agricultural goods and the monopolistic power of the State as the seller of non-agricultural goods. Indeed, the use of monopsonistic power was supplemented by the imposition of compulsory delivery quotas on rural producers. The main justification for the strategy was the lack of an alternative source of capital to finance socialist industrialisation in a pre-capitalist country in which socialist revolution had taken place.[5]

It appears that the main Central Asian cash crop, cotton, was no exception to this strategy in the very early years. The price offered to the growers was very low and, as a consequence, output fell. It was not too difficult, especially once collectivisation got under way, to increase the area under cotton and thereby raise production to the pre-revolution peak and beyond. But the disincentive of low price was too strong an impediment to promote the necessary effort to restore the yield per hectare to anything like the pre-revolution level. Yields continued to decline and by 1932 output per hectare was 35 per cent below the level of 1913.

For a period attempts were made to compensate the cotton growers by offering them grain, tea, sugar, seeds and fertiliser at fixed prices, but in January 1935 these deliveries at fixed prices were discontinued and a major shift in policy was initiated by nearly quadrupling the procurement price of cotton. The result, in terms of production and yield, was dramatic: by 1937, in Uzbekistan, the production of raw cotton was 1,522 thousand tons – nearly three times the pre-revolution peak – and yield per hectare was at an all-time high of 1.6 tons. The result in the rest of Central Asia was similar.

For the next two decades cotton retained this extraordinarily favourable position in comparison to the other major agricultural products, which continued to be subjected to 'non-equivalent exchange' through the imposition of compulsory delivery quotas at extremely low prices. For the 1930s and 1940s actual procurement prices for agricultural goods are not available to us. Information about such prices is available from 1952 onwards. In 1952 relative procurement prices of the major agricultural goods still retained the same general pattern as they did over the two preceding decades. Thus, an examination of the relative procurement prices in 1952 should give us a general impression of the relative advantage enjoyed by cotton during the period under review.

In 1952 the procurement price per ton of cotton was nearly 37 times that for grains. No estimates of relative costs of production in those days are available, but in recent years the average cost of production per ton of cotton was about seven times that for grain.[6] It is possible that the ratio of costs was different in those years, but such a difference could not have been very great. Thus net return per ton was many times higher for cotton than for grain. Indeed, the net return on grain was negative and that on cotton highly positive.

For grains and meat the average procurement price paid to the producers in the USSR in 1952 was less than one-seventh of the international price. For cotton the procurement price paid was nearly a third above the international price. Thus, relative to the production of other major agricultural goods (viz., grains and meat), the production of cotton was being subsidised (or taxed far less heavily).

The first important effect of the exceptionally favourable terms of trade for cotton was the sharp shift of sown area away from grain into cotton. In the pre-revolution days grain was the main crop in Central Asia both in terms of area and physical volume of production. In 1913 about 75 per cent of the sown land in Central Asia consisted of grain and only 15 per cent of cotton. By 1965 the share of grain had fallen to 41 per cent and that of cotton had risen to 36 per cent.

This remarkable shift in cropping pattern was the result not of coercion or administrative fiat but of a systematic use of price incentives. This constitutes an outstanding exception to the strategy of squeezing out surplus from agriculture that is usually attributed to the USSR.

Labour requirement per hectare is on average six times higher for cotton than for grain in Kolkhoz in Uzbekistan. The labour requirement for grain cultivation has fallen quite dramatically over the last eleven years: in Uzbekistan it fell by more than 50 per cent while in the rest of the USSR the decline was as much as 70 per cent. In comparison, there has been a very slow reduction in the labour intensity of cotton cultivation. Over the corresponding period it fell by about 12 per cent in Uzbekistan and by about 13 per cent in the rest of the Central Asia. Thus the gap in the labour requirement between cotton and the other crops has been increasing over time.

It is clear, therefore, that the increased specialisation in cotton has led to a much greater demand for labour in agriculture in Central Asia than would be the case otherwise. This is probably one of the most important factors contributing to the lower rate of urbanisation for the Central Asian republics over recent decades.

In order to make the increased demand for labour effective, it was necessary to offer workers a high enough income to induce them to stay on the farm. It is here that the favourable terms of trade for cotton played a crucial role. After the mid 1930s agricultural incomes grew very fast and the income payments, especially to the Kolkhoz workers, were high enough to render the pull of wages offered by the urban industries relatively weak.

V CHANGES SINCE 1953

Beginning in 1953 the policy of extremely low procurement prices for agricultural goods began to change. Over the next decade the prices of grains, meat and milk were increased steadily and rapidly and the rise in the prices of livestock products continued at a rapid rate to date. By 1962 grain prices had risen more than eightfold over the 1952 level, while prices for meat and milk increased, respectively, by more than 15 and 4 times. During this period procurement price of cotton remained virtually unchanged.

By 1962 the procurement price per ton was only 4.76 times higher for cotton than for grains. The cost of production per ton of cotton is 7.42 times that of grains for the USSR as a whole. Thus the price/cost ratio had altered sharply in favour of grains.[7]

As a result of the sharply lowered relative incentive for cotton its production and yield ceased to grow as rapidly as in the earlier decades. In many areas production and yield fell between the early 1950s and early 1960s. The effect on peasant income was severe. During these years the Sovkhoz specialising in cotton were making substantial losses.

After unsuccessfully trying out various administrative methods of persuading the cotton growers to produce more, the procurement price was increased substantially in 1963 after a long period of stagnation. Thereafter prices were increased in a number of further steps and such increases have generally been at a higher rate than that for grains, the main competing crop. By 1976 some of the relative price advantage lost over the 1953–62 period was restored. Especially in the Central Asian republics the relative procurement prices of cotton and grain were carefully balanced to keep the price/cost ratio higher for cotton.

But, clearly, cotton had lost the extraordinary privileged position it had until 1953. This is reflected in the comparatively slower rate of expansion in cotton production in recent decades. In both Uzbekistan and Tajikistan the rates of growth of cotton production have been declining steadily over time. In Uzbekistan the growth rate in the output of grain has been substantial over the last decade – nearly twice as high as for cotton – as compared to the negative or negligible rates of growth in the preceding four decades.

Several aspects of the system of procurement pricing deserve attention. First, it is an instrument for providing collective incentives. There is a basic price for the given quota that the collectives are expected to fulfil and a 50 per cent premium on the quantity that a collective voluntarily sells to the State in excess of the quota.[8] This system provides an incentive to exceed quota sales by obtaining an appropriate expansion in output. Secondly, procurement pricing is an instrument for the reduction of inter-regional inequality. The procurement price of any product is not uniform all over the USSR, or even within each republic. For grain, for example, there are 17 procurement zones in the USSR. For cotton there are three procurement zones within the Uzbek Republic alone. Price is lowest for the Ferghana-Tashkent zone where conditions are best and highest in the semi-arid Karakalpak-Bokhara zone where conditions are worst.[9]

As is well known there is no land rent in the USSR. From what is known about the principle of differentiating procurement prices between regions it appears that this practice is a substitute for land rent in preventing polarisation in regional income inequality arising out of vast regional differences in the quality of land. Had procurement prices been uniform the differential rent of land in a fertile region would have augmented the income of the workers of the region.

VI PRODUCTIVE EFFICIENCY

Soviet agricultural performance is frequently indicted by critics for low factor productivity. This critique does not apply to cotton, the overwhelmingly dominant product of Central Asian agriculture, so long as output per hectare is used as the indicator.[9] By all standards the achievement in terms of output per hectare has been remarkable. In comparison with the pre-revolutionary level of 1.22 tons (and only about 0.8 ton at the beginning of the 1930s) the output of raw cotton per hectare reached the level of three tons in 1976. Table 11.3 shows that the Central Asian republics have the highest yield per hectare of all the significant producers of cotton in the world. Even within the USSR these republics, which supply the bulk of the cotton, are far above the rest in terms of yield per unit of land.

In the republics the level of tractorisation is considerably above that for the USSR as a whole, where an average collective farm had 11 tractors per thousand hectares of sown land in 1976. What is even more surprising is that the over-all rate of tractorisation in Central Asian agriculture would appear to have been greater than that in the highly capital-intensive agriculture in the USA, since in 1972 in the USA there were 33 tractors per thousand hectares of cropland (see Table 11.4).[10]

In spite of its vast geographical expanse Central Asia is in short supply of cultivable land. In 1976, in Uzbekistan, there were only 1.6 hectares of cultivated land per Kolkhoz worker. This was less than a quarter of the corresponding figure for the USSR. Indeed, this is less than the amount of land available per agricultural worker in Pakistan. In Tajikistan the amount of cultivated land per Kolkhoz worker is 1.9 hectares – only a little higher than in Uzbekistan. It appears that an augmentation in the supply of cultivated land is very costly in terms of resources. Expensive irrigation projects have to be undertaken to bring new land under cultivation. Moreover, one could argue that the supply of labour is probably less of a constraint at present. The rate of population growth has been accelerating and, so far, there is no sign of deceleration in growth. Moreover, the region has a positive rate of net immigration.

TABLE 11.3   Major cotton producers of the world (1976)

Country	Total production (thousand tons of lint equivalent)	Yield per hectare (tons of raw cotton)
USSR	2,800	2.82
China	2,400	1.47
USA	2,298	1.35
(Uzbekistan)	(1,800)	(3.00)
India	1,146	0.46
Pakistan	515	0.84
Turkey	470	2.10
Brazil	390	0.66
Egypt	386	1.95
(Tajikistan)	(288)	(3.00)
(Turkmenistan)	(356)	(2.13)
(Kirghizia)	(71)	(2.88)
Total world	12,695	1.16

Sources: Uzbek, Tajik and USSR data have been quoted from NK SU 60. Data for the other countries have been compiled from FAO, Production Yearbook, vol. 30 (Rome 1977).
Note: For the world as a whole the ratio of lint to raw cotton is about 0.35. For the USSR the ratio is 0.34. These ratios have been used to convert raw cotton into lint (and vice versa) in deriving the figures shown in the table. In 1976 only three countries had a higher yield per hectare than the USSR. These were Guatemala (3.35 tons), Israel (3.21 tons) and Sri Lanka (3.00 tons). Each of them is a small producer. Their outputs, in lint equivalent, were respectively 100, 50 and 2,000 tons.

TABLE 11.4   Mechanisation of Kolkhoz and Sovkhoz in Uzbekistan and Tajikistan

| | Uzbekistan (1976) | | Tajikistan (1973) | |
	Kolkhoz	Sovkhoz	Kolkhoz	Sovkhoz
No. of tractors per thousand hectares of sown land	47	30	34	30
Cotton harvesters per thousand hectares of cotton land	15	20	10	13
No. of workers per tractor	13	10	16	11

Source: The estimates have been based on the data in NK Uz. 60 and ST 50.

Thus, in years to come, the rate of increase in the labour supply is likely to continue to accelerate.

It is natural that Central Asian agriculture, with a resource endowment very different from the average for the USSR and the USA, would use much more labour per unit of land and thereby have a lower output per unit of labour, but to ensure continued progress in the living standard of the rural population it will be necessary to improve output per worker by reducing labour requirements per unit of cotton and of other agricultural produce.

Grain crops

Table 11.5 shows the yield of grain crops per hectare. In every republic of Central Asia there has been a very large increase in output of grain per hectare in recent decades, with a phenomenal increase in recent years. Much of this growth must have been the result of the policy of improving incentives for grain cultivation. During the 1960s yields in the Central Asian republics, with the exception of Kirghizia, ranged between 60 and 70 per cent of those in the USSR as a whole. By 1976, the average yield in Central Asia was above that for the USSR, and Tajikistan – a minor

TABLE 11.5   Grain yield per hectare in metric tons

	1940	Average 1961–5	Average 1966–70	Average 1971–5	1976
USSR	0.86	1.02	1.37	1.47	1.75
Central Asia Average	–	–	–	–	1.82
Uzbekistan	0.41	0.67	0.74	0.95	1.69
Tajikistan	0.57	0.61	0.66	0.83	1.14
Kirghizia	0.76	1.02	1.56	1.87	2.28
Turkmenistan	0.57	0.72	0.86	1.40	2.10
All Asia	–	–	–	–	1.69
India	–	–	–	–	1.22
Iran	–	–	–	–	1.27
Iraq	–	–	–	–	0.97
Pakistan	–	–	–	–	1.44
Turkey	–	–	–	–	1.89
Afghanistan	–	–	–	–	1.31

Source: Soviet data quoted from: *NK SU 60*. The rest quoted from FAO, *Production Yearbook*, vol. 30 (1977).

producer contributing less than 8 per cent of the region's grain output –
was the only Central Asian republic that lagged significantly behind the
all Union average. This was a remarkable achievement.
Productivity per hectare in Central Asia is still well below that
achieved by Japan (5.28 tons per hectare), Korea (3 in North and 4.5 in
South), Europe (3.1) and North-Central America (3.1). But compared
to its more immediate Asian neighbours the performance must be rated
as highly satisfactory.

VII   COLLECTIVE AGRICULTURE AND PERSONAL PLOTS

The issue of personal plots has been a controversial one in Soviet
agricultural development. The performance of this sector has been the
basis of criticism levelled against the Soviet system both from the right
and the left. Western economists have long argued that personal plots
have a much higher output per hectare than collective agriculture. This,
according to such economists, is undisputed testimony to the greater
efficiency of private, as compared to collective, agriculture. The critique
from the left has been based on the argument that the continuation and
prosperity of personal plots is inconsistent with the avowed objective of
a transition to communism – a society in which distribution should be
based on need and not on unequal entitlements based on unequal
capacities to produce.
   The Soviet answer to these criticisms has been to claim that the
produce of personal plots, as a proportion of total marketed farm
output, has been declining and that by now this sector is not of much
quantitative significance. Unfortunately, the scanty time series data
published by the official sources refer to the USSR as a whole.[11] Our
discussion of Central Asia must be based on the small amount of data
that we generated for the five Kolkhozy and some comparative figures of
an aggregative nature for the republics.
   Personal plots in the Central Asian Kolkhoz are on average much
smaller than the ones in the rest of the USSR. The average sizes in
Uzbekistan and Tajikistan are respectively 0.12 and 0.13 hectares as
compared to 0.33 in the USSR. This is probably due to the relatively
adverse land/man ratio in Central Asian agriculture. The average size of
a personal plot in the five Kolkhoz we examined is 0.14 hectares, which is
marginally higher than the corresponding averages for the two
republics.
   If the data from the five Kolkhozy are representative, the contribution

of personal plots to family income certainly is not small. Income from a personal plot, including self-consumption, varies rather widely, namely, from 18 to 40 per cent of the total household income from collective Kolkhoz labour, earnings from employment outside and income from personal plot (excluding items such as imputed rental value of owner-occupied house and collective consumption). There is a perfect negative rank correlation between this ratio and family income from collective Kolkhoz labour. Although the 'sample' is very small one is tempted to note a strong negative association between high collective prosperity and low income from personal plots.

The value of output per hectare in a private plot is, on the average, more than four times as much as the value of output on collectively farmed land. There is a lot of variation even for our very small 'sample', however. This is a ratio that needs to be explained.

The produce of collective farms is largely sold to the State at fixed prices. The State in turn sells these goods at controlled prices to urban and rural buyers through State retail outlets. The produce of private plots does not have to follow the same route but can be taken by the Kolkhozniki to the 'Kolkhoz Markets' in nearby towns. At these markets, prices are freely determined by the interaction between buyers and sellers. It is well known that prices at these Kolkhoz markets are higher than the prices ruling at the State shops, often located on the same premises, frequently by as much as 100–200 per cent. Thus, even if output per hectare were the same on collective and personal land, the *value* of output, defined in this case as the actual sale proceeds, would be greater for the personal plots.

How can one explain the difference in prices? One possibility is a shortage and consequent rationing at the State retail shops. This probably is responsible for a large part of the price difference between the State shops and Kolkhoz markets. The difference in revenue due to this factor must be seen as the result of a concealed tax on collective production by the State procurement machinery – a tax that is passed on to the consumers as a subsidy through the State retail shops.

But part of the difference in price is due to the inherent difficulty encountered by a centralised procurement and marketing agency in dealing with certain goods of a perishable nature. Thus, one is struck by the remarkable difference in quality for vegetables, fruits and similar items between the State shops and Kolkhoz markets. The price difference is highest for these products.[12] Sometimes the high revenue is due to the non-competitive nature of the goods, e.g., home processed food, sold by the Kolkhozniki.[13]

To the extent that the difference in revenue is due to such factors one must treat the higher revenue from personal plots as a return to the Kolkhozniki labour as traders and manufacturers. Indeed, there seems to be a tendency on the part of the personal plots to specialise in the goods in which such activities add considerably to retail prices. Thus, in the case of the five collective farms, there seemed to exist a pattern of specialisation in items such as vegetables and fruits.

It must be recognised that apart from these factors, there would be an incentive for the Kolkhozniki to apply greater effort to personal plots because the value added by collective labour is subject to deductions for taxation, collective accumulation and provision for social services. The weighted average of the ratios of labour payment to value added in the five collective farms was 0.69. Thus, even if an individual Kolkhoznik has no additional uncertainty about the process of collective production, he would allocate his effort between collective and personal plots in such a way that the product of the marginal unit of labour was lower in the latter. As a result labour input and volume of output would tend to be greater per unit of personal plot than per unit of collective land.[14]

VIII   THE DISTRIBUTION OF INCOME

The degree of inequality among collective farms

Even given the limited variation in the natural conditions among the five collective farms that the authors visited a good deal of inequality in average incomes and earnings can be observed. The basic information has been summarised in Table 11.6. Payment per man day from work in the collective farm in the richest Kolkhoz is about three-quarters above that in the poorest of the five. The difference in earnings per worker is even greater due to the greater average intensity of employment in the richer farms. The difference farther widens in terms of per capita collective income because the richer farms are able to employ or attract a higher proportion of the available family labour. The difference in terms of per capita income from all sources is smaller because earnings from non-Kolkhoz employment and personal plots exert a strong equalising influence.

For the Central Asian region as a whole the difference in average earnings and incomes is likely to be greater among the collective farms. In Uzbekistan payment per man day in an average Kolkhoz in 1976 was 4.96 rubles. The lowest such payment in any Kolkhoz was reported to be 3.50 rubles while the highest known rate was 11.00 rubles, the ratio of

TABLE 11.6 Earnings and incomes in five collective farms (in rubles)

Name of the Kolkhoz	Average payment per man-day	Average annual earning from collective labour	Per capita annual income from collective labour	Per capita annual income from personal plot	Per capita annual earning from outside employment	Per capita total annual income
Leninism	7.00	1,287	386	102	81	569
Kholkabad	6.15	1,187	321	103	118	542
Karl Marx	5.49	783	237	137	89	463
XXII Party Congress	4.07	721	170	138	87	395
Rossiya	4.02	681	69	155	168	392

Note: The last column includes income from Kolkhoz labour, outside employment and personal plots.

the highest to the lowest being 3.14.[15]

Not enough quantitative information is available to analyse the impact of State policy on the inter-Kolkhoz income differentials. But on the whole, such policies may have reduced such inequality. There are at least three instruments which have substantially promoted this objective. The first of these is the procurement price which has been regionally varied to mop up the 'differential rent' (and perhaps a part of the cost advantage due to the favourable endowment of resources other than land) in the regions with more favourable conditions and thereby to compensate for the cost disadvantage of the regions with unfavourable conditions.

The details of the operation of the system of taxation are not available but it is known that the collective farms with low profits (below 15 per cent) are exempted from taxation. Thus of the five collective farms for which detailed information is available one paid no tax in 1976 because of low profits.

The final instrument in equalising income among collectives is the contribution of the State to the collective consumption and pensions of the Kolkhozniki. These contributions are distributed far more equally than are the incomes of the collectives.

Intra-Kolkhoz inequality

Each Kolkhoz has a guaranteed minimum pay. For 25 days of work such pay in most Kolkhoz is 70 rubles per month, although in some it is only 60 rubles. Since not all Kolkhozniki work a minimum of 25 days on collective labour the *actual* minimum payment per month may be less than this guaranteed minimum. But those who work fewer than 25 days a month on the farm are usually able to find work for the remaining days, frequently at a wage higher than the minimum guaranteed by the Kolkhoz.[16] Thus, in effect, no Kolkhoznik appears to receive a money income which is less than the guaranteed minimum. Such an income probably is adequate in most cases to secure the basic human needs given that the unfavourable dependency ratio (one worker for 2.5 to 3 members) is partly compensated by the payment of family allowances, that housing is provided at low costs, that personal plots add considerably to the income of the family and that adequate provision for health and education are made by the Kolkhoz and the State.

It is difficult to generalise about differences in income among various categories of employees of a Kolkhoz. Even among the five collective farms studied, the pattern seems to vary quite a bit.

One may distinguish three different categories of Kolkhoz employees. At the top are the chairman, members of the Kolkhoz Board and specialists such as chief agronomist, chief economist and chief book-keeper (some of these specialists are members of the Kolkhoz Board). These employees are on a fixed monthly salary. In the middle category are the technically skilled workers such as tractor drivers. In terms of income, middle-level officials such as ordinary economists and agronomists and the brigadiers appear to be at the same level, although these officials are paid fixed monthly incomes. At the bottom are the 'field workers', the production workers with little or no specialised skill. These workers are all paid on the basis of piecerate work.

Little is known about the dispersion of earnings among field workers. It is known, however, that there are six grades of such workers and that there are significant differences between the grades. Some idea of such differences is conveyed by the fact that the *average* earning of a field worker is about twice as high as the *minimum* earning.

In the three Tajik collective farms the earnings of one belonging to the middle category – a tractor driver or a brigadier – are one and three quarters to twice as high as that of a fully employed field worker. The ratio appears to be much lower in the two Uzbek collective farms.

The chief specialists are relatively highly paid. The chairman, frequently himself a specialist, is the only official who receives a salary higher than that of the chief specialists. The chief specialists are paid more than twice as much as a *fully employed* field worker. The Chairman's salary is three to four times that of a *fully employed* field worker. But the true income of a chairman is not fully reflected in the salary. Frequently he or she is provided with a rent-free house of generous proportions and, in the case of the prosperous collectives, personal cars. In some of the collectives the authors studied such privileges were also given to the chief specialists.

On the whole one is left with the impression that there is considerable, but not excessive, inequality in the distribution of earnings. Indeed, it is frequently admitted in discussions that differences in remuneration are kept sufficiently large to promote incentives.

Personal plots and income distribution

Incomes from personal plots in a Kolkhoz must be fairly equitably distributed. This is because the size of the personal plots is based on the criterion of allocating roughly the same amount per *person*. Thus the system may be compared with one of peasant farming with an absolutely egalitarian per capita distribution of land, a ban on the hiring of labour and a compulsory quota on each household for collective labour. It is not surprising that the resulting distribution of income is highly egalitarian, although complete equality is ruled out by the inter-family differences in quality and quantity of labour available to work on personal plots.

Between collective farms, as we have already observed on the basis of our small 'sample' of five, the rank correlation of per capita earnings from personal plots is almost perfectly negatively correlated with per capita collective income. If this is representative of the region as a whole, then the contribution of the personal plots to inter-Kolkhoz income distribution must be one of equalisation. There are reasons to suggest that this, indeed, is the case. There is very limited variation in the average size of personal plots between collective farms. The range of feasible technologies would also be limited in view of the very small size of the plots. The lower the return from collective labour the greater will be the incentive to work the personal plots intensively. All these factors would tend to combine to make the effect of personal plots an equalising one in so far as the inter-Kolkhoz distribution of income is concerned.

It may seem paradoxical that the distribution of income in the non-socialised part of the Kolkhoz is possibly more egalitarian than in the socialised part. The distribution of income in the socialised sector, *in principle*, is proportional to the individual member's capacity to work. Individuals differ in terms of their capacity. In the socialised sector their differences in capacity are expressed fully as individuals work with the relatively large amounts of socially owned capital and resources. Thus the resulting distribution of income can be as unequal as the distribution of the ability of individuals.

In the non-socialised sector there are such severe limitations on the volume of the means of production per person that the differences between the capacity to work of individuals cannot be fully translated into differential results of work. As a consequence the distribution of income can be less unequal than that of ability to work. Thus, the result surmised by us on the basis of highly inadequate evidence is not unexpected. What must be noted is that the equalising influence of earnings from personal plots is due to the strictly egalitarian limitation on the size of such plots – a limitation that arises from the fact that most of means of production in the economy are socially owned.

IX ACCUMULATION

We have discussed the fact that Central Asian agriculture in the past had
been subjected to a very low rate of surplus extraction compared to the
rest of the USSR. Direct taxation of Kolkhoz income in Central Asia
continues to be low. The weighted average rate of income tax in the five
Kolkhozy was 4.1 per cent of value added in 1976. The highest rate of 6.6
per cent obtained in the prosperous Kolkhoz Kholkabad while Kolkhoz
XXII Party Congress, because of its low rate of profit, paid no taxes at
all.

Whether the terms of trade between collective agriculture and the
State is a mechanism that represents a concealed tax or not is very
difficult to say both because of difficulties in establishing criteria for
quantifying such an extraction of surplus, and because of the inadequacy of available information. The burden of our preceding
discussion, however, has been to show that the prices received by the
products of collective agriculture in Central Asia probably represent no
substantial degree of concealed taxation. Whether such taxation is
incorporated in the prices of the products sold to agriculture is
unknown.

Whatever the amount the State extracts on the aggregate must be
balanced against a substantial State contribution to the collective
consumption and investment of the Kolkhoz. The contribution to
collective consumption takes the form of payments for teachers, doctors
and staff at the Kolkhoz schools and hospitals and a major share of the
costs of pensions and family support allowances. The contribution to
investment consists of the financing of large-scale irrigation and land
improvement projects.

As far as we could determine, it is not the usual practice to charge the
users for water or other benefits of such State-financed projects. Yet
another form of State contribution is cheap long-term credit to finance
capital investment. The rate of interest on such credit is only 1 per cent
while the repayment period can be as long as 20 years.

On the whole collective agriculture appears to be making a fairly low,
and perhaps zero, aggregate transfer to the State. The inadequacy of
information on which the conclusion is based must be emphasised
yet again. But the available evidence does not suggest that the situation is one of 'primitive socialist accumulation' imposed on agriculture.

The information that we have about the savings and investment
behaviour of collective agriculture refers only to the five Kolkhozy. The

weighted averages of the relevant magnitudes for the five Kolkhozy were as follows for 1976 (all percentages of value added):

Total investment	21.1
Increase in reserve	3.1
Internal saving	20.4
Gross long term borrowing from credit institutions	3.8

The rate of investment is quite high, especially when one considers that the data do not include any large-scale development projects undertaken by the State. The internal saving rate also is very high, viz., over 20 per cent of value added. While three of the five Kolkhozy borrowed from the financial institutions, the weighted average of *net* borrowing for all five Kolkhozy was less than 1 per cent of value added.

Behind the average picture depicted above there was considerable variation among the five collective farms. The saving rate ranged from 10 per cent to 30 per cent of value added and the rate of investment from 14 per cent to 41 per cent. Over a single year variations of this magnitude are to be expected for enterprises engaged in such an inherently volatile activity as agriculture. But it is not known how far the weighted average for the five Kolkhozy is a reasonable approximation of the behaviour of collective agriculture in Central Asia.

X SOME CONCLUDING OBSERVATIONS

The Soviet Central Asian republics were a backward and poor region as recently as four decades ago with a living standard not qualitatively different from that of their immediate neighbours such as Afghanistan. Within a relatively short period these republics achieved a remarkable transformation.

This has taken place during a period of a high and accelerating rate of growth of population. The high population growth not only raised the required rate of growth in over-all income for a given rate of growth in per capita income but also raised the dependency ratio and made it necessary to devote a greater proportion of resources to education, child care and various related services.

Prosperity in the Central Asian republics has been achieved not through the classical path of industrialisation but through rural development. The industrial progress of the region has been very substantial, but rapid growth in agriculture has been a key element in the progress of the republics. A distinctive and related feature of their experience has been the continued predominance of the rural sector.

What the Central Asian republics experienced was rapid agricultural growth leading to a rising standard of living in the rural areas and the consequent absence of a push out of the rural sector. The rising living standards in rural areas also made it possible to keep a low urban-rural income differential – a factor which weakened the pull of the urban areas. Thus Central Asia experienced economic development with rural development and in this sense deserves to be studied carefully by those countries which cannot hope to develop through the classical type of industrialisation.

The chief explanation for the material progress of agriculture was the specialisation in cotton. This was characterised both by a very high rate of increase in yield per hectare and by a growing area. Starting from a low level, the region soon surpassed all other significant producers of cotton in the world in terms of output per hectare. The specialisation and prosperity in cotton were brought about through very high price incentives. While collectivised agriculture in much of the rest of the USSR was squeezed by a policy of 'primitive socialist accumulation', cotton was not subjected to adverse terms of trade.

The truly remarkable nature of the Central Asian agricultural growth is fully revealed only in the context of the vast institutional change that preceded it – the kind of institutional change that is known frequently to have produced at least temporary disruptions in output elsewhere. In less than a decade Central Asia experienced a transition from backward feudal relations to institutions such as collective and State farms with only a very brief interregnum during which private peasant ownership existed.

There was a period of hesitation and decline in yield until policies towards agriculture changed from discrimination to encouragement through incentives. The exceptional experience of Central Asia probably demonstrates that advanced forms of organisation such as the collectives can be introduced successfully only if the over-all policies provide appropriate incentives and rewards. That so many experiences of collective agriculture in the last half century have failed to serve as vehicles of agricultural growth is probably due more to inappropriate over-all policies towards agriculture than to any inherent difficulties with collective institutions.

Collective agriculture has facilitated growth with a relatively egalitarian distribution of income. Poverty as it exists in much of Asia is unknown. The relative egalitarianism in the distribution of income has been reinforced further by the provision of social consumption which is perhaps even more equally distributed.

All this is not to deny the existence of significant inequalities in the distribution of earnings. The spread between real earnings of the top management and the earnings of the field workers would appear to be quite large. Similarly, skill differentials seem to be considerable. Such differentials are officially justified by the need to provide material incentives for work and higher productivity.

While the productivity achievements of the system have been truly remarkable in terms of output per hectare of land (which, contrary to an impression of a vast expanse of territory, is a relatively scarce factor), output per worker continues to be very low compared to the agriculture in advanced countries. There are also some important questions concerning the efficiency of utilisation of scarce capital inputs such as tractors. For further material progress the collective agriculture of Central Asia must overcome these problems and challenges.

NOTES

1. Kolkhozy and Sovkhozy are plurals of Kolkhoz and Sovkhoz respectively. Similarly, Kolkhozniki is the plural form of Kolkhoznik (which means Kolkhoz member).
2. These two republics respectively account for 60 and 15 per cent of the population of the entire Central Asian economic region.
3. *Novy Mir*, 10/59, quoted in A. Nove and J. A. Newth, *The Soviet Middle East* (London: George Allen and Unwin, 1967) p. 103.
4. Per capita earnings from personal plots are probably lower in Central Asia than in the rest of the USSR. Average size of the personal plot per household is 2.36 times higher in USSR than in Central Asia where the household size is considerably larger than in the rest of the USSR.
5. Perhaps the most cogent statement of the doctrine that was to be implemented later is contained in the writings of E. Preobrazhensky *The New Economics* (Clarendon, 1965). He forcefully argued, in this book first published in 1924, that to develop a socialist economy in the Soviet Union, resources must be extracted from the then non-socialist parts of the economy – the petty bourgeois and, above all, the peasantry. Besides considering taxation, profits from foreign trade and borrowing, he proposed the method of 'non-equivalent exchange' as the most powerful instrument to effect such transfer. Non-equivalent exchange between the town and country would occur through the manipulation of the prices offered by the State to the peasantry and the prices charged by it on the sale of industrial goods to the peasantry. For an account of this theory and how it became a reality in the Soviet Union a few years after the publication of Preobrazhensky's book see (in addition to Preobrazhensky's own work) M.

Lewin, *Russian Peasants and Soviet Power* (London: George Allen and Unwin, 1967) and A. Ehrlich, *The Soviet Industrialisation Debate* (Harvard, 1967). Stalin's own account of the justification for the implementation of such a policy is to be found in J. V. Stalin, 'The Right Deviation in the C.P.S.U. (B)' in *Problems of Leninism* (Moscow: Foreign Languages Publishing House, 1953).

6. This is the all USSR ratio for 1976. For Central Asia the ratio was lower.
7. The cost ratios of cotton to grain in the Central Asian republics are as follows:

Uzbekistan	3.53
Tajikistan	3.62
Kirghizia	5.69
Turkmenistan	4.03

But the grain prices are higher in these republics than in the USSR on the average. We have no information on the grain procurement prices in the republics in 1962, but it is quite certain that the price/cost ratio in these places had also become more favourable for grain by 1962.

8. At the Central Asian Institute of Scientific Research on Agricultural Economy the authors were told that this system was instituted in March 1965 to replace a previous system of incentive payments. At present, cotton, wheat, rice, meat, wool and milk are covered by such a system of incentive payments.
9. These facts emerged through the discussion the authors had with the staff members of the Central Asian Institute of Scientific Research on Agricultural Economy, Tashkent. We recognise that a comparison of efficiency must be based on a more general measurement and not on the output per unit of a single factor. But to arrive at more general measures we need to quantify relative social scarcities of different factors. On this we have few guidelines either for Central Asia or for the countries with which comparisons are to be made. Later in this chapter we shall try to guess which factors in Central Asia are relatively more scarce and, on that basis, arrive at some tentative judgments on the question of efficiency.
10. The US figures have been calculated from CIA, *USSR Agriculture Atlas* (Washington, DC 1974).
11. These all USSR data do not provide convincing evidence of the decline in personal plots. Compare, for example, the data shown in Morosov, *Soviet Agriculture* (Moscow, 1977). The contribution of personal plots to marketed output of all crops declined from 13 per cent in 1940 to 11 per cent in 1960 and 10 per cent in 1975. In view of the steady decline in the labour intensity of agriculture over the period, such a minor reduction is probably quite consistent with a fairly rapid increase in the output of personal plots per household. In meat, milk and poultry the shares decline more sharply. But these are the sectors in which collective agriculture experienced a rapid acceleration in growth in recent decades and new available technology is frequently more suitable to large-scale production.
12. At the huge Tashkent Kolkhoz Market the authors saw tomatoes selling at 12 kopecs per kg. at the State shop (located inside the market) and at 60 to 70 kopecs at the stalls set up by the Kolkhozniki. The quality difference was

striking. For cucumber the price difference was 50 per cent and the difference in quality was less striking.

13. At the Dushanbe Kolkhoz market the authors saw the Kolkhozniki selling a wide variety of home-made goods, e.g., honey, jam and jelly.

14. There is a considerable theoretical literature concerning the allocation of labour between collective and personal land in a Soviet type Kolkhoz under alternative assumptions about the behaviour of the entities involved. The interested reader is referred to E. D. Domar, 'The Soviet Collective Farm as a Producer's Co-operative', *American Economic Review* (September 1966); W. Oi and E. Clayton, 'A Peasant's View of a Soviet Collective Farm', *American Economic Review* (March 1968); and M. Bradley, 'Incentives and Labour Supply on Soviet Collective Farms', *Canadian Journal of Economics* (August 1971).

15. These figures were supplied to the authors by the Kolkhoz department of the Ministry of Agriculture, Uzbekistan.

16. As the authors found, it is usual for the Kolkhoz management to organise such work in slack seasons. They provide transport to take 'surplus' workers to construction sites and generally try to take advantage of lucrative outside work by making internal adjustments.

12 Payments Systems and Third World Development: some Conclusions

FRANCES STEWART

Much discussion of income distribution and technological choice assumes a given institutional framework, focussing attention on factors affecting incomes and technology within a particular system. It is widely believed that the question of institution is outside the purview[1] of the economist – and also, in a way, of the politician – being a feature of the system determined by historical/sociological forces and not a day-to-day policy matter. Yet, as argued in the first chapter of this book, from both a theoretical and an empirical standpoint institutions and 'rules of the game' are critical determinants of access to work and therefore of employment, and of the income generated by work and therefore of income distribution. As a form of shorthand we have described the set of rules and institutions which determine access to work and income as the 'payments system'.[2]

While the payments system is a major influence on *primary* income distribution, or the distribution of income arising directly from the system of production, *secondary* (or after tax/benefits) income also depends on the distributive effects of government activity via the tax system. Traditionally, it has been assumed that governments could achieve any secondary distribution they liked – *irrespective of the primary distribution*. Hence to the extent that it is secondary income distribution, not primary, which is the main focus of interest in terms of household or individual welfare, the only variable that is important is the total level of income, *not* its primary distribution. With the two assumptions – (i) that governments may redistribute to achieve any secondary distribution; and (ii) that from a welfare point of view only secondary distribution matters – the payments system is only a relevant factor for study to the extent that it affects the total level of income, and hence the amount available for redistribution. But it has become apparent that both these assumptions are illegitimate. In the first place human welfare depends not only on levels of income, but on *how* income is acquired. Employment is an accepted objective in its own right and not simply as a means to acquiring income, while the nature of work (its content/organisation etc) also affect human wellbeing.[3] Secondly, it has become evident that the State – especially but not only in developing countries – is very ineffective in transferring income and thus in making the secondary income distribution very different from the primary distribution. The study of Taiwan (Chapter Four) strongly supports this view: 'even in the overall highly egalitarian situation of Taiwan the taxation system seems to be approximately neutral with respect to income distribution'. While direct taxes tend to be progressive, indirect taxes are regressive and 'transfer payments are likely to be very small in quantity and, even more interesting, to be regressive'. Evidence from other countries – e.g. Nigeria, Malaysia[4] – supports similar conclusions.

Thus it seems that the determinants of primary income distribution must be the central focus of studies of income distribution in LDCs. This was one of the main conclusions of Chapter One, that formed the starting point for the essays in this book: 'Inequality can only effectively be tackled at the sources where it arises – viz. by attacking the mechanisms making for primary inequality.' A second major conclusion of Chapter One was the significance of the institutional rules – the payments system – interacting with economic and technological variables, in determining primary income distribution. The aim of the essays in this book has been to explore further how this interaction operates in a wide variety of cases. If changes in institutions/rules are to play a major part in policies designed to tackle poverty and maldistribution of income it is essential to find out precisely how different rules affect the outcome.

The essays in this book have covered a wide range of cases: in terms of the development of the economy as a whole, we have examples of Taiwan, the Philippines and Peru; studies at a more micro-level encompass the various cooperative institutions in Israel, the communes in China and the Kolkhozy in Russia, the public corporation in Bangladesh, cooperatives in Peru, the informal sector in Argentina, and land tenure in traditional Iran. Since each of these cases has some unique historical features, it is not possible to come to definitive conclusions, applicable to all countries, on the basis of them. But the essays do suggest some quite powerful conclusions which are of considerable relevance to reform of the payments system. This chapter does not claim to provide a complete guide to these conclusions, but briefly highlights some major findings.

The worsening of income distribution that normally accompanies economic development in the initial stages, summarised statistically in the 'Kuznets curve'[5], forms the background to these studies. In the 'normal' mixed economy case, income distribution tends to worsen and absolute poverty often increases (in terms of absolute numbers at least) as development proceeds. This, it was argued in Chapter One, is largely the result of the replacement of traditional payments systems by market payments systems: poverty and maldistribution of income tend to emerge because with a market or capitalist system, traditional rights to income and work are replaced by a system in which people's incomes depend on their ability to acquire earnings through the market system. As land accumulation/decumulation proceeds accompanied by rapid population growth, a class of wage labourers emerge whose incomes depend primarily on their ability to acquire wage employment, and on market determined wage-rates. In a competitive market system, wage rates are related to marginal productivity of work which may be very low (and even falling over time) in a labour surplus situation.

According to this view of the process growing inequality and maldistribution of income could be avoided or mitigated by *institutional changes*, which transformed the way in which people gained access to work, assets and income, or by *economic changes*, which (in a market system) altered the terms on which people acquired work by reducing/eliminating surplus labour. The various essays in this book shed some light on the process of change as economic development proceeds and explore how differing payments systems and differing economic situations and policies affect the process. They show, as might be expected, that the processes involved are often more complex than the brief description just given; they also show a wide variety of outcomes – cases where payments system reform has been more or less completely ineffective in bringing about change in income distribution (Peru, Bangladesh) and cases where there have been varying degrees of success; there are cases where one can observe the normal deterioration in a mixed economy – Peru, Argentina and the Philippines – and one case where economic policies (combined with land reform) have avoided the expected deterioration and even led to improvement in income distribution during the process of development (Taiwan).

The chapter on Iran is the only case study of a 'traditional' system. It cannot in any way be taken as typical of traditional systems in general since it has a number of unique aspects. Nonetheless the essay illustrates certain features of traditional systems which seem to have wider application. First, rights to work with particular assets (especially land) are determined by historic hereditary custom. However, those who did not have hereditary access to work on the land 'were forced either to abandon their rural living or to develop other non-agricultural activity within the village'. Thus the hereditary system provides guaranteed access to work and income (albeit often at low levels) for those within the system; but for others it may be more restrictive than a capitalist system. Among the poorest groups there is a remarkable tradition of highly egalitarian and almost 'communistic' behaviour among the traditional classes of smallholders and sharecroppers. Mutual cooperation may thus support individual households in times of personal misfortune. But, in Iran, the cooperative element tends to break down when innovations are introduced. Secondly, the traditional system may generate very great inequalities. But while inequality is great, the role of custom determining shares may maintain this inequality at a roughly constant level, except where new elements – e.g. population pressure or technical innovation – enter the picture. Thirdly, as powerfully illustrated in this essay, the system tends to be stagnant. The methods of allocating income and work responsibility are such as to discourage innovation/investment. The converse of the stratification in a feudal/traditional system then is a lack of dynamism, well illustrated in the case of Iran with 'an almost complete stagnation in the technological, socio-economic and political development of rural Iran' in that period.

This feature of a traditional system is of course one reason why it tends to break down with population pressure and innovations, and give way to market relationships. As it gives way both the protective elements of the system (those that guarantee access to work and incomes) as well as the sterile elements are swept away; the outcome in terms of poverty and income distribution then depends on whether the new dynamism can be sufficiently strong (and labour-using) to offset the abolition of hereditary rights to access to assets. In this book, three chapters illustrate the tendency for a deterioration in income distribution in mixed economies, as a market/capitalist system develops. In the Philippines, while average incomes per capita rose between 2 and 3 per cent per annum between 1950 and 1975, the share of income of the bottom 20 per cent fell from 4.9 to 3.9 per cent (1956–71) while the Gini coefficient remained at around 0.5, indicating considerable inequality.

In Peru, the share of income of the bottom 20 per cent fell from 3.0 to 2.5 per cent between 1961 and 1972, while the share of income of the top 5 per cent rose from 26 to 33 per cent.

Tokman's chapter refers to evidence showing the validity of the Kuznets hypothesis for Latin America as a whole. But his evidence suggests that much of the deterioration in income distribution that occurred in the 1960s in Latin America was due to an increase in the share of income among upper deciles, rather than a deterioration in the position of the poorest. He shows that introducing the informal sector into the analysis – which had previously been thought of in terms of a two-sector model – delays the turning point when income distribution might be expected to start to improve and increases the level of inequality when the turning point occurs.

These three chapters provide strong support for the view that in the 'typical' case, income distribution will not improve and will probably worsen in the early stages of development in a mixed economy. They also throw more specific light on why this process occurs. John Weeks analyses developments as being an essential aspect of the 'transition to capitalism' with market relationships replacing feudal; 'labour power becomes a commodity on a growing scale' and 'The seller [of labour power – i.e. the wage earner] is thrown into a monetary world in which the condition of his continued existence depends upon not just his capacity to work but his *sale* of that ability.' Although the terminology differs, the analysis is very similar to that outlined above. The extent of poverty then depends on the labour market and wage determination. In Tokman's analysis, income distribution in the economy as a whole depends on developments in the various sectors: on the extent of oligopoly/protection in the modern sector, preserving differences in incomes and productivity between it and the informal sector, and pressure of population on resources in the rest of the economy. While Ranis provides a more detailed breakdown of various elements determining income distribution in the Philippines, his overall conclusions are not dissimilar to either Weeks or Tokman: capital-intensive industrialisation behind heavy barriers – with a land reform increasing the number and worsening the situation of landless labourers – leads to a low and deteriorating share of wages in the urban sector. The interesting contrast however, between the analysis of Ranis and that of Tokman and Weeks, is the emphasis Ranis places on the role of economic policies. While the Philippines story is very similar to the Latin American stories – the 'typical' Kuznets story – Ranis does not believe this to be an inevitable stage in the transition to capitalism, but rather a feature of the particular policies followed and one which could be avoided by a different set of policies, *even in the context of a mixed economy.*

This conclusion is based on his analysis of the very different experience of Taiwan: in Taiwan during a period of rapid economic growth, inequality decreased quite markedly from a high level (Gini of 0.57 in 1950) to remarkable equality (Gini: 0.28 in 1970), while the income share of the poorest 20 per cent rose from 2.9 to 8.8 per cent. There are, as Ranis shows, a complicated and interacting set of factors responsible for this development with differing initial conditions and historic heritage, land reform and government policies each playing a part.

There was at the outset a very successful land reform: the Gini of land ownership declined from 0.62 (1950) to 0.46 (1960), while, even more remarkable, 'full owners' who represented about 36 per cent of farming families in 1950 represented 80 per cent by 1974. This is a total reverse of the normal development of social relations in agriculture (of growing inequality in land ownership and the development of a class of landless labourers). Extensive (and increasing) land ownership acts as con- siderable safety net, preventing extremes of poverty. Thus the land reform in itself would probably have been a very significant element in preventing too sharp a deterioration in income distribution, in the absence of other special factors. But given the other developments in the Taiwanese economy during this period, it may not have been as important an element as one would normally expect: rapid labour-using and productivity-raising growth in agriculture, a fast growth in rural non-agricultural employment opportunities and rapid growth in urban employment opportunities led to an economic situation in which the balance of demand and supply of labour was such that income distribution tended to improve. The urban wage share rose sharply, while the shift to non-agricultural activity in the rural areas improved rural income distribution. The land reform may well have contributed to the great success in agriculture which in turn provided opportunities for industrial and service activities in the rural areas. But government policies towards the terms of trade between agriculture and manufacturing, credit and infrastructure (favouring decentralised ad- ministration with an unusual rural emphasis) were also an essential feature. Government economic policies were – Ranis argues convincingly – mainly responsible for the rapid growth in labour- intensive manufactures, which led to a growth in demand for labour in manufacturing of 5.4 per cent per annum during the 1970s, thus eating into the labour surplus. The package of policies followed by Taiwan which favoured 'export substitution', in contrast to the more 'normal' import substitution phase II, included reduced protection, and competitive interest rate policies.

Despite the difficulty of disentangling the various elements responsible for the Taiwan story, it does appear that economic policies may lead to a pattern of growth which avoids the normal Kuznets deterioration – thus contradicting the apparently inevitable story of deterioration in income distribution in a mixed economy, during the transition process, that appears from the Latin American examples. The main elements of the policies include: emphasis on labour-intensive agriculture; decentralisation of administration, infrastructure etc; and the package of policies conducive to export-oriented labour-intensive industrialisation, rather than highly protected phase II import substitution. It must be added, however, that while (given appropriate political conditions) the direction of developments in Taiwan could be duplicated elsewhere, it seems heroic to assume that the magnitude of success could be (e.g. a growth of over 200 per cent in agricultural labour productivity and a sustained growth of manufacturing production of over 15 per cent p.a. over twenty years). These magnitudes are important in determining the balance of demand and supply for labour and the level of real wages. With more moderate results, it is likely that the Kuznets story would be modified rather than contradicted, and changed institutions (especially access to land) would be necessary to prevent the emergence of poverty. Moreover, Taiwan did have a very successful land reform. But the Taiwan case does provide an important perspective in underlining the significance of economic policies in determining developments in a mixed economy.

Changed economic policies provide one approach to modifying the usual conflict between growth and equality which occurs in capitalist economies. An alternative is to change the rules determining entitlement to income, by changing the way in which people get access to work and the allocation of income from work. It is, as argued above, the way in which access to work and income from work is determined in a market economy which is fundamentally responsible for the poor (and often deteriorating) income distribution in the sort of economic situation typical of many developing economies. Many of the studies in this book represent examples of cases where the rules/institutions have been changed. In general the intention has been to avoid the emergence of poverty and inequality associated with capitalist payments system, while retaining the dynamic accumulation ethos. As the essays on socialist experiments in this book show there is considerable variation in the rules adopted among different socialist systems[6] and (in part in consequence of these differences) differences in their success in achieving the joint objective of an egalitarian and dynamic system.

All the socialist experiments reported on here change the rules of asset ownership, limiting the ability of individuals to accumulate assets and placing assets in collective ownership and control. But the level of ownership and control varies: the State owns and controls operations in public corporations and State farms, although elements of control are delegated to the units of operation. In communes in China and cooperatives in Russia, Israel and Peru, ownership and control are effectively vested in members of the coop/communes. But decisions have to be taken in a framework of State given regulations and influences which often diminish the real independence of the individual units. In the very large units (as in Russia and China) direct democracy is largely replaced by the election of a small group who have effective powers of decision over major areas.

The cooperative ownership of assets gives all members of the cooperative the right (and obligation, normally) to work with these assets and also a right to a share in the output thus produced. Thus no number of a cooperative can be excluded from work access to the productive assets collectively held. Members therefore do not need to seek an employer to get access to productive work; this increases their bargaining power in the system, gives them psychological strength and excludes the possibility of lack of income arising from the absence of work opportunities. But while members are in a stronger position, from this point of view, non-members are not. In systems such as the communes and the kolkhozy it seems that all the relevant population are included as members. In this case, the whole rural population is effectively guaranteed against unemployment, and has a right to work with the community assets. But where membership of the cooperatives is limited, the non-members may be in as weak a position as the assetless in capitalist societies. This is powerfully illustrated by Caballero's description of Peruvian coops, which form a privileged group who employ non-members for very low wages.

The capitalist system has a class of people who own assets and receive profits/rent and a class who sell their labour and receive wages. Competition ensures that wages are broadly in line with marginal productivity. But a collective cooperative system of asset ownership abolishes the distinction between the two classes and, usually, frees decision-makers from the competitive pressures leading to income distribution according to the marginal product of work. Consequently, a cooperative system has considerable freedom in how it allocates its total income. It is not surprising therefore that the rules of distribution vary considerably. At one extreme we have kibbutz where complete equality of consumption is pursued – in some to an almost absurd extent with the same *physical* goods being provided for everyone. At the other, work is the prime determinant, with workpoints being allocated according to duration and productivity of work. In China, the workpoint system can lead to a variation of as much as 2:1 in workpoints, but a range of 8–10 for men, and 7–9 for women is reported as being more typical. In the kolkhoz in Central Asia the differentials appear greater, with specialists being paid $1\frac{3}{4}$ – 2 times an average field worker, and with six grades of field workers. Ghai and Khan report that average earnings of field workers are twice as high as the guaranteed minimum. The system of allocation adopted by the moshavim vary from equal distribution according to needs (i.e. size of family) in the moshav shitufi to distribution according to resources (the moshav ovdim). Within some of the latter very great differentials have been observed – one study showed a ratio of 11:1 between the income of the highest and the lowest farm within a moshav. Within the Peruvian cooperatives, the main difference, as noted, is between members and non-members with the former receiving as much as four times the average earnings of the latter in one rather rich coop.

In a work-related earnings scheme, household incomes tend to vary more than workpoints because of varying household composition. Actual income distribution within any unit depends not only on earnings from the collective but also on alternative earnings opportunities and on collective provisions to prevent extremes of poverty. In both the communes and the kolkhozy private plots have been a quite important source of income accounting from 18–40 per cent of earnings from collective labour among kolkhoz labour, and 10–25 per cent of income among members of communes. But it is reported that whereas income from private plots is a major source of inequality in China, among the kolkhozy it is claimed to be a major equalising element.[7]

Any system of income distribution which is primarily work-related may lead to very low incomes for those households with few workers, or with workers of low productivity. Each of the work-related systems has some sort of safety-net system, to prevent complete destitution and ensure a minimum subsistence for all members. In the Chinese communes this is achieved by the '5 guarantees', a basic minimum grain ration and some consumption provided collectively and free. In the kolkhozy, there is also collectively provided consumption, and a guaranteed minimum pay for 25 work days, and no kolkhoznik appears to receive a money income below the guaranteed minimum, which is estimated to be sufficient to meet basic minimum needs. In the moshav ovdim the principle of 'mutual aid' acts as some offset to inequalities in earnings as does the collective provision of items of consumption. It seems that the provision of a collective safety net of some kind is a general feature of socialist systems, which contrasts with many poor capitalist economies, where generally no such systematic safety net exists. Thus while the rules of payment often allow for quite marked inequality, destitution is thereby prevented. There appear to be two reasons why a 'safety-net' is more often a feature of a socialist system than of a capitalist one – a social reason and an economic one. First there is a social/political principle of collective responsibility towards *all* members: secondly, from an economic point of view the importance of sustaining the life and health of all members is recognised as having significant long run economic benefits since eventually they will contribute to the output of the collective. In contrast, in a capitalist system, the private unit of account – the firm – may not benefit directly from sustaining the health of those it does *not* employ (viz. the family of employees and the unemployed). It is worth noting that the firm does often provide food rations etc. to sustain the productivity of those it directly employs.

In a competitive capitalist system, a major source of inequality and poverty is differentials arising from differences in occupation and marginal productivity of different factors. But, aside from pervasive oligopolistic influences (illustrated by Tokman in comparing the informal and formal sectors), competitive pressures can be expected to produce a uniform wage for a uniform category of worker, so that differences in wages received by farm labourers or unskilled industrial workers should not vary greatly according to the productivity of the individual enterprise.[8] But in socialist systems where mobility of factors (of land, labour and capital) between units is restricted, a major source of inequality can be differences in productivity between units. This is illustrated in each of the studies (see Table 12.1).

For any given degree of differentials *within* a unit, overall inequality will be greater, the greater the difference in average incomes between units. An inverse relationship between inter- and intra-unit inequality might be expected; the less the restrictions on factor mobility between units, the less the likely extent of inter-unit differentials, while greater factor mobility between units is also likely to lead to more market (and

Work, Income and Inequality

TABLE 12.1 Dispersion of income between units

Case	Measure	Dispersion
5 Moshavim	Ratio of income per capita of highest unit: income per capita of lowest unit	3.3
5 Kolkhozy (1976)	,,	1.44
Shanghai County (1974):		
Communes	,,	1.65
Brigades	,,	1.30
Teams	,,	2.70
Kibbutzim (1950s)	Gini coefficient for income distribution	0.11–0.18
Kibbutzim (1968)	,,	0.16–0.20

less social) influences on income distribution within a unit and therefore probably to greater intra-unit inequality.[9] It is not possible to test this hypothesis with the limited evidence presented in Table 12.1: indeed as far as it goes some of that evidence appears to counter it, with the moshavim, for example having considerable inter and intra-inequality, while the kibbutzim have complete intra-unit equality and also a high degree of inter-unit equality. But the equality between kibbutzim is largely due to government and kibbutz policy, rather than 'natural' forces.[10] Over time – unless there is government intervention – inequality between units is likely to become greater as initial differences in average incomes lead to differences in savings and investment within each unit. This appears to be the case, for example, with the kibbutz as indicated in Table 12.1. It also seems likely to happen in China where richer units are encouraged to accumulate more.

This tendency for long run and sharpening inequalities to emerge between units may be offset in one of two ways. First – and the major policy of the left in China – by raising the unit of account – i.e. the unit which earns and shares out income. For any given dispersion in productivity throughout an economy, the higher the unit of account the less the difference in productivity between units. But raising the unit of account may raise serious problems of commitment and incentive. While people can appreciate the significance of their individual effort to the results of the unit as a whole at team level (i.e. roughly 30 households), this is more problematic at brigade (roughly 200 households) or commune level (2,900 households). Despite considerable political pressure in the 1970s in China to raise the unit of account to brigade level, the team has remained the most typical unit of account, it appears. It seems likely that as the unit of account is raised, the need for individual material incentives to obtain worker efficiency and commitment may increase, so that while inter-unit equality may increase, intra-unit equality is likely to decrease.

It is worth noting that the size of kibbutz (20 to 2,000 people) and moshavim is similar to that of the Chinese production team, as is the basic organisational unit (the brigade) in the kolkhozy, although in the Russian case this is the production unit but not the unit of account. It seems plausible to hypothesise that a relatively small size of unit may be necessary to obtain voluntary commitment to a collective form of organisation and income distribution.

The second potential offset to inter-unit inequality is some form of higher-level intervention to prevent inequalities emerging in the first place (e.g. by determination of prices of inputs and output, the allocation of credit etc.) or to correct it when it does happen by taxation and subsidies. In the examples in this book, each of these methods has been tried. In the kolkhozy, differential procurement prices have been used 'to syphon off differential rents', while State contributions to collective consumption and the system of taxation are equalising in effects. In the kibbutz, taxation and subsidies are the main equalising instruments.[11] In China, redistributive measures appear to have been rather weak, with an emphasis on 'self-reliance' and rather limited redistributive measures. The most effective equalising measure appears to be the use of a compulsory purchase quota system, rather than taxation/subsidies. In this respect, it appears that collective units are subject to similar limitations to mixed or capitalist economies: it is necessary to tackle income distribution when it arises – i.e. at the primary level – subsequent State transfers tend to meet considerable resistance and to be of rather minor significance.

It is clear that the effects of various collective payments systems on access to work, income distribution and poverty vary markedly between the different examples. The rules of the system have a significant effect on the outcome, some rules being much more egalitarian than others. The rules of the kibbutz (followed by those of the moshav shitufi) are the most egalitarian of those considered here. It emerges from the discussion above that five subcategories of rules are of especial relevance:

1. Rules on asset accumulation. Restrictions on the rights of individual households to accumulate (or decumulate) assets limit the development of inequality. In the kibbutz and the moshav shitufi all asset accumulation is collective, which means that accumulation can poten-

tially be a source of inequality between the cooperatives but not within them. In the communes and the Kolkhozy, households are restricted to a given size 'personal plot', which limits the degree of inequality arising from this source. But inequalities between teams, brigades and communes may arise through unequal accumulation of capital assets. In the moshav ovdim and olim, individual households are not permitted to accumulate land, which limits the inequality arising from this source, but they may accumulate other assets (farm machinery etc.).

2.   Rules about the distribution of income from the collective. Inequality tends to be greater, the more the distribution of income is related to work and private asset accumulation, rather than related to some concept of need.

3.   Rules on membership of the cooperatives. Where membership is limited, then non-members are left without the right of access to collective assets.

4.   Rules on hiring labour. Where hiring labour is permitted, the members of the coop tend to become entrepreneurs (as with the Peruvian coops) and inequality emerges as between the coop members and the labour they hire.

5.   Rules related to the prevention and/or correction of inter-unit inequality.

    Taken together, these five sets of rules, in interaction with technological possibilities and economic policies, determine the extent of the development of inequality. Because the precise rules are so significant, their formation becomes a highly political issue, not only when they are first introduced but also over time. For example in China the question of rules has been central to much political discussion during the past three decades. Among the seven examples of socialist systems described in this book, three could be described as failures from the point of view of radically changing income distribution, while the remaining four are (to a varying extent) successful, from this point of view. The political element is a quite explicit factor behind the three failures: the general reforms in Peru, the coastal coops in Peru and public enterprise in Bangladesh.
    As Sobhan shows, public corporations in Bangladesh have done little to change income distribution, but have been used by special interest groups to reinforce their positions. He concludes 'the distributive regimes under public enterprise tend to be conditioned by the prevailing

dispensation of class forces'. He believes that the use of public corporations 'as a genuine weapon of class war in the service of the poor . . . would appear to depend on a transfiguration of power within the state'.

Weeks' essay on Peru shows that a number of structural changes in the rules of the payment system explicitly intended to improve income distribution, which were introduced by the military government after 1968, appear to have had no significant effect on income distribution. The reforms included land reform, social property legislation introducing worker's ownership on a small scale and profit sharing extensively, and quite large scale nationalisation. The proportion of the gross domestic product under State ownership rose from an estimated 13 per cent in 1968 to 22 per cent in 1975 (and 35 per cent if agricultural cooperatives are included). Yet, 'The statistics overwhelmingly indicate that the post-1968 reforms had no discernible impact on the functional income distribution, except perhaps towards greater inequality.' Weeks concludes, 'While the Peruvian case does not demonstrate the impossibility of distributional reform, it does clearly demonstrate the weakness of such reforms in the face of the economic cycle intrinsic to the capitalist mode of production.' Caballero's examination of agricultural cooperatives in Coastal Peru provides a detailed example of how the Peruvian reforms failed, in terms of changing income distribution.

Weeks' findings with respect to public enterprise in Peru are similar to those of Sobhan for Bangladesh: public enterprise as such does little to change income distribution in a mixed economy. This finding is common to other studies of public enterprise.[12] It is not very surprising: public ownership as such does not introduce a new power base with new objectives into a mixed economy; in fact in a way it introduces a sort of power vacuum, which will be used by whatever interests happen to be powerful in the State and the economy. A similar situation arises with marketing cooperatives, which rarely do anything to transform the existing structure of power and distribution.[13]

In contrast, cooperatives where the workers' own the assets do potentially change power and objectives. Even there external pressures of various kinds may limit the change brought about. Competitive pressures may force the cooperative into a mould which is very similar to that of capitalist firms;[14] pressures from external interests may reduce the extent and impact of the changes, as in Peru. Moreover, the members of the coop itself may choose an inegalitarian pattern of allocation, as with some moshavim and the Peruvian coops. The three 'failures' just described underline the difficulties of achieving change in the context of a mixed economy; but the successes of the cooperatives in Israel and the land reform in Taiwan show that payments system reform can be effective within a mixed economy.

Over a long period, the dynamic qualities of a system can become more important than its static distributional rules in determining the real incomes of the poor. The evidence from the examples in this book suggest that collective systems can be efficient and dynamic. The examples in Soviet Central Asia show a remarkable and sustained growth in productivity and incomes that have resulted in standards of living in these areas comparable to those in industry in Russia. The productivity of the cooperative and state farms are vastly greater than those in rather similar neighbouring Asian countries. In Israel too it appears that both kibbutzim and moshavim have enjoyed rapid growth of output and incomes. It is not possible – from the evidence collected here – to come to conclusions about 'efficiency' in terms of social costs and benefits: these institutions have been favoured with special prices/subsidies and at international prices their output may prove to be less than at market prices. Nonetheless in volume terms there has been a very dramatic and sustained growth rate, following high investment rates. It does not seem reasonable to deny their dynamism. The land reform in Taiwan was also followed by an extremely rapid rate of growth of agricultural output and labour productivity. It is much more difficult to conclude anything much on the limited evidence available from China. We do not know, and perhaps never will, whether the recent reversal in egalitarian policies is due to economic failure or political pressure or both. The Bangladesh case and the Peruvian coops, appear to be examples of highly inefficient production, on the limited evidence. They seem to have succeeded in combining 'socialist' institutions with inequality and stagnation. Similar (but capitalist) outcomes can be identified in some Latin America countries. Thus no one type of institution can claim invariable success or failure with respect to efficiency, to growth or to equality and poverty elimination.

CONCLUSION

The first chapter of this book set out the hypothesis that the payments system – i.e. the set of rules determining how people acquire work and income – was of major significance to the determination of income distribution and poverty. Each of the essays in this book was designed to shed some light on this hypothesis. This chapter has not fully summarised the results of each study, which contain far richer and fuller insights than could be included here. The book has covered only a portion of the available evidence, and that from a number of different angles, which reduces the systematic nature of that evidence, although it increases its breadth. Nonetheless, I believe we can reach some fairly firm conclusions.

First, modifications in the payments system can reduce inequality and poverty, in any given economic system. Secondly, we can identify the type of modification in rules likely to lead to this result. Thirdly, egalitarian changes in the payments system need not lead to reduced dynamism and therefore need not threaten the long run prospects for growth of incomes. Fourthly, some cases of payments system reform have not improved income distribution and from this point of view might be regarded as a failure; these failures tend to be related to the politics of rule formation. Because the rules of the system *are* potentially so significant for distribution, their formation is a highly political question as with any factor influencing income distribution significantly. Fifthly, while in general, the essays support the view that capitalist payments systems tended to be more inegalitarian and generate more absolute poverty than socialist systems, the Taiwan example showed that a capitalist (mixed) economy could avoid the normal conflict between growth and equality, given a particular set of economic policies and very rapid economic growth in all the main sectors of the economy.

Payments system reform should be of central concern to any strategy aimed at achieving more egalitarian economic development. Economic reforms are also of major importance, both in themselves and through interactions with the payments system. Thus in Taiwan, land reform supported the economic package which itself favoured a different sort of capitalism, with less oligopoly and less privilege for the large scale sector. As Tokman shows, the oligopolistic and privileged nature of the 'modern' sector was mainly responsible for great inequality in a number of Latin American countries, while the much more competitive informal sector was more egalitarian. But the relevant economic policy changes challenge existing interests perhaps as much as some payments system reforms and are thus equally subject to political obstacles, as illustrated in the discussion of the Philippines. The next stage of analysis therefore requires a systematic examination of the political conditions necessary to achieve effective reforms in both dimensions – the economic framework and the payments system.

NOTES

1. There are of course notable exceptions to this – e.g. Meade (1972) and Vanek (1970) discuss the economic consequences of workers' cooperatives.
2. See Chapter One. The payments system describes all those rules which determine access to and income from work – in this respect it is similar to Sen's (1980) entitlement approach which focusses on 'that combination of economic, political, social and – ultimately – legal arrangements that affect people's entitlement'.
3. For a fuller discussion see Stewart, (forthcoming).
4. See Sahota (1980); Meerman (1979).
5. See Chapter One, p. 14.
6. There are of course many socialist collective systems not described in this book. See also, e.g. Ghai, Khan, Lee and Radwan (1979); and Ardelan (1980).
7. This, perhaps, surprising finding may be due to the fact that in each system, inequalities arising from personal plots are limited because the size of the personal plots are roughly the same for each person – but because of the greater inequality in collective income in the kolkozy the effect is *relatively* equalising there in contrast to the communes, where collective income is more equally distributed.
8. In practice a wide dispersion in earnings of the *same* factor of production is often observed among capitalist enterprises. Theoretically, these differences may be attributed to various market imperfections. Thus the distinction made above between the two types of system is not as clear in practice as it appears in theory. See Knight and Sabot (1981).
9. A safety-net system whereby everyone is prevented from falling below a given minimum income could also act in this direction, since if there are large differences in average incomes between units, the floor system will act to reduce differentials in the poorest units.
10. See Chapter 9.
11. There is an attempt to equalise consumption among kibbutz by publishing a 'minimum standard of consumption', but this has the effect (as does similar influences in China) of increasing inequality in savings and investment and therefore making future inequality more marked.
12. E.g., Frank.
13. See e.g. Apthorpe and King.
14. The John Lewis Partnership provides a British example. See Oakshott.

REFERENCES

Apthorpe, R. J. (ed.), *Rural Cooperatives and Planned Change in Africa*, (Geneva: UNRISD, 1970).
Ardelan, C., 'Workers Self-Management and Planning: The Yugoslav Case', *World Development*, 8, 9 (1980).
Ghai, D., 'Income Distribution and Labour Utilisation Under Different Agrarian Systems', paper for the Sixth World Congress of Economics (1980).

Ghai, D., Khan, A. R., Lee, E. and S. Radwan (eds), *Agrarian Systems and Rural Development* (Macmillan, 1979).

ILO, *Poverty and Landlessness in Rural Asia* (Geneva, 1977).

King, R., 'Cooperative Policy and Village Development in Northern Nigeria', in J. Heyer, P. Roberts and G. Williams (eds), *Rural Development in Tropical Africa* (Macmillan, 1981).

Knight, J. and R. Sabot, 'Why Wages Differ' (World Bank, 1981).

Meade, J. E., 'The Theory of Labour Managed Firms and Profit Sharing', *Economic Journal* (1972).

Meerman, J., *Public Expenditure in Malaysia, Who Benefits and Why* (OUP, 1979).

Oakshott, R., *The Case for Workers' Coops* (Routledge and Kegan Paul, 1978).

Sahota, G. S., 'The Distribution of the Benefits of Public Expenditure in Nigeria', (World Bank (mimeo), 1980).

Sen, A. K. (1980), 'Famines', *World Development*, 8, 9.

Stewart, F. 'Work and Welfare' in Streeten (ed.), *Proceedings of the Sixth World Congress of Economists* (forthcoming).

Vanek, J., *The General Theory of Labour-Managed Market Economies* (Cornell University Press, 1970).

Index

Accumulation, *see* Asset accumulation

Adelman, I., 3

Agriculture
centralised in Philippines, 88
Chinese: aid to collectives, 254–5; characteristics, 246; collectives during 1970s, 252–6; household economy, 253; income differentials, 254; intensification in 1950s, 246–7; planning, 256–7; *see also* Communes
cooperatives: equilibrium, 179–80; in China, 250–1; in Israel, 189–214 (growth of settlements, 194; types, 189–91, 215–17; *see also* Kibbutzim; Moshav); in Peru, 168–88; in Taiwan and Philippines, 88–9; in USSR, 282–4; income distribution variations, 314–15; members' lack of motivation, 184–5; problems of ensuring effort, 181; rules affecting inequalities, 317–18; wages, 174
effect on income of decline in employment, 98
farmers' associations in Taiwan, 88
in Bangladesh, 152–4; state programmes, 145
in Iran: degradation of land fertility, 53; problem of indebtedness, 53–4; property rights, 35; restructuring, 56; role of landlords, 52
in Peru: effects of land reform, 65
in Soviet Central Asia, 279–305; *see also* Kolkhozy

in Soviet Union: and primitive socialist accumulation, 286–8; changes since 1953, 288–90; private plots, 293–5, 298–9; productive efficiency, 290–3; share in national income, 281
Israeli participation in development programmes, 210

Ahluwalia, A. H., 3, 20, 131

Asset accumulation
attempts by bourgeoisie in Bangladesh, 144
cumulative, with technological development, 11
in Chinese collectives, 259–61
in mixed economies, 7
in socialist economies, 8
in Soviet Central Asia, 300–1
in Taiwan, 88
kibbutz and moshav rules, 317–18
'primitive socialist', 286
relationship with consumption, 261
rules governing, 6
socialist experiments, 313
under capitalism, 7

Bacha, E., 129, 131

Bain, J. S., 117

Balance of payments of informal sector of economy, 114–15

Bangladesh
agricultural sector, 152–4
GDP from public sector, 145
growth through state expenditure policies, 146
income distribution unaffected by public enterprises, 318, 319
loans to private industry, 145
middlemen, 154–60

324

Index